THE COLLECTED
PRESTONIAN LECTURES
1975–1987

(Volume Three)

LONDON

LEWIS MASONIC
IAN ALLAN GROUP

Other volumes in this series:
The Collected Prestonian Lectures Volume One 1925–60
The Collected Prestonian Lectures Volume Two 1961–74

© 1988
Quatuor Coronati Lodge, London
Published by
Lewis Masonic for Ian Allan Regalia Ltd
Terminal House, Shepperton, TW17 8AS
who are members of the Ian Allan Group

First published in collected form in England, 1988
by kind permission of
The Board of General Purposes
of the United Grand Lodge of England

British Library Cataloguing in Publication Data
  The Collected Prestonian Lectures, 1975–1987
  1. Freemasons
  I. Freemasons. *Quatuor Coronati Lodge*
  366′ .1   HS395
ISBN 085318 157 8

CONTENTS

List of Illustrations

The Lecturers
1975–1987

1975   W Bro R. Theodore Beck, PDepGSupt Wks
1976   W Bro Brig. A.C.F. Jackson, *CVO*, *CBE*
1977   W Bro R.A. Wells, PAGDC
1978   W Bro Charles MacKechnie-Jarvis, PSGD
1979   W Bro G.E. Walker, *OBE*, PAGReg
1980   W Bro F.J. Cooper, *TD*, PSGD
1981   W Bro Cyril N. Batham, PAGDC
1982   RW Bro Sir James Stubbs, *KCVO*, PSGW
1983   W Bro Richard H.S. Rottenbury, PAGDC
1984   W Bro I.H. Mendoza, PAGDC
1985   W Bro Sinclair Bruce, PAGDC
1986   W Bro Prof. Wallace McLeod
1987   W Bro Christopher Gotch, PAGSupt Wks

INTRODUCTION

EXTRACT FROM THE GRAND LODGE PROCEEDINGS FOR 5 DECEMBER 1923.

In the year 1818, Bro William Preston, a very active Freemason at the end of the eighteenth and beginning of the nineteenth centuries, bequeathed £300 3 per cent. Consolidated Bank Annuities, the interest of which was to be applied 'to some well-informed Mason to deliver annually a Lecture on the First, Second, or Third Degree of the Order of Masonry according to the system practised in the Lodge of Antiquity' during his Mastership. For a number of years the terms of this bequest were acted upon, but for a long period no such Lecture has been delivered, and the Fund has gradually accumulated, and is now vested in the MW the Pro Grand Master, the Rt Hon Lord Ampthill, and W Bro Sir Kynaston Studd, PGD, as trustees. The Board has had under consideration for some period the desirability of framing a scheme which would enable the Fund to be used to the best advantage; and, in consultation with the Trustees who have given their assent, has now adopted such a scheme, which is given in full in Appendix A [See below], and will be put into operation when the sanction of Grand Lodge has been received.

The Grand Lodge sanction was duly given and the 'scheme for the administration of the Prestonian fund' appeared in the Proceedings as follows:

APPENDIX A

SCHEME FOR ADMINISTRATION OF THE

PRESTONIAN FUND

1. The Board of General Purposes shall be invited each year to nominate two Brethren of learning and responsibility from whom the Trustees shall appoint the Prestonian Lecturer for the year with power for the Board to subdelegate their power of nomination to the Library, Art, and Publications Committee of the Board, or such other Committee as they think fit.

2. The remuneration of the Lecturer so appointed shall be £5 5s 0d for each Lecture delivered by him together with travelling expenses, if any, not exceeding £1 5s 0d, the number of Lectures delivered each year being determined by the income of the fund and the expenses incurred in the way of Lectures and administration.

3. The Lectures shall be delivered in accordance with the terms of the Trust.

One at least of the Lectures each year shall be delivered in London under the auspices of one or more London Lodges. The nomination of Lodges under whose auspices the Prestonian Lecture shall be delivered shall rest with the Trustees, but with power for one or more Lodges to prefer requests through the Grand Secretary for the Prestonian Lecture to be delivered at a meeting of such Lodge or combined meeting of such Lodges.

4. Having regard to the fact that Bro William Preston was a member of the Lodge of Antiquity and the original Lectures were delivered under the aegis of that Lodge, it is suggested that the first nomination of a Lodge to arrange for the delivery of the Lecture shall be in favour of the Lodge of Antiquity should that Lodge so desire.

5. Lodges under whose auspices the Prestonian Lecture may be delivered shall be responsible for all the expenses attending the delivery of such Lecture except the Lecturer's Fee.

6. Requests for the delivery of the Prestonian Lecture in Provincial Lodges will be considered by the Trustee who may consult the Board as to the granting or refusal of such consent.

7. Requests from Provincial Lodges shall be made through Provincial Grand Secretaries to the Grand Secretary, and such requests, if granted, will be granted subject to the requesting Provinces making themselves responsible for the provision of a suitable hall in which the Lecture can be delivered, and for the Lecturer's travelling expenses beyond the sum of £1 5s 0d, and if the Lecturer cannot reasonably get back to his place of abode on the same day, the requesting Province must pay his Hotel expenses or make other proper provision for his accommodation.

8. Provincial Grant Secretaries, in the case of Lectures delivered in the Province, and Secretaries of Lodges under whose auspices the Lecture may be delivered in London, shall report to the Trustees through the Grand Secretary the number in attendance at the Lecture, the manner in which the Lecture was received, and generally as to the proceedings thereat.

9. Master Masons, subscribing members of Lodges, may attend the Lectures, and a fee not exceeding 2s may be charged for their admission for the purpose of covering expenses.

Thus after a lapse of some sixty years the Prestonian Lectures were revived *in their new form* and, with the exception of the War period (1940–46), a Prestonian Lecturer has been appointed by the Grand Lodge regularly each year.

It is interesting to see that neither of those extracts announcing the revival of the Prestonian Lectures made any mention of the principal change that had been effected under the revival, a change that is here referred to as *their new form*. The importance of the new form is that the Lecturer is now permitted to choose his own subject and, apart from certain limitations inherent in the work, he really has a free choice.

Nowadays the official announcement of the appointment of the Prestonian Lecturer usually carries an additional paragraph which lends great weight to the appointment.

The Board desires to emphasize the importance of these the only Lectures held under the authority of the Grand Lodge. It is, therefore, hoped that applications for the privilege of having one of these official Lectures will be made only by Lodges which are prepared to afford facilities for all Freemasons in their area, as well as their own members, to participate and thus ensure an attendance worthy of the occasion.

The Prestonian Lecturer has to deliver three 'official' lectures to lodges applying for that honour. The 'official' deliveries are usually allocated to one selected lodge in London and two in the provinces. In addition to these three the lecturer generally delivers the same lecture, unofficially, to other lodges all over the country, and, on occasions, to lodges abroad. It is customary for printed copies of the lecture to be sold – in vast numbers – for the benefit of one or more of the masonic charities selected by the author.

The Prestonian Lectures have the unique distinction, as noted above, that they are the only lectures given 'with the authority of the Grand Lodge.' There are also two unusual financial aspects attaching to them. Firstly, that the lecturer is paid for his services, though the modest fee is not nearly as important as the honour of the appointment.

Secondly the lodges that are honoured with the official deliveries of the lectures are expected to take special measures for assembling a large audience and for that reason they are permitted – on that occasion only – to make small nominal charge for admission.

In 1965 a collection of 27 Prestonian Lectures was published entitled *The Collected Prestonian Lectures 1925–60* and this was reprinted in 1984. It covered the period from the time of the revival of the lectures until 1960 with the exception of the following three lectures that were omitted because of their esoteric content.

1924	W Bro Capt. C.W. Firebrace, PGD	– The First Degree
1932	W Bro J. Herron Lepper, PGD	– The Evolution of Masonic Ritual in England in the Eighteenth Century
1951	W Bro H.W. Chetwin, PAGDC	– Variations in Masonic Ceremonial

Editorial versions of these three lectures were published by *Quatuor Coronati Lodge* in volume 94 of *Ars Quatuor Coronatorum*.

In 1983 *The Collected Prestonian Lectures 1961–74* was published and all fourteen lectures covering the period were printed in full.

This third volume contains all of the lectures from 1975 to 1987 and therefore brings the collected series as up to date as is possible. With the exception of the three lectures mentioned above the remaining 54 lectures are now contained in these three collected volumes. It should be emphasised that the opinions expressed and the accuracy of the statements made are the responsibility of the individual lecturers. Most of those honoured by the United Grand Lodge of England in being appointed as Prestonian Lecturers had previously distinguished themselves, not only as masonic scholars, but in other aspects of masonic life. Many of the lecturers were, and are, Past Masters of Quatuor Coronati Lodge and in this book which contains thirteen lectures, no less than eight are members of the lodge.

It must be pointed out that not only this collection but also the individual lectures are copyright. In every case permission to publish these lectures has been

obtained from the authors, their heirs or assigns and the publishers are indeed grateful for their help and co-operation in making this publication available.

1988   The Publishers

ANTHONY SAYER, GENTLEMAN THE TRUTH AT LAST

THE PRESTONIAN LECTURE FOR 1975

THEODORE BECK

INTRODUCTION

When I informed a very learned brother of the Title of my Paper it immediately produced the following comments 'That a Biographical Study was very unusual for a Prestonian Lecture and that the subject was a challenging one'. He also implied that it was likely to be provocative and explosive and I readily accept these observations as 'Fair Comment'.

It will I hope be clear to Brethren why I chose biographical research when I say that to me the development of Speculative Masonry is the history of men and it is the individual's construction and interpretation of ritual that makes it memorable, exciting and alive. The Challenge and the Sting stem from the following pungent comments made some time ago when discussing Anthony Sayer with a Masonic Scholar many years my senior who pontifically pronounced as follows:

(a) That although our knowledge on Sayer was of the slightest all that could be known was known.
(b) That no man with hands like that could be a gentleman (he was of course referring to the Mezzotint of the lost painted portrait by Joseph Highmore).
(c) That he was a nobody.
(d) That being Grand Master didn't do him any good.

My immediate reaction to his remarks was as follows:

(a) Utterly untenable.
(c) Whatever his detractor might say he did reach the top of the tree.
(d) The Apotheosis or glorification of Anthony Sayer was not the purpose of the exercise.
(b) So far as (b) was concerned a delayed reaction to this came after I had shown the mezzotint to a group of medical experts who unanimously pronounced that the unusual hands revealed a man severely afflicted by arthritis.

As the story develops we shall deal with these and other aspects in depth.

One of the most difficult but essential factors in understanding the spirit and condition of the times in which Sayer found himself is to recreate the atmosphere or perhaps a better word is the smell of these times and in the 17th and 18th centuries Cities and populous places did smell strongly and abominably. It has long been my considered opinion that not only was Speculative Masonry of

1

English birth alone but also that it was the result of a sudden explosion in the first decades of the 17th century and not of gradual development from operative Masonry.

The three principal characters involved were utterly unaware of the influence their works would play in this particular field although they created enormous effect at the time in the realms of their own particular choice.

These individuals were:

(1) Palladio of Vicenza, that immortal Architect.
(2) Dr John Dee, Scientist, Occultist, Alchemist and Secret Agent to Queen Elizabeth I.
(3) Christian Rosencreutz (Rosie-Crucian is almost certainly an Anglicised and bastardised version of the Rosenkreuzes 'Mythical' followers of this 'mythical' person.

The influence of these persons lies not only in their writings but how others wrote on them and of them. Editions of their books or commentaries on them appeared in the 17th century. All the books in this connection to which I shall refer, or most of them, were published in the life time of Sayer's father.

You may well wonder where this argument is leading and I am now permitted to inform you that Anthony Sayer was by profession a Bookseller and is so described even when at the point of death. The mists of obscurity now slowly begin to clear.

The Books of Palladio exerted an enormous influence on the English scene. The most influential was *I Quattro Libri Dell' Architettura* and the edition of 1601 published in Venice largely owed its practical precedence to the high standard of fine illustrations and printing which until then had not been achieved. Inigo Jones owned a copy of this edition which he annotated. Palladio's system enabled the English Nobility and gentlemen of taste and intelligence to design buildings from the scale of Somerset House to that of the elegant country seat of the well to do and provided the catlyist between this moneyed class and the operative masons. The amateur of taste and the operative mason each could make a valuable contribution to the project. The former was glad to embrace the practical side of building and the latter had an opportunity to study design and be accepted on more or less equal terms by his employer.

John Dee (1527–1608) A great mathematician and very extraordinary person in the repubļiç of Letters and in the Occult. To quote his own words: 'Anno 1542 I was sent by my father Rowland Dee to the University of Cambridge there to begin with Logic, and so to proceed in the learning of good Arts and Sciences.' His assiduity in making astronomical observations, which in those days were always understood to be connected with the desire of penetrating into futurity, brought some suspicions upon him, which was so far increased by a very singular incident which befell him, as to draw upon him the imputation of a conjuror or magician, which he could never shake off for 60 years after.

This incident was soon after his removal from St John's College on being chosen one of the Fellows of Trinity where he was assigned to be the under-reader of the Greek tongue. 'Hereupon' says he, 'I did set forth, and it was seen of the University,

a Greek comedy of Aristophanes named in Latin *Pax*; with the performance of the scarabaeus or beetle, his flying up to Jupiter's palace with a man and his basket of victuals on her back; whereat was great wondering, and many vain reports spread abroad of the means how that was accomplished.'

Disturbed with such reports he left England but later returned and was accepted at the Court of Elizabeth. Nevertheless his credit at Court was not sufficient to overcome the public odium he lay under on the score of magical incantations which was the true cause of his missing several preferments. At Mortlake where he had made his home, he was greatly feared as a practitioner in Black Magic and the mob set about his house scattering and destroying the bulk of his vast library which contained many manuscripts. That he was greatly feared is understandable from his close associations with one Edward Kelley, a notorious sinister figure and a dealer in necromancy of whom John Weaver writes in his *Ancient Funerall Monuments* published in 1631 Chapter IX 'Of such malefactors ... who violated sepulchres. This diabolicall questioning of the dead, for the knowledge of future accidents, was put in practice of the foresaid Kelley; who, upon a certaine night, in the Parke of Walton in le dale, in the county of Lancaster, with one Paul Waring (his fellow companion in such deeds of darknesse) invocated some of the infernall regiment, to know certaine passages in the life, as also what might bee knowne by the devils foresight of the manner and time of the death of a noble young Gentleman, as then in his wardship.' Kelley, who had previously inquired 'what corse was the last buried in Low-churchyard, a Church thereunto adjoyning', was told that a poor man had been buried that very day. Kelley, Waring, together with a servant of the young Gentleman, an assistant who was well paid and who 'did helpe them to digge up the carcass of this poor caitiffe', betook themselves to the lonely churchyard at dead of night, and after certain conjurations over the cadaver they had so profanely and beastly disinterred, 'by their incantations, they made him (or rather some evill spirit through his Organs) to speake, who delivered strange predictions, concerning the said Gentleman. I was told thus much by the said Servingman, a secondarie actor in that dismall abhorrid businesse. And the Gentleman himselfe (whose memorie I am bound to honour) told me a little before his death, of this conjuration by Kelley: as he had it from his said Servant and Tenant; onely some circumstances excepted, which he thought not fitting to come to his Master's knowledge,' 'The blacke ceremonies of that night being ended', Kelley and Waring packed away, leaving their wretched accomplice a prey to great horror. Weever justly comments: 'These injuries done against the dead who ought to sleepe in peace untill the last sound of the Trumpet, have ever beene, even amongst the very Pagans themselves, esteemed execrable.'

The new century saw the beginning of a reversal from the enlightenment and enquiring liberalism of the neo-Platonists and Renaissance Magia and the mounting of a nation wide drive against all suspected of witchcraft and black magic.

King James I himself was vehemently opposed to witchcraft and in fairness to the King he had good reason to be. There certainly was a secret society practising magic as a weapon against the King and all these incidents led to James writing his *Three Books on Demonalogy* which he based on his personal examination of

witches who had confessed. It is therefore not surprising that in the first year of his reign on 19 March 1604 James asked Parliament to enact a Statute which would help 'uproot the monstrous evils of encharters'. It was a far more drastic law on this subject than any that had preceded it. 'If any person,' it stated, 'shall use practise, or exercise any invocation or conjuration of any evil and wicked spirit, or shall consult, covenant with, entertain, employ, feed or reward any evil and wicked spirit, to or for any intent and purpose, or take up any dead man, woman or child out of their graves or the skin, bone or any part of any dead person, to be used in any manner of witchcraft, sorcery or enchantment whereby any person shall be killed, destroyed, wasted, consumed, pined or harmed in his or her body, or any part thereof; that then every offender, their aiders, abettors and counsellors shall suffer the pains of death.' Though the Bishops of the House of Lords found the Statute 'Imperfect', it was rushed through Parliament and put on the Statute Book on 9 June 1604. James was taking no chances.

Dee was seized with a blind panic and took steps to establish his innocence by presenting a petition to Parliament urging them to pass 'An Act Generall against slander, with a specific penal order for John Dee, his case'. Certainly his plea for a Law against slander was not out of place for it would have been a safeguard for the innocent and feeble minded who for years to come were to suffer cruelly from the Witchcraft Statute which was often cited under pretexts of personal vengeance, sadism and terrorism resulting in diabolical persecution and the stoning and burning of harmless lunatics condemned of these malpractises.

Dee continued his invocation until 7 Sept 1607, which is the last date in the journal which was published by Meric Casaubon D. D. Lond in 1659 under the title of *A True and faithful Relation of what passed for many years between Dr John Dee, a Mathematician of great Fame in Queen Elizabeth and King James, their reigns and some Spirits ... out of the original copy written with Dr Dee's own hand, kept in the library of Sir Thomas Cotton Knt Baronet.*

Casaubon's view was that Dee was deluded by Devils and little better than a black magician be that as it may the Government of the day endeavoured to suppress the book but was defeated by the speed with which the book sold.

It is unfortunate for Dee's reputation that his curious cabbalistic Treatise on the elements was later to be used as a basis for a revival of black magic in the 18th and 19th centuries. It is also of significance that it is alleged it was a basis for Rosi crucianism.

Certainly it would seem there are certain parallels between the aims and principals of Rosicrucianism and the ideas set out by Dee in his writings. Theosophy and the principals of reincarnation appear to form the modern elements of Rosi-crucianism and both Dee and the Roscicrucians drew on ancient Egypt for their inspiration. To the uninitiated it would seem that man can experience 'momentary flights of the soul and become one with the universe and receive a flow of great understanding.'

That highly successful man Elias Ashmole who on the 16 October 1646 was elected a brother of the Free and Accepted Masons snapped up any scrap of information on John Dee and Aubrey states that 'John Dee's printed book of Spirits is not above the third part of what was writ, which were in Sir Robert

Cottons Library, many whereof were much perished by being buried, and Sir Robert Cotton bought the field to digge after it'.

Dee's influence on those seeking to penetrate the veil of futurity was enormous. Indeed Dee's influence on Ashmole caused the latter to publish in 1650 a treatise by Dr Arthur Dee (eldest son of John) relating to the Philosopher's Stone together with another tract on the same subject by an unknown author. He published these pieces under a fictitious name; the title runs thus: *Fasciculus Chemicus or Chemical Collections expressing the Ingress and Egress of the secret hermetic science ... whereto is added the Arcanum or grand secret of hermetic Philosophy.*

It is clear from the study of the minutes of early Lodges that the members were voracious for information on every possible subject particularly the secrets of futurity and were prepared to obtain them by any means. A late example of which is exemplified by Dr Stukely F.R.S. who in 1717 removed to London and was one of those who revived the Society of Antiquaries. Considering these were some remains of the eleusinian Mysteries in Freemasonry, he gratified his curiosity and was constituted Master of a Lodge in 1723. He became Rector of St George's, Queen Square, London and died 3 March 1765 and was buried at East Ham, Essex. When Stukeley's grave was accidentally discovered in 1886, his coffin found at a depth of about six feet was found to be in a good state of preservation. On it was a brass plate bearing a simple inscription in Latin and ornamented with scroll work and a goat's head. To the Antiquary and all versed in black magic the goat was a potent and exceedingly sinister symbol. The survival of the Noah tradition and necromancy are still evident in the Third Degree.

The famous Statute against witchcraft of 1604, 1 Jas 1, remained in force until 1736, Stat 9, Geo II but though England has repealed the laws against witchcraft The Divine Law she cannot repeal 'Thou shalt not suffer a Witch to live'.

1. THE UBIQUITOUS SAYERS

The surname Sayer has variants as Sawyer and even Sare though the last form is rare. There are centres for the surname in Norfolk, Berkshire, Kent, Durham, York and Surrey. The name appears in many London Parishes and the Liberties thereof and in many Parish Registers SAYER and SAWYER are used for the same person and in the minutes of Old King's Arms Lodge (in Anthony's time in King's Arms Lodge) both Sayer and Sawyer are used. In spite of the surnames' wide distribution a compensating factor is that the Christian name Anthony is most unusual. In the case of the Berkshire Sayers four Anthonys in successive generations (c 1624–1770) occur but in the case of the Norfolk Sayers 'a very old county family' only one Anthony occurs being born in 1698. In both counties the name was an import through marriage. In the former case the Pyseley's in the latter the Oldfields.

Now two golden rules for genealogists are:
1. Verify your references.
2. Beware of probabilities.
Let us begin by verifying-Anthony Sayer's burial entry:
Church of St Paul's Covent Garden Parish Register No. 4 Burials 1739–1767.

1742 Jan 5th Anthony Sayer from St Giles in the Fields.

Now let us turn to the obituary which is extracted from the *London News* of Saturday, January 16th to Tuesday, January 19th 1742. 'Buried St Pauls Church Covent Garden. A few days since died, aged about seventy years. Mr Anthony Sayer, who was Grand Master of the most Antient and Honourable Society of Free and Accepted Masons in 1717. His corpse was followed by a great number of gentlemen of that Honourable Society of the best quality, from the Shakespears Head Tavern* in the Piazza in Covent Garden and decently interid in Covent Garden Church.'

It is a matter of considerable interest to compare the obituaries of James Anderson the author of the *Constitutions* (first issued in 1723 with a second edition of 1738) with that of Sayer's already quoted:

The York Courant No 712 29th May to 5 June 1739
Deaths
The Rev and Learned Dr James Anderson, at his house in Exeter Court, a noted Dissenting Minister. Author of the Royal Genealogical Tables and of several Theological and Historical Works, and the Constitutions of the Ancient and Hon. Society of Free and Accepted Masons lately published (1738). He was a Person of great Learning and Abilities, and reckoned a very facetious Companion.

The Newcastle Journal No 10 Saturday 9 June 1739
Last night was interr'd in Burnhill Fields the corpse of Dr Anderson, a Dissenting Teacher, in a very remarkable deep grave. His Pall was supported by five Dissenting Teachers, and the Rev Dr Desaguliers. It was followed by about a Dozen of Free-Masons, who encircled the Grave; and after Dr Earle had harangued on the Uncertainty of Life, etc without one Word of the deceased, in a most solemn dismal Posture, lifted up their Hands, sigh'd and struck their Aprons three Times in Honour of the Deceased.

The impression left after reading these obituaries is strikingly different. Sayer though in greatly reduced circumstances clearly still commanded loyalty and affection from those with whom he mingled and the phrase 'decently interid in Covent Garden Church' bears witness to a social status. Whether we approve or not there was a social convention in the 18th century of burial precedence e.g. Chancel, Central Nave, Aisles etc and finally Churchyard. A license had to be paid for and the Rector or Vicar benefitted thereby. Additional fees were also required for monuments or monumental inscriptions and grave stones and inscriptions *c.f.*.

Jan 13th 1743 An account of money received for laying grave stones. Received of Mr William Reason for the Liberty of laying a grave stone over the grave of Mrs Margaret Oldfield in the Deans Walk 8.8.0.

I made a careful search of the Churchwardens accounts covering the years 1742–1744 inclusive for any comparable reference to Sayer but without success. In the normal course of events the Parish Clerk would have submitted details of all burials and the charges made for same. These items would be submitted as 'vouchers' but once the totals had been approved by the Churchwardens and Vestry Clerk would either be stored or in due time destroyed. The result here is

*At which the Stewards Lodge was meeting at this time.

that we have quarterly totals (with a few exceptions as above) under the recurring heading 'An account of money received for Burials in the Church and Churchyard and use of the Palls in ... '

However on searching the Church Wardens Accounts for 1742 I was rewarded by discovering the following:

An A/C of money received for Pews and Seats Church Wardens Accounts March 5 1742 (the quarter in which Anthony died).

"MR SAYER the Bookseller, being a Gift to the Poor for his seat in the Church, having no Warrant 1-1-0'.

We have here for the first time proof of Sayer's profession. Through the courtesy and assistance of the Clerk and Assistant Clerk of the Worshipful Company of Stationers and Newspaper Makers I was enabled to search their records from 1600–1750. They concurred with me in my opinion that relaxations took place in the Company after The Great Fire and that whilst Publishers, Printers and Book Binders had to be Free of the Company Book-sellers did not.

The following Sayer entries were found:

Christopher Sayer Bound 28 Jan 1616/7
Christopher Sayer sonne of John Sayer of Batersey in ye County of Surrey, gent, lately putt himself in apprentice to Laurence Lisle Citizen and Stationer of London for ye terme of 8 years from this day of his Master Lawrence Lisle, Bookseller. We know as follows, he was bookseller in London 1607–1626 The Tigers Head, St Paul's Churchyard, Son of William Lisle of Paddington, Co Middlesex, yeoman. Christopher was living in 1623 but never became Free of the Stationers Company.

Robert Sayer, Mapseller, Freedom by Redemption 6th September 1748. For details of which the Chamberlain's Court of the City of London kindly allowed me to inspect the Certificates.

Robert Sayer, Printseller, by Redemption, Ladbroke, Mayor.

Tuesday 6th day of September 1748 in the twenty second year of the reign of King George II of Great Britain, etc. Freedom of this City by Redemption in the Company of Stationers. Paying into Mr Chamberlain for this City's use the sum of Forty six shillings and eight pence. If this is not presented in three months it is void.

Son of James Sayer, late of Sunderland in the County of Durham, Gent, deceased.
Thos. Shackleton, Haberdasher
Elias Jones, Carman
Robert Walton, Vintners   7th September 1748
Andrew Broson,   Partridge
                    Thomas Longman, Warden.

Robert Sayer had a very full and successful career, he was received in to the Livery in 1753 and became a member of the Court in 1783 his last appearance on which is 1791. He was publisher, map and print seller from 1751–1794. He succeeded Philip Overton at the Golden Bush, opposite Fetter Lane, Fleet Street; (afterwards No 53 Fleet Street). One of the leading publishers in his day, his publication of maps and prints were very numerous, among them being *a general view of the City of London 1751, a view of the Monument 1752, The Small British Atlas 1753 ... an Atlas of the Mundern System 1774.*

John Bennett entered into partnership with Sayer in 1775 and together they

published several works. *The American Atlas: The North American Pilot: The West Indian Atlas:* and *The Large Map of Yorkshire.* Bennett remained in partnership until 1784; from that date to 1794 Sayer continued to publish various maps and charts and was finally succeeded by Lawrie and Whittle.

James Sayer, mapseller, son of Robert. Became Free by Patrimony 4th July 1775, A member of the Livery 22nd December 1778. Died 10 Dec 1803, at Richmond Surrey.

His addresses are listed Fleet Street 1786–1794, Queen Square Bloomsbury 1795–1798, Bedford Row 1799, Richmond Co, Surrey 1800–1803.

Thomas Sayer Apprenticed 3 December 1754, Son of John Sayer of Eastcheap (Haberdasher, Hats) to Thos. Crump of Warwick Lane. Bookbinder. Free 1 November 1763.

William Sayer Apprenticed 5 August 1755. Son of Mark Sayer* of Academy Court, Chancery Lane, Taylor, to Robert Sayer printer. Thomas did not obtain his Freedom of the Company.

From the foregoing names it will be noted there were Sayers associated with printing and the Book Trade from the beginning of the 17th up to the beginning of the 19th century, with Anthony Sayer mid way in time between Christopher Sayer gent, of Surrey and Robert Sayer gent whose father was of Sunderland, Co. Durham.

Many books were published in the 17th and 18th century on the theme 'does trade extinguish gentry' and the accepted view was that it did not. Conversely it was not easy for a tradesman (unless highly successful) to be accepted as a gentleman. In the case of Christopher and Robert both could claim the right to bear a Coat of Arms and what is more the Arms were the same.

2 THE PORTRAIT

There is an old and true saying 'Show me a portrait and I can save you a thousand words' and fortunately although the portrait by Joseph Highmore is lost we have an excellent and rare mezzotint by John Faber taken from the portrait. It is this mezzotint which has on it the following engraved wording *Anthony Sayer, Gent, Grand Master of the Masons.*

This evidence of the wording is in my view of enormous significance for at this time Sayer was in contact with a wide cross section of the community for the City of London and of Westminster. The upper crust being composed of the nobility and gentry. The last Heralds Visitation was admittedly in 1688 but snobbery and privilege were rife and styling himself a gentleman if his claim was false would have brought upon him that cruellest of penalties; ridicule. I have come across no example yet of this print where erasure or omission of the word has occurred.

To searchers for the portrait I would offer one word of warning, it may not show Sayer with the apron (the flap of which is upturned in the mezzotint). The reason is as follows: In the possession of the District Grand Lodge of the Punjab there is a 'Proof before Letters' of the engraving. In this particular example no

---

*In the Burial Register of St Giles in the Fields is the following 1741 May 10 Catherine of Mark Sayer (presumably his wife).

apron is shown and I am convinced this implies that in Highmore's portrait the apron may be lacking.

It is my considered opinion that the mezzotint was executed in 1717. There are two reasons for this (1) The wording refers to 'Grand master' which we know was in 1717 and (2) Prints are produced to sell and the year when Sayer was at his Masonic Zenith was when sales were likely to be the highest. The fact that Sayer himself was a bookseller with doubtless many bookseller friends would be certainly no hindrance to sales.

Searchers after the Sayer portrait should be reminded that in 1926 the following advertisement appeared in *The Times, No 44331*, London, Friday, July 23rd, on the front page (Adverts), it ran thus: Freemasons' – Painting, Anthony Sayer, First Grand Master, by Highmore. Price £100.—Write box 34,953. The Times 42 Wigmore Street W.1.

Bro Albert F. Calvert examined this painting and satisfied himself conclusively that it was a contemporary portrait touched up and definitely not Sayer and that the wording thereon had been recently faked.

NOTE

In 1762 Joseph Highmore for the reason given below moved to Canterbury and as a consequence decided to sell his collection of paintings. The Sale took place at LANGFORD'S, GRAND PIAZZA, Covent Garden on the 5th March, 1762. It had been suggested that Sayer's Portrait had been included in this sale. I therefore approached the Keeper of the Library of The Victoria and Albert Museum, South Kensington and in addition to the details mentioned above was informed that only one copy of the catalogue was recorded in LUGT'S *Repertorie* of Sales and that copy was in the Cabinet des Estampes of the RIJKSMUSEUM, Amsterdam.

On writing to that Museum I had a most courteous reply from the Assistant Librarian the gist of which was 'I would like to inform you that I can not trace the portrait of Anthony Sayer. There are however many portraits but often without a name.'

BIOGRAPHICAL NOTES

These notes prove that the painting of the Portrait and the execution of the Mezzotint could both have been produced in 1717.

Joseph Highmore Esq

An eminent painter he was born in the parish of St James Garlickhithe, London, June 13, 1692, being the third son of Mr Edward Highmore a coal-merchant in Thames Street. Having such an early and strong inclination to painting, that he could think of nothing else with pleasure, his father endeavoured to gratify him in a proposal to his uncle, who was serjeant painter to King William, and with whom Mr (afterwards Sir James) Thornhill had served his apprenticeship. With good reason the offer was declined, and he was articled as clerk to an attorney on July 18, 1707 but this was so much against his own declared inclination, that in about 3 years he began to form resolutions of indulging his natural disposition in

his favourite art by having continuously enjoyed his leisure hours in designing and in the study of geometry, perspective, architecture, and anatomy; all without any instruction except books. He had afterwards an opportunity of improving himself in anatomy, by attending the lectures of Mr Cheseldon, before entering himself at the Painters Academy in Great Queen Street, where he drew for 10 years and had the honour to be particularly noted by Sir Godfrey Kneller. On June 13, 1714 his clerkship expired and on March 26, 1715, he began painting as a profession and settled in the City. In 1761 on the marriage of his daughter to the Rev Mr Duncombe, son to one of his oldest friends, he took a resolution of retiring from business and disposing of his collection of pictures, which he did by auction during March 1762. Soon after he moved to his son-in-law's at Canterbury where he spent the remainder of his life. He died on March 3rd 1780 and was buried in the South aisle of Canterbury Cathedral leaving one son Anthony, educated in his own profession.

Highmore was Junior Grand Warden in 1727 when he was described as a 'Painter'.

(The rate books show that in 1739 he was living in Newton Row)

John Faber

This artist was a native of Holland and at first practised portrait painting on vellum, but afterwards he applied to Mezzotint in which line he executed a number of plates. He resided for many years in England and died at Bristol in 1721, leaving a more famous son who died in 1756.

The following description of the manner in which Sir Cecil Wray's portrait came to be painted may be of interest. It is taken from the Minutes of Old King's Arms Lodge of which Sayer was Tyler until his death in 1742.

Monday December 1st 1735

A Motion was made that the Foot Cloth made use of at the Initiation of new members should be defaced on Acct. of convenience. Carried Nem contradicente.

A Second Motion was made that our Right Worshipful Brother Sir Cecil Wray's picture late DGM and the cloth mentioned should be applyed to that purpose and that our Bro West* should be appointed to draw the same and that the Lodge do pay for it when done.

Bro West was pleased to desire that he might have the pleasure to present the Lodge with Sir Cecil's Picture if his Worship will do him the Honour to sit for him, this was a most acceptable proposition to the Society and Bro West's Health was proposed and drank to with great satisfaction.

Monday 7 June 1736

Bro West was pleased to bring his kind Present of our late Friend and Venerable Master Sir Cecil Wray according to his proposal of Dec 1st last which happened to be finished but just before it pleased Almighty God to call him to Himself which appeared to the Society to be done with so much Dexterity and Happiness that it was by a Majority carried that in Order to make this worthy Bro some sort of amends and to show a decent gratitude for the same it would be proper to make him a present of ten guineas which with some fourteen pounds that the frame and case came to and which the Lodge ordered should be handsomely done suitable to the subject and the goodness of the picture at the last Chapter.

In order that this necessary Expense should not sink the funds of the Lodge too far that

*Robert West, Face painter in Holborn, initiated in Old King's Arms Lodge 4 November 1734.

the following Motion be inserted in the next circular Letter to be distributed in July that none may plead ignorance thereon, viz;
It is thought proper by the Lodge for the support of the public Fund and the Honour of the Lodge to raise a general contribution of one half guinea each. It has already been carried once. Your special Attendance is therefore desired on this Occasion to give your Assent or Dissent on this Head.

3. A BREEDING GROUND OF THE MASONIC HIERARCHY

An area where the most intense masonic activity was taking place in the 17th and 18th centuries extended from St. Paul's Churchyard in the East, to Westminster in the West, And St. Giles in the Fields from the North to the River Thames in the South. Further afield, and entered on the first pages of the original Minute Book of Grand Lodge were, regular constituted Lodges at Edgware, Acton and Richmond the first due to Desaguliers and the last due to the influence of Sayer.

Examination of Parish registers in the above mentioned area indicates that Sayers, whether related to Anthony or not, were moving westward. In the 17th century the area around St. Giles in the Fields was an aristocratic one but later it became so densely populated and so notorious that to dwell in a garret in St. Giles was a symbol of utter destitution or degradation. Indicative of the fearful conditions was the building of St. George's in Bloomsbury to enable the gentry and better quality to avoid the risks of attending church at St. Giles in the Fields. Sayer, latterly, certainly worshipped at St. Paul's Covent Garden.

The limits of area quoted above contained four Lodges which we know were invoked in the formation of the First Grand Lodge in 1717. Their places of meeting were:

1. The Goose and Gridiron Ale-House in St. Paul's Churchyard (now the Lodge of Antiquity No 2).
2. The Crown Ale-House in Parker's Lane (Lodge erased in 1736).
3. The Apple Tree Tavern in Charles Street, Covent Garden, Anthony Sayer's own Lodge (now the Lodge of Fortitude and Old Cumberland No 12).
4. The Rummer and Grapes Tavern in Channel Row, Westminster (now the Royal Somerset House and Inverness Lodge No 4).

The location of others can be plotted from the early lists of Lodges.

It is acknowledged that Grand Lodge in 1717 was an innovation applying with close limits to the Cities of London and Westminster only. The idea behind the project was for the principal officers of the few Lodges within these narrow bounds to meet together quarterly in brotherly communication and once a year hold a Grand Assembly and Feast. Outside these gatherings Grand Lodge did not exist except as an ethereal or abstract image consisting of the Grand Master and his two Grand Wardens only. So far as a central controlling body was envisaged it was only of strictly limited territorial control – as described above – within the Cities of London and Westminster and their immediate environs.

There is to me more than a possibility that the germ of co-operation may have sprung from the idea of the so called 'territorial lodges' which can be traced in Scotland to the beginning of the 17th century. These did not appear in England

at that time. In the North of England however at the beginning of the 18th century there do appear lodges of a 'territorial' type but with no official status, eg those at Alnwick in Northumberland and Swalwell County Durham. There are various indications of co-operation among Scottish Lodges. The so called St. Clair charges of 1601 and 1628 show that five lodges united in 1601 and seven in 1628 then finally nine lodges to support the claim to exercise jurisdiction over the Masons of Scotland. From the beginning of the 17th century there was without question an intermingling and transference between England and Scotland. The counties of Northumberland and Durham – particularly the latter – played a big part, for Sunderland was a Port by which many Scots entered England. James Sayer father of Robert, as we have seen came from Sunderland and it was from the North that the 'Mason Word' became increasingly used in the South and was a foretaste of the ritual change to come. Of the four old Lodges already mentioned No 4 easily outstripped the other three in aristocratic membership, to have it in control over the other three would have caused umbrage but a nebulous 'Grand Lodge' of three individuals was acceptable to all. The increasing coastal coal trade between Durham and London no doubt played its part in introducing Northern masonic influence. The coal trade played an important part in the economics of the City of London, and levies made on its sale in London were used to finance many projects including the building of Churches. It also brought South some Northern influences. Joseph Highmore's father was an eminent coal merchant. Robert Sayer the distinguished bookseller received his Freedom of the City on September 1st 1748 and the Stationers Company described his father as James Sayer, late of Sunderland in the county of Durham, gent, deceased. Robert became one of the leading Publishers in his day and succeeded Philip Overton at the Golden Buck, opposite Fetter Lane, Fleet Street. He lived in Queen Square Bloomsbury, Bedford Row and died at Richmond. Between the years 1618 and 1748 we have, including Anthony, no fewer than five Sayers; publishers, bookbinders, printsellers and map sellers. I consider it not unlikely that Anthony was associated with John Overton. All these Sayers lived and worked in the area described and the Piazza Covent Garden is referred to again and again.

4. THE INFLUENCE OF INDIVIDUALS ON A FRATERNITY

If my earlier statement that 'accepted or speculative Masonry is the history of Men' is accepted, the first three Grand Masters are admirable examples. ANTHONY SAYER, GEORGE PAYNE AND DR JOHN THEOPHILUS DESAGULIERS. These three men, all of them commoners, merit the classification of Grand Originals. The last named, DR DESAGULIERS is the best known and most eminent of the three – both in his career and as a mason. He was elected a Fellow and Curator of the Royal Society in 1714. He introduced the reading of lectures in experimental philosophy to the Metropolis and was Chaplain to the Duke of Chandos and to the Prince of Wales. He also played a great part in reorganising ritual and originated the formation of a General Charity. Information on his career is readily accessible.

Of the Second Grand Master, GEORGE PAYNE, much less is known. He has

generally been described as a learned antiquarian but no evidence is available that he was ever elected a Fellow of the Society of Antiquaries. I did however find the following in the Minutes of Old King's Arms Lodge. Monday, August 1 1737 'Part of the Architecture of Palladio were read by the Master to which the Society were very attentive and the late Grand Master our Bro Payne thereupon gave the Lodge a curious Acct. of the manner of building in Persia'. Little has been discovered of Payne's private life his will is dated Dec 8 1755 and was proved by his wife on March 9 1757. He died on Jan 23 1757. He is described as of St. Margaret's Westminster. He died at the house in New Palace Yard, was Secretary to the Tax Office and was comfortably off. He was deeply respected by the brethren of the 'Old Lodge at the Horn' and the craft generally. He compiled the General Regulations which were afterwards finally arranged and published by James Anderson in 1723. His last appearance in Grand Lodge was in November 1754.

ANTHONY SAYER – Gentleman and Bookseller – was elected and invested First Grand Master on St. John Baptist's Day 1717. The only record of the proceedings has to rely on an account by James Anderson, who as a historian must be considered suspect. The account is too well known to require repetition but the following points must be borne in mind. The proceedings opened by the senior past master present, taking the chair for the show of hands. It is clear from this there were other names (or name) submitted, probably Payne or Desaguliers or both. Sayer won, by what margin we know not, was proclaimed and invested. Anderson (always suspect) states four Lodges were present, names them and refers to other past masters being present. Samuel Prichard (author of *Masonry Dissected*) gives the number as six lodges and is probably right. On election not only was Sayer concerned with the problem of co-operation and co-ordination but with providing Speculative Masons with an acceptable image to the public at large. There is no doubt at this time that speculative masonry was highly unpopular, mistrusted and feared. The argument of the following unique Broad Sheet of 1698 is not easy to refute.

To ALL GODLY PEOPLE
in the CITIE OF
LONDON

Having thought it needful to warn you of the
Mifchiefs and Evils practifed in the Sight of GOD by
thofe called Freed Mafons. I fay take Care left their
Ceremonies and fescret Swearings take hold of you;
and be wary that none caufe you to err from
Godliness. For this devllifh Sect of Men are Meeters
in fecret which fwear againft all without their
Following. They are the Anti Chrift which was to
come leading Men from Fear of GOD. For how
fhould Men meet in fecret Places and with fecret
Signs taking Care that none obferve them to do the

Work of GOD; are not thefe the Ways of Evil-
doers?
Knowing how that GOD obferveth privilly them
that fit in Darkness they fhall be fmitten and the
Secrets of the Hearts layed bare. Mingle not among
this corrupt People left you be found fo at the
World's Conflagration.

Set forth as a Warning to this Chriftian Generation
by M. Winter, and Printed by R. Sare at Gray's Inn-
gate, in Holbourn, 1698.

It must be made clear that 'Antichrist' is not used in the Anti Popery sense but
in the terms of St. John's Epistle 1, 2:18–22.

In order to realise the pervading belief in the occult at this time it is sufficient
to mention *Pandaemonium*, or the *Devils Cloyster* by Richard Bovet 1684 (probably
born 1641 and described as Richard Bovet, Armiger, Wadham College, Oxford)
described by those who should know, 'as without question one of the most
extraordinary works in the immense library of occult research.' Here is reported
the belief (also by St. Clement and St. Augustine) that the flood was to be the cure
of devil worship. Shem and Japhet followed Noah in good works but Cham or
Ham instituted his own son Mizraim into the forbidden science incurring Noah's
curse. Bovet also refers to 'the idolatry of the Great Ages after the Flood'.

Sayer's real problem and those of his successors in title was to change the
vestiges still remaining of necromancy and the occult into an acceptable form by
speculative explanation.

Thus the age old tradition of Noah's three sons raising the corpse of their dead
father 'for to try if they could find anything about him for to lead them to the
vertuable secret which this famous preacher had, for I hope all will allow that all
things needful for the new world were in the ark with Noah'. This was transformed
into the five points of fellowship with its speculative and moral explanation stage
by stage. The dire warning is that the Master or Magician questioning the spirits
must remain in the circle, the barrier and protection against evil and not be enticed
out by any pretext or illusion – this becomes watered down to – that being a point
from which a master mason cannot err. The essential secrets of the operative
mason were retained (a) How to form a right angle. (b) How to lay levels and
prove horizontals. (c) How to erect uprights whilst fixing them on their proper
bases – these were the essentials for the operative mason and all these three are
essential to ensure stability. This was the title stability which Sayer selected for his
ritual. His goal for the order was however more than stability it was respectability.

5. SAYER'S IMPACT ON RITUAL

Sayer's election as Grand Master from amongst other strong contestants for that
office was due to the following factors:

(a) He lived and worked in the vicinity

(b) He was a gentleman, possibly the only one in style and background from amongst three out of the four Lodges.

(c) As a bookseller he possessed a degree of learning and erudition

(d) A natural reluctance from the three lodges of widely varying cross section – operative masons and tradesmen to be bossed by a member of a lodge consisting of members of the nobility and highranking members of the armed forces.

It is more than possible that he originally formulated the need for Lodges to co-operate and confer.

Always bearing in mind that it takes time for an idea, however excellent or revolutionary, to be implemented it is not easy and sometimes impossible to pinpoint the Individual responsible. These factors soon became evident after 1717 ie masonry must be given a boost Historically. A more interesting story and climax reflected in the ritual with more involvement of individuals and a universality by omitting references to the Trinity, the latter an integral part of the Guild and Operative masonry by Mediaeval times.

From time out of mind the traditions of masons had been expressed by the Rule of Three (three times three) (1) Noah, Shem and Japhet two of his sons and Cham or Ham the third son who incurred the curse of Noah. (2) Moses, Aholiab and Bezaleel. (3) Solomon, Hiram King of Tyre and Hiram Abif. That splendid and exciting Graham MS dated 1726 gives us the truest picture so far discovered of the pre trigradal ceremony, the latter form introduced in the lifetime of Sayer. The only major corrupt section of the Graham MS is the reference to a King Alboyne and his two sons being associated with Bezaleel, and the omission of Moses. Alboyne is a corruption of Aholiab and to overcome this problem two sons were attributed to Alboyne to maintain the pattern of three. In the formation of a three degree tradition Noah and the practice of necromancy by the three sons and its suggestion of evil magic and all other occult references were banished, the craftmanship of Bezaleel is added to a completely fabricated Hiram Legend, Bezaleel is omitted, and with the drama intensified by the death of Hiram under conditions bordering on the ridiculous, and all references to the blessed Trinity disappears in favour of Deism. Everything being done to encourage universality of appeal. The reference in the Graham MS catechism, 'what is your foundation words at the laying of a building where you expect that some infernal wandering spirit hath haunted and possibly may shake your handiwork' is symptomatic of the belief in the 17th and 18th centuries of good and bad spirits or angels in continual universal strife *Job 1:7* 'And the Lord said unto Satan, from whence comest thou? Then Satan answered the Lord, and said, From going to and fro in the earth, and from walking up and down in it.' After the first two decades of the 18th century the age of reason began to take over, scientific explanation began to take command and scientifically explain and question the Biblical Story.

There are, I think, few who would dispute that the late Dean Inge must be regarded as an example of an extremely advanced master of the Modernist School. On Sunday 6th March, 1932, when preaching at St. Marks, North Audley Street,

London, the Dean said: 'Liberal theologians may jeer and philosophers scoff but there it is. We cannot get rid of the Devil. "Deliver us from the Evil One" is the right translation. I have not the slightest doubt that Christians are enjoined to believe in a positive, malignant, spiritual power. Two reasons alone would make the Graham MS vitally interesting (1) That it entirely bears out Dean Inge's belief and (2) It is completely non-operative in essence and the ideas behind it are exceedingly impressive.

One is left with the inescapable conclusion that until the beginning of the 18th century Bezaleel was the outstanding personality and not Hiram. The following baptismal entry in the Parish Registers of St. Clement Danes, Strand, London- Vol. 5, Baptism 1671/2–1700 would seem to confirm this '1672, May 9th, Basalael Jellyman the son of Basalael and Elizabeth.' I would expect to find that the father was an operative or speculative mason of standing and the surname Jellyman may well be known to specialists in Building history of the period. After 1700 Hiram would have taken precedence.

But who can doubt that Sayers misfortune prompted one of the most unforgettable incidents in the First Degree as we know it ... it cannot be denied we have many members of rank and opulence but some who perhaps from circumstance of unavoidable misfortune or calamity are reduced to the lowest ebb of poverty and distress. I will touch on this again under 'Charity'.

To sum up, Sayer witnessed and participated in a working of two degrees; was in the midst of a dramatic reform when three degrees were elaborated out of the elements of two degrees and a dramatic change made in emphasis, in personality, and in drama. He also saw a nebulous Grand Lodge, of three persons only, become a powerful working entity and the Craft put on a sound financial and commercial basis before he died in 1742.

6. SAYER'S IMPACT ON THE CHARITIES

There is little doubt that individual lodges were highly suspicious of centralisation and this extended to their attitude towards a suggested joint charity. This was no doubt influenced by a natural desire to assist brethren one knows personally rather than to a general fund where the recipient is in many cases a complete stranger. The early minutes of Old King's Arm Lodge show that to their own brethren assistance was forthcoming by grants from the lodge and the odd guinea from members themselves if their compassion was aroused. Sometimes Legacies came from testators to be administered as certain persons named thought fit. The Will of John Sayer of Crownthorpe, Norfolk is an example (1719). After bequests to Ann his wife and his sons Samuel and John he makes the following 'then I give to poor friends belonging to our monthly meeting at HINGHAM in the county aforesaid, the sum of five pounds of like lawful money to be paid into the hands of John Stacy and Robert Myles Sen. within six months next after my Decease and leave it to their discretion to Dispose of the same'.

Anthony became Tyler of Old King's Arms Lodge (1731) and the following Minutes on the General Charity are between the years 1737–40, two years before his death, and present a fair picture of the then general attitude.

MONDAY FEB 6 1737/8. PROPOSED BY BRO GASCOIGNE.

That this Lodge has been liable to the inconvenience of hazarding its Right of attending at the Committee of Charity by not contributing in due time to the general Charity; for want of a Proper Regulation concerning the same. A discretionary power to be lodged in the master of contributing to the Charity (at any Quarterly Communication) what sum he should think fit not exceeding one guinea, providing always that no public Chapter of the Lodge be held between the Time of such Quarterly Communication and that of receiving the summons thereto.

MONDAY THE 1ST DECEMBER 1740.

A letter from the Grand Secretary to the Master was read imparting that there would be a committee of Charity held at the Queens Head in Great Queen Street, on tomorrow night, when the Lodge was all of opinion that the Rt. Worshipful Master should attend.

MONDAY JAN 5 1740/41.

Our Rt. Worshipful Master acquainted the Lodge that next Wednesday will be held a Quarterly Communication at the Devil Tavern, Temple Bar, and desired to know if one guinea shall be carryed in for Charity from this Lodge which was unanimously agreed to and Bro Curzon ordered to attend then with the Warden. The Rt. Worshipful Master not sure that he will be engaged upon other business.

It had been at the Quarterly Communication of November 1724 that the centralised Charity Scheme was first brought forward. A special committee was then appointed to consider the proposal; its report was submitted to Grand Lodge and to the Private Lodges and was adopted by Grand Lodge on 28 February 1726. A committee for the Charity was appointed in June 1727 but it was not until the end of 1729, after Desaguliers had reported in March of that year, that the spirit of Charity began reviving in several Lodges and contributions began to trickle in. The misfortune of Sayer had brought reality home to them.

LATTER DAYS

That his misfortune left him clear of all stigma or loss of caste is amply shown by the fact that during the remainder of his life he was Tyler of at least four famous lodges. About 1731 he was appointed Tyler of King's Arms Lodge and Lodge of Friendship No 6. In both these Lodges the indefatigable Martin Clare FRS and a great friend of Sir Cecil Wray was a leading light and one who must have felt great sympathy with Anthony. In the Lodge he is always referred to as 'Our Tyler'. During March 1739/40 he received an additional gift of money, 'In consideration of the late hard weather' and received compassionate consideration. In March 1741/2 a few weeks after Sayer's death his widow was granted financial relief. This is the last occasion she is referred to and I identified her with Elizabeth Sayer, widow, in the burial register of St. Giles in the Fields some six months after Anthony's death.

At the time of Sayer's death the membership of King's Arms Lodge reads like the pages of *Debrett*. He was buried in the Church of St. Pauls Covent Garden and as I have shown was quite an expensive business, I consider it certain the Lodge paid for his funeral and a great number of members of this Lodge and Grand Stewards lodge saw him laid to rest. Whether they paid for an inscription

I could find no evidence nor whether they paid for his widow's burial in the parish of St. Giles. It is strange that the lives of the Sayers of Pulham St. Mary, Norfolk and those of St. Mary's Battersea, Surrey, failed in the male line at this time.

Between 1719 and 1724 Sayer suffered financial disaster and was in fact one of the first recipients to receive financial assistance from Grand Lodge on the 21st November 1724. On the 21st April 1730 he was again a petitioner. The appeal sets forth his misfortunes and great poverty. This state of affairs is made even more poignant because on 29th January 1730, the Duke of Norfolk was invested and installed at an Assembly and Feast held at Merchant Taylors Hall in the presence of a brilliant Company. No fewer than nine former Grand Masters attended on this occasion and walked in the procession – juniors first, viz Lords Coleraine, Inchiquin and Paisley, the Duke of Richmond, Lord Dalkeith, the Duke of Montague, Dr Desaguliers, George Payne and Anthony Sayer.

If Sayer's position was embarrassing from the financial angle in April, it was even more so at the end of the year for on December 15th 1730, Bro Sayer attended to answer a complaint made against him; after hearing both parties – some of the brethren being of opinion that what he had done was clandestine, others that it was irregular – the Question was put whether what was done was clandestine, or irregular only, and the Lodge was of opinion that it was irregular only, whereupon, the Deputy Grand Master told Bro Sayer that he was acquitted of the charge against him, and recommended to him to do nothing so irregular in the future.

At this meeting the powers of the Committee of Charity were much extended. All business referring to Charity was delegated to it for the future, and the committees were empowered to hear complaints, and ordered to report their opinion to Grand Lodge.

Sayer's position had brought home to masons at large that a common charity fund was essential. They had seen a brother struck down by an undeserved calamity.

As to the charge of irregularity its form has never been agreed upon but in the fresh knowledge that Sayer was associated with the book trade my own view is that it was linked with the publication of Samuel Prichards *Masonry Dissected*, which proved a best seller.

I hope it will be appreciated why the opening pages are taken up with a description of the time. Pictorially of course the engravings of Hogarth's Industrial and Idle apprentices are quite superb in this respect. How forcibly Anthony Sayer's chequered life reminds us of those thought evoking words of

Ecclesiastes 5:11.

> I returned and saw under the sun, that the race is not
> to the swift, nor the battle to the strong, neither yet
> bread to the wise, nor yet riches to men of understan-
> ding, nor yet favour to men of skill, but time and
> chance happeneth to them all

PRESTON'S ENGLAND

The Everyday Life of Masons of the late XVIII Century

THE PRESTONIAN LECTURE FOR 1976

Brig. A. C. F. JACKSON

1. William Preston was born at Edinburgh in 1742 of middle class parents, his father being a Writer to the Signet. He was apprenticed to a printer, but moved to London in 1760. Here, he was immediately employed by the King's Printers, and he remained with this firm all his working life.

A few weeks before his 21st birthday, he was initiated into an Antient lodge, but within months he and several others of its brethen changed their allegiance to the Moderns. He soon became a fine ritualist and Master of his lodge. However, he found himself unsatisfied with the rather elementary ceremonies then in use, and began their revision. By 1772, his work had progressed sufficiently for him to hold a 'Grand Gala' at which he demonstrated his new system before many distinguished Masons.

In the same year, he started a course of instruction in his Lectures, and published his book, *The Illustrations of Masonry*. This explained his Lecture system, and also revised and brought up to date the history of the Craft, written by Dr. James Anderson in his books of Constitutions in 1723 and 1738. The early part of this revised history, i.e. pre-1717, can best be described as 'traditional' but the later part adds to our knowledge of XVIII century Masonry. *The Illustrations of Masonry* ran into many editions and can be found in most Masonic libraries.

Except for a period of ten years, when he was in trouble with Grand Lodge, Preston continued with his Masonic teaching until forced to give it up owing to ill-health. He died, after a long illness, in 1818 and was buried in St. Paul's Cathedral. Among his bequests was an endowment to finance the delivery of an annual lecture to teach the Masonic system he had developed. This was given for some years but fell into abeyance. The Prestonian Lecture was revived in 1924 and a lecturer is chosen annually by the trustees of the fund. Now, however, the lecturer may choose any Masonic subject he wishes.

2. The object of my lecture is to show what the Masons of Preston's period were like; and how they lived in and out of lodge. I have chosen this subject as I believe that, in our studies of early Masonry, we have been too inclined to treat Masonry as if it existed in a vacuum, and to neglect the social and economic background which motivated the individual Mason and directed his daily life and his Masonry. The XVIII century is well documented and, to keep the lecture within bounds, I will deal primarily with the Middle class Masons of London, of the type of William Preston, and shall seldom refer to the rich or poor; though few of the latter were Masons.

PART I – THE BACKGROUND TO MASONRY

Historical Note

3.   Until the Napoleonic Wars started at the end of the XVIII century, it was generally a peaceful period, particularly in the second half when the only major war – that of the American Revolution – had little effect on life in England. It was also a period of economic growth with the Agricultural Revolution bringing a higher national prosperity. The Industrial Revolution was yet to come, but the improvements in communications, which were to make it possible, were starting in the last decades of the century; and were also adding to the country's wealth.

With the increased prosperity of the upper and middle classes came the opportunity to enjoy leisure and the social life. Communities in the various levels of society were small enough for everyone to know everyone else. One of the results was that, in the English taverns and coffee houses, there arose little dining clubs formed by people of similar interest. Into this framework, the Masonic lodge fitted extremely well. A lodge had all the advantages of a club without the excessive gambling and drinking; and Masonic brethren, with a Tyler, could ensure a privacy for themselves which the ordinary club could not guarantee for its members.

4.   The first half of the century provided the biggest changes in the whole history of Masonry. Operative Masonry had virtually disappeared, while the comparatively few lodges of the XVII century had multiplied into a number of Grand Lodges controlling many hundreds of lodges all over the civilized world. The *Old Charges* in their *Manuscript Constitutions* were developed into a printed *Book of Constitutions* and an unwritten system of three degrees. These three degrees, in their turn, had become comparatively unimportant; the main 'work' being the Lectures.

The second half of the century should have been a period of Masonic consolidation and, in many respects, it was so. In England, however, Masonry was bedevilled by the feud between the premier Grand Lodge (the 'Moderns') and the Grand Lodge of the 'Antients', the latter started by Masons who were unwilling to accept the premier Grand Lodge's authority. Each accused the other of mutilating the ceremonies, but the real differences were small. As a generalization, the Antients may be considered as being mostly drawn from the artisan classes with their lodges tending towards being benefit societies, while the Moderns were of a higher social standard with their lodges less formal and more convivial.

5.   It was not an age of political or religious toleration. Masonry, however, was in advance of contemporary thought. Masonry could not have continued at all in England through the period of the Civil Wars of the previous century if politics had entered into it. It is hard for us now to appreciate what a courageous step forward towards universal brotherhood had been the 1723 *Book of Constitutions* which opened Masonry to men of all religions. As was intended, Masonry now became possible to non-Christians, but it also brought together in lodges all shades of Christianity, ignoring the legal barriers designed to keep the different sects apart. Anderson, the Presbyterian Dissenter; Desaguiliers, the Huguenot Protestant; Daniel Deville, the Jewish snuff merchant; and the Roman Catholic Duke of Norfolk could all be members of lodges.

The laws of England forbade the same tolerance in civil life. Penal laws against Roman Catholics had been enacted in the reign of Queen Anne and, by the Test Acts, neither Catholics nor Dissenters could enter a university or hold public office without receiving Holy Communion according to the rites of the Church of England. In 1780, an Anglican member of Parliament, Henry Beaufoy, tried to get the laws changed:

> 'The Saviour of the World instituted the Eucharist in commemoration of his death, an event so tremendous that afflicted Nature hid herself in darkness; but the British legislature has made it a qualification for gauging beer barrels and soap boiler tubs, for writing Custom's dockets and debentures and seizing smuggled tea'.

His motion was defeated, and these sectarian laws were not repealed for another 50 years. Nevertheless, the Mason of Preston's day would not think it unusual to meet Presbyterians. Methodists or Jews in his lodge, though owing to the Papal Bulls of 1738 and 1751, there were few Roman Catholics in Masonry.

The Start of The Day

6.   The daily life of the middle class Mason of Preston's time was generally one of leisure and comfort, but it had its discomforts; one of these must have been getting up in the morning in winter in a Georgian house. In summer, this was no hardship, though many things that we would now look on as essential were missing. In winter, it would be most unpleasantly cold and dark. There were fireplaces in most bedrooms but their use was considered an indulgence reserved for sickness. Coal, however, was coming into general use in domestic fireplaces though it was expensive, of low grade and smoky. There were still no efficient matches. The flint and tinder box, carried by the majority, was difficult to work in the dark while the matches that had been invented, usually some combination of phosphorus and sulphur, were as dangerous as a Molotov cocktail. However, in the meanest household, there was a servant who started the day in even greater discomfort, and it was her duty to blow up the embers of the never extinguished kitchen fire, and light candles. When the time came for calling her employers, she would heat water and, candle in one hand and water jug in the other, go round the house waking its occupants and lighting their candles.

In the early XVIII century, nightclothes were seldom worn by either sex but, by the 1770s, the custom of wearing a shirt or a shift was starting. Nightcaps had always been worn and were a real necessity for those whose heads were often shaved and who slept in a room where, in winter, the water was frequently frozen in the basin.

7.   London was reputed to be the healthiest city in the world, even if the standard was not high. Many of its houses, outside the slum areas, already had running water on all floors. Nevertheless, washing in the morning was infrequent and bathing did not become a normal custom until the middle of the next century, possibly then encouraged by Gladstone's removal of the heavy tax on soap which had been imposed by Cromwell. The morning toilet of the middle class man would therefore be scanty. He may have washed his hands and face, but that would be all. In *The Diary of a Country Parson, 1758–1802*, the Rev. James Woodforde

gives details of everyday existence over nearly 50 years but never mentions washing or bathing. Most men shaved themselves, though it was difficult to keep razors sharp, and many who could afford it had themselves shaved on their way to business. Those who wore wigs had to have their heads shaved, so barbers shops were very numerous; and most combined a lucrative trade in minor medicine and surgery with their normal work.

In spite of London's reputation for health, its sanitary measures, by modern standards, were appalling. Any house that had a garden or yard had an outdoor pit system W.C. which was politely called the 'Necessary House' or 'House of Office' – Parson Woodforde calls his the 'Jerico'. Where such an arrangement was not possible, the outlet of an internal privy was the gutter of the street outside. In the poorer parts of the city, the night-soil was merely dumped in the road or thrown out of the window. Here it lay piled, together with the waste from all shops, until it was washed away by rain, sank into the mud, or was removed by the very infrequent rubbish collectors.

8.   With such a low standard of hygiene, it was inevitable that contagious diseases, such as typhoid and dysentry, should be endemic; and many suffered from skin diseases. It is outside the scope of this paper to deal with doctoring in the XVIII century. It is enough to say that its second half saw the start of scientific medicine with, in England, such men as Jenner who discovered vaccination; Pringle who reformed hygiene; Lind who cured the Navy of scurvy; and the Hunter brothers, perhaps the first true surgeons. It was, nevertheless, generally believed that diseases were caused by impurities or foulness in the air; and there were plenty of bad smells to substantiate this theory. There were no anaesthetics, and it was still the age of traditional remedies, of clysters, purges and emetics, or bleeding and cupping by the barber surgeons. When Parson Woodforde had a sty in his eye, he rubbed it with the tail of a black cat. This seemed to help: 'I cannot but conclude it to be of the greatest service to a Stiony on the Eye-lid. Any other Cat's Tail may have the above effect in all probability – but I did my Eye-lid with my own black Tom Cat's Tail'.

XVIII Century Dress

9. The wide disparities of dress between the various classes of the Commonwealth and Restoration had disappeared. All had adopted the clothing of the middle classes – knee-breeches, stockings and shoes – which had been in fashion for more than half a century, but the coat was now cut away and much longer. To fill the gap, waistcoats, coming half-way down the thighs had been invented. When going out of doors, the *surtout*, a loose greatcoat with a cape-like collar was worn in bad weather.

10.   At the start of the century, men's hair was cut very short or shaven and, at home, a turban or night-cap was worn. The earlier full-bottomed wigs had always been very expensive and, except for officials or state occasions, were disappearing in favour of the small wig tied at the nape of the neck. Even before Preston's time, however, men began to wear their own hair, powdered and often with a pigtail. In 1795, a tax on powder of a guinea a head, imposed by Pitt to pay for the

Napoleonic wars, caused a complete change of fashion; and powdered heads and wigs disappeared for ever.

The cocked hat (*tricorne*) was a mark of standing, and distinction from the lower classes who wore their hats uncocked i.e. with the brim not turned up. Hats were worn indoors, even at meals. It was only in the presence of someone of a much superior station that the hat was removed. This custom, so odd to us now, could have been the reason why the Master of the XVIII century lodge alone wore a hat when the lodge was open.

11.   In theory, it was the privilege of gentlemen to wear swords, but in practice, men of all classes, except perhaps the lowest, wore them. An unfortunate result of this habit was the prevalence of duels, especially after a few drinks had made a gentleman's solicitude for his 'honour' overrule his normal common sense. It is probably for this reason that swords were forbidden in most Modern lodges while the Antients, drawn from the artisan classes, had no need for this rule.

London Town

12.   When the Mason of Preston's time left his house and went out into the streets of London, he was entering what was fast becoming the most important city in the world. It already had a population approaching a million, nearly an eighth of the whole population of England, and ten times bigger than the next city in the country, Bristol.

Small in extent by modern standards, those living in its centre were compressed into appalling overcrowding in slum tenements where several families might live in a single room without light or water. Typical was the area near Seven Dials, north of Covent Garden, and a few hundred yards from Freemasons' Hall, into which it was unwise to go, unless forced by poverty to live there. So close together were the tenements, huts and sheds that it was possible to pass from one end of the area to the other without seeing the light of day. Such places were the private empires of gang bosses, where crimes of violence could be committed with impunity and where criminals were safe from justice. The only police, the Bow Street Runners, started by the magistrates, the Fielding brothers, in 1749, were so few and the town watchmen were so ineffectual that the forces of the law could not enter these areas at all.

The middle classes were spreading from the centre of the City into the nearby villages of Kensington, St. Pancras, Islington and Bethnal Green on the north side of the River Thames; and beyond Southwark and Lambeth to its south.

Thus London was the great urban community of the kingdom, the only place where town life and rural life were completely separate; where the country visitor was a being from another world, and probably a figure of ridicule. To the stranger, and even to the Londoner, it was a city of glamour. The River was crowded, day and night, with small boats taking passengers across to such landing places as Rotherhithe or below London Bridge to Wapping, where the forest of masts stretched for ten miles. The congested streets were a pageant of private and hackney carriages, carts laden with country produce, and sedan chairs, each fighting its way towards various destinations and carrying all classes of society. Business was transacted in hundreds of little shops and offices, often grouped by

trades, as in a modern Eastern bazaar. In the streets were hawked all the necessities of life – the food no doubt being highly insanitary. Each trade had its special cry and each seller was prepared to exchange repartee with rich and poor alike.

Preston's London was at the same time a miracle of wealth and splendour, and a cesspool of poverty and vice. However, it was a city of endless opportunities, drawing into its slums each year a stream of country people who more than made up for the thousands that it killed by its diseases and overcrowding:

'Such London is, by taste and wealth proclaim'd,
The fairest capital of all the world,
By riot and incontinence, the worst'

(William Cowper, 1785. *The Task.*)

The Pleasures of The Table
13.   Breakfast was a light meal, usually eaten at home. At the start of the century, it had only been a piece of bread and a draught of light ale. With the opening up of trade of the East, tea though still expensive, even when smuggled, had become the standard drink of all classes at breakfast, with chocolate being a comparatively rare alternative restricted to ladies and high society, Dr. Johnson's breakfast, a standard one for the middle classes, was bread and butter, and tea. As the dinner hour became later towards the end of the century, more food was eaten at rising or there was a midday snack.
14.   The principal meal of the day was dinner for which the fashionable time was 3 p.m. but those who worked longer hours had a less elaborate meal which they took later. Most wage earners worked very long hours indeed and it was an age of sweated labour for children. All these ate when they finished work. The middle classes, which included most of the professions, had a comparatively formal meal in the late afternoon. This they ate either at home or at one of the many eating houses or taverns which London provided.

During the century, food and cooking was improved in standard and in variety by the use of the potato, coffee, plenty of sugar, more spices, better meat, and the introduction to London of such country cheeses as Stilton, Double Gloucester and Cheddar. Any dinner would include roast meat, fowls and possibly game. Fish, except by the sea or near a river, had to be salted, but oysters, cockles and mussels were sold to all classes in huge quantities by the street sellers. Vegetables were few in variety and somewhat monotonous, with dried peas and beans, and cabbages being common. 'Plumb' pudding and similar heavy puddings or pastries concluded meals. A certain French influence, in such matters as sauces, was becoming popular with the fashionable, but was treated with contempt by the conservative.

By modern standards, the dinner meal was enormous, even as the only real meal of the day. It was usually of two courses, both somewhat similar. In 1770, William Boswell describes how he and Dr Johnson and two ladies had a modest Sunday dinner of 'a very good soup, a boiled leg of lamb and spinach, a veal pye and a rice pudding'. The 'pye' was baked at a public oven, and this was commended as it allowed the servants to go to church. Parson Woodforde, who took a great interest in his food and recorded in detail the dinners of the last twenty years of

his life, describes a dinner for eight at which the first course was 'some fresh water fish, Perch and Trout, a Saddle of Mutton rosted, Beans and Bacon, a couple of Fowls boiled, patties and some White Soup – 2nd Course – Pigeons rosted, a Duck rosted, Piggs Pettytoes – Sweetbreads – Raspberry Cream, Tarts, Puddings and Pippins'. His normal dinners were on the same scale with he and his niece on their own often sitting down to two joints. Masonic lodges only had a formal dinner at their annual feast and this was certainly on similarly heroic proportions.

Dinner at the Old Dundee Lodge in 1749 for some dozen brethen was:

	£.	s.	d.		£.	s.	d.
Ducks				Pease, 3 Qts., Beans, 6			
		8.	0.	Qts.		6.	0.
Necks of Veal				Colliflowers and Cab-			
		6.	0.	bages		2.	0.
1 Ham		8.	6.	Bread, Sauce, etc.		9.	0.
Wine	1.	5.	0.	Dressing		5.	0.
Rum, Lemons & Sugar		8.	6.	French Horns (Music?)		10.	6.
Beer and Tobacco		7.	6.	Tarts		7.	6.
Tyler		2.	6.	Servants		2.	6.
					£5.	7.	6.

15.   For some unexplained reason, smoking in fashionable society declined after the middle of the century. 'Smoking has gone out' said Dr. Johnson in 1773 (Boswell, *Tour of the Hebrides*); and continued so for eighty years. In contrast, there was a steady increase in the use of tobacco by the rest of the population and smoking was normal in all lodges. It was the age of the churchwarden pipe, provided automatically in the type of inn where lodges met; as the tobacco to smoke in it. Many used snuff or chewed tobacco soaked in rum.

16.   There was some heavy drinking among the upper classes and it was the era of the 'three bottle man'. Nevertheless, nationally, the second half of the century was a big improvement on the preceding fifty years. Hogarth's engraving 'Gin Lane' and signs outside drink shops such as 'Drunk for 1d, dead drunk for 2d, clean straw for nothing' dated from before the Act of 1751 which had spectacularly raised the duty on spirits. This turned the poor back to beer, and equally spec-tacularly reduced the death rate, but it only had a marginal effect on the middle and upper classes who could afford and obtain any form of drink, except possibly whisky which had not yet started to be exported from the Highlands.

The usual drinks at table were port wine – fortified with cheap brandy for the English taste – claret, burgundy, and brandy shipped direct from France, even in wartime. Rum from the West Indies was popular, particularly at seaports, but it was also drunk in the form of 'punch', comparatively recently introduced by 'nabobs' and seamen returning from the East. (Named after the Urdu word 'Panch' for five, was composed of rum, sugar, lemon, spices and water). There was a lucrative trade in smuggling the heavily taxed wines and spirits, and also tea. These duties were unpopular and the smuggler was welcomed, even by respectable members of society. Many households, particularly in the rural areas,

had smugglers who visited them regularly much in the same way as Americans, during the years of Prohibition, had their own bootleggers.

Masons certainly drank no more than the general public, and often very much less. In practically all lodges, there were by-laws ruling that brethren 'disguised in Liquor' should be fined or, for repeated offences, excluded. The *Shrewsbury Chronicle* of 19 September 1877 reported:

> 'We learn that last week the new Salopian Lodge of Freemasons was regularly con-
> stituted ... by Major Charles Shirreff, Deputy Provincial Grand Master for this country;
> when an excellent dinner was provided and the afternoon spent with that sober hilarity
> and with that edifying conversation which becomes and always should distinguish Free &
> Accepted Masons from men of dissolute and disorderly manner'.

On the other hand, the Lodge of Amity Song Book of 1778 included the following:

> 'Let every man take a glass in hand,
> Drain bumpers to our Master Grand
> As long as he can sit or stand
>   With decency'.

Perhaps it was symptomatic of the drinking habits of the age that the Georgian sideboard had a specially constructed space big enough to hold a chamber pot to save a long and possibly unsteady journey to the Necessary House!

Sports and Pastimes
17.   For the majority of Englishmen, the formal dinner did not degenerate into the traditional drinking bout, reputed to end with the participants sliding under the table or being carried to bed by the footmen. This may have been not infrequent for the country squire who had hunted, fished or been on his land all day, and who had nothing else to do in the evening. The townsman was normally reasonably abstemious, and after dinner either joined the ladies for cards and conversation, or went out into the town to take part in its many attractions, such as the theatre, or to a coffee house to gossip or gamble; the latter being a far worse middle class vice than drinking.

At the week-end, the Londoner took his pleasures further afield. Every inn or eating house within reach of London turned itself into a Sunday resort. There were also hundreds of cheesecakes and bun shops, the best being by the river at Chelsea, patronized by royalty and giving the name to the Chelsea bun. There was the trip up and down the river, or a visit to one of the many gardens; those at Ranelagh or Vauxhall being the most fashionable. In such gardens, there was music, usually dancing and most had a bowling green. At Vauxhall, the Mason of Preston's time could have heard the infant prodigy, Wolfgang Amadeus Mozart – a future member of the Craft – at the age of eight, playing his own compositions. Other popular attractions were the lions at the Tower of London, the waxworks, the newly opened British Museum or, for 2d, taking tea with the lunatics at Bedlam (until 1770).

For the younger people, football and cricket, with rules very different from the present ones, were played. Football had been the sport of the apprentices of London since mediaeval days and the ball, a leather-covered pig's bladder, was

unchanged since the time when King Henry V's bowmen used to get into trouble kicking one about instead of practising their archery. Cricket, first played in the villages in Stuart times, was now popular with all classes, and many grounds were available around London, including one at Mr Lord's tavern at Marylebone and another in the City at the Artillery Ground.

18. Of spectator sports, there was a big choice, duck-hunting, badger-baiting and cock-fighting. The latter was legal and got such a hold on Georgian Englishmen that much of the slang of the cock-pit has passed permanently into the language. 'Pit against', 'show a clean pair of heels', 'cut out for', and 'battle royal', when a number of cocks are pitted together, for examples. The real 'fancy-man' if he could avoid the efforts of the local magistrate, might attend and bet on a prize-fight, but he ran the risk of ending the day in a general mêlée between the supporters of the contestants and the Army.

Racing was for royalty, the nobility and the owners of the new country houses being built with the profits of the agricultural boom. It was not of much interest, as yet, to the middle classes of London, but it was starting to become important with the first running of the St Leger in 1776, the Oaks in 1779 and the Derby in the following year.

19. The most important of the public spectacles, and one of the most popular because it was free, was the public execution. The penal system of England still had its mediaeval cruelty, and men and women could be sentenced to almost indefinite imprisonment for the smallest offences. Unless they could bribe their gaolers to feed them, all but the strongest starved to death. The crimes punishable by hanging increased throughout the century until they numbered some two hundred, and included the most trivial offences. This severity often defeated itself, with juries refusing to convict for minor offences which would lead to execution. As the police were so inadequate, the worst criminals never were caught and, for those that were, it required the King in person, advised by the Lord Chancellor, in Privy Council, to confirm a death sentence. However, many criminals were hanged. In London, in 1785, there were 97 hangings at Tyburn, all attended by large crowds who would pelt the prisoner with stones and rubbish.

From the Masonic aspect, the most interesting execution was that of the Rev. William Dodd, LL.D. who was Grand Chaplain at the consecration of the new Modern Grand Lodge in May 1776. At the ceremony, Dr. Dodd selected the anthem and delivered an oration which lasted about half an hour. A few months later, he was arrested for forgery and convicted. In spite of petitions in his favour, the sentence was upheld by George III. On the Sunday before his execution, he produced a sermon which he wished to preach to the other convicted criminals, as was the normal custom, but he was not allowed to do so as public opinion was so strongly in his favour that a riot was feared. After his execution, his body was cut down and unsuccessful efforts were made by doctors to resuscitate him. As it was the law that the bodies of executed criminals should be taken to Surgeons Hall for dissection or hung in chains, one can assume that Dr. Dodd's influential friends had their way to some extent, even though they were not able to save him from execution. The Sunday service held in prison was also a public exhibition to which admission could be bought. The convicted criminals sat in a dock in the

centre with a coffin. The sermon was usually preached by the prison chaplain who appears to have had a share in the takings. The non-Masonic story of Dr. Dodd is given in *The Macaroni Parson*, by Gerald Howson, 1973.

The Character of the Middle Class Georgian
20.   The manners of the XVIII century were a curious mixture of coarseness and elegance. The Georgian, particularly in the presence of ladies of his own class, might bow and posture and turn a compliment with the most courtly grace. The same man on occasions would use the most violent and obscene language not only to his equals among men, but also to women of any class inferior to his own. In similar circumstances, many women used just as bad language. References to the natural functions of the body and details of sex, in ordinary conversation, were so frequent and commonplace that they must have become as meaningless as the four letter words of the present day. When his anger was aroused, the upper or middle class man was inclined to get involved in the most unnecessary brawls, often ending in duels with a fatal result.

Costly laces and elegant clothes were worn by people who were frequently dirty and whose personal habits, by modern standards, were most unpleasant. The lack of indoor toilet facilities may have contributed to this, and any lady or gentleman, unable to find the Necessary House, or unwilling to go out of doors, would have no scruples in using the fireplace or a corner of the room.

There were, of course, many people of better manners, but it must be appreciated that the men of this period were liable to indulge in the coarsest of pleasures, and the chastity of any woman, of a level of society lower than his own, was a challenge to the virility of the Georgian male. In the country houses, the chief sport of the young gentlemen of the family seems to have been the seduction of the female servants, a pastime as much enjoyed by the quarry as by the hunter. The young woman concerned, if fortunate enough to have a child could, under the Bastardy Act of 1733, demand marriage – which was unthinkable – or be kept in comfort for the rest of her life.

21.   It is only fair to give the other side of the picture, as it was far from being an irreligious age and there were many whose private lives were irreproachable. The Christian doctrines of the period laid down rules of conduct far stricter than in previous centuries. Churches, particularly in the country, were well filled and the proportion of communicants remarkably high. The majority of Anglican parsons took their duties seriously, looking after their parishioners and holding regular services. Unfortunately, this was not always the case. Clergymen, once appointed, were virtually irremovable and those with rich livings could not be forced to tend them and many left a poorly paid curate to do the work. Even Parson Woodforde, one of the better type of incumbent, thought nothing of leaving his parish in the care of a curate for four or five months each year. The London parson had no need to do more than preach once on Sundays if so inclined, spending the rest of his time in society or in the coffee house.

The Nonconformist ministers appear to have been more conscientious and closer to the people than their Anglican counterparts, and the revivalist teaching of the Wesley brothers reached expanding areas previously neglected by the

Anglican Church or the State. As he moved across the country, John Wesley formed his supporters into small self-governing congregations able to look after themselves; and so gave permanent roots to revivalism. Wesley's Methodism was well suited to the new towns springing up in the coal and iron areas in the North and Midlands; towns which had no tradition or background with Anglicanism. Masonry also put down roots among the middle classes in such areas which were, in due course, to become strongholds of the Craft.

22.   The XVIII century saw the start of organized private charity, mainly in the provision of hospitals which the poor could attend free. Guys, Westminster, St. George's, London and Middlesex all date from this period, while there was a corresponding wave of building of small clinics and dispensaries in the counties. A general increase also in the provision of charitable schools, mostly for found-lings, was perhaps the stimulant for such Masons as the Chevalier Ruspini to found the Girls School and for the Antients, a few years later, to open the Boys.

PART II – MASONRY IN PRESTON'S TIME

The Masonic Lodge and its Furnishings

23.   The Mason of Preston's time would receive his summons by hand from the lodge Tyler. Meetings were held fortnightly or monthly. On the day, there was no need to hurry over dinner as, except at the annual feast when the proceedings would include a meal, the normal time of opening the lodge was six o'clock or after.

After 1776 a few lodges met at the newly built Freemasons' Hall, but the majority remained in one of the many inns which catered for small club gatherings. In the public room of the inn, the early arrival, meeting another brother could stop for a glass of ale before going upstairs to the lodge. At the door, he found the Tyler, possibly an old Mason, but equally likely to be one of the waiters of the inn, specially initiated for the office.

The average size of XVIII century lodges, particularly in London, was small; a dozen members at a meeting being a good number. The lodges were small because the brethen, probably used to the intimacy of the small clubs of the period, liked it that way. A candidate, made in a lodge, did not necessarily become a member of it, and had to be balloted for as such after a formal proposition. Cases of initiates being black-balled are not unknown. There was little urge for lodges to have more than the occasional candidate as there was plenty to do in 'working the Lectures' without having to spend time on the degree ceremonies. London lodges, if they made many Masons, presumably did so because they wanted the fees to swell their funds. Country lodges, inclined to be larger, appear usually to have taken their initiates as members but, in all lodges, the ceremonies of making Masons, though essential, were of comparative unimportance.

The Old Dundee Lodge at Wapping had a special 'Making Room' from 1763, and only those concerned with the ceremony went into it, other members remaining in the lodge room if they wished. In the 1780s, the Whitchurch Lodge By-laws laid down that no Mason could be made, except at an emergency meeting, for which the candidate had to pay all expenses. Visitors, however, could always

demand admission to any lodge. If proved, they were admitted on payment of a small fee to cover the food and drink they might consume.

24.   Towards the end of the XVIII century, lodges were comfortable places. Thanks to woodworkers like Chippendale, and to French influence, furniture was no longer the stools and benches of the previous century. Most lodges kept their own furniture at the inn where they met, and provided their Master and Wardens with large, padded arm-chairs, carved with Masonic symbols, while the other brethen sat on well-made chairs. For lighting, wood or brass candlesticks, elaborately carved in the richer lodges, were used for illumination and for the symbolic lighting. It was still an era of smoky candles which had to be snuffed at regular intervals. Gas was not to come for several decades and electricity for nearly a century. The first mention of gas in a lodge that the writer has been able to find is in the Minutes of the Cannongate Kilwinning Lodge No. 2, dated 15.6.1818, when 'owing to the great expense of lighting the lodge room with wax and tallow candles, Resolved that the Secretary and Treasurer wait upon the Manager of the Gas Company'. In winter, a good fire of wood or coal, possibly in a mantlepiece copied from one made by the Adam brothers, made the lodge a pleasant place in which to pass an evening.

Masonic Clothing

25.   Masons in lodge wore white gloves and an apron as a compulsory uniform. Towards the end of the century, a white stock was also to become 'Masonic' in many lodges, and brethren refused admission if wearing any other colour. The 1750s were a period of change for the apron. Earlier, the plain white lambskin, as used since 'time immemorial' was worn in private lodges and was lodge property. In lodge Minutes, there are frequent references to motions for 'The Lodge to be new Cloathed' or 'New Aprons to be bought' when presumably the lodge bought a new set. After the middle of the century, the apron tended to become the personal property of the individual who began to decorate it as he thought fit. This was particularly so among the Antients. The two pillar *motif*, surrounded by Masonic emblems, was popular while a number of shops sold transfers which could be superimposed on the white skin. Many of the designs were colourful and elaborate, and examples of the later types can be seen in the Museum of Grand Lodge.

26.   It was not known when Masonic jewels first began to be worn. London Companies wore regalia from very early times and, in Scotland, the officers of the Incorporations may have worn insignia of office from the XV century on. Lodges possibly copied these examples and started the custom of Masonic jewels. However in England by 1727, jewels for Masters and Wardens were usual enough for Grand Lodge to have to make regulations for their use and for the colours of the ribbons from which they could be suspended. In Preston's time, all officers, including Past Masters, wore jewels and occasional presentations of special jewels were made. Those worn by the rival Grand Lodges differed.

The Masonic Ceremonies

27.   In the middle of the century, the ceremonies for making Masons and working the Lectures, though varying in lodges, were basically the same. Two decades later

i.e. when Preston started teaching, some development had taken place. A lodge opened with the Right Worshipful Master (The title changed to 'Worshipful Master' in English lodges at the Union of 1813) in the theoretical East. Opposite him, in the West, was the Senior Warden. In some lodges, he still had the Junior Warden on his left, but by 1770 the JW's place was tending to become fixed in the middle of the South. In Modern lodges, the other officers usually were the Secretary, Treasurer, one or two Stewards and the Tyler. Lodges of the Antients and some of the Moderns had in addition two Deacons who helped with the degree ceremonies by doing duties otherwise performed by the Wardens or Stewards. It will be seen that, in small lodges, some 50% of the brethren had to take an active part in the work of the lodge.

The Master was an important figure and did 'rule and direct his lodge'. Besides conducting the comparatively short and simple degree ceremonies, he had to work the Lectures. As these were liable to develop into *extemporare* discussions, he needed sufficient Masonic knowledge to teach symbolic Masonry and to keep the work within the Landmarks. Masters were often in office for several years, or shared it by taking turns with other experienced brethren. The influence of a Master can be seen in the story of the Lodge of Antiquity. In a poor way about 1775, the Lodge invited the experienced Preston to join and become its Master. His teaching of the Lectures he had recently developed was so popular that the Lodge at once picked up. Unfortunately his success led to trouble through the jealousy of a few of the older members.*

28.   The lodge met round a long table and, when the opening ceremony ended, the Master opened the Bible which he had in front of him, put on his hat and sat down. After any lodge business, if there was a degree ceremony to be done, the officers and any brethren who wished to take part, left their seats. The Master took up the Bible while others moved the necessary symbolic lights and stood round a diagram previously laid out on the floor by the Tyler. In early days, this diagram had been drawn with chalk or charcoal, and the candidate had later to wash it out, using a mop and pail. By Preston's time, most lodges had metal or wood plates to represent the appropriate symbols, or a floorcloth with a design on it.†

Working the ceremony only took a few minutes. Then the candidate removed the diagram and retired to 'restore himself'. The brethren returned to their places round the table and, when the candidate re-entered the lodge, the remainder of the ceremony was quickly completed. Then the brethren settled down to the serious business of the evening, the Lectures.

29.   There was probably little difference between the Lectures used by the two Grand Lodges except that, up to the time Preston and other Masonic teachers started their elaborations, the Moderns' were probably shorter.‡ The Lectures referred to the symbolism of the making ceremonies, the form and contents of the lodge, and the duties of Masons. Symbolic references to architecture, particularly in relation to Solomon's Temple, were stressed. They were worked in catechism

* The story is given in the *History of Freemasonry* by R. F. Gould, Vol II, pp 422–8, and in the Prestonian Lecture for 1947 by G. Y. Johnson.
† For details of the mid-XVIII century ceremonies, see the author's *English Exposures of 1760/62, A.Q.C. 84.*
‡ The Prestonian Lecture for 1928, Masonic Teachers of the XVIII century by J. Stokes covers this subject.

form with the Master usually asking the questions. There were a number of stock questions and answers, with catch phrases, which had been in use for decades, but there was plenty of opportunity for extemporization.

30.   The proceedings were leisurely and companionable, and accompanied by the eating of snacks, drinking and smoking. In some lodges, this freedom was restricted to periods when the lodge was called off. Calling-off was frequent, so there was ample time for the drinking of toasts and the singing of songs. Contemporary Masonic books published lists of toasts, and the health of all those in the lodge was probably drunk at least once during the evening. Loyal toasts, often with the wording 'The King and the Craft' were normal* and usually the whole royal family was also toasted. 'The ladies', 'our fair sisters' and other romantic sentiments figures among the non-Masonic toasts.

31.   Hardly a Masonic book was published in the XVIII century without an appendix of songs. The 1723 *Book of Constitutions* had songs; the 1738 edition added others. For the Antients, their book, *Ahiman Rezon*, 1756, had 128 pages of songs and poetry out of 224 pages. In his *Bibliography of Freemasonry*, 1844, Dr. G. B. F. Kloss catalogues 213 Masonic songbooks in various languages between 1734 and 1837. By modern standards, these early Masonic songs are almost uniformly bad, with faulty scansion, indifferent rhyming and turgid sentiments. Hardly any of the music was original, most of the songs being set to existing tunes of which the majority, perhaps fortunately, have disappeared. The only song that is still in general use, the Entered Apprentice's Song, has a sentimental attachment for all Masons but, by any standards, it is no masterpiece.

A musical programme of the Dundee Lodge, dated 1784, gives an idea of the jingoistic sentiments of a period which actually was remarkably peaceful. The music played was 'God Save the King', 'Britons Strike Home', 'Rule Britannia', 'See the Conquering Hero Comes', and 'Hearts of Oak'. Songs included 'This Day a Stag must Die', 'Land of Potatoes' – perhaps there was an Irish brother present – 'Wine cannot cure', 'The Joys of a Humble State', and 'What Folly Boys to be Downhearted'. However, they all seem to have given the brethren of Preston's time a great deal of pleasure, usually ending with an enthusiastic toast and Masonic fire.

Singing was a nationally popular form of entertainment and it seems a pity the songbooks did not include some of the better songs which, in a musical period, did exist. However, the audience was a sympathetic one and it would be rare for a singer to be without an accompaniment. Few people could not perform on some musical instrument and some brother would produce a flute or a fiddle from under his chair to add encouragement. Perhaps some of the wealthier lodges might already have possessed one of the newly invented pianofortes or owned a harpsichord.

And so to Bed

32.   When the lodge business was ended, some of the brethren would take supper together in the inn while others went home. It was no longer the London of Hogarth's picture 'Night' of 1738 which shows a drunken Master of a lodge being

---

* An interesting reference to this toast and its meaning appears in the *'Freemason's Guide and Compendium'*, by Bernard E. Jones.

helped home by an equally drunk Tyler. Of course, there were Masons who drank too much but the majority did not and, like Major Shirreff, writing to the Grand Secretary in 1788, could refer to themselves as 'not a supper man' preferring bread and cheese in their own lodgings to a meal in a tavern and a late return home through the streets of London.

Until the 1800s, there was no effective police force, and travellers on all roads, not only in the country but in and around London, were liable to attack. In the early part of the century, it had been the sport of fashionable, though unpleasant, young men calling themselves Mohocks or Scowerers to assault pedestrians or upset peaceful gatherings in inns. These had mostly disappeared by Preston's time, but highway robberies were still committed almost daily on all routes leading out of London. Some roads were so dangerous that armed horsemen were available for hire to protect travellers.

The streets of London were no place in which to be after dark. Because of open fires and the many urban industries which used coal, a noisome yellow fog, restricting visibility to a few feet, was an almost nightly occurrence in winter. Even by day in summer, there was a perpetual haze over the city. If he had to be out at night, the wise man walked with care, hand on sword or pistol, listening for following footsteps and avoiding any figures which might loom out of the darkness and, as quickly, be swallowed up once more by the fog.

Few men went unarmed but, at night, mere personal protection was inadequate against the gangs which infested the streets. The sensible Mason returning home from lodge joined a group, took a cab or a sedan-chair. If he could afford no more, he could hire, for a few pence, a link-boy or girl who, with torches of tar or resin, would light him home; at least keeping his feet out of the filth of the streets. The ordinary, peaceful Londoner was always thankful to get to the safety of his own home; itself closely shuttered against evil-doers and the sulphorous atmosphere.

Conclusion

33.   The increase in Masonry in the latter half in the XVIII century was remarkable. Masons came from all levels of society. A contemporary list would start with most of the Royal Family, and would continue with many members of the peerage and of the social and intellectual life of the country. Some of these men had disreputable sides to their characters, but many were of probity and benevolence. Nevertheless, the most solid and responsible members of the Masonic community, and its greatest strength were the middle class merchants and professionals of the type of Preston and his associates. None of their names appears in the history of their country and few in the history of Masonry, but there is no doubt that, at this not particularly praiseworthy period of English history, such men gave the Craft a powerful influence – an influence that it had never been able to exert before and possibly will never achieve in the future.

THE TYLER OR OUTER GUARD

THE PRESTONIAN LECTURE FOR 1977

ROY A. WELLS

Whilst there has been a surfeit of speculative writing on the subject of the Tyler, including probable derivations of the word and its applications, nowhere do we find an official reason for the Masonic adoption of that title. In the early period he was referred to as the 'Doorkeeper' or 'Guarder' and it is not until comparatively late in the development of organized Freemasonry that the word 'Tyler' appears. Details of his duties arise only in piecemeal fashion but there is ample evidence that they developed similarly to those of the Beadles employed by City Councils and Trade Gilds.

Although several of the early composite Gilds included the trade of Tyler in the title, e.g., *Tylers, Carpenters and Masons; Tylers and Bricklayers; Tylers and Plasterers,* it does not mean that any one craft would have been involved in the internal affairs of another. From mediaeval times onward skilled workers jealously guarded their separate crafts and strictly observed lines of demarcation between their own and allied trades. Posting a sentinel was a well established pattern for trade meetings and stonemasons were no less anxious to protect the mysteries of their craft.

In 1730 Samuel Prichard quoted a Masonic catechism that may well have described an earlier trade practice:

Q. Where stands the Junior Enter'd Prentice.
A. In the north.
Q. What is his business.
A. To keep off all Cowans and Evesdroppers.
Q. If a Cowan (or Listner) is catch'd, how is he to be punished?
A. To be placed under the Eves of the House (in rainy Weather) till the water runs in at his Shoulders and out at his Shoos.
(*Masonry Dissected.*)

Delegation of that duty to the 'Junior Enter'd Prentice' was quite practical as not only could he be spared from trade discussion but no doubt would have been the most nimble footed to chase an offender. It is an interesting derivation of the word eavesdropper.*

We find another reference which may also have its roots in trade meetings:

How was you admitted a Mason.
By three Solemn Knocks at the Door the last a double distance of Time and much larger.
At the door before you are admitted stands an Entred Prentice with a drawn sword to
guard against droppers, as they call them, from Hearkening. For in this they are very

* *Oxford English Dictionary* (See examples from 15th cent.) 'Euesdroppers vunder mennes walles or wyndowes ... to bere tales.'

Andrew Montgomery, 'Garder of ye Grand Lodge' (1738).

cautious and the Question is frequently ask'd is the House Tiled? If safe from hearing the Answer is T' is Tiled. If not or any Person in Company not a Mason. Untiled. (*Dialogue between Simon and Philip*, c. 1725.)

EARLY OFFICIAL REFERENCES

Organized Freemasonry of today is in direct line of descent from the formation of the premier Grand Lodge in London in 1717. Within a few years a form of behaviour and government was established through the co-ordination of material from the various *Old Charges* and *Regulations*. It was edited by Rev. James Anderson following a collection made by George Payne (Grand Master in 1718 and again in 1720). Anderson's first *Book of Constitutions* was published in 1723 and Regulation No. XIII in that book deals with our subject:

> ... Another Brother (who must be a *Fellow-Craft*) should be appointed to look after the door of *Grand-Lodge*; but shall be no member of it.

The next official reference to guarding the door appeared in 1728, but it stemmed from a Resolution that was passed in Grand Lodge on 24 June 1727:

> Resolved Nem Con that in all private Lodges and Quarterly Communication and Generall Meetings the Maʳ and Wardens do wear the Jewells of Masonry hanging to a White Ribbon (Vig.ʳ) That the Maʳ wear the Square the Senʳ Warden the Levell and the Junʳ Warden the Plumb Rule.

It was to lead to an interesting incident recorded in the Minutes on 26 November 1728:

> It being told to the Deputy Grand Master that a Brother (who was a Warden of a Lodge) attended without in expectation of his Master's coming who had custody of the Jewels of their Lodge, and for want of which he could not gain admittance; on several Members present vouching for him, the Deputy Grand Master Ordered the Officer who kept the Door, to admit the said Brother, who accordingly took his place in the Lodge.

Whether or not the Doorkeeper entered Grand Lodge to take his order directly from the Dep. Grand Master or that it was conveyed to him through a Member is subject to conjecture. Notwithstanding, his vigilance was commendable.

DOORKEEPERS AND GUARDERS

In a large number of Lodge records we find references to 'Doorkeeper' or 'Guarder' and those descriptions continue to be used long after the appearance of the term 'Tyler'. Specimen entries on these lines are as follows:

> Br. Johnson be desired to attend to gard the Lodge every Lodge night, and that he be allowed eighteen pence and one pint of wine for his attendance.
> (*Minutes, 10 March 1731, Swan & Rummer, then No. 39, Erased 1751.*)

In other Lodge records the 'one pint of wine'; might well read 'one quart of ale'.

Andrew Montgomery is described as 'Garder of Ye Grand Lodge', according to an engraving of 1738; the Lodge meeting at the Two Black Posts, Maiden Lane,

London, in June 1738 officially instructed 'Bro. the doorkeeper to lock up all aprons'. (*Minutes, 22 June 1738, then No. 163, Erased 1801.*)

Generally speaking, Doorkeepers and Guarders were 'Serving Brethren' and quite often were landlords of premises where meetings were held. In many cases they did not rise above the grade of Entered Apprentice and, although there are some classic exceptions, very few were members of a Lodge. As the years went by and Lodge procedure developed an Entered Apprentice was insufficiently qualified so the Tyler was Passed and Raised. Here is the way one Lodge dealt with that situation:

> The Lodge was convened for the purpose of raising Bro. Joshua Evans, Tyler to the Lodge, and it was agreed that he is to receive no payment for this night's attendance. (*History Indefatigable Lodge No. 237, p. 110, n.d.*)

And in the *Rules and Orders*, 1775, of Grand Masters Lodge No. 1, we find:

> ... a Brother well skilled in the Master's part shall be appointed and paid for Tyling the Lodge Door during the time of Communication.

TYLER AS A TITLE

The first official use of Tyler as a specific title appears in Grand Lodge Minutes of 8 June 1732. It is included in an account of a complaint from several Grand Stewards against a Bro. Lewis whom they had engaged as an attendant for the Grand Feast that was due to follow the previous meeting of Grand Lodge. Lewis had been entrusted to lock up thirty dishes of meat which were for that banquet, but because of his carelessness and neglect of duty they had been taken away 'by those who had no manner of Right to the same'. Upon being faced with the charge Bro. Lewis was insolent and in consequence was called before Grand Lodge where he made only 'a frivolous and trifling defence'. He was about to receive an official censure when it was observed that Bro. Lewis was 'Tyler' to several Lodges and 'if the Grand Lodge should Strictly pursue their Resentment it might deprive him of the best part of his subsistence'. The incident ended with Bro. Lewis publicly asking pardon of both the Grand Lodge and the Grand Stewards, faithfully promising to take greater care and 'behave decently', as it was so expressed, in the future. From 1732 there are countless references to Tylers and the title became common-place.

In 1738 Rev. Anderson published the New *Book of Constitutions*, and the 'Old Regulation XIII' dealing with the appointment of '... a Fellow-craft' to look after the door of Grand Lodge was altered to '... another Brother and *Master-Mason* should be appointed the *Tyler*, to look after the Door; ...'

In this edition Anderson included an account of the setting-up of the premier Grand Lodge in 1717 and wrote:

> Sayer *Grand Master* commanded the *Master* and *Wardens* of Lodges to meet the *Grand* Officers every *Quarter* in *Communication* at the Place that he should appoint in his Summons sent by the *Tyler*.

That was written and published twenty-one years after the event, before a Free-masons' Hall had come into existence; in the early period Grand Lodge had no fixed place of meeting. In using the word 'Tyler' and describing the distribution of the Summonses, Anderson may well have been influenced by development that had been consolidated as general practice.

DELIVERY OF SUMMONS

According to the records the Landlord of the Queen's Arms, St. Pauls Churchyard, in 1736, was 'Allowed 12d each Lodge night for carrieing ye Letters to each Member'. That was changed the following year to:

> Ordered that the Tyler for the future do deliver out the Summons for the meeting of this Lodge, and be paid for the same One Shilling exclusively of his money for the Tyling. (*Minutes, 3 July 1744, Lodge of Antiquity, No. 2.*)

Payment for 'Carrying Somonds' was raised to two shillings the next year.
    It is of interest to note that Lodge of Felicity, No. 58, had reversed this situation six years previously:

> July 12th 1738. This night the Lodge took into consideration the Great Expence of the Tyler and came into the following Resolution nem. con: the House [by which was meant the Gun Tavern, Jermyn Street] shall send the Summons to each Member one day before the Lodge night and that the Tyler shall have one shilling only for Tyling the Lodge.

Delivery of matter other than, or in addition to, the Summons was quite normal but one case is on record where that extension was unacceptable. A Brother resigned from Lodge of Unity, No. 69, because his Lodge Certificate had been given to the Tyler for delivery. This apparent indignity has not been dated by the Lodge historian but it was probably in the early 19th century.

DUTIES AND PAYMENT

The most comprehensive outline of duties required of the Tyler is contained in the 1737 By-laws of Lodge of Friendship, No. 6:

> The Doorkeeper is to have Twelvepence ev'ry time of his Attendance. He is never to be off Duty in Lodge Hours, nor be anyhow negligent or remiss in it. He is to take care of the Clothing of the Members, and Utensils of ye Lodge. He is to offer a List to be subscri'd by the Members as Visitors shall call for, to cause them (being vouch'd for) to enter their names in his List, with ye particular Lodge to which they belong, & set down who the persons are that recommend them. He is also before their admission to receive Twelve-Pence apiece from such Visitors, and to produce ye said List and receipts to the Master or Wardens before the Lodge is closed; He is to keep the Key of the Apron Box etc. and be ready with it always in good time; or failing in any of these, he shall lose his pay for the Night.

Comparison between Lodge records in different parts of the country and between By-laws of different dates enables us to build up a picture of changing attitudes and developing procedure. Compare the last example, from London in 1737, with this one from Halifax thirty years later:

There is also to be a Tyler appointed out of the Brotherhood to stand at the door of the Lodge, with a naked sword in his hand, for the security of the same, and to give notice to the Lodge when any visiting brother shall desire admittance; he is also to refuse admittance in Lodge hours to any brother he thinks is disguised in liquor, until he has acquainted the Master therewith. He is also to attend the Master, or in his absence the Deputy Master, twice a week to receive his orders and he is to have one shilling every Lodge night for his trouble. He is to refuse admission to any member of the Lodge who is not clean and decently clad with a white cloth.
(*1767 By-laws, Lodge of Probity, No. 61, Halifax.*)

The injunction for Brethren to appear 'decently clad with a white cloth' was certainly not confined to Halifax nor to that period as an item dated in 1812 from Newport, Monmouthshire, will shew:

Bro. Hy. Griffith fined 6d for appearing in the Lodge in a coloured Handkerchief contrary to Regulations.
(*Minutes 26 June 1812, Royal Cambrian Lodge, then No. 135, Erased 1830.*)

Now let us look at the duties and fees that were paid in a London Lodge in 1798:

After the other Officers are invested and have taken their Stations, a Tyler shall be chosen and the Master shall give him charge of the Jewels, Furniture and Ornaments of the Lodge, that he keeps neat and clean, and also guards the Door and Avenues to the Lodge. To prepare two Lodges each night of Meeting, Summons the Members at least Four days before the regular Lodge nights, for which he shall be allowed the sum of Ten Shillings and Sixpence, and for every Lodge of Emergency Five Shillings, exclusive of One Shilling and Sixpence for each Badge and Collar the whole to be paid from the Funds of the Lodge.
(*1798 By-laws, Bedford Lodge, No. 157.*)

'DRAWING THE LODGE'

The requirement 'To prepare two Lodges each night of Meeting' indicates that it was also part of the Tyler's duties to set out, on the floor of the Lodge room, designs and symbols appropriate to the Degree to be conferred. In the early period they were drawn with chalk or charcoal, and clay models were used with great effect. Payment for this duty was usually separated from other fees:

The Tyler's remuneration was fixed at one shilling and sixpence each Lodge night for tyling the Lodge, and two shillings and sixpence for forming a Fellow Craft or Master's Lodge.
(*By-laws, n.d., Jerusalem Lodge, No. 197.*)

From the same Lodge we find an item that can only have arisen from a mis-understanding or through lack of communication; a situation that Tylers do meet on occasions:

The Tyler having made a mistake in forming the Entered Apprentices Lodge, the Raising was deferred till Lodge night after next.
(*Minutes, 16 September 1772.*)

Among the various descriptions of Floor Drawings perhaps the best comes from *Jachin and Boaz* which was published in 1762:

> He (the Candidate) is also learnt the step, or how to advance to the Master upon the Drawing on the Floor, which in some Lodges resembles the Grand Building, termed a Mosaic Palace, and is described with the utmost Exactness. They also draw other figures, one of which is called the Laced Tuft, and the other, the Throne beset with Stars. There is also represented a perpendicular Line in the Form of a Mason's Instrument, commonly called the Plumb-Line; and another figure which represents the Tomb of *Hiram*, The First Grand Master, who has been dead almost Three Thousand Years. These are all explained to him in the most accurate manner, and the Ornaments or Emblems of the Order are described with great facility.

Tape and nails were used to form the larger items, and templates to outline some of the symbols were used by the inartistic. However, many Tylers possessed outstanding talent and ability, an example of which is shewn by this record:

> The Lodge being this Evening opened and drawn and illuminated with much dexterity by the skill of Bror. Bossemberg the Tyler of the Lodge.
> (*Minutes, 22 February 1742, Lodge of Friendship, No. 6.*)

In this instance we are entitled to think that coloured chalks were used justifying the description 'illuminated'.

It can be fully appreciated that in the various perambulations in Lodge, Brethren would not be permitted to walk across the Floor-Drawing. Thus we have a logical reason for 'Squaring the Lodge', though not exaggerated to the extent that is sometimes performed today.

In July 1778 Laurence Dermott, Grand Secretary of the 'Antients', could not resist a tilt at the 'Moderns' on the subject of Floor-Drawings:

> Nor is it uncommon for a Tyler to receive ten or twelve shillings for drawing two sign-posts with chalk, charcoal, etc. and writing Jamaica upon one and Barbadoes upon the other; and all this, I suppose for no other use than to distinguish where these liquors are to be placed in Lodge.
> (*Ahiman Rezon, 3rd Edn., 1778, et seq. Laurence Dermott.*)

Although it was usually the Tyler's duty to 'draw the Lodge' sometimes it would be illustrated by a Member well skilled in that art. It is of interest to note that whilst the practice of 'Forming the Lodge' in this manner continued for many years in various parts of the country we do find a record of a painted cloth as early as 1737:

> Brother William Goudge this night made a present to this Lodge of a painted cloath representing the several forms of Masons Lodges.
> (*Minutes, 14 March 1737, Medina Lodge, No. 35, Cowes.*)

Henry Sadler states this was probably the first substitute for the old custom of 'drawing the Lodge' on the floor and it was the forerunner of Tracing Boards. (*Thomas Dunckerley, p. 160, London, 1891.*)

In a description of a Masonic procession which took place in Madras in 1787, William Preston recorded that it was headed by 'Two Tylers with drawn Swords'

but, lower down the list, 'The Lodge (i.e., Tracing Board), covered with white satin, carried by four Tylers.' (*Illustrations of Masonry, 1788 Edn.*)

According to *Jachin and Boaz* the Tyler was not responsible for scrubbing out the drawing:

> The Ceremony now being ended, the new-made Member is obliged to take a Mop out of a Pail of Water brought for that Purpose, and rub out the Drawing on the Floor, if it is done with Chalk and Charcoal. Then he is conducted back, and every Thing he was divested of is restored; and he takes his Seat on the Right Hand of the Master. He also receives an Apron, which he puts on, and the List of the Lodges is likewise given to him.

LODGE LISTS AND APRONS

In an age when spurious and clandestine Freemasonry was rife it was necessary for Brethren to have information of dates and places of meetings of Regular Lodges on the Register of Grand Lodge. It was yet another duty of the Tyler to provide the List:

> ... the said Tyler being obliged to present to each New-made Brother with a List of the Lodges.
> (*By-laws, 1757, Lodge of Antiquity, No. 2.*)

At first the List was a crudely printed pamphlet but as the number of Lodges increased and the need even greater, particulars were then printed in Masonic magazines and Calendars. In principle they were the forerunners of the modern *Year Book*.

The List was much needed by the Tyler when attending to his duties obtaining from a visiting Brother necessary Lodge details. That information would be checked against the official List and any cases of doubt would be reported to the Master. Admission to the meeting would depend upon an investigation by a responsible member of the Lodge; a pattern that still applies.

In the early period aprons were the property of the Lodge and in some instances Candidates were required to 'clothe the Lodge' i.e., to provide new in replacement. They were purchased in bulk the cost being about 1/6d each:

> To purchase $3\frac{1}{2}$ dozen aprons for the use of the Lodge.
> (*Minutes, 18 November 1742, Lodge at Crown and Anchor, Seven Dials, London.*)

Safe-keeping of aprons was another responsibility of the Tyler:

> The Doorkeeper to take care of clothing of members and utensils of the Lodge and to keep the key of the Apron Box etc. ...
> (*By-laws, n.d., Lodge of Friendship, No. 6.*)

There was no difference between the aprons worn in Lodge and those worn by stonemasons at work. Indeed, in 1741 a Brother was fined for wearing his working apron (*Minutes, 21 January 1741, Lodge at Duke of Bedford's Head*). The aprons shown in all early illustrations and engravings are long ones with a bib and reached from chest to knees or lower.

The long aprons are depicted in vastly different circumstances and one of great interest is the frontispiece of Anderson's *Book of Constitutions* which shows the

Duke of Montagu, Grand Master in 1721, handing the Constitutional Roll to his successor the Duke of Wharton. Several persons are in attendance but because none are specifically mentioned it has given rise to speculation. However, one has some long aprons draped over his right arm and some white gloves are grasped in his left hand. I cannot think that a senior Grand Officer would be in charge of such items for it is a task more in keeping with those allocated to the Doorkeeper or Guarder.

Another engraving to note is by Benjamin Cole and is dated 1726. In the background it portrays building work in progress with three persons standing in the foreground. One holds a square, one has a plumb-line, the centre figure not only holds the compasses but is wearing a long working apron. The upper part is not buttoned to the chest and this seems to indicate that, not being engaged upon shaping or fixing masonry, the wearer has no reason to fully protect his finery.

Yet another excellent illustration is Hogarth's painting *NIGHT*. It depicts the Master of a Lodge being assisted from the Rummer and Grapes Tavern by a Brother similarly clad who has a drawn sword under his arm and a key suspended from the waist. This Brother may well have been the Tyler and the key the one that locked the apron Box.

UPPER AND UNDER TYLERS

In 1763 the number of Brethren attending meetings of the Lodge at the Dundee Arms Tavern at Wapping had increased so much that 'Upper' and 'Under' Tylers were appointed to share the work. Payment to the 'Upper' Tyler varied from eight to twelve guineas a year whilst the 'Under' Tyler was paid slightly less. The accounts for 1765 show that sixpence was paid for supper for each member but for the Tylers it was only fourpence each!

Two Tylers were employed by Lodge of Antiquity, No. 2:

> One Shilling and Sixpence shall be paid each Lodge-Night to the Head Tyler, who has the benefit of all Formations, and is to take care of the Lodge's Furniture; and Three Shillings shall be paid to the Under Tyler who is to carry the Lodge-Letters to the Members.
> (*By-laws dated 1760.*)

In 1820 their Tyling strength was increased by yet another:

> By-law XXVIII. There shall be two Tylers and an Assistant Tyler. The Upper Tyler shall be allowed Seven Shillings, the Under Tyler Five Shillings, and the Assistant Tyler Four Shillings, for each meeting of the Lodge ...

Ample scope for speculation is provided by an item in the records of Mount Moriah Lodge, No. 34: – Bro. Binks acted as I. Guard and Tyler'. (a) Did he remain outside the door of the Lodge? (b) Inside the Lodge with the door closed? (c) On the threshold and, as a compromise, leaving the door half open? No prizes are offered for the most elaborated guesswork on this subject!

According to an article in *Miscellanea Latomorum* (Vol. XXV, p. 141), 'A Minute of Lodge of Love and Honour, No. 75, Falmouth states – November 1st, 1808, Bro. Tresider proposed that there should be two Tylers, Williamson to act at the door inside and Symons without ...' In the next volume (p. 72) 1814 is the

year given as the earliest date for Inner Guard 'as previously there were two Tylers'. Also that a sword 'for the Inside Tyler was opposed but a Trowel was provided'.

A silver Trowel suspended from his collar was worn by the Inner Guard of Duke of Normandy Lodge, No. 245, Jersey, and this continued right through to 1906.

In Northumberland it was a custom for the Inner Guard and Tyler to be presented together, invested with 'Jewels, Collars and Aprons as emblems of their respective offices' and according to the closing words in a ritual *MS* of pre-union vintage, they were then instructed to take their respective stations, 'the one within, and the other without the door of the Lodge'.

CLOTHING, UNIFORM, AND PROCESSIONS

Distinctive clothing, livery, or just protective clothing for Tylers are described in wide variety. In 1742 *The Westminster Journal* printed a 'Key to Procession' which had the following:

> Two Tylers, or Guarders. In Yellow Cockades, and Liveries, being the Colour ordained for the Sword-Bearer of State. They, as youngest enter'd Prentices, are to guard the Lodge with a drawn Sword from all Cowans and Eaves-droppers, that is Listeners, lest they should discover the incomprehensible Mysteries of Masonry.

A letter published in *St. James' Chronicle* on 9th August 1764 gave a report of a Masonic procession at Taunton which included this account:

> ... First came a Man with an Heroic Aspect. His Hat under his Arm, and carrying a large drawn Sword who I was told was the Doorkeeper ...

On St. John's Day, December 27, of the same year and in the same town, the members of the Lodge meeting at the Fountain Hotel proceeded from the Lodge to the church. They were headed by the town Beadles – 'to clear the way'; next came a 'Grand Band of Musick'; then '3rd – the head Tyler'; lastly, after a long list, the 'Under Tyler closed ye Procession'.

The Minutes record 'That a letter of Thanks be wrote to the Right Worshipful Master of the Lodge at the Jerusalem Tavern, Clerkenwell, for the use of the Tylers Dress'. Obviously the dignity of the Lodge was preserved by matching his appearance with that of the Town Beadles, even though he was arrayed in borrowed finery.

The following week partial independence was gained when the Master presented a 'Tyler's Cap, trimm'd with Gold Lace and Fur'. On 1 November 1765 the members 'Ordered that ye Tyler have forthwith a Watch Coat provided for him ...' (*A.Q.C. Vol. 62.*)

In 1794, Lodge of Friendship, No. 277, Oldham, provided a Tyler's coat, cap and sashes 'at a cost of £1. 0. 7 for making and 17/–d for material'. Two years later they purchased 'Jewels for Wardens and a Tylers Trowel'.

From the history of Restoration Lodge, No. 111, Darlington, we have:

22 Feb. 1784. For the purpose of enhancing the dignity of the Lodge it was agreed and ordered that the W. Master should provide a great coat of Blue Cloth with Red Cape and Cuffs, which is to belong to the Lodge and to be made use of by the Tyler when Tyling the Lodge only.

A full description of a uniform is supplied by the following from Leicester:

That the Tyler be clothed at the expense of the Lodge, with a blue coat and waistcoat and corderoy breeches, the whole with yellow buttons, pair of white stockings, and a three cornered hat; also that he be furnished with a hairy cap to wear on public occasions, the latter to remain the property of the Lodge.
(*Minutes, 15 May 1791, St. John's Lodge, No. 279, Leicester.*)

Countless entries regarding the supply of articles of clothing either for protection or for ornament are to be found in Lodge records. On 14 December 1774 Lodge of Probity, No. 61, Halifax, 'Paid one shilling for Mittens for the Tyler' and five years later 'Order'd that a coat for the Tyler be provided before the next Lodge'. In 1754, Unanimity Lodge, No. 89, Cheshire, purchased for the sum of five shillings 'a mitre of pigskin suitably ornamented with a crossed sword motif'. A Lodge in Cornwall resolved:

that the Tyler shall have a great coat provided him at the expense of the Lodge, not to exceed two pounds in value ... which coat the Tyler is to wear on being at our several Lodges, also to make use on all other decent occasions.
(*Minutes, 27 December 1814, Druids Lodge of Love and Liberality, then No. 127, Redruth, Erased 1834.*)

On 23 January 1755 the members of Old Dundee Lodge, No. 18, meeting at Wapping Old Stairs on the banks of the Thames, were not so generous:

A motion made last Lodge Night 'That the Tyler should be provided with a Cap and Cloak to shelter him from the inclemency' was balloted for and rejected.

On the subject of clothing a rather tragic note appeared in the accounts of another Lodge:

Burying Bro. West £2. 17. 0d, and a burying suit for the Tyler, 10/–.
(*Lodge Benevolence, No. 336, Cheshire.*)

Dignity and respect at all times were prime factors among Brethren and it is of interest to note the tributes that were paid to many faithful Tylers. The following is an excellent example:

He was buried by the Lodge with all honours, the Brethren attending in Black, full and compleat, with White Gloves, Black Stockings, Black Buckles or Shoe Strings. New aprons were provided, the jewels and ribbons being cleaned for the occasion.
(*History of Lodge of Probity, No. 61. Hanson. 1939.*)

SWORDS FOR TYLERS

Mention of swords in Freemasonry is in either ceremonial or procedural context; I have not discovered an instance recorded of where one has been used in defence or for protective purpose. However, one cannot overlook an item in the accounts

of Lodge of Relief, No. 42, Bury, for 1843, which included – 'By Bro. Warburton for grinding sword ... 2/6d'. A blunt sword for that Lodge was undesirable! Dangers in dark alleys and narrow turnings could not be ignored. Hogarth portrayed quite a few in his celebrated painting *NIGHT*. The dangers of the lonely journey from Hampstead to London at night were given as the reason for one Tyler to refuse to act for a Lodge unless provision for accommodation was included. The following item appeared in their accounts – 'Tyler's Lodging, 2/6d'. (*Historical Notes, St. Johns Lodge, No. 167.*)

Reports of Tylers 'with drawn sword' in Masonic processions are plentiful but one unusual description is – 'Tyler with sword in mourning'. One assumes that black ribbon had been tied on it. (*History of Prov. Grand Lodge of Gloucestershitre, p. 30.*)

Freemasons often formed part of Trades processions and the following, which was reported in the *Manchester Mercury* in 1802, may be taken as typical:

> A Lodge of Freemasons in the town, called Peace and Unity followed in full dress. The Bible was carried before them on a velvet cushion. This part of the procession finished with an officer called a Tyler. He was dressed in scarlet with a hairy cap, and carried a drawn sword.
>
> ('Preston—The Gild and the Craft', F. L. Pick, *A.Q.C. 59, p. 108.*)

The funeral of a well respected Tyler in Somerset was treated as a Provincial 'Occasion'. At an appropriate point in the ceremony the Tyler's wand and sword were broken and cast into the grave by the Prov. Grand Secretary and Master of the Lodge respectively with what is described as 'the customary exclamation "Alas, our brother"'. The Brethren returned in procession to the Lodge to conclude 'the Masonic duties of the day'. (*Freemasons' Quarterly Review, 1850, pp. 106/7.*)

All varieties of swords are mentioned, from the wavy edged, purporting to represent the 'Flaming sword' or sword of the 'destroying Angel' of Biblical tradition, military sabres, naval cutlasses, to the scimitar used by the Tyler dressed in Turkish costume as reported in the history of Lodge Scoon at Perth in Scotland.

Quaint use of the Tyler's sword was, and maybe still is, made in some parts of Lancashire. In answer to the Master's question – 'Has every Brother had his due?', the Senior warden replies – 'All except the Tyler, and I will see that he is attended to'. An extension to that form has occurred, viz., the Master sounds his gavel to summon the Tyler who, on entering the Lodge, salutes with his sword, proceeds to the Brother upon whom a Degree has just been conferred and, with flat side uppermost, points the sword to him. That Brother places one shilling on the blade, it is taken by the Tyler who then salutes the Master and retires from the Lodge.

GRAND TYLER'S STAFF OF OFFICE

It has to be pointed out to many Brethren that the Grand Tyler does not 'tyle' Grand Lodge, neither does he carry a sword. The sword that is carried into Grand Lodge is borne by the Grand Sword Bearer which is an office dating from 1730 when 'the Sword of State' (by tradition the property of Gustavus II Adolphus, King of Sweden, 1611–1632) was presented to Grand Lodge by the Grand Master, the Duke of Norfolk.

The Grand Tyler bears a Staff of Office which is surmounted by the Arms of the United Grand Lodge of England. He follows the two Deputy Grand Directors of Ceremonies who head processions into and from the Grand Temple. The Grand Tyler is not elected but is appointed by the Grand Master. Certain amendments regarding his position were promulgated in 1939:

> The Grand Tyler is to be an Installed Master (instead of a Master Mason) and to continue in office during the pleasure of the Grand Master (instead of Grand Lodge).
> (*Grand Lodge Proceedings, 7 June 1939, p. 347.*)

The *Rules and Orders* adopted by the Antients' Grand Lodge on 17 July 1751 contain reference to 'Pursevant and Tyler of ye Grand Lodge'. The Moderns referred to the position as 'Tyler of Grand Lodge' and it is not until the turn of the century that we find reference to 'Grand Tyler'.

Attendance at Grand Lodge is under the control of appointed scrutineers who are in charge of the Registers of Grand Lodge and it is against these that a Brother's qualification to attend is checked. Negligence in forwarding a Lodge Return can sometimes produce an embarrassing situation for a newly appointed Warden. The earlier 'List of Lodges' is hidden in the shadows of the Registers of today.

THE 'SILENT TYLER'

In the period when the slogan 'Go West young man' was bandied around, Freemasonry also went West! Barkerville, British Columbia, was a town in which there were some wild men and some equally wild, wild women. The local Masonic Hall had a unique device known as the 'Silent Tyler'. It was a built-in safeguard consisting of a hinged stairway which led from the ground floor to the floor on which the Lodge room was situated. The stairs could be raised to cut off all access from the floor below and it was done by means of a wheel in the Tyler's room above. No Inner Guard was appointed in that Lodge for the first ten years because the Tyler was able to fill both duties quite comfortably. (*History of Grand Lodge of British Columbia, J. T. Marshall, 1971.*)

UNUSUAL DUTIES

Tylers have been men of many parts and in some cases they were Brethren with particular Masonic skill. The Minutes of Somerset House Lodge, No. 4, in 1787 were kept by the Tyler and he was voted two guineas for his trouble. A Minute in 1792 of Mount Lebanon Lodge, No. 173, states that the Tyler gave 'a Lecter in the first part, under an agreement made to allow him for his duties in the Lodge and attend the books 5s each night provided he found one outside to do that duty'. Mount Moriah Lodge, No. 34, has a record in 1783 that 'a lecture was given by Bro. Aldhouse, Tyler'.

It is commonly known that Summonses were delivered by Tylers but what is surprising is that in certain cases it was part of their duty also to write them and to indicate any special or urgent business that was to be dealt with at the meeting.

The interest of the members of Lodge of Felicity, No. 58 had become so slack

that the Tyler had to be called in to open the Lodge for the meeting on 6 June 1827.

Many Lodges required their Tyler to collect the dining charge from visitors. The following is an excellent example:

> ... 'Tis agreed that the Tyler shall take the Visitors' money at the Door and bring it to the Mr. to save the trouble of the Jun. Warden and Secty.
> (*Minutes, 5 Aug. 1740, Lodge of Antiquity, No. 2.*)

According to a Resolution adopted in 1785 by a Norfolk Lodge the Tyler was well involved in the 'Calling Off' and 'Calling On' procedure:

> I. That for the future Dinner be on the table exactly at 4 o'clock each Lodge Day, and that the Tyler gives notice to the Wardens one Quarter of an hour before it is taken up. To wait Dinner for no Body.
> II. That the Tyler for the future shall come into the Dining Room with his Sword exactly as the clock strikes six, leaving a Brother to tile the Lodge Room in his absence, and shall acquaint the Senior Warden with the hour; the Senior Warden with an Audible Voice shall inform the Master that 'the Duties of the Lodge require the Attendance of the Members in the Lodge Room', upon which the Master and Members are to retire immediately.
> III. That after the above notice of the Senior Warden if the Master and Wardens do not return to the Lodge Room in five Minutes, they shall be fined a Gallon of Claret each for the benefit of the Lodge.
> (*'The Great Lodge, Swaffham, Norfolk', Hamon le Strange, A.Q.C. Vol. 20.*)

Items causing offence to Lodge members were always committed for disposal or destruction by the Tyler. Generally they were letters or circulars but on one occasion a portrait was ordered to be burned (*Temple Lodge, No. 101*). From the *Records of Lodge of Antiquity, No. 2*, we have two examples which may be taken as typical:

> ... An anonymous letter addressed to the Mr. of this Lodge was read and considered— whereupon a Motion was made that it should be burnt by the Hands of the Tyler ...

and another in which William Preston, the originator of the system of Lectures from which has evolved the Grand Lodge appointment of Prestonian Lectureship, wrote a pamphlet entitled *A State of Facts* that was unpalatable to the members. They recorded that it was '... torne and burned by the hands of the common Tyler'.

NEGLECT AND IRREGULARITIES

Neglect of duty has reared its ugly head from time to time and according to the gravity of the offence met with reprimand, loss of pay, or dismissal:

> It being observed by the R.W. Master that several members had entered the Lodge without giving the regular masonic notice of approach. A motion was made and seconded that the Tyler be ordered in and reprimanded for his inattention to the duties of his office.
> (*Minutes, 2 March 1784, Royal Lodge, then No. 201, united with Alpha Lodge in 1824, now No. 16.*)

At one meeting in 1763 Old Dundee Lodge, No. 18, recorded 'Tyler dismissed' but no details of his offence appear. The next meeting has 'Tyler re-admitted'. Four years later they have 'Tyler reprimanded' and in the same year 'Tyler to clean the Lodge in 3 days or wages stopt'. In 1774 they have 'Tyler dismissed' and this time they meant it because a new one was appointed.

The Tyler failed to turn up for the meeting of Lodge of Felicity, No. 58, on 15 January 1849 and as he had the keys the members went their several ways. In April of that year it was reported that one Brother's absence during the preceding twelve months was because the Tyler had not delivered a Summons to him for any of the meetings, so the members voted a refund of his subscription.

Authority for the Master to take immediate action was given by another Lodge:

> The Tyler shall be elected annually in the regular monthly meeting in November immediately after the election of the Treasurer, but if at any time he be accused of improper conduct a Vote of the Lodge may dismiss him and elect a new Tyler, or he may be suspended by the Master, if negligent in the discharge of his duty.
> (*By-laws, 1819, Lodge of Peace and Harmony, No. 60.*)

Their Minutes in November 1850 record that the Tyler's resignation had been received and the Secretary has added the comment – 'which the Lodge was pleased to accept'.

Perhaps the strangest irregularity of all came to light when circumstances branded the Tyler as an 'Eavesdropper':

> 23 February 1815. The Tyler was discharged & paid for this Evening & likewise for the Arch. The Transactions of this Lodge having been repeated, divulged to the other Lodge in this Town [Halifax] and turned into Ridicule and as every Member declares his Innocence, it was thought that the Tyler must have been the Tale Bearer; in consequence a Ballot took place when he was by the unanimous consent of the Members discharged ...
> (*Minutes, Lodge of Probity, No. 61, Halifax.*)

Freemasonry certainly does not transcend the frailties of human nature nor does it claim to be free from those who yield to temptation. Lodge property has been fair game at all times with collars and jewels mostly at risk:

> Previous to this Lodge Bro. Haggard the Tyler made his exit. On enquiry being made after the Jewells of the Lodge found from Necessitous Circumstances he had raised money on them. A motion was made and secd and Carrd that they should be redeemed at the Expense of the Lodge. Consequence of the above mentioned Unfortunate affair no Tyler attended the Lodge there not being sufficient Notice to Provide one.
> (*Minutes, 9 Feb. 1785, The Grenadiers Lodge, No. 66.*)

According to the Minutes of the next meeting the cost of redeeming the jewels was £1. 13. 9, and a new Tyler elected.

At Marlborough Police Court in 1850 a man was convicted of illegally pawning the jewels of all the Lodges of which he was Tyler. Regretfully, only some of the jewels were recovered. (*History of Salisbury Lodge, No. 435.*)

British Lodge, No. 8, was robbed of its jewels by their Tyler and although a member of the Lodge called at his house every day he was unable to influence the restoration of the property. The Secretary of the Lodge wrote to the President of the Board of General Purposes stating that the members were anxious to avoid a

scandal and unwilling to prosecute; nevertheless they felt the Board should be informed in order that other Lodges who engaged him might be protected.

Robert Montgomery, son of the well-known 'Garder of ye Grand Lodge' followed the same profession as Tyler but fell somewhat short of the standard. In 1764, Lodge of Emulation, No. 21, traded in their old jewels and with a cash balance of £26. 14. 6 purchased a new set. Soon afterwards the jewels were missing and, unfortunately, so was Brother Robert. He was caught, clapped into Wood Street prison and there confessed that he had pawned them. Some items were recovered but we have no record of the sentence meted out to him. In those days it could have been very severe as theft was considered a most serious crime and the punishment for it was deportation. Only the year previously the Tyler of Lodge of Friendship, No. 44, was transported for theft of Lodge property.

From W. J. Hughan we learn of one Tyler for whom we must all have some sympathy as he was assigned the role of 'whipping boy'. The incident is mentioned in a *Memorandum* dated 20 November 1799 written inside the cover of the records of a Lodge which met in Rome from 1735 to 1737:

Pope Clement the XII, having published a most severe edict against Masonry, the last Lodge held at Rome was on 20th August, 1737, when the Earl of Wintoun was Master. The Officer of the Lodge (i.e., Tyler), who was a servant of Dr. James Irvin, was sent, as a terror to others, prisoner to the Inquisition, but was soon released ...
(*The Jacobite Lodge at Rome, 1735–7, pp. 23, 35.*)

That Brother was certainly more sinned against than sinning.

FROM GRAND MASTER TO TYLER

Reference has been made to the account in Anderson's *New Book of Constitutions* (1738) of the setting-up of the premier Grand Lodge in 1717, with Anthony Sayer, 'Gentleman', as the first Grand Master. They were circumstances which held the prospect of dignity and prosperity but strangely this was not to be for Anthony Sayer. After his term of office he was required as a Grand Officer only once; as Senior Grand Warden for 1719. By comparison, his successor as Grand Master, George Payne, served as Junior Grand Warden in 1724 and 1725 and served as Senior Grand Warden in 1735.

Sayer must have headed into difficulties quite early because the Minutes of Grand Lodge for 21 November 1724 state: 'Brother Anthony Sayers Peticon [sic] was read and recommended by the Grand Master.' A similar situation arose at the meeting of 21 April 1730:

Then the Petition of Brother Anthony Sayer formerly Grand Master was read setting forth his Misfortunes and great Poverty and praying Reliefe, the Grand Lodge took the same into Consideration and it was proposed that he should have £20 out of the money received on Acct. of the General Charity, others proposed £10 and others £15. The Question being put it was agreed he should have £15 on Acct. of his having been Grand Master.

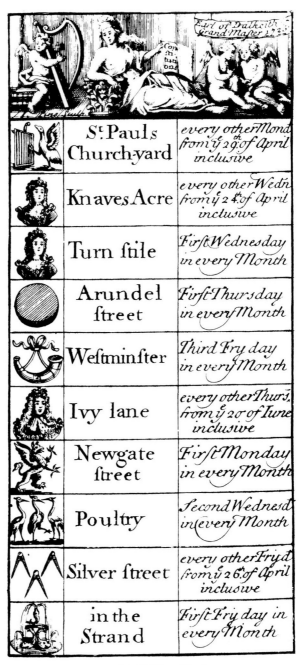

	St Pauls Church-yard	every other Mond from ỹ 29.ᵗʰ of April inclusive
	Knaves Acre	every other Wedn from ỹ 24ᵗʰ of April inclusive
	Turn ſtile	Firſt Wednesday in every Month
	Arundel ſtreet	Firſt Thursday in every Month
	Weſtminſter	Third Fryday in every Month
	Ivy lane	every other Thurs. from ỹ 20 of Iune inclusive
	Newgate ſtreet	Firſt Monday in every Month
	Poultry	Second Wednesd in every Month
	Silver ſtreet	every other Fryd from ỹ 26.ᵗʰ of April inclusive
	in the Strand	Firſt Fryday in every Month

First page of 1723 List of Lodges.

THE SIGNS AND LODGES IDENTIFIED

Goose and Gridiron, St. Paul's Churchyard
Now LODGE OF ANTIQUITY, No. 2.

Queen's Head, Knaves Acre, Wardour Street
Now LODGE OF FORTITUDE AND OLD CUMBERLAND, No. 12.

Queen's Head, Turnstile, Holborn
This Lodge originally met at the Crown Ale House, Parker's Lane, and was
No. 2 of the Four Old Lodges of 1717. *Erased 1736.*

Cheshire Cheese, Arundel Street
Lapsed before 1725.

Horn Tavern, Westminster
Now ROYAL SOMERSET AND INVERNESS LODGE, No. 4.

King's Head, Ivy Lane
Now LODGE OF FRIENDSHIP, No. 6.

Griffin, Newgate Street
Now LODGE OF EMULATION, No. 21.

Three Cranes, Poultry
Erased 1745.

Three Compasses, Silver Street
Lapsed before 1729.

Fountain Tavern, Strand
Now ROYAL ALPHA LODGE, No. 16.

The one-time Grand Master was Tyler of various Lodges over a number of years but his efforts were not always crowned with success:

> Mr. Sawyer [Sayer], happening to tyle the Lodge at Forrest's Coffee House on the night whereon this society meets, disqualifies him from his regular attendance on this and the person he sometimes sends in his place not giving satisfaction on general acts. It was resolved since Mr. Sayer neither came nor sent to justify himself on this night that he be dismissed from tyling the Lodge. A new Tyler was appointed this night.
> (*Minutes, 9 October 1738, Lodge of Friendship, No. 6.*)

In December 1730 Sayer was summoned to attend Grand Lodge to answer a complaint lodged against him. There is an irritating lack of detail regarding this, but it is recorded that after hearing both parties – 'some of the Brethren being of Opinion that what he had done was clandestine, others that it was irregular' – Sayer was told by the Deputy Grand Master that he was acquitted of the charge and recommended to do nothing so irregular in the future. Sadler comments, 'This reads very much like a verdict of "Not Guilty, but don't do it again!" ' (*Masonic Facts and Fictions*, pp. 42/3). Because of the appearance of the word 'clandestine' in the charge and the fact that Sayer was down on his luck, there is every possibility that in addition to acting as Tyler for Lodges on the Register of Grand Lodge he had acted for one that was not. Such Lodges were termed 'clandestine'.

Destitution pursued Sayer because the members of Old Kings Arms Lodge, No. 28, gave him £2. 2. in 1736 – 'to mend his circumstances' – and in 1740 the sum of 10s. 6d. – 'in consideration of the late hard weather'.

KNOCKS TO SUMMON THE TYLER

Knocks by the Master to summon the Tyler find their origin, in principle, in Gild practice. In his Inaugural Address as Master Quatuor Coronati Lodge, No. 2076, (*A.Q.C.* 74.), Bernard Jones quoted a Minute dated 15 June 1644 from the records of the Cutlers Gild relating to Upper and Under Beadles:

> Ordered that from Henceforth ... the Beadles ... stay att the outward doore until they shall be called in And to come in to attend the will of the Court att the knocke of the Hammer.

Bro. Jones commented – 'Can there be the slightest doubt that the Guild Beadle has, in the Craft, become the Lodge Tyler?' and with that statement I am in complete agreement. The double knock is merely a created variation from those in use in the several Masonic ceremonies.

THE TYLER'S TOAST

The Tyler's Toast is not ritual but is a pleasant Masonic custom having a wide variety in presentation. An early indication of the form familiar to most Brethren is to be found in one of the Toasts in *Ahiman Rezon* (pp. 148–50 1756 Edn.), following a song composed by Laurence Dermott:

> To all Ancient Masons, wheresoever dispers'd or oppressed around the Globe, etc.

The 'etc' denies us the full wording but indicates that the Toast was so well known that it did not justify printing in full. Similar treatment was given to other Toasts.

Jachin and Boaz (1762) has 'The Entered Apprentice's Lecture' in catechetical form which was interspersed by various Toasts drunk with 'Three Times Three'. Among the Toasts was 'To all Brethren wheresoever dispersed'.

The earliest printing of the Toast in full was by George Claret in 1840 in *The Whole of Craft Masonry*. It appeared at the end of the Third Section of the First Lecture:

The following is the charge,

To all poor and distressed M .... s, wherever scattered over the face of Earth and Water; wishing them a speedy relief from their misfortunes, and a safe return to their native country if they require it.

ALL POOR AND DISTRESSED M .... S

In common use nowadays is the form 'if they desire it' but Dr. E. H. Cartwright quotes an addition to that: 'if they desire and deserve it'. (*A Commentary on the Freemasonic Ritual, f/n, p. 81.*) This may well have been a wish on behalf of those Brethren unfortunate enough to have been press-ganged but it eliminated the Brother who had been transported!

It should be noted that the Tyler is not associated with any of the examples quoted.

EPILOGUE

The attention of those Brethren who may be interested in an examination of ritual, procedure and duties pertaining to the Tyler, is drawn to 'The Work of the Tyler', chapter four of Dr. Cartwright's book.

'Doorkeeping' has developed far beyond the duty allocated to the Junior Entered Apprentice, whose main function was to guard against 'Evesdroppers' and possibly to catch any offenders. The position has grown into one of trust, of dignity, of understanding, of sympathy, of tolerance, and of dedication. It is because of the exercise of some, if not all, of those qualities that many Tylers rose to eminence, lived respected, and died regretted.

Despite all the changes the future may hold, and no doubt there will be many, let us earnestly hope the same qualities will ever distinguish the Brethren who will be elected to carry out the manifold duties of – 'The Tyler or Outer Guard'.

GRAND STEWARDS 1728–1978

THE PRESTONIAN LECTURE FOR 1978

CHARLES MACKECHNIE-JARVIS

The year is 1715 and the place is London. The uncertain reign of Queen Anne has closed with the death of the Queen at the early age of 49.

The political situation is confused and the Hanoverian dynasty has commenced amid manifestations of unpopularity and mistrust. Jacobite Clubs exist in London and their meeting places and aims are being exposed by the pamphleteers. Accusation and counter accusation are rife in print and achieve reality in the abortive uprising which followed the landing of the Pretender at Peterhead in December, 1715. The outcome is well known and was greeted with relief and thanksgiving and an era of stability ensued in which Freemasonry undoubtedly played its part.

Although the transition from operative to speculative freemasonry is outside the scope of this Lecture, some account of the early years of Grand Lodge and in fact some reference to the years preceding its actual formation are material to the general theme. In matters of history generally, the bare statement of apparent fact can seldom be accepted without qualification of some kind and in this respect the history of freemasonry is no exception.

Our ancient brethren true to their obligations left little written record of their activities and some accounts written after the establishment of the Premier Grand Lodge in 1717 must be questioned.

There is positive evidence of the existence of speculative as distinct from operative masonry in the 17th Century. Lodges of freemasons at this period are believed to have been largely occasional in the sense that they were summoned at irregular intervals according to circumstance. Nevertheless the making of masons continued in London and in the Provinces with sufficient regularity to preserve a knowledge of the procedures and tenets of the Craft.

It is permissible to say that the upsurge in speculative masonry giving rise to the as yet unknown events which led to the formation of Grand Lodge occurred in London and the accepted facts are that four Lodges then meeting at Taverns in London came together and agreed to establish a Grand Lodge. We do not know whether agreement was achieved at one meeting or whether discussion was extended over months or over a year or longer, but we do know that the Premier Grand Lodge was established on June 24th, 1717 when a Feast was held at the Goose and Gridiron, this being St John's Day.

The four lodges in question were those which met,

    (*a*) At the Goose & Gridiron Ale-house in St. Paul's Church-Yard, now Antiquity No. 2.

    (*b*) At the Crown Ale-house in Parker's-Lane near Drury-Lane.

(c) At the Apple-Tree Tavern in Charles-Street, Covent-Garden now Fortitude and Old Cumberland No. 12.

(d) At the Rummer & Grapes Tavern in Channel-Row, Westminster now Royal Somerset House & Inverness No. IV.

SOME STATISTICS

The strength of the four Lodges in 1717 is not known but for later years the figures are:

	1723	1725
(a)	22	15
(b)	21	20
(c)	15	14
(d)	72	71

Of the four original lodges in this context, Lodge (b) ceased working around 1736. The other three, now operating under the appellation of 'Time Immemorial' can, apart from a prior place, each claim distinction on different grounds.

Thus Lodge (a) can justifiably declare itself to be the most ancient of the four and to have links with the Wren and Strong families, both prominent in connection with the rebuilding of St. Paul's Cathedral.

Lodge (c) supplied the First Grand Master, Anthony Sayer.

Lodge (d) was probably the largest of the four and certainly remained so for a number of years. George Payne (G.M. No. 2) and Dr. Desaguliers (G.M. No. 3) were among its members.

This recital of facts prompts certain questions:

Firstly, why did the four Lodges, one of whom (Antiquity) had, it is believed been meeting in London for more than 25 years, suddenly decide that a Grand Lodge was needed? Secondly, were there other Lodges who did not respond to a general call or perhaps, being newly formed, were not invited?

Probably the true answer is that interest in the Craft was changing in tempo to such an extent as to give the older masons cause for concern. A governing body could hardly be justified for just four Lodges but if a sharp increase in numbers of Lodges was foreseen or perhaps was anticipated the question takes on a fresh aspect.

Support for this concept is found in the growth statistics reflected by the Masonic Census figures of 1723 and 1725 as recorded in the Minutes of Grand Lodge.

1723		1725	
Lodges	*Members*	*Lodges*	*Members*
52	900	77	1490

Note: An assumption has been made for lodges on the Register of Grand Lodge making no return, and an allowance for multiple membership.

It has always been accepted that certain of the Lodges which applied for a Warrant from the Premier Grand Lodge had been working for some time previously.

The surviving Minutes of Grand Lodge commence in 1723 and for detail relating to the earlier years from 1717 we are largely dependent upon Dr. James Anderson (1680?–1739) the author of the printed Constitutions of 1723 and 1738. In the latter Anderson writes thus:

> Accordingly
> On St. John Baptist's Day, in the 3rd Year of King George I, A.D. 1717, the ASSEMBLY and Feast of the Free and accepted Masons was held at the foresaid Goose and Gridiron Alehouse.

The day was of course the 24th of June, an anniversary long associated with operative masonry. In succeeding years, the Annual Assembly and Feast continued to be held on June 24th at the Goose and Gridiron until 1721 when in consequence of the larger attendance expected, upon the election of the first noble Grand Master, John 2nd Duke of Montagu 1690–1749 Grand Lodge met at King's Arms Tavern and the brethren afterwards marched in procession to the Stationers Hall 'in proper clothing and due form' where the Feast was held and 'where they were joyfully received by about 150 true and faithful, all clothed'. This was probably the first of the public processions to which further reference will be made.

So far there has been no reference to the ordering of the Feast which on the limited scale possible at the Goose and Gridiron, could be handled by the Grand Wardens in conjunction with the staff of the Inn. Now however a change was envisaged. To quote Anderson in connection with 1721: 'Then the Grand Wardens were order'd, as usual, to prepare the Feast, and to take some Stewards to their Assistance, Brothers of Ability and Capacity, and to appoint some Brethren to attend the Tables; for that no Strangers must be there. But the Grand Officers not finding a proper number of Stewards, our Brother, Mr. Josiah Villeneau, Upholder in the Burrough Southwark, generously undertook the whole himself, attended by some Waiters. . . .'

THE FIRST STEWARD

Josias Villeneau (?-1753) who has the distinction of being the first named Steward in masonry was by family name and context a Huguenot refugee.

His date of birth has not been traced and it is probable that he was born in France and came to London as a child (with others of the same name) about 1685, the year of the Revocation of the Edict de Nantes. He became an Anglican and lived for most of his life in the Parish of St. Saviours, Southwark, but his name occurs as a Godparent to a child of Jean Villeneau at the French Church at Crispin Street, in 1707. Incidentally a John Villeneau was a Grand Steward in 1746.

Josias was married at St. Saviours, now Southwark Cathedral, in August 1703 and his children were baptised there. He is described in all except one of the documents seen as an Upholder, a term which possesses several conflicting definitions. His Will (Canterbury Prerog. Records) however declares him to have been an Upholsterer. His name appears from time to time in the Minutes of Vestry Meetings and on several occasions as one of the Parish Constables appointed under Vestry powers. Finally, by a large majority he was in 1744 elected Parish Clerk, a post which he retained until his death. The Office was a coveted one for

which there were 6 contenders and Brother Villeneau secured upwards of 60% of the votes. His certificate of appointment has been preserved and a xerox copy has been placed in Grand Lodge archives, by courtesy of the Southwark Diocesan Registrar. Josias was buried in St. Saviours parish on December 7th, 1753.

At the investiture which followed the Feast of 1721 Bro. Villeneau was appointed Senior Grand Warden. He served the office of Right Worshipful Master of Antiquity (then No. 1) in 1723 according to the Grand Lodge list.

The position in regard to 1722 is somewhat uncertain and some authorities follow Anderson who infers that no Feast was held and that a gathering at the Stationers Hall on June 24th of that year was unofficial.

For 1723 we are given more positive advice:

> The Tickets for the next Feast were order'd to be Ten Shillings each, impress'd from a curious Copper Plate, and seal'd with the Grand Master's Seal of Office, to be disposed of by the Grand Wardens and the Stewards.
>
> ASSEMBLY and Feast on Monday 24th June 1723, at Merchant-Taylors-Hall.
>
> The Committee appointed to keep out Cowans came early, and the Stewards to receive the Tickets and direct the Servants.
>
> About 400 Free Masons, all duly clothed, dined elegantly in due Form.

A landmark of this meeting was the appointment of William Cowper (16......– 1740) of the Horn Lodge, Westminster (now No. IV) as Secretary to the Grand Lodge, being the first holder of this important Office.

The 1723 Feast was served by six Stewards among whom was Edward Lambert acting for the first time. In 1724 the Feast was again held on June 24th at the Merchant Taylors Hall and the Grand Wardens were assisted as in the previous year by six Stewards. The arrangements for the Feast had evidently been under active review because at the meeting of Grand Lodge on 28th April 1724 it is recorded that

> It is the Grand Ma^{rs} Order that the following Regulations be Observed at the next Annuall meeting:
>
> 1st That No Wine be opened till Dinner be Laid on the Table
>
> 2nd That the Money or Ticketts be return'd to the Stewards about 14 Days before Midsummer.
>
> 3rd That the Members of Each Lodge Sitt together as much as possible at the Grand Feast.
>
> 4th That the Price of Each Tickett shall be ten Shillings.
>
> 5th That the Company shall have no Wine from the Stewards after Eight of the Clock at Night.'

At the General Meeting held on the 24th June, the day of the Feast it was ordered:

> That the Stewards do prepare a List (for the Grand Masters perusall) of twelve fitt persons to Serve as Stewards at the next Grand Feast, And that they do make up their Accounts with all Convenient Speed that the Same may be Audited.

The next Feast was held at Merchant Taylors Hall on the Anniversary day of St. John the Evangelist on the 27th of December 1725, postponed no doubt on account of the serious illness of The Grand Master, the Duke of Richmond. According to Anderson '– No Stewards being appointed G. M. Richmond desired our brother John James Heidegger to prepare the Feast in the best Manner'.

Brother Heidegger (1659–1749) was a colourful figure in the financially uncertain world of the theatre, who would to-day be termed an Impresario. Heidegger (sometimes called John Jacob) was a Walloon (Netherlands) Protestant according to Grove's Dictionary of Music, or son of a Swiss Clergyman (D.N.B.). Musicians denigrate him and claim that he exploited Handel, for a time his partner. The latter however, notwithstanding his justifiably great fame as a composer contrived to make life impossible for our Brother in quarrelling with the Singers. Historical record shows that Handel received large sums from Heidegger whose charitable disposition is supported by contemporary comment.

Heidegger, minuted as the Grand Steward, chose two brethren to assist him one of whom was Brother Edward Lambert (16......–1736 N.S.) a Confectioner resident in Pall Mall. The arrangements for this Feast were again discussed at the Quarterly Communication held on the 27th of November 1725 and the Order concerning procedure made on April 28th, 1724 repeated. In the following year Edward Lambert was apparently appointed sole Grand Steward, although Anderson says 'No Stewards; but Brother Edward Lambert undertook the prepare the Feast.' Perhaps Lambert was acting in a professional capacity as Caterer? According to the Minutes of the Quarterly Communication held on Monday the 12th of December 1726, Lord Paisley, Grand Master presiding:

> His Lorp then acquainted the Lodge that he designed to hold a Grand feast on St. Johns Day next ensuing [*i.e.* December 27] at Merchant Taylors Hall Upon which Mr. Lambert was called in being the Grand Steward appointed for the Sd. feast.
>
> The Grand Mar. read the Regulations agreed on by the Grand Lodge held next before the last Grand feast which were agreed to by this Grand Lodge with the alteration that the Ticketts not taken are to be returned by Monday next.

The Quarterly Communication and Feast appear in fact to have been held two months later on February 27th 1727 at the Hall of the Mercer's Company but no explanation for the postponement and change of venue is given.

It will be noted that the good intention of appointing twelve Stewards as planned in 1724 could not yet be given effect presumably owing to the reluctance of the Brethren to undertake the Office under the certain conditions obtaining.

The state of affairs prevailing at that time was ventilated at a special meeting of Grand Lodge held on Tuesday December 19th 1727 when the arrangements for the forthcoming Feast to be held on St. John the Evangelist's Day, December 27, 1727 were considered. Grand Lodge had been summoned by the Deputy Grand Master William Cowper, who presided in the absence of the Grand Master Lord Inchiquin in Ireland.

Anderson's account is as follows:

> D. G. Master Cowper in the Chair, eloquently excused the Grand Master's Absence in Ireland, and his sudden Calling them together; for that the Feast drew nigh, and that the Grand Master had, by letter, impower'd him to propose, for his Successor, the Lord Colerane Master of a Lodge, who was forthwith saluted as Grand Master Elect.
>
> No Stewards being appointed, Brother Lambert again undertook to prepare the Feast.

The Minutes of Grand Lodge treat the matter somewhat differently and at much greater length. After the preliminaries, the Deputy Grand Master 'proceeded to give the Grand Lodge an Account of his Reasons for Summoning them at this time in the manner following Viz:'

[Here follows an unusually long speech reported fully, in which our Brother discloses that of the 500 tickets printed, only 81 have been paid for. Some Lodges have not received any tickets and others not enough. With only ten days to go there was clearly an element of panic prevailing.]

The Deputy Grand Master blamed 'your present Secretary' but appears to concede that his own inaction has also contributed to the confusion which has arisen. Brother Nathaniel Blackerby, Treasurer of Grand Lodge

'taking notice of the Method used by some Brethren of taking Tickets at the Hall Door, as also of the neglect complained of by the Deputy Grand Master, in the distribution of the Tickets, for the ensuing Grand Feast, proposed that the same might be taken into consideration by the Grand Lodge on St. John's day next ensuing at Mercers Hall, and desired a Minute might be made thereof'.

'The Motion being made, and the Question put the same was agreed to Nemime Con. And the Brethren present were desired by the D. G. Master to come prepared with such Schemes as they should Judge proper and necessary for preventing such Irregularities for the future'.

'The Motion being made that Brother Lambert may have Liberty to advertize in the publick News Papers, That Tickets will be deposited with him till Saturday. The Question was put, and it was unanimously agreed That he may advertize the same in such manner as he shall think proper'.

The 1727 Feast appears to have been successful as the Minute includes the following:

'The other regular Healths were drank, as also Brother Lambert's with Thanks for his Care in the entertainment of the day'. The Secretary to Grand Lodge for the previous year was not reappointed!

THE FIRST BOARD OF GRAND STEWARDS

The question of Stewards was not raised again until the Quarterly Communication held on the 26th November 1728 and then the Grand Lodge Minutes read as follows:

'Then it was proposed that a Grand Feast should be kept on next St. John's day as Usual, which was likewise agreed to. The Deputy Grand Masters then declared he would keep the said Feast at Stationers Hall:'

'And Dr. Desaguliers proposed (that in order to have the same conducted in the best manner) a certain Number of Stewards should be chosen, who should have the intire Care and Direction of the said Feast (together with the Grand Wardens) pursuant to the printed Regulations, which, being seconded by Mr. Collis'.

'The Deputy Grand Master desired that all those who were willing to accept the said Office of Steward would advance to the Table & declare the same by signing their Names before the Chair'.

'The Earl of Inchiquin was thereupon pleased to offer himself in a very obliging manner to be one of the Stewards on that Occasion. But his Lordp. having been so lately Grand

Master, the Lodge thought it would be too great a trouble to, as well as too great a Condescention in his Lordp. to accept that Office, therefore would not suffer it. But at the same time exprest their utmost Gratitude for the Great Honour and Love his Lordp. had shown for the Brotherhood and the Craft'.

'Then the several Brethren hereafter named advanced to the Table and signed their Names respectively, to be Stewards at the next Grand Feast, in Number Twelve and in the Order following, *vizt*:

1. Mr. Cesar Collys of the Lodge at the Rose in Mary la Bone.*
2. Mr. John Revis Master of the Globe in the Strand.
3. Mr. Samuel Stead Master of St. Pauls Head in Ludgate Street.
4. Mr. William Benn Master of Mag Pye without Bishopgate.
5. William Tew of D°.
6. Mr. Gerard Hatley of Bishopgate Coffee House.
7. Mr. Thomas Alford Master of the Rose and Rummer in Holbourn.
8. Mr. H. Smart of the Cross Keys in Henrietta Street.
9. Mr. Thos. Reason of Tottenham high Cross.*
10. Mr. William Hopkins Rummer Pater Noster Row.
11. Mr. William Wilson Ship Fish Streethill.
12. Mr. Theodore Cherriholme St. Paul's Head Ludgate Street.

The Healths of the twelve Stewards was proposed and drank with twelve alluding to the twelve Signes of the Zodiack as well as to their Number which they returned Jointly in like manner'.

'The Stewards likewise propos'd Dr. Desaguliers Health for reviving the Office of Stewards (which appeared to be agreeable to the Lodge in general) and the same was drank accordingly.'

James Anderson's record differs slightly in emphasis. 'Brother Desaguliers moved to revive the Office of Stewards to assist the Grand Wardens in preparing the Feast, and that their Number be 12, which was readily agreed to.' As will be seen later, from this time onwards until modified at the Union, the 12 Stewards acted as a Board, acquiring valued privileges in return for their services. 1728 is therefore regarded as the first Board constituted as such, on the proposal of Bro the Rev Dr Desaguliers.

John Theophilus Desaguliers (1683–1744) was a freemason and scientist of outstanding ability who followed his friend George Payne (168...–1757) into the Grand Master's Chair in 1719 and served the Office of Deputy Grand Master 1722–24 and 1726. He was born at La Rochelle, a town on the West coast of France and was the son of a Huguenot Clergyman who escaped from France during the oppression which preceded the Revocation of the Edict de Nantes in 1685. His father having entered the Church of England (whilst retaining his position as Pastor of one of the French Protestant Chapels in London) J.T. Desaguliers was enabled to enter Oxford University where he graduated B.A. in 1710.

He was ordained into the Anglican Church in 1712 and became Chaplain to the Duke of Chandos in 1714. Dr. Desaguliers was elected F.R.S. in 1714 and as in due course some 10 members of the Horn Lodge bore this distinction it has been suggested that they were perhaps recruited by him. Desaguliers' career as a

* The Lodge at The Rose is now the Old King's Arms Lodge No. 28 and the Swan at Tottenham High Cross is the Castle Lodge of Harmony No. 26. The others are now extinct.

scientific lecturer commenced at Hart Hall, Oxford where from 1710–1712 he was deputising for John Keill F.R.S. He established himself in London in 1713 and advertised his lectures as follows:

> A Course of Mechanical and Experimental Philosophy, consisting of 4 parts, *viz.*
> Mechanicks, Hydrostaticks, Pneumaticks and Opticks to be perform'd by John Theophilus Desaguliers of Hart Hall in Oxford, A.M. at Mr. Brown's Bookseller at the Black Swan and Bible without Temple Bar.

Catalogues of the experiments to be performed were obtainable from several addresses including that of Mr. George Payne at the Leather Office in St. Martin's Lane and Mr. Desaguliers at the French School at Islington.* This establishes that George Payne and J. T. Desaguliers were close friends as early as 1713 since it is unlikely that Payne, a young civil servant would have allowed the use of his office address to a casual acquaintance. George Payne's Brother, the Rev. Thomas Payne was a fellow student with J. T. Desaguliers at Christ Church College, Oxford and the two future Grand Masters, both of whom became members of the Horn Lodge (now Royal Somerset House and Inverness No. IV) may have met through Thomas Payne.

Although a procedure whereby 12 Stewards were to be appointed annually had been agreed by Grand Lodge in 1728, a difficulty arose the following year at the November meeting when an objection was raised to some of the volunteers who responded to the call for Stewards. The Deputy Grand Master, Nathaniel Blackerby, having ascertained that 5 Stewards from the 1728 Board were willing to serve again provided that they could have the liberty of filling the vacancies, it was agreed by Grand Lodge that this proposal was acceptable. At the same meeting, a Stewards suggestion that St John's Day (December 27th) was somewhat inconvenient to many of the Brethren was accepted and it was agreed to hold the Feast a month or six weeks later.

The Minutes of Grand Lodge show that the expenses of the annual Feast were proving something of a burden to the Craft generally and once again it fell to a Deputy Grand Master to attempt to rationalise the position. Thus at the meeting of Grand Lodge on December 15th, 1730, the Deputy Grand Master proposed that as the second course (at the Feast) 'is very expensive to the Stewards, and discouraging to the Brethren undertaking to serve that Office might be omitted and to encourage Brethren to come to the Feast, that the Tickets might be reduced from 10s. to 7s 6d. apiece and acquainted them that the second of February was a Law Holy Day and that both Houses of Parliament did not sit that day and therefore it was reasonable to expect a greater Number of Masons would come to the Feast upon that day, nor any other in Term or Parliament time'. It is to be hoped that the cost of the second course was more than half a crown or the Stewards would be out of pocket to an even greater extent! Perhaps they were, because although both propositions were accepted by Grand Lodge 'Nemine con', the call for Stewards which followed produced only 5 names.

Once more the assistance of the Stewards of the previous Board was sought and the six Junior Stewards asked to attend upon the Deputy Grand Master 'who is

---

* Text of Advt. is given by Miss M. E. Rowbottom in a paper on Desaguliers in Trans. Huguenot Society 1965 and has been verified.

desired to fix this affair in such manner as he shall think fitt'. It is made clear at the next meeting of Grand Lodge that 'when it was left to the Six Junr. Stewards who served last year to provide Stewards for the ensuing Feast that twelve Brethren had accepted the Office....' The Feast which was 'concluded with Mirth and Unanimity' was held at the Mercers Hall in Cheapside on March 27, 1731.

We are not told how the members of the Board of Stewards for 1732 were recruited but the arrangement for the Feast to be held on April 19th of this year were discussed at the March Quarterly Communication, when the names were given, the date of the Feast was fixed for April 19th and the price of the tickets agreed at half a guinea.

LANDMARKS ...

Bro Colonel John Pitt, one of the newly appointed Stewards proposed a Motion 'that the twelve present Stewards, shall after dinner at the said Grand Feast each of them choose his Successor for the year ensuing which being Seconded. The Question was put and carried in the affirmative'.

'It was likewise proposed that the said Method of electing Stewards for the future shall be in the same manner and the same was agreed Nemine con'.

In March 1735 Grand Lodge considered the proposal of Dr J. Anderson to reprint the Book of Constitutions and desired him to print the names of all the Grand Masters 'together with a List of the Names of all Deputy Grand Masters, Grand Wardens, and the Brethren that have served the Craft in Quality of Stewards, which was thought necessary Because it is Resolved ; That for the future all Grand Officers (except the Grand Master) shall be selected out of that Body'.

This Resolution was of extreme importance at the time since it rendered the Office of Steward not only desirable but essential to those seeking preferment in the Craft. As will be seen later the decision of Grand Lodge was qualified by another Resolution passed in 1779 but the policy of recruiting Grand Officers through this channel was abandoned at the time of the Union in 1813.

'An Address from the Body of the Gentlemen who had served the Society in the Quality of Stewards directed to the Grand Lodge was then read praying certain Priviledges in consideration of such their Services &c.

The status of the Stewards was further abated at the Quarterly Communication held on the 24th of June in 1735 when:

1.   That they might meet monthly or otherwise as a Lodge of Master Masons (under the Denomination of the Stewards Lodge) and be enrolled among the Number of the Lodges as usual with the times of their Meeting

2.   That they might be so far distinguished (since all the Grand Officers are for the future appointed to be chosen out of their Number ; and in order to qualify themselves to the right discharge of those Officers, when called to the same) send a Deputation of twelve from the whole Body of Stewards to each Quarterly Communication, all the twelve to have Voices, and all that come to pay half a Crown apiece towards the Expence of that Occasion

3.   That no person who had not served the Society as a Steward might be permitted at a Quarterly Communication or elsewhere to wear their coloured Ribbonds or Aprons But.

That such as had been Stewards might be indulged with wearing a particular Jewel by

way of distinction suspended in their proper Ribbond wherever they appear as Masons the pattern of which they then offend. These were granted them upon a Division. 45 of the Assembly being on the affirmative side and 42 on the Negative.

It was also Declared That

The twelve Stewards for any current year might attend in their proper colour, &c paying as usual for four Lodges*, but they are not allowed votes, nor are to be heard in any Debate unless something relating to the ensuing Feast be under Consideration.'

It will be seen that the Stewards were here proposing some innovations in that, to quote Bro. Songhurst, they sought to obtain sanction to include in the composition of Grand Lodge certain Brethren who were not of necessity Masters or Wardens, and the wearing of jewels (and by inference collars) by those who were not actually holders of office. The jewel is traditionally that designed by the artist William Hogarth who served as Grand Steward in 1734, and is now worn by the Master and P.M.s of Grand Steward's Lodge. William Hogarth (1697–1764) was a member of the lodge meeting at the Bear and Harrow, Butcher Row, Temple Bar in 1730, now St George's and Corner Stone No. 5.

The account of what transpired at the next meeting of Grand Lodge held on December 11th, 1735 may be viewed in various ways. The Grand Master, Viscount Weymouth, was absent and all the principal officers were acting *Pro tempore*. The acting Deputy Grand Master informed the Brethren that the Grand Master 'had received an Express this morning from Paris concerning the Death of his Lordp's Grandmother, so that he could not with decency attend the Society this Evening according to his Intention and hoped they would excuse him on account of the melancholy Occasion that detained him.'

Business appears to have proceeded normally until:

'A Petition and Appeal was presented and read signed by several Masters of Lodges against the Priviledges granted to the Steward's Lodge at the last Quarterly Communication. The Apellants were heard at large and the Question being put whether the Determination of the last Quarterly Communication relating to this matter should be confirmed or not. In the course of the collecting the votes on this Occasion there appeared so much Confusion that it was not possible for the Grand Officers to determine with any Certainty that the Numbers on either side of the Question were, they were therefore obliged to dismiss the Debate and close the Lodge.'

The implied disorder gave rise to a new set of rules for the governing of the proceedings in Grand Lodge, proposed and adopted at the next meeting.

And that none might plead Ignorance herein it was Resolved that these Rules of Conference shall be audibly read by the publick Secretary at every Quarterly Communication after the opening of the Lodge.

An Uncommon Appearance of Harmony –

From the excerpts from the Minutes of Grand Lodge already quoted it would appear that our Masonic forbears were ever ready to express appreciation for services rendered and the necessaries for such toasts must have been readily available.

---

* Each private lodge was permitted to send to each Quarterly Communication 3 representatives, *viz.*, W.M. and 2 Wardens.

In 1729 or thereabouts Captain Ralph Farr Winter of the Lodge of the Queen's Arms, Newgate Street, now the Lodge of Emulation, No. 21, went overseas and soon afterwards became Provincial Grand Master of East India. At the Quarterly Communication held on the 13th December 1733 Brother Thomas Edwards, a Warden of the Horn Lodge of Westminster (now Royal Somerset House and Inverness Lodge No. IV) 'informed the Grand Lodge that our Rt. Worshipful Brother Capt. Ralph Far Winter Provincial Grand Master of East-India &c, had sent over a Chest of Arack for the Use of the Grand Lodge, and ten Guineas to the General Charity being the Contribution of our Brethren in East India.

The Healths of Br. Winter and the Brethren in East India were drank with Thanks for their handsom Present.'

The beverage was apparently permitted to 'settle' for a year until the Quarterly Communication of the 31st March, 1735. With the Grand Master, the Earl of Crauford in the Chair, it is recorded that

> The General Healths being drank and his Lordp's in particular with the greatest Unanimity and affection, attended with Thanks for his Excellent and acceptable administration. Which his Lordp was pleased to return in good Wishes for the Prosperity of the Craft, and was pleased to say that what he had done in this matter he took to be no less his Duty than it had been his Inclination.
>
> His Lordp was pleased to Order a large Quantity of Rack, that was made a Present of from Bengall in the East Indies to the Grand Officers to be made into Punch and to be distributed among the Brethren.
>
> All Business being over the Grand Lodge was closed with an uncommon appearance in Harmony.'

Brother Farr Winter served as Grand Steward at the 1735 Festival and later became Master of the Stewards' Lodge.

GRAND STEWARDS' LODGE

The history of Grand Stewards' Lodge which will be due to celebrate the 250th anniversary of its foundation in 1985 is largely outside the scope of this Lecture. As at the time of its constitution in 1735, it bore the name Stewards' Lodge and was numbered 117. By subsequent renumbering it became successively numbers 115, 70, 60 and in 1780, number 47. In April 1792 it was ordered to be placed at the head of the list of Lodges without number, which position of honour it continues to occupy.

It is constituted as a Master Masons Lodge the membership of which is restricted to those who have served the Office of Grand Steward, subject to proposal and regular election. The Lodge has no power to initiate, pass or raise Masons. The Lodge meets before each Quarterly Communication of Grand Lodge and after closing the Brethren present proceed to the Grand Temple where they occupy seats reserved for them, in compliance with Rule 37 of the Book of Constitutions. The Installation meeting takes place in the ordinary way and is an open function to which Masonic guests may be invited. The Lodge holds an Emergency Meeting in October of each year at which the Investiture of Officers of London Grand Rank takes place and also assists Grand Lodge on the occasion of Special Festivals.

Today, Grand Stewards' Lodge is in a sound position but there have been several occasions in the past when support was lacking. Thus enthusiasm dwindled in the later 1700s and in February 1779 the Officers of Grand Stewards' Lodge successfully petitioned Grand Lodge complaining that Brethren who had served the Office of Steward were tending to neglect all attendance upon the Stewards' Lodge afterwards as members and failed to pay their subscriptions. To remedy this a Resolution was passed by Grand Lodge requiring 'That in future no Brother be appointed a Grand Officer until he shall have served the Office of Steward at a Grand Feast Nor unless he be an actual subscribing Member at the time of such his appointment'. This Resolution qualifies that of March 1735, already quoted, and continued in force until the Union of 1813.

Grand Stewards' Lodge is virtually an association of those members of the 19 Red Apron Lodges who have served as Grand Stewards and its Officers are chosen from the 19 in turn, there being no regular progression or succession as in normal lodges. The Mastership alternates in successive years between the most senior of the Grand Officers of Right or Very Worshipful Status and Worshipful Brethren, all being Past Grand Stewards and members of the Lodge.

THE OFFICE OF STEWARD

Bro Bernard Jones* has drawn attention to a number of precedents adopted by Freemasons from the mediæval Craft Guilds and among these is the Office of Steward. In some Guilds, more senior members of the Livery were required to serve as Stewards and to accept a financial obligation as a pre-requisite for candidature for a seat on the Court. Brethren will note some similarity of procedure in regard to promotion in our Craft Lodges.

The modern English word 'Steward' is supposed to have been derived from the Anglo-Saxon : stig = house and weard = keeper. The precise meaning of 'stig' is apparently uncertain, presumably because it rarely stands alone and other words are more usual for 'house' but 'steward' has been with us for many centuries covering the range of related concepts with which we are familiar. Compound forms such as High Steward, Great Steward and Lord High Steward, etc., are likewise ancient but the form Grand Steward first used in Grand Lodge Minutes in 1725 appears to be peculiar to Masonry.

In all forms the appellation 'Steward' implies service and responsibility. In Masonry it was and is an Office carrying both obligation and privilege but it is fair comment that in the early days while the former was obvious, the latter was somewhat unclear, and no doubt accounts for the reluctance of the Brethren to accept the nomination!

The original function of the Stewards in Grand Lodge as covered by the Constitutions of 1723 was as follows:

Rule XXIII 'If it be thought expedient, and the Grand-Master, with the Majority of the Masters and Wardens, agree to hold a Grand-Feast, according to the ancient laudable Custom of Masons, then the Grand-Wardens shall have the care of preparing the Tickets, seal'd with the Grand-Master's Seal, of disposing of the Tickets, of receiving the Money

* Freemasonry's Debt to the Guilds. *A.Q.C.* 1961.

for the Tickets, of buying the Materials of the Feast, of finding out a proper and convenient Place to feast in ; and of every other thing that concerns the Entertainment.

But that the Work may not be too burthensome to the two Grand-Wardens, and that all Matters may be expeditiously and safely managed, the Grand-Master, or his Deputy, shall have power to nominate and appoint a Certain Number of Stewards, as his Worship shall think fit, to act in concert with the two Grand-Wardens ; all things relating to the Feast being decided amongst them by a Majority of Voices ; except the Grand-Master or his Deputy interpose by a particular Direction or Appointment.

RuleXXIV The Wardens and Stewards shall, in due time, wait upon the Grand-Master, or his Deputy, for Directions and Orders about the Premises ; but if his Worship and his Deputy are sick, or necessarily absent, they shall call together the Masters and Wardens of Lodges to meet on purpose for their Advice and Orders ; or else they may take the Matter wholly upon themselves, and do the best they can.

The Grand-Wardens and the Stewards are to account for all the Money they receive, or expend, to the Grand-Lodge, after Dinner, or when the Grand-Lodge shall think fit to receive their Accounts.'

It will be seen that under this arrangement any deficit on the finances of the Feast will fall on Grand Lodge. Clearly this situation was untenable and must have been changed by mutual consent in return for the privileges granted to the Stewards from time to time by Grand Lodge. The 1723 Constitutions were amended and reprinted in 1738 by Anderson with the 'Old Regulations' and 'New Regulations' side by side.

Rule XXIV (New Regs) reads as follows: 'The Stewards now take the whole Affair upon themselves and do the best they can.

Nor are their Accounts now audited by the G. Lodge; for that generally the Stewards are out of Pocket.'

The Operative Regulation in the present *Book of Constitutions* is Rule 36 which may be paraphrased as follows:

> The Grand Master shall appoint 19 Grand Stewards annually, one brother being recommended by each of the 19 Lodges currently enjoying that privilege. If for any reason the Bro. recommended declines to serve or is unacceptable, the Lodge in question must nominate a substitute forthwith. Failure of a Lodge to comply with this Rule normally results in forfeiture of its privilege.

The Grand Stewards rank as Grand Officers during their year of office but a Past Grand Steward is not a Past Grand Officer. The Rule continues as follows:

> The duties of the Grand Stewards are to regulate the Grand Festival under the direction of the Grand Master, and to assist in the arrangements for the Quarterly Communications and other meetings of the Grand Lodge under the direction of the Grand Director of Ceremonies. They shall so regulate the Grand Festival that no expense shall fall on the Grand Lodge and no Lodge shall, under the penalty of forfeiting the privilege of recommendation, contribute towards the expense to be incurred by any Grand Steward in the discharge of his duties. Any Grand Steward who shall accept of moneys towards such expenses, or shall neglect to pay his proportion of the necessary expenses shall forfeit all privilege or distinction acquired in consequence of his serving that office.

Shortly after their appointment the new Stewards are summoned to a meeting under the Chairmanship of the Grand Secretary who after suitable introductory

remarks reminds them that they are to regard themselves as constituting a Board for which purpose they would require to elect from among their number a President, a Treasurer and a Secretary. These Officers being elected, the Grand Secretary vacates the chair in favour of the new President and withdraws. From now on the Board acts in a corporate capacity meeting from time to time for the purpose of discussing the arrangements for the next Grand Festival working closely with the Grand Secretary and his staff.

The Minutes of previous Boards are available for their inspection and there is, of course, a degree of continuity maintained by contact with previous holders of the Office in the individual Lodges. By and large, however, the new Stewards are unknown to each other, but are soon working in close harmony. According to time honoured custom, the business meetings are followed by private dinners at which during the year the Board are usually honoured by the presence of the Grand Master and other Grand Officers and in this way maintain an ancient custom observed since the beginning of recorded history of the Grand Stewards.

During their year of Office the Stewards are on duty at the Quarterly Communications of Grand Lodge and lead the processions in and out of the Grand Temple. They are at the disposal of the Grand Master for attendance at such other Masonic functions as he may desire and the Annual Investiture and the Investiture of London Grand Rank are two such occasions.

While the Grand Stewards are required to make good from their own pockets any shortfall as between revenue from the sale of tickets and costs incurred, they have no authority to vary the price of the tickets for the Grand Festival from that fixed by Grand Lodge. This point was decided by the Committee of Charity in 1794 when the action of the Board of Stewards for that year in raising the price of tickets from half a guinea to one guinea was declared improper.

DRESS AND REGALIA

As well as adopting practices derived from the ancient Guilds of the City of London, Masonry has acquired something from the noble Orders of Chivalry. It is a matter of common knowledge that prominent members of the Craft have been Garter Knights and that Garter blue is the colour specified in the *Book of Constitutions* for Grand Rank regalia except that of the Grand Stewards, for which crimson is laid down.

It is generally considered that crimson follows the usage of the Order of the Bath which was revived in 1725 by King George I. According to the detailed account given in the British Chronologist (1775), the King appointed the Duke of Montagu to the rank of Great Master and created 36 other Knights among whom were the Duke of Richmond (M.W.G.M. 1724) and the Earl of Inchiquin, who was appointed our Grand Master in 1726. John, Duke of Montagu had been our Grand Master in 1721.

The earliest surviving references to the Stewards' crimson appears to be that in the Minutes of Grand Lodge for 17 Mar. 1731.

Dr. Desaguliers [Grand Master 1719] taking Notice of some Irregularities in wearing the Marks of Distinction which have been allowed by former Grand Lodges.

Proposed.
That none but the Grand Master, his Deputy and Wardens shall wear their jewels in Gold or Gilt pendant to blue Ribbons about their Necks and white Leather Aprons lined with blue Silk.
That all those who have served any of the three Grand Offices shall wear the like Aprons lined with blue Silk in all Lodges and assemblies of Masons when they appear clothed.
That those Brethren that are Steward shall wear their aprons lined with red Silk and their proper Jewels pendant to red Ribbons.
That all those who have served the Office of Steward be at Liberty to wear Aprons lined with red Silk and not otherwise.
That all Masters and Wardens of Lodges may wear their Aprons lined with White Silk and their respective Jewels with plain White ribbons but of no other colour whatsoever.
The Deputy Grand Master accordingly put the Question whether the above Regulation should be agreed to.
And it was carried in the affirmative Nemine con.

Notwithstanding some modification in the size and shape of the Apron apparent from some surviving contemporary portraits and prints, and of course, expansion in the composition of Grand Lodge, this Resolution is largely unchanged in so far as the clauses relating to the Stewards are concerned.

Grand Stewards acquire sanction to wear red upon appointment to their office. Members of a Stewards Lodge, of which to-day there are 19, whether by initiation or joining, wear normal Craft clothing until receiving such an appointment which may follow upon nomination to the Grand Master by their Lodge. A pre-requisite of any nomination is an undertaking by the Grand Steward Elect to fulfil the obligations entailed. The Grand Master possesses the right of veto which has, albeit rarely, been exercised.

Grand Stewards of the year wear plain red collars as also do the Officers and Past Masters of Grand Stewards' Lodge. Past Grand Stewards collars are edged with silver (or gold in the case of two lodges). Since 1835, the Grand Stewards' Jewel has been a cornucopia between the legs of a pair of compasses.

In 1797 a Grand Steward for the year proposed that 'every Member of this Board should wear a plain Blue Coat with Yellow Buttons and the initials G.S. engraved on each button, a white waistcoat and black silk breeches. . . .'. On a show of hands this 'appeared to be unanimously agreed' and Bro David Gwynne the W.M. of the Old King's Arms Lodge and a Grand Steward in 1793, who happened to be present by invitation in connection with a totally different matter 'took the directions to make the same accordingly'. This style of dress was adopted again in 1798 and perhaps continued for some years but uncertainty arises owing to the absence of the Board's Minutes for several years.

The next reference to clothing appears in the Board's Minutes for 1811 when it was decided that the Stewards should wear black suits with white gloves. Reaction set in the following year when the dress approved is once more a blue coat with gilt buttons, white waistcoat, etc. Fashion however decreed that in 1813 the formal wear of 1811 should be chosen and continued henceforth.

CEREMONIAL

We are indebted to Bro Dr Anderson for much of our knowledge concerning the Annual Assemblies of Masons in the years immediately following the establishment of the Premier Grand Lodge in 1717.

He makes frequent allusion to Ancient usage and custom and first mentions perambulations in connection with the Feast of 1721.

As a 'Specimen to avoid Repetitions' he describes in detail the procedure at the Annual Feast of 1724 in the following terms:

> After Dinner G. Master Dalkeith made the
> first Procession round the tables, *viz.—*
>
> Brother Clinch to clear the Way
>
> The Stewards 2 and 2 a Breast with white Rods.
> Secretary COWPER with the Bag, and on his Left
> The Master of a Lodge with One Great Light.
> Two other Great Lights born by two Masters of Lodges.
> Former Grand Wardens proceeding one by one, according to Juniority.
> Former Grand Masters proceeding, according to Juniority.
> SORELL and SENEX the two Grand Wardens.
> DESAGULIERS D.G. Master alone.

On the Left Hand	On the Right Hand
The Sword carried by the Master	The Book of Constitutions on a
of the Lodge to which the	Cushion carried by the Master
Sword belong'd	of the Senior Lodge
Richmond Grand Master Elect	Dalkeith Grand Master

During the Procession, 3 Times round the Tables, the Brethren stood up and fac'd about the regular Salutations; and when return'd Brother Dalkeith stood up, and bowing to the Assembly, thank'd em for the Honour he had of being their Grand Master, and then proclaim'd aloud the most Noble Prince and Brother Charles Lennos Duke of Richmond and Lennox GRAND MASTER of Masons!

The Duke having bow'd to the Assembly, Brother Dalkeith invested him with the proper Ensigns and Badges of his Office and Authority, install'd him in S's Chair, and wishing him all Prosperity, sat down on his Right Hand. Upon which the Assembly join'd in due Homage, affectionate Congratulations and other Signs of Joy.

After the investiture of the Deputy Grand Master, Grand Wardens and the Secretary of Grand Lodge:

> 'Richmond Grand Master made the 2d. Procession round the Tables like the First, except that Brother Dalkeith walked first as the youngest late Grand Master, close after the former Grand Wardens; and Richmond walk'd alone last of all, with his Deputy immediately before him, and his two Grand Wardens before the Deputy, and before them the Sword and Constitutions.
>
> When return'd,
>
> The Grand Master began to toast the regular Healths, the due Respects to our noble Brothers present and absent, particularly to our last good Grand Master Dalkeith.
>
> After which, the usual Expressions of Joy, Love and Friendship went round; and the

Assembly was most agreeably entertain'd with Orations, Musick and Mason Songs, till the G. Master order'd his Warden Payne to close the Lodge in good Time'.

Some variation is seen in the Account of the perambulation given in the Minutes of Grand Lodge for the Feast held on January 29th, 1730, which reads:

'Lynch to clear the Way
The 12 Stewards 2 and 2

Left	*Right*
A Master of a Lodge bearing	The Secretary bearing
one of the Great Lights	the velvet Bag
Junior G. Warden	Senior G. Warden

Two Great Lights born by
Masters of Lodges in Breast

Deputy Grand Master

The Sword born by the same	The Book of Constitutions born
persons as before	on the Cushion as before

Grand Master

Those who have been G. Masters, Deputy G. Masters and
G. Wardens, two and two the Seniors going first after
the G. Master

The Marshal

N.B.—The Brethren sitting at the several Tables must have Directions to face about as the Procession is made, and to take the Candles off the Tables and to hold them in their hands (above their Heads) at proper Distances that the Ceremony may be more Conspicuous.

The Marshal, Mr Pyne is to bear a Truncheon painted blew and tipt with Gold'.

So much for the proceedings relating to the Festive Board. Of much greater moment were the controversial public processions which were a regular feature of the Annual Assembly and in which the Stewards took part. Again we turn to Anderson who informs us that on June 24 1721 a Grand Lodge was held at King's Arms Tavern in the morning where, having elected the Duke of Montague as Grand Master for the ensuing year 'they made some new Brothers, particularly the noble Philip Lord Stanhope, now Earl of Chesterfield : And from thence they marched on Foot to the [Stationers] Hall in proper Clothing and due Form'.

This as already mentioned was the first occasion on which the Quarterly Communication and the Feast were held in separate buildings. By 1723 the 'Assembly' (Quarterly Communication) and Feast were once more being held in the same building (Merchant Taylor's Hall) but the Procession was retained for another reason. 'Dalkeith Grand Master with his Deputy and Wardens waited on Brother Richmond in the Morning at Whitehall, who with many Brothers duly clothed, proceeded in Coaches from the West to the East, and were handsomely received at the Hall by a vast majority.' (Anderson).

The Grand Master referred to was Francis, Earl of Dalkeith, later 2nd Duke of Buccleuch. Brother Richmond was Charles, 2nd Duke of Richmond and Lennox. 'Whitehall' refers to Richmond House, which until demolished in 1819, stood on

the riverside at the west end of the Privy Garden, a position now occupied by Richmond Terrace.

The records contain a number of accounts of the Processions from the London homes of the Grand Masters Elect, of which the following are typical:

1729. 'Assembly and Feast at Merchant-Taylor's Hall on Thursday, 29 Jan. 1729/30, in the 3d Year of King George II.'

'Kingston Grand Master with his Deputy and Wardens, attended the Grand Master Elect in the Morning, at his Grace's House in St. James's-Square; where he was met by a vast Number of Brothers duly clothed, and from thence they went to the Hall Eastward in the following Procession of March, *viz*.

Brother Johnson to clear the Way.
Six of the Stewards clothed proper with their Badges and White
Rods, Two in each Chariot.
Brothers without Distinction duly clothed, in Gentlemen's Coaches.
The noble and eminent Brethren duly clothed, in their own Chariots.
Former Grand Officers not noble, clothed proper,
in Gentleman's Coaches.
Former noble Grand Masters clothed proper, in their own Chariots.
The Secretary alone with his Badge and Bag, in a Chariot.
The Two Grand Wardens clothed proper with their Badges,
in one Chariot.
The D.G. Master alone clothed proper with his Badge in a Chariot.
Kingston Grand Master clothed proper with his Badge,
Norfolk G.M.Elect clothed only as a Mason,
in one Coach.
The Duke of Norfolk's Coach of State Empty

The Stewards halted at Charing-Cross till the Messenger brought Orders to move on slowly and till the Rest follow'd ; And when the Grand Master moved from the Square, Brother John Pyne the Marshal made haste to the Hall to conduct the

Procession of Entry at the Hall-Gate, *viz*.
The 12 Stewards standing, 6 on each Side of the Passage,
with their White Rods, made a Lane.
Brother Johnson to clear the Way.
Former Grand Wardens walk'd one by one according to Juniority.
Former D. Grand Masters walk'd by one according to Juniority.

Former Grand Masters by Juniority, *viz*.

Lord Colerane, Earl of Inchinquin, Lord Paisley, Duke of Richmond,
Earl of Dalkeith, Duke of Montague, Dr. Desaguliers,

George Payne, Esq., and Mr. Antony Sayer.
Then the Stewards closed, walking Two and Two.
The Secretary alone.
The Two Grand Wardens together.
The D. Grand Master alone.

On the Left Hand	On the Right Hand
The Sword born by the Master	The Book of Constitutions
of the Lodge to which it	on the fine Cushion carried by the
belonged.	Master of the Senior Lodge.

    Norfolk Grand Master Elect   Kingston Grand Master.
         Marshal Pyne with his Truncheon Blew, tipt with Gold.

In this Order they decently walk'd into the Lodge Room (while the Others walk'd into the Hall) and there the Masters and Wardens of Lodges received their G. Master with Joy and Reverence in due Form. He sat down in his Chair before the Pedestal, cover'd with the rich Cushion, upon which were laid the Constitutions and the Sword ; and the G.M. Elect on his Right Hand.

After opening the Lodge, the last Minutes were read by the Secretary, and the Election of Brother Norfolk were solemnly recogniz'd.

                Adjourn'd to Dinner, a Grand Feast indeed!

Assembly and Feast at Mercer's-Hall on Saturday 30 March, 1734. D.G.M. Batson with his G. Wardens attended the Grand Master Elect at his House in Great Marlborough-street, with Noble Brothers, and many Others, all duly clothed in Coaches, and made the Procession of March Eastward to the Hall with a Band of Musick, *viz.* Trumpets, Hautboys, Kettle-Drums and French Horns, to lead the Van and play at the Gate till all arrive. . . . '

1737.   "Loudoun G. Master with his Deputy and Wardens, the noble Brothers, the Duke of Richmond, the Earls of Craufurd and Weemes, Lord Grey of Grooby, the Stewards and many other brothers all duly clothed, attended the Grand Master Elect at his House in Pall-Mall, and made the Procession of March Eastward to the Hall in a very solemn Manner, having 3 Bands of Musick, Kettle-Drums, Trumpets and French Horns, properly disposed in the March. . . .

Doubtless these processions were popular with many of the Brethren of the day and were in keeping with the pageantry of the City. They did however provide material for the cartoonists and others ill disposed towards the Craft and were abandoned in 1747.

SUCCESSION

For many years Grand Stewards named their successors according to their own inclination, sometimes choosing a Brother belonging to a Lodge other than their own. In this way, the coveted Red Apron went to and fro, frequently, and not always, returning to a member of the earlier Lodge. This procedure led to the holding of multiple nominations. Thus in the late 18th Century and early years of the 19th up to the Union of the Modern and Ancient Grand Lodges in December 1813 the Brethren of Somerset House Lodge No. IV controlled three and those of Friendship, No. 6, two Red Aprons. Gradually, however, the Red Apron Lodges tended influence those of their members who became Stewards to accept a Lodge nomination for a successor, thus endeavouring to retain of the privilege within the Lodge.

The appointment of 12 Stewards continued from 1728 to 1812/13 in which year the Annual Feast was held on the 27th of December. The momentous year of the Union of the Grand Lodges of the Moderns and the Antients is approaching and although Stewards for the year 1813/14 were nominated by their predecessors, they apparently did not serve and instead, in compliance with Article VII of the Articles of Union the Grand Stewards were delegated by the Stewards' Lodge from among their Members 'existing at the Union'.

The uncertainty of the future of the Grand Stewards at this time and the fact that in any event, future Grand Officers would no longer be chosen exclusively from the ranks of Past Grand Stewards appears to have tempered the enthusiasm of Brethren to accept the Office and of the 10 who met for the first time on the 12th April, 1814 to prepare for the Feast in May of that year, 7 were Past Stewards and 3 were from among those nominated by the previous Board. In order to make the appointment more attractive in this important year, it had been decided by the Grand Master, H.R.H. the Duke of Sussex, 'that the price of the tickets should be increased from 15/- to One Guinea and that, in order that the Stewards should not be put to any expense, the balance of the cost and that of the incidentals would be defrayed out of the funds of Grand Lodge.'

The Stewards for the following year, were nominated by the Grand Master and 18 were appointed. Thereafter nomination has continued to rest with the group of selected Red Apron Lodges, initially to the number of 18 and subsequently 19.

The original 18 Lodges were:

Grand Master's	No. 1	*Globe	No. 23
Antiquity	No. 2	Castle L. of Harmony	No. 26
*Royal Somerset House	No. 4	*Old King's Arms	No. 28
& Inverness		*St. Alban's	No. 29
*St. George's &	No. 5	Felicity	No. 58
Corner Stone		Peace & Harmony	No. 60
*Friendship	No. 6	*Regularity	No. 91
British	No. 8	*Shakespear	No. 99
Tuscan	No. 10	Pilgrim	No. 238
*Emulation	No. 21	Prince of Wales's	No. 259

The Lodges marked* regularly nominated Stewards before the Union. Three others, Royal now Royal Alpha Lodge, No. 16, London Lodge, No. 108 and Jacob's Ladder Lodge which ceased working in 1800, each provided Stewards for a consecutive period of years in pre-Union days. Other lodges can justifiably claim to have provided a Steward occasionally but without success.

The Pilgrim (German : Pilger) No. 238 was founded in London in 1779 as a lodge working in the German language. It received its Red Apron in 1813 and retained its right of nomination until the 8th February 1834 when the Secretary wrote to the Grand Master as follows:

'M.W. Grand Master, the most kind and gracious manner in which your Royal Highness was pleased to bestow upon the Pilgrim Lodge the distinguished privilege of returning one of the Grand Stewards has ever been prized by its Members as a most valued Jewel and they trust the selection they have periodically made has been such as to evince their gratitude and to afford satisfaction to your Royal Highness.

The change of circumstances, however, as far as the numbers are concerned, resulting from the few resident Germans in London during a period of peace, rendered it impossible for the Lodge to avail themselves longer of this much valued privilege, and they are therefore under the painful necessity of returning it into the hands of the M.W. Grand Master. In doing so they venture to hope that your Royal Highness will do justice to their motives and believe that the Pilgrim Lodge will ever retain a grateful sense of the kindness and condescension which your Royal Highness has always shown to their Body.

I have the honour to subscribe myself,

Your Royal Highness most obedient Servant,
by order of the W. Master of the Pilgrim Lodge,
John Schmidt, Secretary

The return to the right to nominate was received with great regret and the privilege placed at the dispoal of Jerusalem Lodge, No. 197.

It has already been stated that the failure of a Lodge to provide an effective nomination, could result in the loss of the privilege and this in fact happened in 1852 in the case of the Old King's Arms Lodge which failed to nominate a Grand Steward for this year. The right to nominate was transferred to Old Union Lodge, No. 46, thus restoring the strength of the Board of Grand Stewards to the number of 18 as laid down in the Book of Constitutions then in force.

The circumstances relating to the failure to nominate are recorded in the history of the Lodge and in short are that a new Lodge Secretary of a few months standing overlooked passing the name of the Brother chosen by ballot in open lodge, to the Grand Secretary. No-one can question the correctness of the subsequent action but many must have been suprised at the severity of the attitude of the Grand Master and that the apparent oversight had not been queried.

It is quite possible that the decision to 'work to rule' in this case arose out of an incident involving a member of this Lodge some 40 years or so earlier when a Brother acting as Secretary to the Board of Grand Stewards refused to pass on the Minute Book to the succeeding Board, as a result of which one year's Minutes have been lost. An unsigned note of his 'contumacious conduct' probably in the hand of the Grand Secretary Bro. W. H. White appears in the Minute Book.

This may appear to some to be a highly improbable suggestion but the fact remains that the Grand Secretary whose authority was flouted in so flagrant a manner happened still to be in office in 1852!

The White family, five of whom were members of Emulation were prominent in masonry from the late 18th Century until late in the 19th. William White (1747–1821) was initiated into Royal Somerset House Lodge, No. IV, served as Grand Steward in 1774 and was Secretary to the Board. He became Joint Grand Secretary in 1781 in which year he was W.M. of the Grand Stewards' Lodge, Grand Secretary in 1784 and again Joint Grand Secretary with his son in 1809. He joined the Lodges of Antiquity, No. 2 and Emulation, No. 21.

William Henry White (1777–1866) served as Grand Steward for Emulation in 1805 and was Secretary to the Board, and again as Grand Steward for Somerset House in 1809. He was appointed Joint Grand Secretary with his Father in 1809, and was Grand Secretary from 1813 to 1856.

Of course the Lodge made strenuous efforts to have the decision revoked and at least one attempt was made in later years. In the event, the privilege was restored in 1904 largely it would seem owing to the eloquence of Brother E. A. Ebblewhite of Shakespear Lodge, No. 99, President of the 1903 Board, and support of Brother John Smithers, the W.M. of Grand Stewards' Lodge. The occasion was a discussion on four notices of motion to modify the Rules to permit an increase in the number of Grand Stewards from 18 to 30, a motion which was withdrawn. A further motion to increase the number of Stewards from 18 to 19 was passed and at the next Festival the privilege was restored to the Old King's Arms Lodge, No. 28.

This very early lodge, formerly the Rose in Mary-le-Bone shares with Tuscan No. 14, formerly the Lyon in Brewer Street, the distinction of having on its roll of members Brother Caesar (Cesar) Collys whose name heads the list of Stewards who volunteered to form the first Board in 1728.

NO NUTS – NO SODA WATER!

It is not without interest to consider the conduct of the Feast and the legislation enacted by successive Boards to meet the administrative situations encountered.

Among the constantly recurring problems which caused anxiety and gave rise to elaborate precautions were the following:

(a) *Quality of wine served in relation to that tasted and ordered.* It was evident that the stipulation that these should be of the best quality was found to be inadequate and for a number of years the wines were checked by a Deputation from the Board of Stewards 'and brought up in Black Bottles into a Room adjoining the Hall and there decanted under the superintendence of the Wine Steward'. In 1832 however, a Minute reads 'The Board declined a taste of sample of the Wines, the President informing Mr. Cuff (Landlord of F.M. Tavern) that the Board should rely upon his Honour to furnish such as would be creditable to himself and satisfactory to the meeting'.

(b) *Quantity of Wine actually consumed against that charged for.* An elaborate system of wine tickets was an established custom by 1775, these being held by the Stewards, the rule being that tickets be provided to be delivered for the wines at the Grand Feast by the members of the Board but that no Ticket be given on any account till the Wine brought up and delivered by the Waiters'. Occasionally other brethren were recruited to assist the Stewards but this too had its shortcomings. Thus, after the Festival of April 1812, the Secretary reported that 'Bro. Dow to whom the charge of the Wine Store was assigned at the Grand Festival had, through inadvertency or from inattention to the Regulations prescribed to him by the Board, been led into error in his account of Wine consumed on that day and that consequently improper charges were introduced in the Tavern Bill on this as well as on other Accounts, contrary to the engagement entered into by the Secretary on behalf of the Board with Messrs. Thorn and Cuff [Landlords] – that he had remonstrated against and conjointly with the President and Treasurer had resisted the payment of such charges and in performance of this duty had been subject to much abuse and scurrilous language from Thomas Hoggray one of the Servants of the Tavern and for which he had demanded an apology and proper concession to be made, that instead he had received a letter purporting to be an acquiescence in his wishes but which contained so much additional insult as considerably to aggravate the original offence – he thereupon demanded the interference of Messrs. Thorn and Cuff and received in answer from Mr. Cuff 'that he regretted the obstinacy of his Servant in refusing to offer a becoming Apology and that he could do no more unless Mr. Percy required him *in writing* to dismiss the Offender from his Service', that from such supineness or indifference on the part of Mr. Cuff nothing

was effected until Mr. Thorn's return to Town who being made acquainted with the disgraceful occurrence manifested a very different feeling and adopted that firm decision and becoming line of conduct which ultimately succeeded in bringing the Servant to a proper sense of his Duty and that he now had the authority to state, if the Board considered an ample Apology would be sufficient atonement, the same would be submitted to in such terms as should be dictated. The Members present having given their opinion upon the subject, Mr. Cuff was called in and the President in strong terms animadverted on the insult and indifference with which the Secretary as their Representative had been treated, and declared that nothing but the most unqualified submission would be satisfactory to the Board which Mr. Cuff assuring the Meeting would be complied with. Thomas Hoggray [Clerk to Messrs. Thorn and Cuff] was introduced who humbly begging pardon for his Offence was dismissed with a suitable reprimand and admonition'.

The question of Wine Tickets was taken very seriously.

Yet another Board varied the procedure by stipulating that 'each Steward do have attached to him a Waiter with a basket and that whenever Wine is wanted a Steward shall accompany the Waiter to the bar of the Wine Room and see that the same is received and brought into the Hall and deposited on the table for which Wine the Steward will give Tickets . . . That proper persons be engaged to attend the Wine Room to decant and deliver out the Wine and receive the Tickets: such persons to be paid 10s. 6d. each and 3s. 0d. for Dinner . . . That each Steward do see to the empty decanters and on no account to suffer any Waiter to remove them.'

A regulation adopted by many of the Boards restricted the wine served to that selected in advance and declared that 'no Steward be allowed to give 2 or more Wine Tickets (or 1 Ticket with any sum of money) for the purpose of obtaining any other Wines under a penalty of a fine (to the Board) of £10'.

(c) *Extras.* At most functions these arose and our early brethren became well aware of the methods available to the management to increase the bills. Periodically the minutes of Boards displays bouts of indignation and in 1806 we read 'Recommended to the next Board of Grand Stewards that they be particular in their agreement with the Landlords of the Tavern to include everything in the price mentioned and that no extras be introduced in the Bill such as Bread, Beer, Broken Glasses, Carpenter, etc., etc., etc.' This recommendation was duly expressed in the form that 'the Prices quoted for the Dinner are to be inclusive of Bread, Beer, Broken Glass and every other kind of charge . . .'.

(d) *Ladies.* It is not possible to determine exactly when entertainment and refreshment were provided for a limited number of wives and sweethearts but the practice appears to have started prior to the year 1775 and to have continued without break until 1939, except for the period 1915–18 when activities generally were curtailed. The number of tickets available for ladies varied from time to time but was about 80–100. It was the custom for each Steward to be permitted to invite an agreed number of ladies (varying from two to five) and to allow some tickets for the use of the Grand Master's party. The

ladies had at their disposal the Gallery and Glee Room for which singers were provided. The Gallery door was properly 'tyled' by a Steward who was instructed to allow Ladies to pass upon presentation of a ticket 'signed by a Steward naming the Lady to be admitted' and shall admit none without. Boards of Grand Stewards governed their proceedings largely by precedent, the Resolutions which were considered by the successive Boards being varied as experience might demand. Thus in 1798, no gentleman was to be admitted to the company of the Ladies unless introduced by a Steward but by 1846 an instruction from the Grand Master to the Stewards in respect of the Ladies stated that '2 Grand Stewards and no greater number be appointed to attend to their accommodation, and on no account shall any other member of the Board, except the President (should his presence be called for) be permitted to go to the Ladies Room until after the Grand Master or other presiding Officer shall have quitted the Banquet Hall'.

(e) *Music*. There are many references to music at the Feast of which the Minute for 1811 is typical. 'Bro. Samuel Wesley [Grand Organist 1813–17] be engaged to perform upon the organ in the Glee Room and that each Member of the Board be entitled to 4 invitation tickets, the President 6.' On this occasion '12 Professional Gents' were engaged 'for their Vocal Performance at the Grand Festival'. It was also resolved that the 'usual Military Band consisting of 12 Masons be engaged from the Guards, conducted by Mr. Horne of the Coldstream Regiment.''

In 1817 The Board was informed that the Duke of Kent's Band was disembodied, which lamentable situation was met by an under-the-counter deal with the late Band Major!

Musicians were as temperamental then as they sometimes are to-day and Boards have been known to run into difficulties when they tried to break up groups of singers by excluding some to whom they had objection. There also appears to have been a tendency to run up the fees. In the 1830s there were frequent and lengthy exchanges of letters between the Secretary to the Board of Grand Stewards and Sir George Smart, Grand Organist 1818–1843. The letters, framed in the most courteous terms were firm and to the point, reinforced on both sides with the implication that the contents had been approved by His Royal Highness the Duke of Sussex, Grand Master 1813–1843. It was finally agreed that whilst the Board fixed the fee, the conduct of the music and the musicians was the prerogative of the Grand Organist!

The 1863 Board was on firmer ground when they took exception to the action of the Grand Organist of the day who produced at the Festival a singer clad as a mason and who was discovered to be a Cowan.

Music was discontinued in 1939 and has not been provided subsequently.

(f) *Exuberance*. The toasting and other customs of the Festive Board are outside the scope of this Lecture but there is no doubt whatever that the Grand Feast of the 18th and early 19th Centuries was an occasion for great rejoicing and it has to be said that occasionally the proceedings tended to get out of hand.

As long ago as the year 1815 the Boards of Stewards included in their Resolutions 'that neither soda water nor nuts be allowed in the Hall' but no

reason for the decision is given. This Resolution was repeated year after year.

At the Grand Festival in 1846 when owing to illness only 16 Stewards were on duty, irregularities and disorder occurred and following an investigation, the Board of General Purposes reported that the arrangements of the Board of Grand Stewards were totally inefficient for the occasion. The Board of Grand Stewards' Minutes make reference to 'A numerous party of Brethren' from a group of Lodges which must remain nameless and at this distance in time it does appear to be a little unreasonable to blame 16 (or for that matter 18) Stewards at a gathering of nearly 400 plus the Ladies.

As a result however the Grand Master, the Earl of Zetland issued a series of guidelines for future Boards which although reiterating the spirit of the Resolutions of successive Boards do not appear to be directed against those who caused the disturbance. It may well be that the Minutes are incomplete and that nuts and soda water were unfortunately available!

NOT WITHOUT CHARITY –

However romantic and exciting the earlier years of the Craft may have been, there is at least one daunting aspect, namely the peril of loss of income from whatever cause arising. The early Minutes of Grand Lodge are noteworthy both for the constant exhortation by Dr. Desaguliers and others to the Lodges to support the Grand Charity, as well as for the frequent calls upon the limited funds available for the relief of indigent Brethren.

Anthony Sayer our first Grand Master in 1717, Thomas Morrice or Morris Junior Grand Warden in 1718–19, William Reid, Secretary to Grand Lodge 1727-33, and North Stainer, (Grand) Steward in 1724 were all in later life petitioners for assistance, the two last appealing from Debtors Prisons. Truly does the Tyler's Toast acquire a positive significance against such a background of misfortune.

Ever mindful of the needs of the Brethren, the Doctor in April 1730 acquainted Grand Lodge that 'the Directors of the Infirmary at Westminster, out of their regard to Masonry (several of them being Masons) had offered to take care of any poor Brother who may happen to be disabled by broken Limb, etc., from following his Employment....'

'Whereupon it was proposed that five Guineas be paid Annually to the said Infirmary.... [agreed]'.

A vellum Roll of Subscribers to the Infirmary, later Westminster Hospital, from 1719–1733 has survived and contains the names of a number of the masons of the time comprising several Grand Masters, including Dr. Desaguliers, and Stewards: Edward Lambert, Henry Prude, Capt. Sam Tuffnell, Dr. Meyer Schomberg, Dr. Wm. Graeme and others.

It was an age in which public conscience was being awakened and two very different persons, George Frideric Handel the Composer and Brother Wm. Hogarth the Artist supported the Foundling Hospital Scheme of Captain Coram, *circa* 1739, with great enthusiasm.

Yet another Charity served by a long line of masons and a number of Grand Stewards is the French Protestant Hospital known traditionally as 'La Providence'.

Established in London by Huguenot refugees before 1706 and incorporated by Royal Charter in 1718, this foundation is even older than the Premier Grand Lodge.

The Directors of 'La Providence', a number of whom were Past Grand Stewards founded the Huguenot Lodge No. 2140 in 1885, a year chosen to mark the bicentenary of the tragic events of 1685. Claude Champion de Crespigny, a Grand Steward in 1732, who was a member of the Lodge at the Bear and Harrow (now St. George's and Corner Stone, No. 5) and a Director of this Hospital, spent a lifetime in the service of the South Sea Company. His nephew Philip was a Grand Steward in 1781 for Somerset House Lodge.

Still later another Grand Steward, Chevalier Bartholomew Ruspini who served in 1772 for St. Alban's Lodge, No. 29, was instrumental in founding the first of the four individual Masonic Charities, the Royal Masonic Institution for Girls, on March 25th, 1788.

SOME FACTS – SOME SPECULATION

Several references have been made to the Huguenot fraternity and the Edict de Nantes and some explanation may be of interest.

The development of the Protestant movement having as its object the reform of the Christian Church as it then existed, is a feature of the life of Mediæval Europe. Over many contentious years the Reformed Church under various names became well established in England, Germany, Holland and Switzerland but in France, however, there was a long drawn out opposition to more liberal views and the struggles of the 16th Century culminated in the massacre of Protestants on the eve of St. Bartholomew, 24th August 1572 when upwards of 12,000 died in Paris alone and nearly 100,000 in all France. Queen Elizabeth I sent strong protests to the French King and made substantial provision for the reception of the refugees from France to whom the term Huguenot had been applied. In due course the newcomers of this first exodus were largely absorbed.

The Protestant party in France exerted their influence on the king and in 1573 obtained a charter of religious freedom which had become known as the Edict of Nantes. An uneasy peace with periodic bouts of oppression ensued until October 1685 when under pressure from the Church and Council, a not unwilling king formally revoked the Edict and terror ensued. It is estimated that at this time the population of France was about 15 millions of whom some ten per cent were Protestant. 300,000 are thought to have escaped – many to England and southern Ireland. In London the influx is considered to have been more than 50,000 over a period from 1681 (some foresaw the danger ahead) to about 1693.

Now we must turn to the London of the 17th century, in relation to which any comments on population statistics are derived from the area covered by the Bills of Mortality. By this expression is meant an inexact zone of roughly 10 miles radius of London Stone, Cannon Street, with some notable exclusions such as the villages of Chelsea, Kensington, St. Mary-le-bone and St. Pancras, although the term as later applied by Grand Lodge would doubtless have included the entire zone. At the heart of the area are the Cities of London and Westminster which

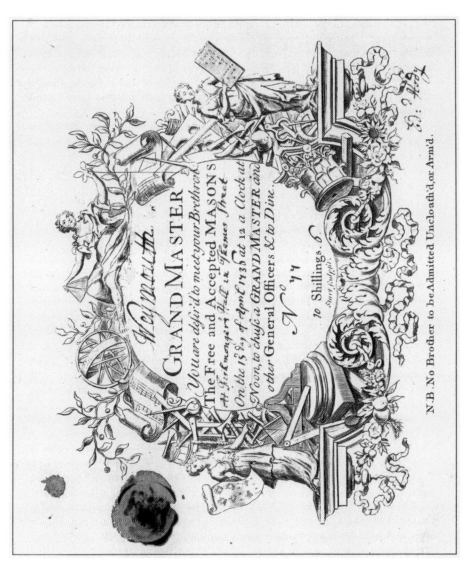

Admission Ticket to Grand Festival 1736 bearing seal of Grand Lodge and signature
of Dr. Edward Hody, M.D., F.R.S., Grand Steward

by the early 18th century were conjoined although they were, as they still are, separately administered. The population of the whole area in 1660 was roughly 300,000 and during the years of the Plague (1664–66) between 69,000 and over 100,000 of the inhabitants died. The first figure is that of the official return but it has always been known that the system collapsed and that the true number was much higher, the second figure being an 18th century estimate. After the Plague came the Fire of 1666 which destroyed 436 acres (eighty-three per cent of the City and part of the built-up districts outside the walls). These two events not only checked the growth of the urban area but drastically reduced the number of inhabitants.

London was therefore peculiarly well-suited to receive an influx of refugees who were not only co-religionists but were for the most part a corpus of people of independent outlook, steadfast in principle and composed of a mixture of hard-working artisans, craftsmen and members of the learned professions. At about this time new areas of central London, then largely fields and market gardens, were being developed and the Berners estate of Soho is an example. Soho quickly became a centre for the Huguenot community just as today it maintains a heterogeneous foreign population. The parishes of Spitalfields, Clerkenwell and Wandsworth also became heavily populated by the newcomers who, in some areas, accounted for more than one in every six or seven of the population. At one time there were in the London district some forty-nine chapels erected or converted from other buildings for their use and the pattern was reflected in other cities such as Canterbury, Rochester, Southampton and Norwich, to name but a few.

This was the London in which the permier Grand Lodge was established in 1717, by which time the progeny of the refugees were of mature age. As a body they must have gloried in their new found freedom in our liberal society and to those who came into contact with them the tenets of masonry must have appealed strongly.

Many of the early freemasons bear the names of families recorded officially in the long lists of denizations and naturalizations extending up to the year 1701 and a considerable number served as Festival Stewards, the numbers tending to increase towards the middle of the 18th century. Thus during a period of five years from 1738 the lists of Stewards include such names as Barret, Beaumont, Bernard, Carne, Caton, Combrune, De Charmes, De Vaux, Du Mouchel, Faber, Foy, Hemet, Le Bas, Le Maistre, Ruck and Vol, amounting to rather more than one in four of the sixty Stewards who served for this period.

There is as well a strong possibility, as yet unproven, that Edward Lambert, several times mentioned as a Steward, was a member of a well known Huguenot family of that name. It is, of course, open to argument that some of these names were in use in both England and France at this time and the validity of this contention can only be resolved by continuing research. The names are scattered over a number of the recorded lodges of the period but the members of three lodges were almost entirely of French descent, these being Solomon's Temple, Prince Eugen's Head and the French Lodge in Long Acre.

Inasmuch as the mason's among the native population were apparently quiescent in the early years of the 18th century, is it possible that the developing interest

of the newcomers in freemasonry was a major factor in producing a reaction which led to the formation of the first Grand Lodge?

This year marks the 250th anniversary of the appointment of the first regular Board of Grand Stewards. Initially born of necessity, the Stewards have been honoured to serve the Craft for a Quarter of a millenium and long may they continue to do so. Their service is typical of that given to Masonry in many ways by the brethren generally.

Freemasonry provides the opportunity – it is for us to embrace it.

'... Who must otherwise have remained at a perpetual distance.'

250 YEARS OF MASONRY IN INDIA

A Study in Resolved Discords

THE PRESTONIAN LECTURE FOR 1979

G. E. WALKER, *OBE*

(This paper was written by the late W Bro G. E. Walker to be the Prestonian Lecture for 1979 and to mark the 250th Anniversary in that year of the first establishment of a lodge in India. He had completed it in draft shortly before his death which occurred with tragic suddenness on 9 December 1977. The Trustees of the Prestonian Fund decided that this paper should still be designated the Prestonian Lecture for 1979 and, *vice* the late W Bro Walker, they invited W Bro G. J. C. Hambling, PDistSGW (Bombay) to deliver it. He, in the sad circumstances, was pleased to accept this task of proxy Lecturer.)

On February 6th 1729, the Grand Lodge of England authorised the constitution of the first Lodge in India. In 1961, when the Grand Lodge of India was formed, there were 186 Lodges in India owing allegiance to the United Grand Lodge of England (plus another 17 in what had by then become Pakistan; there were 79 Lodges belonging to the Irish and Scottish Constitutions; and another 80 or so had had their day and ceased to be.)

With such growth on record, the historian is not likely to be gravelled for lack of matter; but within a limit of three-quarters of an hour's talk – 6,000 words or thereabouts – what he certainly can't do is to produce a complete history. So I must begin by declaring an interest. I was initiated in Madras in 1937, in the Archibald Campbell Lodge, No 4998, a Lodge founded 'to promote better fraternal relationship between Indians and Europeans who have had the advantage of residing in each others' native land'. There were then 39 members, 29 Indians and 10 Europeans.

It is to the circumstances of my Masonic birth and infant nurture that I owe an abiding interest in the growth of Masonry in India from an exclusively Western, Christian organisation into an inter-racial, theist body, of which even 50 years ago the first Lord Cornwallis, then Deputy Grand Master, could write (joyously mixing nationalities and religions):

We have seen as many as five Volumes of the Sacred Law in use at one and the same time, and Brethren of the following among other races, taken at random – Europeans, Parsis, Chinese, Burmese, Hindus, Americans, Ceylonese, Punjabis, Mohammedans, Sikhs,

Armenians, Greeks, Bengalis, Jews, Aracanese, and Madrassis – participating in the Ceremonies. The Brotherhood of Man, under such circumstances, becomes a living reality.

So let us look back 250 years to 1729.

In England: George II, and Walpole restored to power by the Queen's persuasion; in India: the free-for-all that followed the death of Aurangzeb in 1707. The English, French, Dutch and Portuguese Companies were trading and squabbling with the best of them; but they were only lessees of their holdings: none of them then laid claim to empire.

What manner of men were our English Masonic forebears? One must always beware of applying twentieth century moral judgments to eighteenth century behaviour; but one needs to understand something of the differences in circumstance and temperament.

Bro Heron Lepper (*the poor common soldier, AQC* vol 38) has described the period as 'a brutal age that had crude ideas about tolerance and humane dealing and general decency of conduct'[1]; and indeed our Founding Fathers were a strange combination of culture and coarseness, rugged individualism and sycophancy, good taste and ostentation; and they were chauvinist and bigoted, truculent and outspoken.

And if this was the Englishman on his home ground, we can well understand how his natural tetchiness would be aggravated in India by the heat, the humidity, the velvet coats and high neckcloths, and the quenching of his inevitable thirst by his daily tipple of arrack-punch and a bottle (or more) of Madeira.

When I read of the suspensions, the exclusions, the secessions, the blackballing, accusations of murder, of forgery, 42 members suspended for libelling a Past Master (though admittedly 32 of them apologised and were reinstated) – then I confess to making a wry mouth when I hear that this association has been formed and perfected with so much unanimity and concord; it ought to have been; but in fact the discords which our forebears made were not resolved for nearly 200 years.

MASONRY COMES TO INDIA

We are lucky enough to have full details of the constituting of that first Indian Lodge preserved in the minutes of Grand Lodge: first, the petition, presented on December 28th, 1728; then, at the end of the minutes of that meeting, the text of the 'deputation' from the Grand Master, 'to Impower and authorize our Well-beloved Brother George Pomfret.... that he do, in our place and stead, Constitute a regular Lodge, in due fform, at Fort William in Bengall in the East Indies....' This was signed and sealed 'the 6th day of ffebruary 172$\frac{8}{9}$ and in the Year of Masonry 5732' (which shows that Grand Lodge used Ussher's Chronology in dating the Masonic era – as the Grand Lodge of Scotland still do). It is the earliest document of its kind of which any record exists.

The Lodge at 'Fort William' – that is, Calcutta – appears in the Engraved List of 1730 as No. 72; it was called, perhaps after its place of meeting, The East India Company's Arms (of which the crest was a golden lion rampant gardant, supporting between the forepaws a regal crown, proper – irreverently known in the Company's Marine Services as 'the monkey and the coconut').

The Lodge lasted less than thirty years: it was erased in 1756. Perhaps the most interesting thing about it is the application for a warrant from Grand Lodge – then only twelve years old and in its early years aspiring only to regulate the Craft in the cities of London and Westminster. Overseas Lodges in those days tended to come into being by a kind of parthenogenesis: a few Masons met, called themselves a Lodge, made other Masons, and created more Lodges, without applying to anyone for permission.

This is why Provincial Grand Masters began to be appointed in about 1726, 'when the extraordinary Increase of the Craftsmen, and their travelling into distant Parts and convening themselves in Lodges, required an immediate Head, to whom they might apply where it was not possible to wait the decision or Opinion of the Grand Lodge'. The appointment was always a prerogative of the Grand Master, and the Provincial Grand Master originally ranked as a Deputy Grand Master; by 1767 he had become 'a Grand Master in his particular District', who was 'also empowered to appoint a Deputy, Wardens, Treasurer, Secretary and Sword Bearer who are entitled to wear the Cloathing of Grand Officers while they officiate as such within that particular District; but at no other time or place'. In 1784 a Chaplain was added to the list, ranking between the Secretary and the Sword Bearer.

Here, it would seem, is the beginning of the Provincial Grand Lodge as we know it today – though the Article seems rather to constitute a local Grand Lodge than a subordinate Provincial Grand Lodge. Be that as it may, nothing like a modern Provincial or District Grand Lodge sprang into being; the original Provincial Grand Masters were more like the Grand Inspectors of today. (Incidentally, the distinction between 'Provincial' and 'District' wasn't made until 1866; until then, the *District* was the area over which the *Provincial* Grand Master exercised authority).

THE FIRST PROVINCIAL GRAND MASTERS

In 1729, Captain Ralph Farwinter (his name is variously spelt) was appointed 'Provincial Grand Master for East India in Bengal' – and also James Dawson as 'Provincial Grand Master for East India'. No one seems to know why two appointments were made; perhaps because of geographical woolly-mindedness in London; after all, it was only about a dozen years since the publication of Clarendon's glowing reference to 'the Island of Bombay with the towns and castles therein, which are within a very little distance from Brazil'.[2]

Bengal was fortunate in doing things in their proper order: a Provincial Grand Master first, followed by the constitution of private Lodges by him. Lodges were formed in other districts: in Madras in 1752 and 1765, and in Bombay in 1758; but although they appeared in the Roll of Grand Lodge, we don't know how they came into being. Certainly there were no Provincial Grand Masters there to constitute them: Bombay's first, James Tod, was appointed in 1764 (though there is no record of his ever doing anything, and it was 97 years before another appointment was made); and Madras had its first Provincial Grand Master (Captain Edmund Pascal) in 1767. The Punjab didn't have its own Provincial

Grand Master till 1869, and Northern India not until 1951 (as a result of the partition of the sub-continent into India and Pakistan).

By the time of Pascal's appointment, English Masonry was split between the Modern or Premier Grand Lodge and the Antient or Atholl. This isn't the place to deal with that bygone quarrel, beyond saying that the Grand Lodges of Ireland and Scotland leaned towards the Atholl Masons; that Ireland, Scotland and Atholl all specialised in warranting ambulatory or military Lodges, which helped greatly in the spread of Masonry, in India and elsewhere; and that the Atholl and Premier rituals differed radically, especially over the Royal Arch.

The first impact of Atholl Masonry in India was in Madras, where, in the very year after Pascal's appointment, an Atholl Lodge was established at Fort St. George by officers of the army, and soon became the principal Lodge of the Coast of Coromandel; it acted as a Provincial Grand Lodge[3], granting warrants for new Lodges; it built a Masonic Hall and established a Charity Fund.

Bengal, meanwhile, stayed with the Premier Grand Lodge; two of its Lodges are still on the Register: Star in the East, No 67 (1740), and Industry and Perseverenace, No 109 (1761).

EARLY PIQUES AND QUARRELS

But in the 1780s the Premier Masons in both Bengal and Madras got themselves into deep trouble: owing, in both cases, to the human cantankerousness which I have already spoken of.

We can give an account of the Madras troubles in the words of its own Provincial Grand Master (by that time, Brigadier-General Matthew Horne), who wrote, in 1784, of 'the unfortunate Divisions that arose and continued some years in the Settlement, occasioned by the Removal of Lord Pigot from the Government of Madras; and many of our Members becoming warm Adherents of different Parties, their animosity against each other ran so high, that they could not meet as Brethren; and not choosing to exclude either Party, our Lodge ceased'.

Bengal's problems stemmed from a practice which dated back to the beginning of things and went on until the 1890s, by which the overseas Provincial Grand Lodges formally recommended someone whom they would like to have as Provincial Grand Master, for the Grand Master's approval. If there were two or more proposals, there was a vote – and the procedure was misleadingly called an election.

From 1781 to 1785 the Provincial Grand Lodge of Bengal was in abeyance, owing to war in the Carnatic[4] and elsewhere. In 1785 one George Williamson, a Past Provincial Senior Grand Warden, was given a 'deputation' to convene a meeting, to recommend a Brother for appointment as Provincial Grand Master *and* to act himself until a regular appointment was made.

Then the trouble really began. At the so-called 'election', Williamson got four votes, and one Edward Fenwick got six, and was declared elected. Plainly, until the Grand Master confirmed Fenwick, Williamson was the acting Provincial Grand Master; but Fenwick refused to wait, usurped the Provincial Grand Mastership, writing in that capacity to Grand Lodge, and having himself formally installed; while Williamson in return made off with the seal and the books and

papers (his position was somewhat weakened by his being on the run from his creditors).

Grand Lodge took a poor view; Fenwick's installation showed 'too much precipitation'; the brethren had 'no powers of election', so they had better think again, and in the meantime Williamson was to continue in office.

Their letter provoked an outburst of fury which can only be described as outright mutiny, and a monstrous (in both senses) letter was written to Grand Lodge, of which the gems are in paragraphs 26 and 27, which say quite flatly that 'the Masons of Bengal never assented' to the appointment of a Provincial Grand Master being the prerogative of the Grand Master; that they had a 'natural and inherent' right to elect their own Provincial Grand Master, and while they would always communicate their choice to Grand Lodge, this was 'all the submission' that could be 'reasonably required' of them.

The reply to this impertinence is Grand Lodge at its best. It is addressed to Fenwick himself, and says in effect, that as most of the brethren seem to want you as Provincial Grand Master, they'd better have you; then (and how the Grand Secretary must have chuckled as he wrote it!) he hopes that the brethren 'will yet be of opinion that it is only for the brethren to recommend and the Grand Master to appoint his Representative; *and you, Right Worshipful Sir, now standing in that honourable Situation, will I doubt not be mindful of the Rights of the Most Worshipful Grand Master.*'

So the poacher was appointed gamekeeper. But Nemesis awaited him. Within two years he too was on the run from his creditors, and had to resign his office. And on the day he resigned, the Hon Charles Stewart was 'elected' in his stead – *and installed.* Bengal just would not be told.

UNION IN MADRAS

Madras, at this stage, was more statesmanlike. In 1785 the Atholl Lodge at Fort St. George wrote to their Grand Lodge of their 'deepest concern that Freemasonry should be unhappily divided into two different sects' and wishing that 'an union of the Craft could be effected', for 'the evils that attend the disunion of the Craft are many, and in Provinces remote from the mother-country, they are experienced in a degree of which the Brethren in England can have no conception'.

The Atholl Grand Lodge made no reply to this sensible suggestion; and in 1786 their Lodge in Madras got together with Brigadier-General Horne, who had been re-appointed Provincial Grand Master of the opposite faction, and drew up an Act of Union of eleven Articles, under which the Atholl Lodge 'surrender up their Powers and Dignities of a Provincial Grand Lodge' and accept a warrant from the Premier Grand Lodge; 'the United Society' is to instruct all members 'in the essential points that have Distinguished the two Societies'; Lodges warranted by the Atholl Lodges come into 'the United Provincial Grand Lodge' in their present seniority; individual Atholl Masons come into the Union; buildings, books and 'paraphernalia' are handed over, and 'the Cash of both Lodges' becomes a new General Fund – in short, a dignified and honourable treaty, giving Madras a 27 year start over the United Grand Lodge of England. The old Atholl Lodge, under

its new warrant, is still on the Register as the Lodge of Perfect Unanimity, No 150.

FURTHER DISSENSION

It seems a pity that, after such a display of statesmanship, the new Lodge should have treated Provincial Grand Lodge as a closed shop[5]: it was 63 years – in 1849 – before Provincial Grand Lodge was extended to members of what were actually called 'the Inferior Lodges'. Bengal, I'm afraid, did the same kind of thing, the only difference being that their closed shop consisted of two Lodges, Star in the East and Industry and Perseverance; and the rank-and-file Lodges were not 'Inferior' but 'Subordinate'. But whatever the name, these lesser Lodges were not allowed to be present at the opening and closing of Provincial Grand Lodge: they were summoned to give an account of their stewardship and then ordered to withdraw. And they didn't even install and invest their own Master and Wardens: the Province did that. In Bengal, which never did things by halves, four resentful 'Subordinate' Lodges seceded to the Atholl Grand Lodge between 1797 and 1801. This didn't matter in the long run, as in 1813 England followed the excellent example set by Madras, and formed the United Grand Lodge of England.

But this wasn't the end of the administrative problems of Indian Masonry. In 1813, that great and good man, the Earl of Moira (later Marquess of Hastings) arrived in India with a patent as Grand Master 'in and over the whole of India and the Islands in the Indian seas'; and it seems that because there was a Grand Master in India, correspondence with Grand Lodge in England from Bengal 'fell into abeyance', and from Madras, 'from 1801 to 1820 no returns were sent to England'; then in Bengal, by 1820, we have the Province demanding the Grand Lodge dues and returns from the 'subordinate' Lodges – and failing to forward them.

True to form, Bengal mutinied. One Lodge returned its warrant; two others demanded that a committee be set up to report on relations with Grand Lodge; the Deputy Provincial Grand Master refused to allow the motion to be put, on the grounds that it was 'derogatory to the authority of the Provincial Grand Lodge and the respect due thereto by the subordinate Lodges'. On this, 'the movers of the original resolution renewed the discussion with vehemence' – and the Deputy and both the Provincial Grand Wardens resigned their Chairs on the spot[6]. Then six Calcutta Lodges formed themselves into a 'Lodge of Delegates' to prepare a memorial of protest to Grand Lodge – indeed, the only Lodges in Calcutta that didn't join were Star in the East and Industry and Perseverance, which furnished all the officers of Provincial Grand Lodge anyway.

And to make matters worse, the administrative side of Grand Lodge itself broke down; Madras reports that 'from 1822 to 1836 ... no communications were received from headquarters'; Bengal, that Grand Lodge 'withheld certificates and left applications for warrants unattended to'. And there was serious talk in India of seceding from the English Grand Lodge and setting up an independent Grand Lodge for themselves – a suggestion which was still meeting with approval in the Indian Masonic press in the 1850s[7].

PROGRESS

Fortunately, better times were ahead, not only in the two old Provinces of Bengal and Madras, but in Bombay as well; and in each case the better times were due to the emergence of a genuine Ruler in the Craft.

In Bengal, Dr John Grant became Provincial Grand Master in 1840, and restored some of the dignity and high importance of Masonry in his Province for close on ten years. His one blind spot, which I shall come back to shortly, was not as evident to his contemporaries as it is today.

Madras had a kind of false dawn. The handsome, 30 year-old Lord Elphinstone became Governor in 1837 and Provincial Grand Master in 1840. (The gossip of the London Clubs was that Lord Melbourne had shoo'd him off to Madras because he and the 18 year-old Queen Victoria were growing far too interested in each other)[8]. His appointment caused an immediate upsurge of interest in Freemasonry, but not perhaps for Masonic reasons: rather as a means of catching the Governor's eye. The interest did not survive Lord Elphinstone's return to England in 1842; and with the retirement of his Deputy shortly afterwards, the Province was left with only the Provincial Senior Grand Warden in charge. It wasn't until 1848 that John Binny Key was appointed Deputy and put new life into Masonry in South India. Lord Elphinstone remained provincial Grand Master *in absentia* until 1852; he never returned to Madras: Binny Key was the moving spirit.

But the most notable of the three Rulers in the Craft who emerged at this time was James Burnes, a medical officer in the East India Company's service, who had arrived in Bombay in 1821. He was an outstanding man in many ways: a Fellow of the Royal Society, and the last Knight of the Guelphic Order of Hanover to be made by King William IV[9]. ('His great-grandfather ... was elder brother to William Burns, the father of Scotland's immortal poet; and his grandfather was the relation to whom the unfortunate bard on his deathbed appealed for pecuniary relief'.)[10] The Chevalier Burnes (as he was always called) had been initiated in Lodge St. Peter, Montrose, under the Scottish Constitution; he was Master of the (English) Lodge of Perseverance in Bombay, as well as Provincial Grand Master of Scottish Freemasonry: Gould writes that he was one 'whom nature had bountifully endowed with all the qualities requisite for Masonic administration'.

It was the Chevalier Burnes, more than anyone else in India, who was responsible for bringing Indians into Freemasonry: the greatest revolution in the Craft since the formation of the first Grand Lodge.

THE EARLIEST INDIAN MASONS

All the Masonic history books tell us that the first Indian Mason was Omdat-ul-Omrah, the Nabob of the Carnatic, initiated in 1775. Some of them add the Grand Lodge sent him 'a Masonic apron, elegantly decorated, and a *Book of Constitutions* bound in a most superb manner'; the cost was £37.17.6 – reckoning the bullion, the gold leaf and the workmanship (and the VAT), £500 would hardly cover it today. What the books don't say is that Omdat-ul-Omrah is a classic instance of the folly of making someone a Mason solely on the grounds of his social conse-

quence: the early minutes of Perfect Unanimity contain many references to the Nabob's unmasonic conduct – one of the more gently despairing of them says:

> Experience has shown that the solemn obligations of a Mason, and the admonitions of the Lodge, have weighed little with His Highness, in the payment of a just debt to the orphans of a faithful Brother and Servant.

We shall never know whether this first error of judgment delayed the development of Masonry universal; but in the next fifty-nine years I can find the making of only one Indian Mason – in 1812. I can hardly believe that, in the middle of so great an ocean of time, there was just one tiny island of an evening when one single Indian was made; but I have searched all the records in Grand Lodge, of all the Lodges that are known to have existed in India between 1775 and 1834, and only the one name emerges. There were other Lodges, of course, of which no records remain; and even the surviving returns of the eighteenth and early nineteenth centuries are not always as reliable as they might be; so it is possible that time or circumstance may restore some names which now are missing. For the present, we must make do with the one. Happily, we know quite a bit about the circumstances.

The initiate's name was Meer Bundeh Ali Khan, and he was made in the Marine Lodge, now No 232 and meeting at Portishead, but in 1812 an Atholl Lodge meeting in Calcutta; and fortunately the United Grand Lodge has inherited the Atholl Grand Lodge's copy of the minutes of the occasion – a fascinating social document:

> *Monday, 23rd March* 1812
> Lodge of Emergency – at 8 P.M. Opened the Lodge on the 1st Degree Officers protempore proceeded to Initiate Meer Bundeh Ali Khan, And He received the 1st Degree of Masonry – Brs McCoy and Smith Secty would not be present saying that they were obligated not to be present at the Initiation of a Turk Jew or Infidel, And they considered all Mahomedans, *Turks*. Brs Hardie & Wilkins withdrew because they considered him as professing no Religion from his eating at Table with Europeans But their Objections being ridiculous in the extreme and proceeding from extreme ignorance they were permitted to withdraw, but while the Lodge was Engaged in what was serious and Solemn these Brethren were most unworthily and unmasonically employing themselves in ridiculing the Mahomedan Religion, and so near the Lodge room that they were made to leave the place – A Most impressive & Solemn charge setting forth the principles of Free Masonry and the Duties of a Good Mason was delivered on the Occasion By the Worshipful Master in the Chair (Bro Tucker) After which The W. M. & all the Brethren present most cordially congratulated Br. Meer Bundeh Ali, on becoming one of our Brethren – and He in return most Sincerely thanked in such terms as language can scarcely express – At 10 P.M. Closed the Lodge.

Perhaps Marine was ahead of its time in initiating an Indian, as six months later we find the Master, Wardens and Secretary writing to the Atholl Grand Lodge (September 1st 1812):

> It is with sorrow that we have to state that three or four Ignorant Bros have from their Malice and Ignorance, and not being able to appreciate the Meaning of what a Mason ought to be, have been of great Injury to the Lodge, by their having opposed the Making of Br. Meer Bundeh Ali Khan a man Universally respected, for the confirmation of which,

We beg to refer you to the Marquis Wellesley, and we are further sorry to say that these Brethren have had the address, to head away Several Bigoted, though otherwise very Worthy Members who were absent, to their opinion, and we have been informed that these Members have written to England to the Grand Lodge on the Subject, and we have great reason to think that they have put many Signatures to their letter that have never been Authorised....

What we have done has met with the good wishes and Sanction of Lodge No 1 Bengall and a Number of the better Informed Brethren of Lodge No 317 as well as many other very worthy Brethren who have done us the Honor of Visiting us, coming from all quarters of the globe....

There is a certain unconscious humour in this, as 317 was the number of Lodge Humility with Fortitude (now No 229); and in 1838 it was Humility with Fortitude which refused to admit as visitors the next two Indians initiated by Marine – two Muslim Brethren – 'alleging that the Grand Lodge does not recognise their admission'. Marine wrote to Grand Lodge 'requesting information on the point'; and we have the first of a series of letters from Grand Lodge on the theme that 'the Grand Lo: of England and the Craft at large acting under its authority admit of no distinction on the score of Religion or Creed'. (Emboldened by this, Marine initiated another Muslim, an Arab merchant from Muscat, in 1839).

In the meantime, two – possibly three – other Indian Masons had been made. Mahomed Ibrahim Purkar, initiated by the Lodge of Hope in Ahmednagar in 1834, and Mahomed Ismael Khan, Ambassador from Oudh, initiated in 1836 in the Lodge of Friendship, No 6, and immediately invested, by the Duke of Sussex himself, as a Past Senior Grand Warden. There is also a story that Ghazi-ud-Din Haydar, the so-called King of Oudh, had been initiated by Lord Moira, but there is no record of this at Grand Lodge.

CROSS-CURRENTS

There were, of course, many cross-currents at work. First, there was the determination of the Duke of Sussex, as Grand Master, to make Masonry a genuinely universal brotherhood, 'let a man's religions or mode of worship be what it may'. Second, there was the obstinate rearguard action of those who wanted to maintain the Christian ethic of the Craft,[12] which led, after the Duke's death, to the growth of the Christian side-degrees. Then there was the class-consciousness of the English, specially in the Presidency towns which were the seats of Government, and where Masonry tended to become dangerously stratified – as witness the 'Inferior' and 'Subordinate' Lodges, and Gould's account of the 13 non-commissioned officers in Bombay who were 'too poor to establish a Lodge of their own and too modest to seek admittance in what they considered an aristocratic Lodge'. (They were invited to the 'aristocratic Lodge' as guests, but were offered 'refreshments *downstairs*' – and very properly walked out).[13] This preoccupation with social gradations (it was an English disease, not so much a Scottish one) was fortified in India by the genuine belief that Genesis ix, 25, was Scriptural warrant for the superiority of Europeans over all dark-skinned people.

And finally, Bengal had a Provincial By-Law, No 55, which became notorious

later on, in the 1860s, which prohibited the initiation of any Asiatic without the Provincial Grand Master's personal approval. Madras doesn't seem to have had such a by-law, and doesn't seem to have discriminated expressly against Asiatics; but as early as 1804 it had been laid down that the names of *all* candidates must be submitted to the Provincial Grand Lodge before an 'inferior' Lodge could confer any degree. This drew from the Secretary of Carnatic Military (Coromandel No 11) an admirable letter of protest:

> It has from time immemorial been considered the undoubted Privilege of every lodge to elect, pass and raise its own members. Men in similar situations of life naturally associate together, and from such intercourse become the best Judges of each other's habits, dispositions, and general tenor of conduct; possessing this information who can so well as themselves form an Idea whether a man is, or is not worthy of being passed or raised?

The historian Malden says that this order was only one of many unconstitutional acts of the Provincial Grand Lodge of Madras, which 'at the time seems to have violated almost every article of the Constitutions'.[14]

Despite all the difficulties some European Masons would have admitted more Indians; but they were at the mercy of the ballot-box and the Provincial Grand Lodges, and few proposals were successful. But there was increasing interest in the subject – and increasing controversy, conducted to some extent in the public press.

FURTHER PROGRESS

In the end, the break-through came in Bombay, and in the Scottish, not the English, Constitution. In 1843, a Parsee named Maneckji Cursetji, who had been initiated in a French Lodge, A La Gloire de l'Univers, was proposed as a joining member of the (Scottish) Lodge of Perseverance,[15] and was turned down. Thirty brethren, nineteen of them members of Perseverance itself, petitioned Burnes, as Provincial Grand Master, for a Lodge designed expressly 'for the admission of natives into the Craft'; the petition was granted, and Lodge Rising Star of Western India was consecrated under the Scottish Constitution on 15th December, 1843, with Burnes himself as its first Master. Four Indians were proposed for initiation, a Parsee and three Mohammedans (the Parsee, Ardeshir Cursetji Wadia, was the first Indian F.R.S., the Chief Engineer of the Bombay Dockyard, and scion of the famous shipbuilding Wadia family, whose nine line-of-battle ships were the only vessels of their class ever to be built for the Royal Navy outside the British Isles).[16]

SETBACK

At the same time as Burnes in Bombay was moving towards the formation of Rising Star, Grant in Calcutta was asking for a ruling by the Duke of Sussex, on the admissibility of Hindus as Masons. The ruling, given in 1840s, is forthright:

> The initiation of Hindus ... is a question which has occupied H.R.H.'s attention for many years, and it has formed a part of his Masonic creed that provided a man believes in the existence of the Great Architect of the Universe and in futurity, and extends that belief likewise to a state of rewards and punishments hereafter, such a person is fully competent

to be received as a Brother. Previously, however, to swearing any man to secrecy it is necessary to ascertain what religion he professes in order to obligate him in the most formal and solemn manner possible; when once admitted into the Fraternity all questions of religion cease.

Having got the ruling, Bengal rejected it; Grant could not 'contemplate such a possibility without horror', and gave it as his own opinion that Hindus and Mohammedans alike were not eligible for admission 'on any grounds whatsoever'.

Two years later he returned to the charge. His opening remarks are instructive:

When a highly distinguished and respectable Hindu was proposed for initiation by members of one of our Calcutta Lodges, an insuperable difficulty presented itself in the question of how he was to be obligated. This was more especially the case as he was understood to live at variance with many of the rules of caste.

So the unfortunate Hindu, as we say in Yorkshire, can't do right for doing wrong: if he is a strict observer, he's a heathen; if he isn't, he's an apostate – and his distinction and respectability go for nothing.

Later on in his allocution, Grant produces one phrase that seems to be a century before its time: speaking of Indians in general, he says:

Shut up beyond our reach by a strict and impenetrable circle of exclusion, ... of their virtues and vices *behind this iron curtain* what can we know?

His peroration is sorry reading:

After a residence of 26 years in this country ... of all the natives whom I have ever known, two or three fingers would cover the names of those whom I could venture conscientiously to recommend for ... Masonry.

And yet 'we are all sprung from the same stock, partakers of the same nature, and sharers in the same hope': could there have been so few in fact?

HINDUS: THE SPECIAL PROBLEM

But this question of Hindu initiates needs more consideration. The returns of private Lodges show that throughout these early years all Indian initiates belonged to the strictly monotheistic religions: Muslim, Parsee and Sikh. In 1849, one Bhagwandass Beeneeram, a Jain of the Dhondia sect, applied for initiation in Rising Star, claiming to be monotheistic; and the Master confirmed this and said that he knew the Dhondia Jains 'to be so totally different from Hindus'.

The truth was that even the Hindus' well-wishers (and Rising Star was the last Lodge in the world to be against them) were puzzled by their apparent multiplicity of gods: could they be said to believe in The G.A.O.T.U.? And those who made some enquiry into Hindu beliefs, and found that Hinduism was rather a way of life than a revealed religion in the Christian or Muslim sense[17], were further puzzled by the problem of obligating them: what, then, *was* their equivalent of the Bible or the Koran?

As for the anti-Hindu element: violent, vociferous, vituperative – they excelled themselves in a mixture of plain racialism and religious bigotry. Here is a rep-

resentative example of the 1850's, from a journal strangely called *The Indian Freemanson's Friend*: it is, alas! only one of many. Indians, it says, are men

> who are in a transition state, rising from a condition of barbarous idolatry to one of European civilization; who are but half educated, and whose characters are less than half-formed, according to the standard of Christian morality; men who are too well informed to hold to the superstitious religion in which they were born, and yet not sufficiently enlightened to rise superior to the demoralizing and degrading system of faith and practice in which they were trained in their earlier years; whose religion is a non-entity as yet; who see no sacred virtue nor admit a binding claim upon their consciences, whether they appeal to the waters of the Ganges or Shasters, or the Koran or the New Testament, in support of any pledge they take.

One wonders how any Englishman, after a century of the kind of unchristian, unmasonic backbiting of which I have given the merest outline, can have had the blindness to write such stuff. To one who was brought up in a Lodge of many religions, the strangest thing is the Englishmans' intemperately expressed assumption that he had nothing to learn from the Hindus – even if it was only what a modern writer has called the Hindus' 'civilised respect for all religions'.[18] One has to force oneself to remember that nineteenth century Christians were not bred to tolerance:

> Lord, I ascribe it to Thy grace,
>   And not to chance, as others do,
> That I was born of Christian race,
>   And not a Heathen or a Jew.[19]

Wrapped in what Kipling called 'the triple-ringed uninterest of the creed that lumps nine-tenths of the world under the title of "heathen" ',[20] they were unable to realise that there was another point of view than their own: and I'm afraid that if they had realised it, they would have dismissed it with contempt – as Macaulay in a notorious passage[21] dismissed Indian ideas of history and geography – 'kings thirty feet high, and ... seas of treacle' – not realising how foolish his own fundamentalist belief that the world was created in six days would look 150 years later.

So to our brethren of the mid-nineteenth century, Hinduism was simply polytheistic and idolatrous – which is, after all, what those uncompromising monotheists the Muslims think of the Christian Trinity and the saints in stained-glass windows. And if the brethren had thought to inquire instead of ignorantly condemning, they would have found that to the Hindu his many gods are personifications of different aspects of the One God. 'The Nameless and Formless is called by different names, and different forms are attributed to Him, but it is not forgotten that He is One'.[22]

HINDUS ADMITTED

But the door to Hindu Masonry was flung wide – one might almost say, kicked open – in the 1860's by two events: first, the unstoppable determination of one Mr. P. C. Dutt of Calcutta to become a member of the Craft, and second, the

contumacious behaviour of Bros Jordan and O'Mealy of the Lodge of Harmony, No. 438, of Cawnpore.

Mr. Dutt was proposed for initiation in Lodge Courage with Humanity, No. 392, and the Master, in accordance with Provincial By-Law No. 55, applied to the Provincial Grand Master (Hugh Sandeman) for permission. Sandeman referred to the matter in Provincial Grand Lodge in September 1863, when he ruled

> that Hindus were not eligible for admission into Masonry, and further that it was not desirable with reference to social considerations that they should be admitted, and as long as he held a veto under the By-laws he would exercise the power rigidly.

The Master accepted the decision; but Dutt wrote to the Grand Master (then the second Earl of Zetland) asking for a ruling. He didn't get a reply for fifteen months, because in the meantime Sandeman and the Grand Master had been grievously at odds over Bro Jordan's case.

Jordan was Master of the Lodge of Harmony, and he wrote (again under By-Law 55) for permission to initiate Prince Said-ud-Dowlah – which was refused. Three Past Masters of the Lodge, including O'Mealy, then wrote to Jordan and told him to disregard the refusal and initiate the Prince, and they would stand by him; so Jordan did. Sandeman, as one might expect, set about asserting his authority; judging by his photograph, he was a dominating and formidable personality, powerfully built, with a mighty curling moustache and beard, and what John Aubrey, of the *Brief Lives*, would have called 'great goggli eies, not of sweet aspect': a man not to be crossed unadvisedly.[23] Two of the Past Masters quickly made their submission and apologised, but O'Mealy (doubtless of a more determined and atrocious character than the rest) not only refused to recant but stubbornly maintained that he was right. Jordan seems to have lost his head at this point, placed the Lodge in abeyance and made off with its warrant and books, which he refused to deliver up when ordered by the Provincial Grand Master. Provincial Grand Lodge unanimously ordered him to be expelled from the Craft, and O'Mealy to be suspended for a year.

These punishments were duly reported to Grand Lodge by the Province, and Jordan and O'Mealy appealed to Grand Lodge against them – direct, instead of through Provincial Grand Lodge as required by Provincial By-Law 52.

When the Grand Secretary's reply to the Provincial Grand Master came, poor Sandeman must have felt that the heavens had fallen on him. First, By-Law 55 'cannot be upheld or enforced; it is directly opposed to the spirit of our Institution and to the very words of the Antient Charges'. Then (and at least as important, in my view) 'It is the privilege of a Lodge, *and one which cannot be interfered with*, to decide who it will receive – the required formalities ... being duly observed'. But worse: Bro O'Mealy was justified in his advice to Bro Jordan, and 'in asserting and continuing to maintain his opinion on the subject'; and the Grand Master 'directs that Bro O'Mealy be forthwith reinstated'. And worse still: if the matter were to come formally before Grand Lodge the expulsion of Bro Jordan would certainly be reversed, 'seeing that the offence charged against him in the first instance was his refusing to obey an illegal By-Law', so Sandeman had better get

the District Grand Lodge to reverse its own decision, in order to forestall an appeal.

And (as if all this wasn't enough) the Grand Master says that many of the Bengal By-Laws 'are contrary to and inconsistent with the laws and constitutions of Grand Lodge'; and in another letter, he orders By-Laws 52 (Appeals) and 55 (Asiatics) to be struck out.

Despite a private letter from the Grand Secretary to Sandeman urging Bengal not to appeal against these decisions, they insisted on doing so, and were inevitably turned down by Grand Lodge. The rejection of the appeal was announced in District Grand Lodge by the Deputy District Grand Master, with 'a strong expression of regret' at 'the indelicacy of the applause with which the reversal of a decision of this District Grand Lodge was received by members of the Grand Lodge of England' – defiant even in defeat.

One could feel more sympathy for Sandeman if it had not been for his fulsome speech at the initiation of the Maharajah Duleep Singh in Star in the East, in March 1861: '... while Duleep Singh had been admitted ... in Calcutta, another Lodge ... had lately witnessed ... the initiation of a Mohammedian nobleman, while the Rajah of Kapurthala and his brother Bikram Singh were about to join our Order at Lahore. He was also glad to see as a guest ... his noble Brother the Nawab Zulaladin ... Were not these ... ample and convincing proofs that Freemasonry is not an institution for any particular sect or nation or for any one country or religion? And was it not a pleasing thing to know and to feel that there does exist in this world at least one Society where, whatever might be the feelings of race, all could meet as brothers descended from one common parent...' and so on – and on: unexceptionable sentiments; but evidently applicable only to a select few, and flatly contrary to his general principles and practices: 'as long as he held a veto under the By-laws...'

Much that was said in District Grand Lodge about the admission to the Craft of Indians in general and Hindus in particular is best forgotten; some intemperate things, especially, were said (and enlarged on in the Masonic press) about caste being inconsistent with Masonry.

Caste is a subject little understood by Europeans, and it has changed out of all recognition during the past hundred years or so. There has been 'a gradual breaking down of caste barriers, except in some enclaves which are diehards ... a sort of intermixing that is responsible for the indistinct boundaries between the castes in modern times'.[24] The clamour in the 1860s was that Hindus would not only not sit down with men of other religions: the different castes wouldn't even sit down with each other.

But a Hindu who felt so strongly about the caste system would hardly offer himself as a candidate for the Craft; after all, Masonry imposes conditions on its candidates, not the candidates on Masonry. One mustn't generalise: a Hindu who was willing to accept the rules of the Craft was as eligible as any other man. The unfortunate truth is that the outcry against caste was a cloak for more religious bigotry and racialism – which are as inconsistent with Masonry as the caste system at its most rigid. The future was to prove how wrong the cavillers were.

But in the meantime I have kept Mr. Dutt waiting in the wings. After the

removal of By-law 55 had been ordered by the Grand Master, he had a letter from the Grand Secretary to say that there was no objection to his being initiated, although of course, no private Lodge could be *compelled* to accept him.

Mr. Dutt sent a copy of this letter to the District Grand Master, but had no reply. After the rejection of the appeal against By-law 55, Bengal still had a shot in its locker, and ruled that there was no form of oath which would be binding on a Hindu. So the indomitable Mr. Dutt writes to Grand Lodge to enquire 'whether a Hindu can be initiated into the Craft on the same oath as that by which he assumes charge of the duty of a Judge of the High Court or a member of the Viceroy's Council, etc.' And the reply comes back: Yes.

In the end, nine years after he set out on his single-minded pursuit, Mr. Dutt became Bro Dutt in Anchor and Hope, No. 234, in 1872. Twenty-three years later, he was Deputy District Grand Master.

In the more equable South, even before Bros Jordan and Dutt had come to notice, Hindus were being initiated without fuss; the first – the first anywhere, so far as I can discover – were Bros Ranganatha Sastri in Perfect Unanimity, and Murugesa Mudaliar in Universal Charity, No. 283, both of them in 1857;[25] and the answer to the objectors on the score of caste was conclusively provided by Universal Charity and the Lodge of Rock, no. 260; the former, between 1855 and 1869, initiated (besides a Muslim and a Parsee) a Mudaliar, a Chetty, a Pillai, a Naidu, an Iyengar and an Aiyar – six different Hindu caste-names; and Rock, between 1863 and 1877, initiated seventeen Hindus of seven different caste-names.[26] So much for the different castes beng unwilling to sit together.

Reverting for a moment to the oath required of a Hindu: Bro Maduranayakam Pillai, a former District Grand Secretary of Madras, has recorded that 'in the old days, Candidates professing the Hindu religion were obligated by a Hindu priest who was taken into the Lodge, and returned, blindfold'.[27] In modern times, one or other of the Shastras is used: in my own Mother-Lodge, the Bhagavad Gita; in other Lodges, sometimes the Rig Veda.

WEST AND NORTH INDIA

I have been concentrating on the two oldest Districts, Bengal and Madras; it is time to glance at developments in other parts of the country.

After the emergence of the Chevalier Burnes in the 1830s, English Masonry in Bombay went into a decline for a dozen years, and many English Masons transferred their allegiance to Scotland; it was perhaps fair comment (though maybe a bit sanctimonious) for a Scottish Mason to write to the *Freemasons' Quarterly Review*, in 1844:

> Unnatural mothers will ever produce undutiful children; the Grand Lodge of England having proved herself an inattentive and disobliging guardian, a foster-mother has been found who will watch more carefully over her adopted children.

Anyhow, as Gould puts it, English Masonry became 'quite dormant until the year 1848, when a Lodge, St. George, ... was again formed at Bombay, and for some years was the solitary representative of English Masonry in the Province'.[28]

Other Districts, then, mustn't grudge Bombay its later period of glory when H.R.H. the Duke of Connaught became its District Grand Master for fourteen years, before becoming Grand Master of English Masonry in 1901.

Further North, there were Lodges in Simla, Ambala, Peshawar, Lahore, Jullunder and Delhi, all operating under the Provincial Grand Lodge of Bengal; scattered enough even in this age of air-travel (Peshawar is nearly as far from Calcutta as Moscow is from London); in those days, virtually inaccessible. So in 1869 a new District Grand Lodge of the Punjab as formed, with headquarters at Lucknow. It was heavily dependent on the Army for its membership, and individual Lodges had greater ups and downs than those in more settled commercial and planting districts.

Early Indian members in the West and North-West seem to have been mostly Parsees; one of them, Dorabjee Pestonjee Cama, was the first Indian to become an Acting Grand Officer, being elected Grand Treasurer in 1886; and it is good to note that another, Dhanjibhoy Camadore (who later gave his house in Rawalpindi to be the Masonic Hall), was in 1876 unanimously elected Master of Light in the Himalayas, No. 1448, a predominantly European Lodge – good because of the sorry habit of some mainly European Lodges of denyine their few Indian members the Master's Chair – to take only one example: Perfect Unanimity's Ranganatha Sastri was Junior Warden in 1862, Senior in 1863, but never Master.

'OUR NATIVE BRETHREN'

However, even this unbrotherly behaviour had one good result: the establishment in 1883 of a Lodge in Madras 'for the special benefit and convenience of native gentlemen' – the Carnatic Lodge, No. 2031. A circular dated August 1st 1883 was addressed 'to all Native Freemasons' by Bro Pulney Andy, a doctor who had qualified in England, an Indian Christian, who was then Senior Warden of Universal Charity. His photograph shows a distinguished looking man with a patriarchal white beard and dignified gold-rimmed pince-nez, and the opening paragraph of his circular ran like this:

> It is generally reported that natives do not find easy admission into Freemasonry, and that many of our native brethren who were fortunate enough to be admitted to that privilege, on finding that they had no chance for further advancement, were obliged to disconnect themselves from their respective Lodges. It is therefore in contemplation to form a new Lodge for the special benefit of our countrymen.

The Lodge was duly consecrated, and at the next meeting of District Grand Lodge, the Deputy District Grand Master-in-Charge said:

> I trust its members will bear in mind the necessity of keeping a high standard of efficiency and of working in strict accordance with our constitutions, and of carefulness in selection of members.

I can best give an idea of the way his advice was followed, and of the position that Indian Masons achieved in the affairs of their country, by taking just six names from the Carnatic membership list: three prominent in Masonry, and three in public life – goodness knows, they could be matched from other Districts and

in other Lodges; but these were all men I knew; one at least, a close friend – which is both reason and excuse for naming them. First, then, in Masonry: a District Grand Master, T. V. Muthukrishna Aiyar; a Deputy, P. M. Sivagnana Mudaliar; and a District Grand Secretary and later Deputy District Grand Master, S. T. Srinivasa Gopala Chari. Then, in public life, Chakravarti Rajagopalachariar, the first Governor-General of independent India; Sir C. P. Ramaswamy Ayyar, K.C.S.I., K.C.I.E., once Law Member of the Government of Madras, then of the Government of India, and for twelve years Dewan of Travancore; and P. V. Cheriyan, an internationally famous surgeon, one-time Speaker of the Madras Legislative Council, and later Governor of the Province of Maharashtra. Surely such men are an answer to those who tried to keep Indians out of Masonry.

But the increasing entry of Indians into the Craft from the 1860s onwards didn't mean that everything was sweetness and light for ever after; Indian Masons are as capable of folly as their brethren 'neath the western sky. And there were growing-pains to be lived through. Besides, some Europeans were clumsy or thoughtless, and some Indians understandably touchy: about one storm in a teacup, an Indian historian wrote: 'The incident could have been averted altogether by a little more of tact and judgment on the one hand and of forbearance on the other'.[29]

Attacks on Hinduism, too, continued for some time, and must have been galling to men of goodwill; there was a particularly vicious one in the *Indian Masonic Review* as late as 1894. Hindu Masons, however, with the highly developed system of philosophy which was such a feature of their age-long-inheritance, became the foremost contributors to the esoteric and mystical side of Masonry, as anyone who was brought up, eg., on the *Madras Masonic Journal* would agree.

THE SOCIAL EFFECT OF MASONRY

Looking back along the distance of the years, I think Masonry was an unrivalled way of breaking the ice socially. One must remember that Indians of the old rock didn't like the Craft because they didn't want their sons to become 'Europeanised', so the difficulties weren't all on one side. The second Lord Ampthill, when he was District Grand Master for Madras, said in 1901, after referring to the difficulties which social and religious customs then caused in the 'free and informal inter-course' between Europeans and Indians:

It seems to me that here in Freemasonry we have found the common ground on which we can meet in friendly fashion, exchange ideas without restraint or formality, and get to know and understand one another better. If I am right, and if Freemasonry in India is tending to this end, it will be the best influence that the Craft has had on the destinies of mankind.

Social problems in the early days were partly due to embarrassment – such things as not being quite sure of each other's codes of good manners, and being stupidly too proud to ask – and partly a matter of 'what would the neighbours say?' It is true that, after the consecration of the Carnatic Lodge, the visitors were treated to a 'sumptuous banquet' in the dining-room while the members had their own refreshments separately; but my belief is that the members were more concerned

with the reactions of their elders and women-folk than with any personal breach of the strict rules of caste. Certainly all this kind of thing had disappeared by the time I was a young Mason in the Madras of forty years ago: one asked for a vegetarian or non-vegetarian meal at choice, and that was that. Visiting was free-and-easy; one dropped in to other people's Lodges without ceremony: dining was inexpensive, and Indian catering staffs were immensely efficient; an extra dozen last-minute guests were no problem; and invariably on the third rising, the Master would invite all visiting brethren to stay and dine – a far cry from the terse little note on today's summonses in England: no dinner unless you give notice a week in advance.

This informality of visiting and eating together was the more admirable in that Lodges, in the larger towns at all events, tended to be rather tightly knit: as that long ago Lodge Secretary wrote in 1804, 'Men in similar situations of life naturally associate together', and it is a phenomenon by no means peculiar to the old Indian Presidency towns that this Lodge should cater for merchants and bankers, that one for retail traders, the other for lawyers, and so on. It wasn't a matter of exclusiveness, still less, by then, of racial prejudice: it was just the way things were.

INDEPENDENCE AND PARTITION

When I left India in 1946, Masonry had become a stabilising influence amid the political strains of that time; but we wanted no ghost to tell us that British rule was coming to an end, and that there would be radical changes in the Craft as in everything else. With 1947 came Indpendence – and the partition of what we had until then called India into India and Parkistan. Inevitably, the Masonic District of the Punjab was the worst hit, as partition created West Punjab, which was Pakistan, and East Punjab, which was India, and there were of course Lodges on both sides of the border. Lodges in Sind, too, which were in the Bombay Masonic District, now found themselves in Pakistan, with the rest of the Bombay Lodges in India. After some to-ing and fro-ing, the Punjab District absorbed the Sind Lodges, and a new District Grand Lodge of Northern India was formed to take charge of the Lodges in East Punjab; and later, the name of the District Grand Lodge of the Punjab was changed to the District Grand Lodge of Pakistan.

But the British Army had gone; the British members of all the civilian services had gone; restrictions were imposed in both India and Pakistan on the recruitment of Europeans to mercantile and commercial posts – for all practical purposes the British contribution to Freemasonry in 'India' (using that word in its old sense) had come to an end. Some British Masons took their Lodges home with them; others became non-resident members and left their Lodges behind; we may never know what heart-searchings took place, nor how the decisions were reached.

PAKISTAN

But from this point on, we must treat the Craft in India and Pakistan as two stories, not one. Pakistan, from its Masonic dependence on the Army, soon lost several Lodges by transfer to the United Kingdom. But worse was to follow:

Masonry became subject to press and platform attacks, ignorant (as such attacks always are) of the true aims of the Craft, and misrepresenting the Israelitish background of our traditional history as a kind of Israeli fifth column: a manifestation of the age-old distrust of the Children of Ishmael for the Children of Israel. For a time, the Government of Pakistan stood out against the clamour, but eventually they had to give way; and the Craft in Pakistan is now 'suspended' – temporarily, we hope.

THE GRAND LODGE OF INDIA

India's case was different – if only because it had ten times as many Lodges as Pakistan, so it was, in modern jargon, a viable unit. There were experienced brethren who had held all the senior offices in one or other of the Districts, so if they had chosen to go their own way there were plenty of competent officers for a new Grand Lodge. But there was no break-away. There were those among the Indian Lodges of all three parent Constitutions who favoured establishing an Indian Grand Lodge; in the end they proved to be a majority – just. Logic would seem to be on their side; but a strong minority of brethren, even in Lodges by then wholly Indian, preferred to abide by the old ways. Still, the ballot taken on the direct question of establishing a sovereign Grand Lodge of India showed a majority in favour; 96 Lodges of the English Constitution joined it; 71 stayed with the United Grand Lodge of England, though domiciled in India; and still others transferred their meeting-places to England – with more heart-searching, as there must always be in such cases.

The new Grand Lodge was inaugurated in 1961 by the Deputy Grand Masters of England and Ireland and the Grand Master Mason of Scotland; the present Grand Secretary of England, writing a dozen years ago, refers to 'a great atmosphere of goodwill which survives even disputes as to the allocation of funds between old and new'; I can add to this, that many Masons in India today belong to Lodges both under the Grand Lodge of India and under the parent Constitutions – and not only belong, but hold, e.g., Regional Grand Rank under India and District Grand Rank under England.

There I must leave it; some future chronicler may take the story on from there.

CONCLUSION

Looking back again over the years, I feel we must recognise the Chevalier Burnes as the father of Indian Masonry; but although Scotland led the way, the main driving power was the English Grand Lodge with its insistence, against all pressure from English Masons in India, on two absolute fundamentals: that a man is not excluded from the Order, whatever his religion may be; and that no senior authority can interfere with a private Lodge's right to choose its own members. For this we have in the last resort to thank the Duke of Sussex. He has been unkindly treated by historians until Mollie Gillen's recent sensitive biography;[30] but in Masonry we can remember with gratitude that it was his firm guidance which enabled the

Craft to become in reality 'the happy means of conciliating friendship among those who must otherwise have remained at a perpetual distance'.

NOTES

1. J. Heron Lepper, *The Poor Common Soldier, A.Q.C.,* Vol. 38, Part 2, p. 182.
2. Edward Hyde, first Earl of Clarendon, *The History of the Reign of King Charles the Second from the Restoration to the end of the year* 1667, Vol. I, p. 173.
3. 'It was warranted in 1768 simply as an ordinary Lodge. By the 1770s it had assumed Provincial status (we have a blank engraved certificate dated 177– in which it has the title of Provincial Grand Lodge). From the Register it would appear that they were granted a Warrant of Renewal as a Provincial Grand Lodge on 23 May 1778'. Letter from John M. Hamill, Assistant Librarian of Grand Lodge.
4. Carnatic is the name formerly given to the South-East part of India, between the Coromandel coast and the Eastern Ghats. It was the centre of the struggle for supremacy between the French and the British in the eighteenth century, and among the famous names associated with the war in the 1780s were Haidar Ali, Tippoo Sahib, Sir Eyre Coote, and Admirals Bailly Suffren de St. Tropez on the French side and Sir Edward Hughes on the British. The Carnatic came under British rule in 1801 and afterwards formed part of the Madras Presidency.
5. This was not peculiar to Indian Provinces. In 1814 all the Provincial Grand Officers of Lancashire were appointed from the Lodge of Unanimity, now No. 89. *See* M. J. Spurr, *The Liverpool Rebellion, A.Q.C.* Vol. 85, p. 30.
6. The Deputy, William Coates Blaquiere, was something of a despot. He monopolised the Chair of Star in the East for more than a dozen years – the last time in 1844, at the age of 85. He died in 1853. For a more detailed account of the 'mutiny', *see* W. K. Firminger, *The Early History of Freemasonry in Bengal and the Punjab*, chap. ix.
7. *See, e.g., The Madras Freemasons' Herald and Journal of Literature and Science* for May 1850.
8. *Dictionary of National Biography*, art. *Elphinstone, John, 13th Baron.*
9. He must have been the last British Knight ever, as the Order became wholly Hanoverian when the Salic Law prevented Queen Victoria from inheriting the Kingdom of Hanover. *See* art. by J. Hawkes in the Heraldry Society's magazine *The Coat of Arms*, N.S. Vol. II, No. 100, p. 99, and later correspondence.
10. Memoir by John Grant in Dr. Corbyn's *Indian Review* for September 1840.
11. R. F. Gould, *History of Freemasonry*, Vol. 3, p. 335.
12. *See* T. O. Haunch, '*It is not in the power of any man....*' (Prestonian Lecture, 1972) *A.Q.C.* Vol. 85, p. 198.
13. R. F. Gould, *ib.*, p. 334.
14. Rev. C. H. Malden, *History of Freemasonry on the Coast of Coromandel*, p. 181.
15. The controversy about the English and Scottish Lodges of Perseverance is outside the scope of this Lecture. Gould's contention that the English Lodge went over bodily to Scotland (Vol. 3, p. 335) is hotly contested by Scottish Masons; there is a detailed examination of the *tracasserie* in Isaac Shield's MS *History of English Freemasonry in Western India*, in the Grand Lodge Library, pp. 80 *et seq.*
16. There is an excellent biographical sketch of this remarkable man in *The Bombay Dockyard and the Wadia Master Builders*, by Ruttonjee Ardeshire Wadia, Bombay 1955, pp. 332–346.
17. *See* Ninian Smart, art. *Hinduism* in the *Dictionary of Comparative Religion*, ed. S. G. F. Brandon.
18. Dervla Murphy, *On a Shoestring to Coorg.*
19. Isaac Watts, *Divine Songs for Children*, No. vi.
20. Rudyard Kipling, *Kim*, chap. v.
21. Minute dated February 2nd 1835, written when he was a Member of the Supreme Council of India.

22. K. M. Sen, *Hinduism*.

23. The photograph also shows him wearing the collarette of the Ancient and Accepted Rite with his Craft regalia. 'It is only by paying due obedience to the laws in our own conduct...'

24. Letter from W Bro Karamana Padmanabha Ramsami, P.A.G.D.C.

25. In 1852, the Calcutta Lodge Courage with Humanity, No. 392 (now No. 3 under the Grand Lodge of India), initiated a brother whose name appears in the records as Radanauth Sichdar. W Bro K. R. N. Menon, a Past Master of the Archibald Campbell Lodge, has suggested that this is an Englishman's mishearing of Ragunath Sirdar. Ragunath is a Hindu name, and 'Sirdar was commonly used in the Native States as a sort of equivalent of Esquire, but was derived perhaps from indigenous military circles as it used to denote a cavalry troop-leader'. If he was a Hindu, Bro Ragunath is the first on record. But I have been unable to trace either the Provincial Grand Master's dispensation, which would have been essential under By-law 55, or the minutes of the occasion, which might have shown, e.g., how the candidate was obligated. So, bearing in mind the attitude of the Province at that date towards Hindus, I think Bro Ragunath, despite his name, must have been a Christian. It is by no means unusual, even in modern times, for Indian Christians to bear names which are normally associated with Hinduism – for instance, the Rev. Paul Krishnaswami, District Grand Secretary of Bengal until his death in 1976.

26. The use of the caste-name is now less common than it used to be, but a century ago it was an infallible indication of caste. The Hindu system of nomenclature in South India is quite unlike any European system. A man has four names: (*i*) his place of birth; (*ii*) his father's given name; (*iii*) his own given name, (*iv*) his caste-name. Analogy with European names produces some inconsistencies; when the caste-name is retained, it becomes a kind of surname with the given name in the place where a European would expect to find it, as in T. V. Muthukrishna Aiyar. When the cast-name is dropped, the given name is left as the equivalent of the surname (e.g. K. P. Ramsami (Aiyar)), and then the initials of the first two names often become almost a nickname. But as North Indians find Southern names just as difficult as Europeans do, some Southerners carry the process of simplication much further: e.g. T. V. Muthukrishna Aiyar's son, the late Tiruchendurai Muthukrishna Subramania Aiyar, called himself T. M. S. Mani.

27. Rai Sahib C. M. Maduranayakam Pillai, *Old History of the Lodge of Universal Charity*, No. 273, p. 14.

28. R. F. Gould, *ib.*, p. 335. Lodge St. George, No. 549, is still the senior English Lodge in Bombay.

29. T. V. Muthukrishna Aiyar, *History of the Carnatic Lodge, No. 2031. E.C.* p. 77.

30. Mollie Gillen, *Royal Duke*. Sidgwick & Jackson, 1976.

ROBERT FREKE GOULD

Masonic Historian 1836–1915

THE PRESTONIAN LECTURE FOR 1980

F. J. COOPER

The early summer day on Exmoor was drawing to a close, my wife and I, after a picnic lunch had spent the afternoon on the high moors and it was no time to return to our hotel in Dunster. The route we had planned took us into a little steep sided valley and as we approached we noticed below us a farm with a large stone building on a small hill quite near. Yes, it was a church and the notice at the lychgate informed us that it was Stoke Pero, the smallest, the oldest and the highest church on Exmoor.

A glance at the interior showed that it had been loved and cared for by generations of worshippers, in spite of its remote position. There were references to the re-building of the church in the early years of this century and especial mention – and a photograph on the church wall – recorded not the name of the architect nor of the builder who carried out the work, but of the little donkey 'Zulu', who had hauled the materials for the renovation up from the valley below. It was that sort of church.

I was astonished to read in the list of incumbents, the name of Robert Freke Gould. Could this be the writer of *The History of Freemasonry*? I thought that the dates were perhaps a little early for that, maybe it was our Gould's father. It was then that I resolved that at the end of our holiday, I would find out more about *this* Gould and *our* Gould.

In the event the task took rather longer than I had anticipated at that time and the paper which follows is, to me, the sequel to our visit to Stoke Pero Church, a year or two ago.

THE INHABITANTS LODGE, GIBRALTAR

The date was 3 February 1858, the Guard on the Old North Gate of the fortress of Gibraltar, provided by the 31st Regiment of Foot, had just been mounted, the Guard Commander was about to leave the parade ground when the Sergeant of the Guard approached and reported that two sergeants of the Royal Sappers and Miners wished to speak to him. The sergeants were brought to the young subaltern and the younger of the two, the one wearing two Crimea War medal ribbons introduced his companion as Sgt. Searle. He spoke of the efforts that the two of them had made to resuscitate the Inhabitants Lodge, which had been dormant during the previous seventeen years, and asked the young Lieutenant to accept the Mastership of the Lodge for the revival meeting.

It could well have been that he was not the first officer that the two sergeants had approached, but they appear to have carried out all the necessary spade work and it only remained to obtain the consent of the Deputy Provincial Grand Master-in-Charge to hold this first revival meeting, and they may have considered that it would be preferable that a commissioned Officer should approach him for the required permission.

The young Officer, Robert Freke Gould, agreed to accept the office and one week later, on 10 February 1858, the first meeting of the Inhabitants Lodge, after its dormant period, was held with Gould in the Chair and the Sgt., Francis George Irwin, who had been initiated in the Rock Lodge (now Calpe Lodge) No. 325, Irish Constitution, in the June of the previous year, was appointed the Senior Warden.

The first meeting between Gould and Irwin, on the parade ground in Gibraltar on this 3 February was to have far reaching effects on the masonic careers of both. Gould up to this time had shown little interest in the Craft since his initiation at Ramsgate just over two years previously, on 8 December 1855, and on his short period of service in Malta. He had however joined the Friendship Lodge No. 345, now Royal Lodge of Friendship No. 278, Gibraltar in 1857, but his enthusiasm was fired by this first appointment and this enthusiasm for the Craft was to remain with him for the rest of his life.

There is a tradition in Gibraltar that Gould was actuated to resuscitate the Inhabitants Lodge as a result of discovering the Warrant of that Lodge being blown about by the wind in one of the streets on the Rock. From Gould's own account of his involvement in bringing new life to the Lodge, it is obvious that there can be no basis of fact for the story, but it could well be that Irwin discovered the Warrant of Constitution of the Inhabitants Lodge in a somewhat similar fashion because Irwin appears to have considered the Antients Warrant dated 1777 as his personal property. W. J. Hughan tells us that, when visiting Irwin at his home in Bristol, he saw displayed in Irwin's study the old Charter of the Inhabitants Lodge. Hughan persuaded Irwin to give him the Warrant which he sent to Gibraltar and it was formally presented to the Inhabitants Lodge by the District Grand Master in 1877.

This was not the only treasure that Hughan was enabled to send to the Inhabitants Lodge, for in August 1902 he discovered in a second-hand book shop in Plymouth, an old Minute Book of the Inhabitants Lodge, then No. 202 on the Register of the Antients, covering the period 1796–1801. It appears to be more than a coincidence that Irwin had been living in Plymouth from April 1865 until 1868 and in fact the last entry in the book, a certificate authorising a brother to act as Assistant Secretary, and dated 20 October 1859, was in Irwin's handwriting. One can perhaps speculate that Mrs. Irwin was beginning to find the accumulation of her husband's masonic papers a problem which she was unwilling to bear.

FAMILY BACKGROUND AND EARLY YEARS

The two families of Freke, or ffreke, and Gould had deep roots in the counties of Dorset and Somerset, information of their early history is contained in *The Visitation of Dorset, 1623*, edited by Bro. John Paul Rylands, a Founder of Quatuor Coronati Lodge, and published in 1885. The pedigrees which are included in the work tell us that Robert ffreke, the grandson of Robert ffreke of Iwerne Courtney, near Blandford, who died in 1592, on 22 December 1628 married Catherine, daughter of Matthew Ewens of North Cadbury, near Wincanton, an ancestor of the present writer. Their eldest son, Robert Freke of Upwey, near Weymouth, died in 1699 and a grandson Ralph, died in the ship 'Golden Lion' in 1691. The same work contains the Gould pedigree, commencing with a John Gould of Dorchester, gent., aged 65 in 1623.

The first Robert Freke Gould, born in 1755, became Rector of Luccombe, near Minehead, Somerset, in 1783 and held the living for 56 years, until his death in 1838. He was the son of Thomas Gould of Milborne St. Andrew and Frome Billet, Co. Dorset and his wife Mary, daughter of William Freke of Hinton St. Mary in the same County.

Robert Freke Gould's eldest son, John Smith Gould was born in 1799, entered the Royal Navy as a midshipman in 1813 and died at sea on 22 May 1826. His second son, christened Robert Freke Gould, was curate of the parishes of Martinhoe and Trentinhoe, both near Ilfracombe and he was later to give up the livings of these two parishes to take over the Rectorship of Stoke Pero on 4 April 1857. His first son was baptised Robert Freke Gould at Luccombe on 14 December 1835, but died a few weeks later. A second son, *our* Robert Freke Gould, was baptised at Luccombe on 14 June 1838.

There were therefore, at the ceremony of baptism, three present who bore the name of Robert Freke Gould, the child in arms, the father who carried out the baptism, and the grandfather, the Rector of Luccombe.

There can be no question as to the date of Gould's baptism, at Luccombe, 14 June 1838, but there are difficulties in establishing his date of birth. Every biographical note on Gould states that he was born in 1836, but without giving an actual date, and this information must have emanated originally from Gould himself. This date also appears on the Gould family pedigree contained in *The History of Part of West Somerset* written by Sir Charles E. H. Chadwyck Healey in 1901, which notes the date of Gould's birth as 10 November 1836.

Bro. W. G. Fisher, P M of Quatuor Coronati Lodge, in a paper which appears in the *Transactions of the Somerset Masters' Lodge, No.* 3746, for 1951, includes extracts of the Gould pedigree from the West Somerset history but incorrectly copies the date by quoting it as 1837. Later he quotes from the Luccumbe Parish Register, with the marginal note which appears at the side of the entry for 14 June 1838, 'Born 10 November 1837, privately received, 14 December at Ilfracombe'. The present Rector of Luccombe, the Revd. H. L. Bonsey has been kind enough to confirm to me that the date of the marginal note does state the year of birth as 1837.

One is therefore left with the question, was the date 1836 asserted as a result of

a lapse of memory on Gould's part, or did he perhaps increase his age in order to enter the Army, a subterfuge he failed to rectify in later life. It is of course possible that his father made an error when making the note in the Register, an uncle the Revd. George James Gould, who was curate of Luccombe at the time of the christening, was born on 12 May 1805 and not baptised until 27 February 1807, one year and nine months later.

The title of this paper, carrying with it the date of 1836 as Gould's date of birth, was decided before its preparation was complete and the date was in question. However the writer has thought it preferable to retain Gould's traditional date of birth in the title, rather than to alter it to the date shown in the Luccombe Parish Register.

Apart from the fact that Gould attended school for a period at Minehead, little is known of his boyhood but possiblities for interest and adventure must have been unlimited, living as he did in a town just emerging as a popular seaside resort on the edge of Exmoor. His father was the type of man beloved of the Victorian, a sporting parson, and his prowess with the rod and the gun was the subject of affectionate folk memory for many decades after his death. As a fisherman we are told that he made his own flies and on one occasion caught so many trout at Bagsworthy Water that he had to hire a boy and a horse to carry them home, and that once when he walked from Ilfracombe to Allerford to visit his mother, he brought with him forty snipe which he had shot on the way. He was a man of considerable stature and great strength with a reputation of being a master of the art of self defence, who even in old age 'could use his fists on occasion with great effect'. One is left to ponder on the circumstances under which, in addition to the cure of souls, he found it necessary to demonstrate this additional accomplishment.

When Robert Freke Gould, the father, became Rector of Stoke Pero in 1857, he made his home at Doverhay Cottage in the village of Doverhay on the outskirts of Porlock and the records show that in spite of the distance from his home to the little church, services were regularly held there for the first time for over fifty years.

THE ARMY AND FREEMASONRY

In 1855 Robert Freke Gould joined the Army as an Ensign in the 86th Regiment of Foot and in a matter of months transferred to the 31st Foot, later to become the East Surrey Regiment, on promotion to Lieut., stationed at the Regimental Depot at Walmer, pending the return of the Regiment from the Crimea.

Gould's diary for the year 1856, preserved in the Library at Freemasons' Hall, is typical of that kept by any young, newly joined soldier of Gould's time – and probably of every other age. There are references to 'subs' from the 'Governor' of £20, and £5 from Mother, details of the comings and goings of drafts, records of Lodge meetings attended, and a budding love affair.

Whilst stationed at the Depot of the 31st Foot at Walmer, Gould was initiated in the Royal Navy Lodge at Ramsgate on 8 December 1855. Fifty years later it was said of him 'His enthusiasm for Masonry at this early stage of his career was evidently of no mean order for he induced four subalterns to accompany him through the ordeal of initiation the same evening'.

The Royal Navy Lodge, No. 429 was No. 621 when it was founded on 12 October 1835, appears to have taken its name from a previous Lodge, No. 282, constituted at Deal on 8 June 1762, later to take the name of Royal Navy Lodge, which was erased in 1822. There is a local tradition that the original Royal Navy Lodge was formed by personnel of the Royal Navy and that meetings were held aboard a warship stationed in the Downs.

The five subalterns who were initiated at the ceremony on 8 December 1855 were –

>   Robert Place Gould, aged 25, Lieut., 31st Foot.
>   Robert Freke Gould, aged 21, Lieut., 31st Foot.
>   Constantine H. S. Gayner, aged 22, Lieut., 38th Foot.
>   William Hill James, aged 31, Ensign, 31st Regt.
>   Arthur Coleman Hallowes, Ensign, 31st Foot.

Gould was of course under age at the time that he was initiated into the Craft, but he overcame the difficulty by asserting that he was aged twenty-one years. Whereas previously he had two different ages, he now had three, masonically he was twenty-one years old, traditionally he was nineteen years old, but according to the Luccombe Register, he was eighteen years of age.

Surprise has been expressed that Robert Freke Gould should have joined a Naval Lodge, rather than a Lodge with a military tradition, in fact the Royal Navy Lodge in spite of its name at no time had a predominant service membership. There is no reference to a naval rank in the list of the petitioners for the Warrant and in the decade that Gould and his friends were initiated, the trades of the brethren who were admitted to the Craft included Victuallers, Master Mariners, Stationers, Block Makers and Shoe Makers.

On 16 April another companion of Gould's was initiated, Lieut. George John Hamilton and May 14, two Ensigns, Gardiner and Holland. But by this time the group had already commenced to break up for on 6 January, one month after the original ceremony, Lieut. Robert Place Gould and Ensign William Hill James were included in the draft to join the Regiment at Malta. Gould himself was included on the draft which embarked on the steamer 'Sultan' for Malta on 16 October 1856. Four of the little group resigned from the Lodge before being posted and the fifth, who had omitted so to do was excluded three years later.

FREEMASONRY IN GIBRALTAR

Let us return to 10 February 1858, the date on which Robert Freke Gould was installed Master of the Inhabitants Lodge. There are two sources of information from which we can draw to obtain a picture of Gould's active masonic life in Gibraltar following his stay in Malta with the 31st Regiment of Foot where, apart from joining the Royal Arch and the Knights Templar Degrees, he appears to have displayed little interest in freemasonry. The two sources are the Lodge Minute Book, happily rediscovered at a late hour when it had been thought that it had been lost at sea in 1940, and two reports in the *Freemasons' Magazine* for 1858. Bearing in mind that Gould himself states that he started his literary masonic

career as a reporter for that Magazine in that year, we can assume that they were both written by Gould himself.

We learn from the Minute Book that Gould was installed in the Chair by Brother Francis a member of the George William Lodge, attached to the 94th Regt. No. 328 Scottish Constitution, that he appointed Sgt. Irwin as Senior Warden and Irwin's companion Sgt. Searle as Master of Ceremonies. Searle could not have taken his duties at all seriously because he attended the Lodge on only two further occasions during Gould's Mastership, and on the second visit he was included in the list of members not holding office. Members of the Regiment who were appointed to office included Captain Schreiber, as Junior Warden; Staff Sergeant Molony, Secretary; Lieut. Cassidy, Senior Deacon; Armourer Sergeant Beard, Junior Deacon; the Inner Guard being Colour Sergeant Fraser of the Royal Engineers. These officers, together with the members, seventeen in all, became joining members of the Lodge on that same evening.

Gould's report in the *Freemasons Magazine* does not coincide with the record in the Minute Book. He states that a Bro. Deacon, who was raised at the meeting, was appointed Inner Guard and the Inner Guard Fraser as Director of Ceremonies. Searle, who was appointed Master of Ceremonies was simply referred to as having been present. In addition to the Installation ceremony and the raising of Bro. Deacon, the Worshipful Master also carried out a second degree ceremony on Bro. W. H. James of the 31st Foot, who was of course that Ensign William Hill James, one of the four subalterns initiated with Gould three years before in the Royal Navy Lodge, Ramsgate. Gould was to remark 50 years later in 1906, that he and Lieut. Colonel W. H. James were the only survivors of the five.

It is of particular interest that in Gould's report to the press he states that the lodge met for the purpose of installing Bro. R. F. Gould who had been unanimously elected Worshipful Master for the ensuing year at the preceding meeting, when all the evidence points to the fact that the previous meeting had been held seventeen years before when Gould was four years old. Possibly the answer to this mystery could be that Gould was mindful of the fact that reports in the masonic press were read at the highest level, and so he considered that had he concentrated on the story that the Lodge was meeting for the first time for seventeen years, the question of the authority he had for assuming the Chair might be asked by someone in a position to demand an answer. Gould may well have been aware that only five years before Rt. W. Bro. William Tucker, Provincial Grand Master for Dorsetshire, had written a comprehensive report on the proceedings of his Provincial Grand Lodge at Wareham in August 1853 and following confirmation by him to the Grand Secretary, in reply to a query as to the clothing that he wore and sentiments he expressed, found himself discharged from his office.

That Gould's first essay into masonic reporting was not particularly successful is illustrated by the fact that his Senior Warden, Sgt. Irwin is given the name Irvine, and the 'a' of Sgt. Searle's name has been omitted.

Meetings of the Lodge were held every fortnight and the first ten, including one emergency meeting, were held during the period 10 February to 21 May, the Minute Book recording an impressive amount of masonic work that Gould undertook during his Mastership. At the second meeting on 19 February, Lieut.

Rycroft of the 31st was initiated and Br. James was raised. At the third meeting on 3 March there were three initiations, Corporals Dunstan and Davis of the Royal Engineers, proposed and seconded by Irwin and Searle, and a Lieut. Fairfax of the 31st. In addition four applications for joining were balloted for and proposals for joining were made for a further six. At the next meeting on 18 March, there was an initiation and a passing of officers of the 31st and Corporal Dunstan was also passed. At this meeting eight brethren became joining members, three of them, Captains Bedingfeld and Lovekin and Lieut. Pigott of the 48th having been, according to the Minute Book, elected members at the previous meeting. There were also six proposals for initiation as well as four for joining membership. Honorary membership was also proposed for a Bro. Goulden who was referred to as Past Grand Master of Turkey.

There is no record of attendance at the Emergency Meeting on 25 March, but there were three initiations, two passings, and one raising. The first mention of a Lodge Treasurer occurred on 6 April, the sixth meeting of the Lodge, when Bro. Francis who had been Installing Master, and had been made a Honorary Member at the first meeting, was appointed Treasurer, and there were one initiation and five passings, two of which were of Colour Sergeants Aires and Woodward of the 31st, who had joined the same evening. Two of the brethren, a Sgt. Attril of the Royal Engineers and Corporal Moneypenny, Royal Artillery were both initiated at the Emergency Meeting on 25 March, passed at the following meeting and raised on 13 April, nineteen days after their introduction in the Craft.

The accounts of the meeting of 23 April, when four candidates were initiated, and three Brethren raised to the third degree, which appear in the Lodge Minutes and in the *Freemasons' Magazine* very closely coincide, but in Gould's report he does give himself a slight pat on the back when he refers 'which work the Worshipful Master executed in his accustomed masterly style without evincing any signs of fatigue'. His self congratulations on his stamina could refer to the length of the ceremony but it could possibly refer to the fact that the Lodge meeting had been postponed for two days because Gould, together with many members of the Lodge, had taken an active part in a amateur theatrical performance at the Calpe garrison theatre two days previously.

In mid April the 31st Foot had been placed on standby to proceed to the Cape of Good Hope, and at this 23 April meeting, at the end of the business Bro. Irwin, Senior Warden, requested the Master to retire from the Lodge, and the Chair was taken over by a past master. Irwin then reminded the Brethren that the 31st Regiment was on the point of departing to the Cape of Good Hope and that Gould's active participation in the Lodge was shortly to end. He stated that in his opinion there never had been a more zealous or indefatigable Master as the very high state of efficiency of the Inhabitants Lodge best testified, and which had been entirely owing to his unremitting exertions. He stated that he knew from his personal experience that at the time of the resuscitation of the Inhabitants Lodge great difficulty had been experienced in procurring even a sufficient number of masons to fill the Lodge offices, and that now the membership exceeded 50 members enrolled on its books.

He concluded by proposing that, although the Worshipful Master was in the

middle of his year of office and he was shortly to leave, the Lodge immediately obtain a Past Master's jewel from London for presentation to him. Irwin's proposition was carried unanimously, the Worshipful Master was invited to return to the Lodge and informed of the resolution. Gould, while expressing his thanks, told the Brethren that he felt that any money they had, would be better spent on buying Lodge regalia or furniture but on being told that the resolution had been carried unanimously and could not be rescinded he accepted the situation with grateful thanks.

On 21 May, Gould, following a triple Third, made his farewells to the Lodge, and announced the resignation of all the members who belonged to the 31st Regiment. However, another meeting was held three days later on 24 May when Gould carried out an initiation and made his final farewell for the Regiment was embarking the following morning. He was accompanied by the faithful Sgt. Molony, the Secretary, but the other members from the Regiment were obviously too busy to attend and Molony, although he was recorded as Secretary was unable to write the Minutes, Sgt. Searle taking over that duty.

On the first meeting on 10 February seventeen joining members were present and six visitors, making a total of twenty-three. At the second meeting there were nineteen brethren present, but from the third meeting onwards the attendance was always between twenty-five and thirty-five, and by May, the membership of the Lodge had reached fifty. During the first ten meetings of the Lodge Gould had initiated thirteen, passed sixteen to the second degree, and raised fourteen to the third degree, making a total of forty-three in all. In addition, on 7 May he read a lecture to the Lodge which was very well received and, on the proposition of Bro. Ingram, this lecture which 'comprised a most beautiful and concise record of Free Masonry' was ordered to be recorded in the Minute Book of the Lodge, an instruction which unfortunately Staff Sergeant Molony failed to carry out.

There can be no doubt that it was Gould's enthusiasm and drive which turned a moribund lodge in a period of three months into a thriving hive of industry, and one is delighted to realize that the progress of the Inhabitants Lodge has continued from strength to strength to the happy position that it holds today.

POONA INTERLUDE

The stay of the 31st Foot at the Cape of Good Hope was of a very brief duration, and almost immediately on arrival it was directed to India and the station of Poona. Gould's awakened enthusiasm for the Craft was illustrated by the fact that he immediately joined two lodges in Poona, St. Andrew's in the East, No. 343 Scottish Constitution and Lodge Orion in the West, No. 398, now 415. At the time that Gould joined the lodge, on 13 September 1859, plans were being made to re-start it after a period of dormancy and whilst he was not one of the Officers at the revival meeting, there are indications that he was active in the resuscitation of the lodge.

In the same year, 1859, he was a Founder and first Master of the Meridian Lodge, No. 1045, later No. 746, attached to the 31st Regiment and this lodge was to continue as a military lodge until its erasure in 1904.

It was however in the Order of the Knights Templar Degree, he became a member of the Order in the Melita Chapter, Malta in 1857, that Gould appears to have made his greatest impact. The Very Excellent Companion Sir Knight G. S. Judge, Provincial Grand Commander of Bombay had for six years been endeavouring to establish an Encampment of the Order in India, had in fact obtained a Charter in December 1858, but through lack of numbers and interest, had been unable to put his plans into effect. Gould's enthusiasm appears to have been the spark which set the project in motion and on Saturday, 29 October 1859, the first Encampment in Western India, the Mount Zion Encampment, was established with Judge acting as the Eminent Commander and Gould as the First Captain. Judge also appointed Gould to be his Deputy Provincial Grand Commander and at this meeting Gould was able to obtain a Dispensation from Judge to form a second Encampment, to be called the Ascalon Encampment, also to meet in Poona, in which Gould was to be the first Eminent Commander.

The first meeting of the Ascalon Encampment was held on Monday, 5 December 1859 with Gould in the Chair. At the end of the meeting a Sir Knight Woolace, who described himself as a mason of thirty-five years and the oldest mason in western India, told the gathering that he was convinced that the amount of work announced and carried out by the Ascalon Encampment at its opening meeting was unprecedented in the annals of the Order, the installation of ten Companions in a station in a single evening when in the entire Presidency two months previously only five Knights Templars were supposed to exist, was a subject for great exaltation.

In the following month, January, the first meeting of the Provincial Grand Conclave of Bombay was held, in which Gould's appointment of Deputy Provincial Grand Commander was confirmed, as well as a second meeting of the Ascalon Encampment. However, this state of euphoria was short lived, for at the end of the month the 31st Foot was placed under orders for service in China and the order to move was received two months later, on 10 February 1860.

THE NORTH CHINA CAMPAIGN

The 30 Officers and 973 men of the 31st Regiment of Foot formed part of the Expeditionary Force of 13,000 men assembled at Hong Kong on 7 June 1860, the Regiment being the largest of the eight infantry regiments included in the force. Gould was a Company Commander during the campaign and the 31st took part in all the actions which culminated in the capture of the Taku Forts on 27 August, for which he was awarded the campaign medal and clasp. The Regiment took part in the advance on Tien Tsin on the road to Pekin until the truce of 24 October. It then took over garrison duties in Tien Tsin Province from 18 November 1860 until 1862. Gould was selected to recruit, train and discipline one of the two battalions of native Manchu troops to form a part of the garrison. At this time his duties brought him in close contact with Major General (Chinese) Gordon, later to be killed at Khartoum, and sergeants of the 31st Foot were loaned to assist in the training of Gordon's so called 'Ever Victorious Army'.

During the campaign there was little opportunity for Gould to undertake any

masonic activities but he does report that on 17 January 1862 the Meridian Lodge, the lodge attached to the Regiment, met at Tien Tsin when the Master, F. Y. Cassidy, vacated the Chair for Bro. Gould to instal his successor Bro. W. E. Adams. The Meridian Lodge used the Masonic Hall in Shanghai for its meetings in 1862 and 1863.

However active service for Gould had not ended, and he served on General Staveley's staff during the operations against the Taipings in the vicinity of Shanghai in April and May 1862.

Gould joined the Royal Sussex Lodge No. 501 on 11 April 1863, the day of the first meeting of the lodge in Shanghai, which had previously met in Hong Kong where its last meeting had been held in the November of 1858. The Lodge History tells us that 'Bro. Gould had rendered us considerable assistance in the transfer of the lodge from Hong Kong to Shanghai and was the first joining member in Shanghai and was elected the first honorary member of the lodge'.

In the January following, he joined a second lodge in Shanghai, The Northern Lodge of China, No. 570 but apparently he felt that there was a need for a third lodge as immediately after joining, he held meetings at his home of interested brethren with a view to starting another lodge. This was the Tuscan Lodge, No. 1027, the founders were given a local dispensation to hold its meetings which commenced on 18 June 1864. This lodge, now re-named the Shanghai Tuscan, today meets in London.

In the same year 1864, Gould acted as the Installing Master at the Consecration of a Scottish lodge, which was carried out within an English Lodge, the Northern Lodge of China. A Petition had been sent to the Grand Lodge of Scotland to form the first Far Eastern Scottish lodge by three Scottish, three English, six American, one Irish and one German masons, which Charter was dated 7 March 1864, and this first meeting was held at three days notice. At this new Cosmopolitan Lodge, No. 428, Gould after installing the Master, gave the Charges and was elected the first honorary member. Gould was to retain his links with China until his death. For many years he was responsible for obtaining places at the Masonic Schools on behalf of the China lodges and this interest was rewarded by the rank of Past District Grand Warden conferred upon him by the District Grand Lodge of Northern China over 50 years after he had returned to England.

ENGLAND, THE LAW AND MASONIC RESEARCH

The 31st Regiment had embarked for England on 22 June 1863 and was to see no more active service for over 51 years when, as the 1st Battalion, the East Surrey Regiment it was to land in France in August 1914. Before the Regiment had left however, Gould had resigned his Commission when he was the Senior Lieut. of the Regiment to take up the appointment of Secretary of the Municipal Council of Shanghai. In 1864 he resigned the appointment and following a visit to Japan with his friend Hans Peter Hanssen, he returned to England the following year. He studied law at the Inner Temple and was called to the Bar on 6 June 1868, to practice in the Western Circuit. At this time he was living in Russell Square,

London, which he described as most convenient for the masonic researches he was carrying out in the Library of Grand Lodge and the British Museum.

He apparently found this latter work so much more congenial that in 1877 he gave up his practice in the Western Circuit and, a year or two later, vacated his chambers in the Temple and ceased his legal work.

During the 1860s and 1870s the standard of scholarship in the masonic historical field was a source of disquiet to the few masonic historians who rejected the traditional historical concept and were attempting to establish an authentic system, in fact one writer in 1871, prefaced a masonic essay as 'a signpost in a strange land'. Gould was to remark, when referring to the state of scholarship of the period, that the cardinal defect of the great majority of masonic writers, which had made the literature of freemasonry a byword and reproach, was the presentation of statements fully destitute of ordinary proof. Critics and reviewers outside the Craft had argued, not without some show of reason Gould asserts, that the secret of the Freemasons – if they possessed one – must surely consist of the flexibility of the laws of evidence, as interpreted by the masonic historian.

Gould was equally scathing at the standard of instruction given to the young enquiring freemason and he considered that when a reply was given to the seeker for information, too often it was similar to the advice given by the great teacher Annabal Caracci of the Bologna School of Painters, who once told a scholar, 'That which you do not understand, you must darken'.

QUATUOR CORONATI LODGE

The publication of Gould's first book *The Four Old Lodges* in 1879, brought him in contact with the foremost masonic students of the day and as a result of the considerable correspondence in which he became involved, it became obvious to him, as it did to others at the time that their interests, and the interests of the Craft as a whole, would be better served if a Lodge of Research was formed. It was considered that the organisation would have to be a Masonic Lodge, bearing in mind the short life of the Masonic Institute, formed, with others, by Sir Charles Warren, Walter Besant and William Simpson.

Woodford, Hughan and Gould were enthusiastic for the formation of a literary lodge but were disinclined to take action in spite of the more virile approach being advocated by Speth and Rylands. It was only when Rylands invited Gould to meet Sir Charles Warren and Walter Besant at his chambers that the enthusiasm was generated to establish Quatuor Coronati Lodge.

Sir Charles Warren was designated the first Master, Rylands to be founder Senior Warden and Gould Junior Warden. The Warrant of the Lodge was dated 28 November 1884 but before the Lodge could be consecrated, Sir Charles Warren was sent to South Africa on military duty and it was not until 12 January 1886 that it was possible for the consecration to be held. Following Sir Charles Warren's year in the chair, Rylands was unwilling to succeed him, and in fact took no office owing to his bereavement by the loss of his wife, and Gould became the second Master, being installed on 8 November 1887.

The regularity of his attendance at Quatuor Coronati Lodge in its early years

was only exceeded by the Secretary, Speth; he missed only one meeting in the first eight years. It had been the intention of the Founders that they themselves would have filled the various offices in the first instance, taking the Mastership in turn, but it was a disappointment to the more enthusiastic members to find that some of the founders attended the Lodge at rare intervals and the system was obviously impractical. A system was therefore adopted of placing joining members in the various offices, whilst the Founders became a reserve to be called upon in an emergency.

Gould was to contribute probably more than anyone else to the controversial nature of the discussions following the reading of papers to the Lodge. This was a tradition fostered from the commencement of the Lodge and which still exists today. At the dinner following the Consecration ceremony a brother had expressed the hope that the members of the Lodge would, in the words of Shakespeare, 'Do as adversaries do at law, strive mightily but eat and drink as friends'.

At the second meeting of Quatuor Coronati Lodge, Gould read a paper and on vacating the Senior Warden's chair to give his address, he asked a brother who was seated nearby, a retired Army major, to occupy the chair during his temporary absence. At the end of the meeting the brother concerned told Gould that this was not the first time that he had occupied the Senior Warden's chair at Gould's invitation, because he was that Sgt. Irwin who had been Gould's Senior Warden at the first revival meeting of the Inhabitants Lodge thirty years before. Francis George Irwin was to become a full member of Quatuor Coronati Lodge in 1886.

FINANCIAL DIFFICULTIES

It could be that Gould had expectations from the estate of his father who died in 1885, but in this he may well have been disappointed as he had two un-married sisters who lived in Minehead for many years. Possibly he felt that he would receive a reasonable remuneration from his masonic writing but his first book *The Four Old Lodges* published in 1879 was not a financial success for it had a very limited sale and, it has been said, some of his friends purchased the book 'not from a motive of adding to their masonic knowledge, but rather from feelings of charity and good will'. In the United States the book was very favourably received and resulted in Gould forming friendships with many masonic historians on that side of the Atlantic which were to continue until his death.

He received no income from 'The American Edition' of his *History* and by 1890 his financial position was such that he was forced to sell the treasures that he had collected in his library. His friend and fellow member of Quatuor Coronati Lodge, Henry Joseph Whymper bought from him the Freemasons' Calendars covering the period from 1781–1813 and the Grand Lodge Proceedings from 1776–1890. Whymper commented at that time that Gould was under the erroneous impression that his financial position was a secret.

Secrecy, if any, was not to remain for long for six months later at 24 June 1891 meeting of Quatuor Coronati Lodge, with Bro. Bywater, Master and Bro. Col. Sir Norman Pringle, Bart., a member of the Correspondence Circle, as Junior Warden and Gould, Director of Ceremonies, the Minutes of the meeting report –

At the request of the Worshipful Master, Bro. Sir Norman Pringle gave an account of the present financial position of Bro. R. F. Gould and detailed the steps that he and Bro. Speth had taken for his immediate relief and projected a scheme for his further benefit as suggested in the draft of a circular in each brother's hands. Bro. Speth described the steps he proposed to take should the Lodge adopt the scheme. The Worshipful Master moved that he be empowered to sign the circular, which was seconded by Bro. Pratt and supported by Bro. Rylands, put by the Senior Warden and carried unanimously.

This is the only record of the matter in the Minutes of the Lodge, but there is a note in the Minute Book dated six months later, 4 January 1892, which states under the heading 'Gould Annuity' –

£1,000 in Legal and General Life Assurance Soc., Fleet Street.
payable £40.16.8 to Pringle or Golding on 4 January and 4 July yearly.
24 April 1892. ditto. £700 payable 29 September and 29 March.

Jul	4	£40.16.8
Sep	29	£28 — -
Jan	4	£40.16.8
Mar	29	£28 — -

£137.13.4

In the May meeting of the Lodge, Bro. Richardson suggested that his monograph on the poet Burns be re-printed as a de luxe edition and sold for the benefit of the Gould Fund. On the motion of the Worshipful Master, the thanks of the Lodge were tendered to Bro. Richardson and after discussion it was decided to leave the matter in the hands of the publishing committee. Presumably the committee did not consider that the success of this enterprise was assured, as nothing more was mentioned about it, nor in fact anything further of the Gould Annuity Fund.

THE HISTORY OF FREEMASONRY

In 1881, Mr. Thomas Jack of Edinburgh, proprietor of the publishing company of Thomas C. Jack of Grange Publishing Works, Edinburgh and 45, Ludgate Hill, London, realizing the interest and enthusiasm for authentic historical material among the members of the Craft, as the result of the publications and papers being produced by the little group of authentic writers, considered that the time was opportune for the publication of a comprehensive History of the Craft of a standard never before attempted.

He chose as writer of the projected work William James Hughan, then living in Truro who in 1869 had been appointed Provincial Grand Secretary of Cornwall and on 29 April 1874 had received the rank of Past Senior Grand Deacon of England in recognition of his historical researches and literary services to the Craft. Hughan's reputation as a masonic historian at that time was probably unequalled, a contemporary had described him as 'perhaps the best informed masonic archaeologist who ever lived'. Three years previously he had assisted the Revd. A. F. A. Woodford in the production of *Kenning's Cyclopaedia of Freemasonry* and he wrote the section on Freemasonry in the *Encyclopaedia Britannica*.

In December 1884, he was presented with a writing table and a cheque for £364 'in recognition of his valuable contributions to the History of English Freemasonry', at a meeting held at the Freemasons' Tavern presided over by W. Bro. Sir John Monckton, past President of the Board of General Purposes.

Hughan's health, at the time that he was invited by Thomas Jack to write a 'History', was giving him some concern and he felt unable to commit himself to the several years' work which the preparation would entail, and he suggested that the task should be offered to Bro. Gould, equally well known for his masonic researches. Gould fully appreciated that Hughan had a greater claim for consideration as the history's writer than he himself, in fact at the time of Hughan's death, he said –

> Hughan's name will go down to posterity as a great teacher in the Craft, albeit there obtrudes an unwelcome doubt whether posterity will fully realize the measure of his life's work or whether the extent of his labours and the encouragement he gave to others will ever be adequately appreciated, except by those who have been from time to time his colleagues and companions in the thorny path of masonic research.

Gould accepted the commission after being assured by his masonic colleagues of their assistance. In the brochure advertising the forthcoming publication of Gould's *History of Freemasonry*, he acknowledges the help that he has been promised by 'many zealous brethren in both hemispheres, of whose hearty co-operation he has been assured', including the Revd. A. F. A. Woodford, P.G.Ch., Mr. David Murray Lyon, Grand Secretary of Scotland, and Mr. William James Hughan, P.G.D., England.

The first volume of Gould's *History* was published in 1882 and the many collaborators in its preparation were surprised and disenchanted that no mention of their assistance appeared in the work. They no doubt expected that in the Introduction or Foreword, some mention of apprciation would have been made, but unusually the work has no preamble of any sort and, as readers of the *History* will have noticed, Gould immediately moves into the narrative of his first Chapter on the Antiquities of Freemasonry. As this was the nearest approach that Gould made to an introduction, I will quote the commencement in full –

> Up to a comparatively recent period, the History and Antiquities of Freemasonry have been involved in a cloud of darkness and uncertainty. Treated as a rule with a thinly veiled contempt by men of letters, the subject has been, for the most part, abandoned to writers with whom enthusiasm has supplied the place of learning, and whose sole qualification for the task has been membership of the fraternity. On the other hand, however, it must be fairly stated that the few *literati* who have taken up this uncongenial theme, evince an amount of credulity which to say the least, is commensurate with their learning, and by laying their imaginations under contribution for the facts which are essential to the theories they advance, have confirmed the pre-existing belief that all masonic history is untrue. The vagaries of this latter class have been pleasantly characterised as 'the sprightly and vivacious accounts of the modern masonic annalists, who display in their histories a haughty independence of facts, and make up for the scarcity of evidence by a surprising fecundity of invention. 'Speculative Masonry', as they call it, seems to have favoured them with a large portion of her airy materials, and with ladders, scaffolding and bricks of air, they have run up their historical structures with wonderful ease.

It was not however until the publication of the third volume in 1887, five years later, that the collaborators were to receive public acknowledgement of their assistance, for in the very last page of his work, under the heading 'L'Envoi', the belated acknowledgement appears. Among the brethren mentioned are Gould's fellow members of Quatuor Coronati Lodge, Hughan, Rylands, Speth and Woodford.

John Lane is not included in the list and Gould, rather ungraciously, it is thought, comments 'Lane's *Masonic Records*, I regret to say, was published too late to be of any service to me; but had the work appeared a year earlier, my toil would have been much lessened.'

Gould finally salutes the memory of Bro. Thomas Chisholm Jack the publisher of the '*History*', who did not survive to see the publication of the third Volume.

It is not the purpose of this paper to carry out a statistical survey of the separate editions of Gould's *History of Freemasonry*, nor is it to give the mechanics of publication. The reader can obtain this information from the scholarly and comprehensive paper, written by Bro. A. R. Hewitt, entitled *R. F. Gould's 'History of Freemasonry' a Bibliographical Puzzle*, published in A.Q.C.85.

DISAPPOINTMENTS, FINANCIAL AND PERSONAL

Gould was to experience two bitter disappointments in connection with his '*History*.' The first was as a result of his failure to be awarded the Peeters-Baertsoen Prize and the second was the circumstances under which *The History of Freemasonry* was pirated in the United States of America.

The Grand Orient of Belgium had been left a sum of money under the will of Bro. Peeters-Baertsoen to provide three prizes awarded to the writers who, in the opinion of the Grand Orient, published the most meritorious works, from the Masonic point of view, during the previous decade.

The first awards, covering the period 1879–1889 were made in the latter year. Gould, from the international acclaim that his '*History*' had received, was confident that he would win the award. In fact Quatuor Coronati Lodge, at its meeting on 25 June 1888, when Gould himself was in the chair, Hughan, P.M., Simpson, S.W., and Rylands, J.W., Bro. Hughan had moved

> that the members of this Lodge composed exclusively of authors of works on freemasonry ... are of the opinion that *The History of Freemasonry* by the Worshipful Master is the most meritorious work from a masonic point of view published in Great Britain between 15 March 1879 and the present date. That Bro. Gould's work is not only critical but most exhaustive and treats of the origin, progress and present condition of the various branches of the Craft, in both hemispheres, and as the History is practically without a rival that the W.M. be therefore requested to compete for the Peeters-Baertsoen prize, offered by the Grand Orient of Belgium, the Lodge being strongly of opinion that no masonic author so well fitted to uphold the literary honour of England and of the Lodge Quatuor Coronati.

The proposition was seconded by Bro. Simpson, the only brother mentioned who had not made a contribution in the preparation of the '*History*', and carried.

Twenty years later, in 1909, Bro. Gould was to be more successful, on that occasion the jury judged that his *Concise History of Freemasonry* was the most

meritorious work from the masonic point of view published during the decade 1899–1909. The chairman of the adjudicating panel, Count Eugene Goblet de Alviela, Past Grand Master of Belgium, by a happy coincidence had been invited to become a full member of Quatuor Coronati Lodge in 1908.

The second misfortune that Gould was to suffer, was of a considerably more serious nature for on the completion of the publication of the *History* in 1887, it was promptly pirated in the United States, for at that time no international copyright agreement was in force between the two countries. The publication was called *The American Edition* and in addition to Gould's work it included sections on Craft, Royal Arch, Knights Templar and the Ancient and Accepted Scottish Rite history in the United States. The point that affected Gould very deeply, and for many years, was the fact that the writers or compilers of the new sections, who also assisted in the publication, were three correspondents of his, but who had given him no inkling of the action that they were taking.

The three whose conduct had so enraged Gould were Josiah H. Drummond, Past Grand Master of Maine, Theodore S. Parvin, Past Grand Master of Iowa, and Enoch T. Carson, Past Grand Commander, Knights Templar, Ohio. A commentator at the time of Gould's death points out that he had written lengthy biographies of Drummond and Parvin and concluded that over the years passions had subsided but, over twenty years after the event Gould was to write in the American magazine, '*The New Age*' ...

> Some will perhaps share the opinion of the present writer that the circumstances attached to the reproduction in North America of his original *History of Freemasonry*, were of a character that might well bring a blush to the cheek of any honest man in the Great Republic ...

MASONIC HONOURS

Contrary to popular assumption, Bro. Gould did not receive the rank of Senior Grand Deacon of the United Grand Lodge of England in recognition of his literary work, he was appointed to that rank in 1880, for his services on the Board of General Purposes in 1876, 1878 and 1879 as an elected member. From 1880 to 1883 he served by nomination of the Grand Master. He was elected member of the Colonial Board from 1876 until 1879. On 5 December 1877 he was appointed a member of the Special Committee to enquire into, and to report to Grand Lodge on the action taken by the Grand Orient of France in removing from its Constitution the paragraph which asserts a belief in the existence of the G.A.O.T.U., and it is understood that it was Gould himself who wrote that report. He had however written *The Four Old Lodges* and *The Atholl Lodges* in the year previous to his preferment, but the first volume of his *History of Freemasonry* was not to be published until two years after his Grand Lodge appointment.

Following the publication of his '*History*', Gould was acclaimed throughout the masonic world and among the many honours that he was accorded there were two that gave him particular gratification. In 1901 the members of the Inhabitants Lodge, Gibraltar had increased their membership to the extent that a daughter lodge became desirable and to commemorate the work that Gould had carried

out in a previous generation, in resuscitating the lodge, they named the new lodge the Robert Freke Gould Lodge which was given the number 2874.

Five years later, in 1906, the freemasons of Hamburg and the brethren of the Quatuor Coronati Lodge Hamburg Zirkel Correspondenz, on the initiative of Bro. Carl Wiebe, Past Grand Master of Hamburg, decided to present Bro. Gould with a Dedication-Plaque to celebrate his Jubilee of masonic life, which he had reached in the previous December. The presentation was made by the Worshipful Master of Quatuor Coronati Lodge, Bro. G. L. Shackles, at the lodge meeting on 5 October 1906, in the presence of a large and distinguished company. A reproduction of the beautifully executed plaque, cast in bronze, appears in the report on the proceedings contained in A.Q.C.19, page 178.

In the following years, among the honours that Gould received were Honorary Memberships of the Grand Lodges of Ohio, Iowa, British Colombia, District of Colombia, Kansas, South Dakota and later New Zealand and Maryland.

It is with some surprise that one notes that the United Grand Lodge of England was strangely silent on this point and it was not until 1913, some thirty years after the publication of *The History of Freemasonry* during the celebrations commemorating the centenary of the United Grand Lodge of England, that the Grand Master was to confer upon Gould that honour which his friends had earnestly hoped for and which they considered his international reputation had earned him.

So that when this decrepit, half blind, old man was led up to M.W. Bro. Lord Ampthill, the Pro Grand Master to be invested with the insignia of Past Senior Grand Warden of England at the Investiture in Grand Lodge on 3 December 1913 it was too late for him to appreciate to the full the very great honour that had been done to him.

The honour was indeed the highest to which he could attain and had been given very sparingly over the previous years, the brother to receive the rank in the following year was H.R.H. Prince Arthur of Connaught.

Gould, when speaking later of his emotions on attending this Investiture, tells us that his mind continually wandered back to a period forty years before when he was an active member of Grand Lodge and the memory of so many of his distinguished masonic friends, who were no longer alive, and he was conscious that he was the sole survivor of a previous generation.

The Pro Grand Master himself drew attention to the delay in the recognition of Gould's literary work when he commented at the investiture –

> For fifty-seven years Bro. Gould has been a Mason, and all that time he has worked unceasingly for the Craft without asking for, or expecting, any reward. Thirty-three years have passed since he was made a Grand Officer; and his contentment with the position of Senior Grand Deacon has been an example to which I would fain call the attention of those who are actuated by restless ambition.

FINALE

In the early years of the twentieth century Gould's activities had decreased considerably owing to his gradually developing ill health and failing eyesight but he retained an interest in his literary work and only a few days before his death, he

wrote to the Editor of *The Freemason* and referred to his many friendships in England, in Gibraltar and in America.

In his last years he visited only the two Woking Lodges, Wayside Lodge No. 1395 and Bisley No. 2317. At the Way Side Lodge meeting on 19 March 1912, Gould carried out his last masonic ceremony when he took the Chair at an initiation and he commented at the time that the first initiation that he had carried out was in Gibraltar in 1858, 54 years before.

He died on Friday 26 March 1915, at his home Kingfield Green, Woking and as the funeral took place on the following Tuesday, few people had the opportunity of attending, the only relative present was a Mr. J. C. Partridge of Hove. Several London and local lodges were represented, Quatuor Coronati Lodge by Bro. Dring a Past Master, and Bro. W. J. Songhurst the Secretary. The wreath from the Grand Lodge of England was inscribed 'In affectionate remembrance of a distinguished and beloved brother'.

The one point that emerges in the obituaries and letters of regret which appeared in abundance in the masonic press on the death of Robert Freke Gould was the universal affection and respect with which he was held by the members of the Craft. So often in writings of this type one can detect the suspicion that the deceased's character may have had a flaw in some aspect, but in Gould's case this suspicion does not exist, and writer after writer commented on the kindliness of a man always willing to put himself out to be of assistance to others.

Complimentary references to his life's work there were in abundance – 'his writings will live and will have an abiding claim on the thoughtful brethren of this and every other age', but I cannot do better than end this paper by quoting from Bro. W. J. Chetwode Crawley, a fellow member of Quatuor Coronati Lodge and Grand Treasurer of the Grand Lodge of Ireland, who after describing Gould as 'an English gentleman in the true sense of the word', wrote

There has been no-one like unto him in our day, nor is there any probability of a successor that shall outdo his work.

THE GRAND LODGE OF ENGLAND ACCORDING TO THE OLD INSTITUTIONS

otherwise known as
THE GRAND LODGE OF THE ANTIENTS as
THE MOST ANCIENT AND HONOURABLE
SOCIETY OF FREE AND ACCEPTED MASONS as
THE ATHOLL GRAND LODGE and as
THE GRAND LODGE OF THE FOUR DEGREES

THE PRESTONIAN LECTURE FOR 1981

CYRIL N. BATHAM

1. For convenience I refer throughout this paper to the premier Grand Lodge of England founded in 1717 as the 'Moderns' and the rival Grand Lodge founded in 1751 as the 'Antients'. Further, in all quotations I retain the original spelling, punctuation, etc.
2. The Prestonian Lectures are concerned essentially with craft freemasonry and so there is but passing reference in this paper to the Royal Arch and other degrees.

INTRODUCTION

Amongst the fifty Prestonian Lectures that have been delivered since they were revived in 1924 one was devoted specifically to the Grand Lodge of the Moderns and several others have dealt indirectly with it in addition to which there was one paper on 'The Grand Lodge south of the River Trent'. Very little, however, has been written about the Grand Lodge of the Antients and this is surprising in view of its important role in the story of the evolution of speculative freemasonry. It is no exaggeration to say that the craft ceremonies of today would be much the poorer had it not been for the Antients and, in particular, that the impressive installation ceremony might be no more than the Master-elect being invited by the outgoing Master to occupy the chair. Further, the Royal Arch and Mark degrees would probably have survived but certainly not in their present richness of ceremony. It is difficult to understand this neglect. Is it because the Antients were regarded for so long as 'schismatic?' Is is because their founders were considered to be men of inferior social status whose aim was to ridicule and perhaps even to destroy and replace the Grand Lodge of the Moderns? Is it because so many of the compromises made at the time of the union of the two Grand Lodges were in favour of the Antients and consequently it was said that the pure stream of ancient freemasonry had thereby been fouled? Certainly these are matters of the eighteenth and nineteenth centuries, perhaps better if forgotten, but tendencies linger on and in any case these charges can be no more than partially true.

The purpose of this paper, therefore, is to review the position of the Antients from the time they began to emerge as a rival body in 1751 until the union of 1813 though to a large extent their story is that of one man, Laurence Dermott and of his book, *Ahiman Rezon*. However, this cannot be done without giving some preliminary consideration to the Moderns. In this task I must inevitably rely to a considerable extent on those who have already covered part of the ground. I make no apology for this and can only say in the words of Charles Reade, 'I milked an hundred cows for it but the cheese I made is mine.'

THE PREMIER GRAND LODGE OF ENGLAND

For reasons that are hidden from us, four London lodges, viz. the lodges that met at:
1.   The Goose and Gridiron Ale-house in St. Paul's Churchyard,
2.   The Crown Ale-house in Parker's Lane near Drury-Lane,
3.   The Apple-Tree Tavern in Charles-street, Covent-Garden,
4.   The Rummer and Grapes Tavern in Channel-Row, Westminster, and 'some old Brothers' decided, at a meeting held on some unrecorded date in 1716 at the aforesaid Apple-Tree Tavern, to constitute a Grand Lodge and this was done at a subsequent meeting held at the Goose and Gridiron Ale-house on 24 June 1717.

Little is known about this, the Mother Grand Lodge of the world, prior to 24 June 1723 when the first Minute Book was begun. The founding lodges were confined to London and Westminster but there may not have been any firm intention to restrict the authority of the Grand Lodge territorially. The 1725 list includes lodges at Bath, Bristol, Chester, Chichester, Gosport, Manchester, Norwich and Warwick, whilst from 1728 onwards lodges were founded in various countries overseas and appointments of Provincial Grand Masters were made, even for territories abroad where no lodges existed. On the other hand, although information about them is virtually non-existent, doubtless there were lodges in London and elsewhere in the country that, at least for a number of years and in some cases possibly for the whole of their existence, maintained an independent status so that, as from the very inception of the premier Grand Lodge there would be a body of opposition ever ready to challenge its decisions. Nevertheless, had the sweet voice of reason prevailed in its councils at this time and had its attitude to the Antients been less aggressive in later years, the opposition to it might have faded out and the bitterness of more than sixty years might have been avoided.

INTERNAL PROBLEMS

From about 1720 the public began to take a keen interest in freemasonry as it is shown by the increasing number of references to it in the press and elsewhere and by the appearance of masonic exposures, the first of which was *A Mason's Examination*, published as a series of three instalments in April 1725 in *The Flying Post or Postman* but the most notorious of all was Prichard's *Masonry Dissected* which appeared in 1730 and gave, for the first time, details of the third degree. This proved to be immensely popular, three editions being published in the first

eleven days and, on average, there was one new edition every three years for the remainder of the century quite apart from many Continental, Irish and American editions. It was so detailed that anyone making a careful study of it could pass himself off as a member of the craft and this, quite understandably, caused considerable concern to the authorities. Not only did the clandestine making of masons become quite common but it was discovered that these persons by posing as regular masons were able to claim relief and were thus making considerable inroads into the General Charity fund. In addition, members of the independant lodges that did not acknowledge the authority of the new Grand Lodge may well have sought admission to meetings if only out of curiosity. In order to counteract these dangers, at the Grand Lodge meeting of 15 December 1730 it was resolved ' ... that no Person whatsoever should be admitted into Lodges unless some Member of the Lodge then present would vouch for such visiting Brothers [*sic*] being a regular Mason ... '

However, this obviously did not completely solve the problem for at some date unknown, but about nine years later, Grand Lodge took a most unfortunate decision to reverse certain modes of recognition in the first and second degrees so as to render more easily the detection of these impostors. That the undesirable activities of irregular masons were a serious problem is undisputed but the drastic decision taken by Grand Lodge was justifiably regarded by many as interfering with the ancient landmarks, a charge later made with considerable force and effect by the Antients. A more sensible solution would have been to have introduced a secret word, chosen by Grand Lodge and changed every six or twelve months, to be communicated only in open lodge and thereafter to be given by every brother before entering a lodge.

There were other causes for dissatisfaction however. The new and by modern standards still very small Grand Lodge, having a succession of mediocre Grand Secretaries inexperienced in the management of Grand Lodge affairs, proved inefficient, perhaps inexcusably so as it amounted to neglect. As Calvert said (*Grand Lodge Secretaries* p. 9) the Moderns 'had been content to leave its secretarial work to a succession of mediocrities'. If only Laurence Dermott had been Grand Secretary of the Moderns instead of the Antients the whole future of freemasonry would have been altered very drastically and the craft today would doubtless be quite different. This inefficiency applied from the Grand Masters downwards for they neglected their duties as much as anyone. William, 5th Lord Byron, who was Grand Master from April 1747 until March 1752 spent much of that time abroad. During his term of office there were only nine meetings of Grand Lodge and after his Installation he did not attend again until the nomination of Lord Carysfort as his successor on 16 March 1752, only four days before the Installation meeting. As Bernard Jones points out, his absence and that of his deputy became such a scandal that some brethren 'grew so restive that they summoned by advertisement a meeting of the Craft to elect a new Grand Master' but a Past Grand Steward, Bro Thomas Manningham, [Deputy Grand master 1752–6] attended the meeting and persuaded the brethren to be patient.

The resultant discontent was widespread as is shown in a letter written in 1743 by Horace Walpole who was himself a member of the craft: 'The Freemasons are

in so low repute now in England, that one scarce heard the proceedings at Vienna against them mentioned ... [Proceedings following the publication of the 1738 Papal Bull against freemasonry which, however, was not promulgated in Austria] I believe that nothing but a persecution could bring them into vogue here again.' The initial enthusiasm engendered by the formation of Grand Lodge in 1717 had begun to evaporate and by the middle of the century one quarter of the lodges had been removed from its register.

'IRREGULAR' FREEMASONRY

Inefficiency on the part of Grand Lodge and the general apathy on the part of so many members of the craft were not the only problems in the first half of the eighteenth century. As previously suggested, it would be naïve to think that the only lodges existing in 1717 were the four that were the founding lodges of the premier Grand Lodge of England as undoubtedly there were other lodges, equally well-established, whose members had governed their own affairs from inception and who had no intention of submitting to the authority of the recently created body calling itself a Grand Lodge, the like of which had never before been known and which, in their opinion, had no mandate to act as such or to make decisions binding on them or on the craft as a whole. They would regard themselves, in all sincerity, as being just as regular as any other freemasons and of having a perfect and unimpaired 'time immemorial' right to make masons just as they had done prior to 1717 and that candidates who were made masons in their lodges were just as regular as any made in lodges operating by authority of the new Grand Lodge. What is even more likely, especially in view of the widespread public interest in freemasonry following the events of 1717, is that there were recently formed lodges whose members claimed similar powers. There may possibly have been some very loose form of association or consultation between these lodges but that is very questionable and it is more likely that they functioned quite independently, governing their own affairs precisely in the manner they wished.

An example of such a lodge as those just mentioned is the English lodge at Bordeaux, founded on 27 April 1732 by three English naval officers, which not only governed its own affairs and initiated, passed and raised candidates but also constituted other lodges in south-western France before applying for and receiving, on 8 March 1766, a Warrant from the premier Grand Lodge of England. This lodge exists today but is now a French lodge, La Loge Anglaise (204) No. 2 on the register of La Grande Loge Nationale Française, 204 being its former English number.

Unfortunately the records of any such lodges in England have disappeared but there was a masonic music society, the *Philo-Musical et Architectural Societas* that restricted membership to freemasons. It was founded on 18 February 1725 (N.S.) and its last minute is dated 23 March 1727. During that short period of time eighteen persons were initiated 'in order to be admitted Members of This Right (Worshipfull & Highly Esteem'd) Society' and passings and raisings were also performed, in fact the raising of Bros Cotton, Ball and Geminiani on 12 May 1725 may possibly be the first record of a third degree ceremony though R. F. Gould

(*AQC 16* pp. 126–7) and others have expressed considerable doubts about it, suggesting that they were being made Fellow Crafts. Moreover, a second degree ceremony performed on 18 February 1725 was carried out some nine months before the repeal of the 1720 regulation that no one could be advanced beyond the rank of apprentice except in Grand Lodge. It may be that this regulation had not been widely observed, but the fact remains that the members of this London Music Society, operating it might be said under the very nose of Grand Lodge, did not hesitate to act in breach of the rules and regulations of that Grand Lodge on several occasions. Moreover, the said regulation also prohibited the foundation of any new lodge without the Grand Master's Warrant and this was reinforced by several minutes stipulating that no person offending in this way should be admitted 'into Regular Lodges'. The members of the Society may not have founded a new lodge in a strict sense of the word but they were certainly operating as one.

Their activities obviously became known to Grand Lodge for only eight days after the ceremony on 12 May 1725 seven of their members were ordered to appear at the next Quarterly Communication though there is no record of their having done so. However, the minutes of the Society for the meeting on the following 16 December record the receipt of:

> A Letter Datd the 8th Instant from Brother Geo: Payne Junr. Grand Warden directed in form to this Society inclosing a Letter from the Duke of Richmond Grand Master dat. likewise the 8 Instant directed to the Presidt. and the rest of the Brethren at the Apollo in which he Erroneously insists on and Assumed to himself a Pretended Authority to call our Rt. Worshipful and Highly Esteem'd Society to an account for making Masons irregularly for which reasons as well as for want of a Due Regard Just Esteem and Omitting to Address himself in proper form to this Rt. Worshipful and Highly Esteem'd Society.

ORDERED

That the Said Letters do lye on the Table.

Not only did the Society flout in this manner the authority assumed by Grand Lodge but it continued to perform masonic ceremonies. The attitude of the members is nowhere better expressed than in a letter of their President, Bro William Gulston, in which he said: 'I beg leave to recommend to you the Same Cordial Affection and Unanimity which we have hitherto on all Occasions Shown by which we Shall not only Disappoint and Defeat our weak tho inveterate Enemyes but also grow deservedly in great and reall Esteem ...' No doubt that was the attitude of the members of the independent lodges then existing but how many there were or what was the strength of the opposition to the premier Grand Lodge is never likely to be known.

THE BIRTH OF THE ANTIENTS

The Grand Lodge of the Antients was founded by five lodges of Irish freemasons at a General Assembly held at the Turks Head, Greek Street, Soho, on Wednesday 17 July 1751 and was referred to in its minutes as a Grand Committee until 27 December 1753 though the term 'Grand Lodge' was used in the original Rules

and Orders. Presumably the latter title was being reserved until such time as a Grand Master was installed, an event that took place on 27 December 1753 when Robert Turner was installed as their first Grand Master. Obviously there must have been discussions prior to this and obviously plans for its formation must have been laid well before that date but there is no evidence to support the contention of some writers that it had been in existence in committee form since the 1730s.

As already explained the Moderns had been concerned about the activities of members of lodges not under its jurisdiction who, in their opinion, were irregular freemasons, to say nothing of those made in a clandestine manner. As an example of this latter practice there was a London tavern that exhibited a sign 'Masons made here – 2/6d' and later, two brethren named Phealon and Mackay were known to have 'initiated' persons for 'the mean consideration of a leg of mutton'. Nevertheless there is no reason whatsoever to think that these clandestine masons or these unattached lodges were involved in forming the Grand Lodge of the Antients in 1751 or that they were supporters of it subsequently. Moreover although lodges were continually being removed from the Register about this time, at least twenty-six out of a total of eighty being erased between 1725 and 1729, it would seem that this was solely because they had ceased to meet.

Discussions on the problem took place in Grand Lodge in 1723, 1724 (twice), 1730 (twice), 1735, 1739 (twice), 1740, 1749, 1752 and no doubt consideration was given to it on other occasions. What is of particular interest, however, is a minute of the Grand Lodge meeting of 30 June 1739: 'The Complaint referred by the last Committee of Charity concerning the irregular making of Masons was taken into Consideration When the Secry. informed the Lodge that he had given Notice to the several persons complained off to attend & answer the same at this Q.C.' Only one such person attended and in the 1784 *Constitutions*, reference is made to this incident in the following terms:

> The Grand Lodge justly considered such proceedings as an infringement on the original laws, and encroachment on the privileges, and an imposition on the charitable fund of the Society. It was therefore resolved to discountenance those assemblies and to enforce the laws against all brethren who were aiding or assisting in the clandestine reception of any person into Masonry, at any of these illegal conventions. This irritated the brethren who had incurred the censure of the Grand Lodge; who, instead of returning to their duty, and renouncing their error, persisted in their contumacy, and openly refused to pay allegiance to the Grand Master, or obedience to the mandates of the Grand Lodge.
>
> In contempt of the ancient and established laws of the Order they set up a power independent, and taking advantage of the inexperience of their associates, insisted that they had an equal authority with the Grand Lodge to make, pass and raise Masons.... This illegal and unconstitutional claim obliged the regular Masons to adopt new measures to detect these impostors, and debar them and their abettors from the countenance and protection of the regular lodges. To accomplish this purpose more effectually, some variations were made in the established forms which afforded a subterfuge, at which the refractory brethren readily grasped. They now assumed the appellation of Antient Masons, proclaimed themselves enemies to all innovation, insisted that they preserved the antient usages of the order, and that the regular lodges on whom they conferred the title of Modern Masons had adopted new measures, illegal and unconstitutional. Thus by a new

species of deceit and imposition they endeavoured to support an existence, using the necessary precautions taken by the Grand Lodge to detect them, as grounds for a novel and ridiculous distinction of Antient and Modern Masons.

The reference to the Grand Lodge minute is true in general terms but whether the remainder of the statement can be accepted as correct reporting is a matter of some considerable doubt. Other parts are palpably incorrect and that alone throws doubt on the entire passage but there is yet another reason for suspicion. It was written some forty-five years after the event and it is an established fact that the further away an account is from the event it records, the less accurate it is likely to be and the greater the possibility that the writer is advancing, at least in part, some theory of his own. Admittedly, some fifteen years prior to this, in a letter written in 1769, James Heseltine, the Grand Secretary of the Moderns, referred to the Antients as 'a set of men who first made their appearance *about the year 1746*'. Again, not only was this written twenty-three years after the event but it was in the year when Bro Heseltine was appointed Grand Secretary so he was writing about something of which he had no direct knowledge. In addition, the words I have placed in italics are so indefinite as to suggest that he was repeating hearsay.

There is not a single piece of evidence between 1717 and 1751 to support this theory of the existence of the Antients in committee form from the 1730s and there are several reasons for doubting it. In the first place those who founded that Grand Lodge were mainly Irish masons of the artisan type, itinerant and often unreliable. Out of 173 members entered in the 1751 General Register of Members, no less than 53 were struck off, 42 being excluded, almost entirely for misconduct or non-payment of dues, and 11 for having gone abroad, mainly to Ireland. Moreover no less than 31 of the erasures are of 1751/2, 4 of 1753 and 2 of 1754. Nowhere is there any suggestion that those incurring the displeasure of the Moderns prior to 1751 were either Irish or as transient and unreliable as this. In addition, at the first meeting of the Antients' Grand Committee on 5 February 1752, there were present 'the Officers of No. 2, 3, 4, 5, 6, 7, 8, 9 & 10 *being the Representatives of all the Ancient Masons in and adjacent to London* [my italics]. The membership of the first six lodges was approximately eighty, so the total membership is unlikely to have been more than one hundred and twenty, a small number to have caused the Moderns' Grand Lodge so much concern over the years and a very poor return for the activities of any Antients' Committee that was said to have been in existence for more than twenty years, a committee of which there is no record whatsoever and to which there is not a single reference in any of the later writings of Dermott or in any of the subsequent records of the Antients.

Further, neither the first Grand Secretary of the Antients, John Morgan, nor his successor, Laurence Dermott, ever suggested that any of their lodges or any of their members had joined them because of disagreements with the Moderns' Grand Lodge. Certainly there were lodges that changed their allegiance later, also individual masons, but when he published his first edition of *Ahiman Rezon* in 1756 any such evidence would surely have been seized upon avidly by Dermott had it existed. Moreover he, who was always anxious to maintain that his Grand Lodge was the custodian of 'pure ancient masonry,' never attempted to confer

'Time Immemorial' status on any of his lodges nor did he ever refer to their possible existence prior to 1751 though, paradoxically enough, he did claim that the Antients had issued Grand Lodge certificates from time immemorial. Surely one of his temperament, who once wrote that his form of freemasonry was 'not only coeval with the scripture, but in all probability prior thereto', would have claimed prior establishment of his lodges had he not known that any such statement could be immediately disproved. When Warrants were issued subsequently to the founding lodges they were all dated 17 July 1751 and there is no reason to think that those lodges were in existence for any appreciable time prior to that nor did they last for long afterwards, No. 2 being struck off in 1769, No. 3 ceasing to meet regularly as early as the latter end of 1751 and being struck off in 1757, No. 4 lapsing about 1765, No. 5 in 1761 and No. 6 in 1754. Obviously not one of the five was soundly based as would surely have been the case had it been in existence from the 1730–9 period. Moreover, by the end of 1753, after only two and a half years had elapsed, the number of lodges had increased to twenty eight which is yet another indication of what would have been the position in 1751 had a Grand Lodge or Grand Committee existed for twenty years prior to then. It seems therefore, that members of the Grand Lodge of Ireland resident in London, finding themselves unwelcome in English lodges because of their inferior social status, because they were unable to meet the financial obligations that would have been involved in membership, or for other reasons, decided to form lodges for themselves and to organize a Grand Lodge on Irish principles. There was certainly no attempt made to found it on the English pattern or to make it work according to the English system as would surely have been the case had it been founded by existing English lodges. In particular, it seems likely that they wished to establish a Charity Fund of their own to provide them with grants in time of need, also funeral benefits, two items that subsequently became salient features of their organization. Whatever may be the truth of the matter, the General Assembly of Freemasons that met at the Turk's Head Tavern did so in order 'to show posterity how much we desire to revive the Ancient Craft upon true Masonical principles' and this was the official foundation of the Antients though the first Minute Book does not begin until the meeting held at the Griffin Tavern, Holborn, London, on 5 February 1752. The precise wording should be noted. The meeting of this General Assembly, not of a Grand Committee, was to *revive* the Ancient Craft not to improve the administration or to expand it. Why was there no mention of any previous Grand Committee? What had happened to it? Surely the answer is that the Antients had not previously existed in committee form?

For many years it was indeed believed that this was a breakaway move by discontented members of the Modern's Grand Lodge but in 1887 Henry Sadler published his *Masonic Facts and Fictions* in which he showed that most of the founders of the Grand Lodge of the Antients were Irish freemasons who were resident in London but who had never owed allegiance to the Grand Lodge of the Moderns.

The lodges involved in the foundation of the Antients were those subsequently recorded as meeting at:

1. The Turk's Head, Greek Street, Soho,
2. The Criple, Little Britain,
3. The Cannon, Water Lane, Fleet Street,
4. The Plaisters' Arms, Grays Inn Lane,
5. The Globe, Bridges Street, Covent Garden.

In his *Freemasons' Guide and Compendium*, Bernard Jones stated that there were six lodges but he was presumably including the one that met at the Fountain, Monmouth Street, Seven Dials which was not warranted until 29 July 1751, *i.e.* twelve days after the meeting. However, Rule 8 of the Rules and Orders of the Antients stipulated that: 'No Admission or Warrant shall be granted to any Brothers to hold a Lodge until such time they have first formed a Lodge of Ancient Masons and sitt Regularly in a Credible House and then Apply by Petition and such Petition to be Attested by the Masters of three Regular Lodges who shall make a Proper Report of them.' It may well be, therefore, that this sixth lodge had been meeting without a warrant and that members were present at the inaugural meeting but this does not alter the fact that there were only five founding lodges.

The first Grand Secretary was John Morgan and he it was who produced their earliest records in the form of a book that has become known as Morgan's Register. However, before the new Grand Lodge was one year old Morgan resigned to take up a sea-faring career and Laurence Dermott was appointed as his successor.

LAURENCE DERMOTT

Laurence Dermott has been described as 'a great perhaps even the greatest character in the Craft history of the eighteenth century.' Even R.F. Gould, to whom the Antients were an anathema, wrote of him in eulogistic terms:

> Of Laurence Dermott, the first Grand Secretary ... it may be said, without erring on the side of panegyric, that was the most remarkable Mason that ever existed. 'As a polemic' observed a judicious writer, [Mackey, *Encyclopaedia of Freemasonry*] 'he was sarcastic, bitter, uncompromising and not altogether sincere or veracious. But in intellectual attainments he was inferior to none of his adversaries, and in a philosophical appreciation of the character of the Masonic Institution, he was in advance of the spirit of his age.' Yet although a very unscrupulous writer, he was a matchless administrator. In the former capacity he was the embodiment of the maxim, '*de l'audace, encore l'audace, toujours l'audace*,' but in the latter, he displayed qualities which we find united in no other member of the Craft, who came either before or after him. As Grand Secretary and later as Deputy Grand Master he was simply the life and soul of the body with which he was so closely associated. He was also its historian, and to the influence of his writings, must be attributed, in great measure, the marvellous success of the ... [Antients]

He was born in Ireland in 1720 and is said to have been initiated on 14 January 1740 in an Irish Lodge, No. 26, meeting at the house of a certain Bro Thomas Allen in Dublin though this date may be according to the old style of numbering the years and if so, it would be 1741 according to our present style. This seems to be indicated in the General Register of the Antients at the time when he joined

Lodge No. 10 where it is recorded that he was 'made on Jan. 14 1740–1'. There is, however, a mystery about this as, according to Crossle's *Irish Masonic Records*, Lodge No. 26 met at Lestrand in Co. Sligo and furthermore there is no mention of any Lodge No. 26 in Spratt's *General Regulations* of 1741 which gives a list of sixteen regular lodges in Dublin with numbers ranging from 2 to 141. The Lestrand Lodge No. 26 was erased and could have been transferred to Dublin prior to 1740 though there is no record of this other than a statement in the *Pocket Companion for Freemasons* (Dublin 1735) which indicated that Lodge No. 26 met 'at the Eagle Tavern on Cork Hill'. I am indebted to V.W. Bro W.J. O'Brien of the Lodge of Research, Dublin, for the suggestion that it was so transferred and that the members remaining at Lestrand then joined Lodge No. 340 in nearby Strokestown. Certainly members of this lodge showed a very considerable interest in Dermott as subscribers to his 1760 edition of *Ahiman Rezon*.

   The warrant of this lodge was later secured by a military lodge (26th. Foot 1st Bn. the Cameronians) and was surrendered by them in March 1922. It is now the warrant of St. Jude's Lodge, Belfast.

   There is no mention of Dermott in any masonic records in Ireland but this is not significant as unfortunately such records are very far from being complete at that time and in particular the page on which his name would have been entered is missing from the Grand Lodge Register. Further, when he was accused in Grand Lodge on 2 March 1757 by one, John Hamilton, of having been made clandestinely at a house in Long Acre, London, Bro Thomas Allen gave evidence to the effect 'that Bro Dermott had faithfully served all offices [Junior and Senior Deacon, Junior and Senior Warden and Secretary] in a very Reputable Lodge held in his house in the City of Dublin.' Bro Charles Byrne confirmed this and stated that he

had installed him in the Chair of that lodge on St. John the Baptist's Day [24 June] 1746. Moreover, Dermott himself produced a certificate signed by the Grand Secretary of Ireland, confirming the property of his masonic conduct and servitude whereupon Grand Lodge declared itself satisfied and excluded John Hamilton for life. It is thought that he was also made a Royal Arch mason in this lodge and in the same year but this suggestion may be based solely on the fact that entry into the Royal Arch was restricted to Installed Masters. Nevertheless, although the exact date is unknown, Dermott claimed to have been made a Royal Arch Mason early in his masonic career and in the Antient's Register of Members of the Royal Arch he is recorded as having been so made in 1746 and in Lodge No. 26, Dublin. Little is known of his early years but he is thought to have been of humble origin though

he may have been distantly related to the Mac Dermots of Rosscommon. The accompanying illustration is of his book-plate, obviously designed after his appointment as Grand Secretary but whilst still a journeyman painter. It bears a certain resemblance to the armorial bearings of the Painter-Stainers Livery Company but the true source is definitely those of the Mac Dermots as is clearly shown by the following: 'Mac Dermot (Chiefs of Moylurg, Co. Roscommon; an ancient Irish Sept. descended from Maolroona, second son of Teige, King of Connaught, in the seventh century), *Argent*, on a chevron *gules*, between three boars' heads erased *azure*, tusked and bristled *or*, as many cross-crosslets *or*. CREST, a demi-lion rampart *azure*, holding in the dexter paw a sceptre crowned *or* MOTTO (over), Honor et Virtus.

His writings certainly seem to indicate that he was at least reasonably well educated though he is described as a journeyman painter and in the Register previously mentioned his occupation is given as 'Painter Buttlers Alley More fields'. Nevertheless, he is credited with a knowledge of Latin and Hebrew and of an acquaintance with Greek and Roman mythology though it is impossible to say where he might have gained this knowledge. The minutes of the Stewards' Lodge for 21 March 1764 record: 'The petition of George Joseph Frange an Arabian mason with whom the Gd. Sec. conversed in the Hebrew Language ...' though it must be added that this minute was written by Dermott himself and so could have been a question of self-glorification. It is also recorded that when the Grand Master quoted a Latin text to him in Grand Lodge on 12 June 1767, Dermott replied 'Fungor officio meo' [I do my duty].

Exactly why or when he moved to England is unknown but it was probably about the year 1748 and it has been said that shortly after arriving he joined a Moderns' lodge. There is no record of this in the Grand Lodge archives but that is by no means conclusive. It is based solely on his statement, when writing of the Moderns, '... when I was first introduced into that society.' Several writers have suggested that this may mean nothing more than that he attended as a visitor, possibly with the idea of joining it later but the words 'introduced into that society' seem indicative of joining rather than visiting. In any case, the indications are that his reception was not all that he could have desired and if that is true it may account for his hostility to the Moderns which was very early in evidence. It may, indeed, have prejudiced him for a time against freemasonry as a whole for his name is not amongst the founders of the Antients' Grand Lodge though he had been resident in London for three years by then. Alternatively, if he did join a Moderns' lodge he might still have been a member of it at that time.

Bernard Jones states that in 1752 he joined the Antient lodge No. 9 which he soon left to join No. 10 but in this he is in error. According to the General Register Dermott joined Lodge No. 10 on 1 February 1752 and is recorded as resigning from it and joining Lodge No. 9 on 24 February 1752 though in the Grand Committee minutes of 5 February 1752 he is described as 'of No. 9 and 10.' He resigned from No. 9 on 20 June 1752 having been a member for not much over four months and having been a member of No. 10 for only just over three weeks. It must be borne in mind, however, that lodge membership in those days was far from being as firmly established as it is now and it may be that, having been

elected Grand Secretary, he felt the responsibilities attaching to that office were all he could manage and that he would have no time for ordinary lodge affairs. In any case, there is no subsequent record of his being a member of any lodge until we hear of him as a member of No. 11.

It was at the meeting on 5 February 1752 that he was elected Grand Secretary. The relevant minute reads:

> Brother John Margan Grand Secretary, Informed the Committee that he being lately appointed to an Office on board of one of His Majesty's Ships, he received Orders to prepare for his departure and therefore Advised the Grand Committee to chuse anew Secretary immediately.
>
> Upon which Brother John Morris past Master of No. 5 and Brother Laurence Dermott of No. 9 and 10, and Past Master No. 26 in Dublin were proposed and admitted as Candidates for the Office of Grand Secretary. And Grand Secretary Morgan was Ordered to Examine the Candidates separately & report his opinion of their Qualifications.
>
> After a long & minute Examination Relative to Initiation passing. Instalations, and General Regulations &c. &c. &c. Brother Morgan declared that Brother Laurence Dermott was duly qualified for the Office of Grand Secretary. Whereon the Worshipful Master in the Chair put up the Names of John Morris, and Laurence Dermott, separately when the latter was Unanimously Chosen Grand Secretary: and accordingly he was installed (in the Ancient Manner) by the Worshipful Mr. James Hagarty Master of No. 4 then presiding Officer, Assisted by Mr. John Margan late Grand Secretary and the Masters present. After which Brother Morgan (at the request of the president) proclaimed the new Grand Secretary thrice, according to ancient Custom. Upon which the new Secretary received the usual salutes. And then the president and late Grand Secretary John Morgan delivered the books &c &c. into the hands of the new Secretary; upon certain Conditions which was agreed by all parties, and which Conditions the said Worshipful Brother James Hagarty can Explain. The Grand Committee Unanimously Joined in Wishing Br. Morgan Health and a Successful voyage and then Closed with the greatest Harmony. Having Adjourned to Wednesday the fourth of March next.

The minute is in Laurence Dermott's handwriting and without wishing to be unfair to him, the question arises as to whether the voting was unanimous as surely Bro Morris who was a Past Master of No. 5 lodge must have had some support bearing in mind that he, also, was proposed for the post and the retiring Grand Secretary was ordered to examine both candidates and report upon them. Perhaps the explanation is that those present all accepted the recommendation of Bro. Morgan.

However, it seems that even the Antients found him intransigent and difficult to deal with at times but it has to be remembered that in later years he suffered severely from gout and this may well have been the cause of his uncertain temper. On occasions the attacks were so bad that 'he was oblig'd to be carried out of his bed (when incapable to wear shoes, stockings or even Britches) to do his duty at the Stewards Lodge' and it is understandable that this affected his outlook on life. At the Grand Lodge meeting on 6 June 1770 there is a record of a serious dispute between him and the Deputy Grand Secretary, William Dickey Junior, who had resigned as 'he would not serve under such a Man as Mr. Dermott'. The disagreement was referred to at the subsequent meeting and again on 5 December when 'many warm disputes happened ... the recording of which wou'd be of no

service to the Craft nor to the several speakers' but the matter was resolved a fortnight later when Grand Lodge unanimously agreed 'that Brother Dickey has been at fault.' Laurence Dermott continued in office for nineteen years until he was appointed Deputy Grand Master in 1771, an office he held until 1777 and again, after a lapse of six years, from 1783 until 1787. At the Grand Lodge meeting on 27 December 1787, after a short address, the newly elected Deputy Grand Master, James Perry, proposed: 'That the thanks of the Grand Lodge be given to the Rt. Wl. Lau. Dermott Esq. Past Deputy Grand Master who after forty seven Years zealously & Successfully devoted to the Service of the Craft had now retired from the Eminent station which he had held, and to whose masonic knowledge and abilities – inflexible adherance to the Ancient Laws of the Fraternity and Impartial Administration of Office, the fraternity are so much indebted.'

His last recorded attendance at Grand Lodge was on 3 June 1789 and two years later, in June 1791, he died aged 71. No account of his funeral has survived and the place of his burial is unknown. What is even more surprising is that there is no reference to his death in the records of the Antients and indeed the only mention of it is in the proceedings of the Grand Lodge of Pennsylvania which was of Antient origin. On 4 June 1792 it was resolved 'that in order to show the just regard and respect of this Grand Lodge for our late Brother Laurence Dermott, the patron and founder thereof, it be recommended to every member of this Grand Lodge to appear on St. John's Day next, with Aprons bordered with black or other marks of mourning.'

His great contribution to the cause of the Antients was that he organized it on a sound and efficient basis and built it up so that when union with the Moderns became a possibility the Antients were able to negotiate on terms of equality and, indeed, to impose conditions regarding certain aspects they regarded as of particular importance. It has been said that no one person has ever done more for freemasonry than Laurence Dermott nor has anyone's work been more abiding. I would not quarrel with that as a generalization though Anderson, Desaguliers, Dunkerley, Preston and others have their supporters and in any case, if Dermott's work was of such outstanding value, it was work done exclusively for the Antients rather than for freemasonry as a whole.

He was a great disciplinarian, an excellent administrator and a firm believer in the principle and tenets of the craft. As Grand Secretary of the rival Grand Lodge he was in a position where he was an obvious target for criticism and it must be admitted that at times his enthusiasm for his task, as he saw it, led him to make unjustified and unworthy attacks on the Grand Lodge of the Moderns to such an extent as almost to indicate hatred of it. Certainly the Moderns regarded the Antients very much as an irregular Grand Lodge as irregular brethren are looked upon today and it was natural for Dermott to resent this but on occasions his resentment went beyond the bounds of reason. At times he was vindictive in a manner that was crude in the extreme and even he must have had doubts about the truth of some of the statements he made. It is greatly to be wished that the energy he devoted to his campaign of vilification had been devoted rather to healing the breach between the two Grand Lodges.

MORGAN'S REGISTER

This, the official Register and earliest record extant of the Grand Lodge of the Antients, took its name from their first Grand Secretary, John Morgan. It consists of:

1. An index to the Register
2. Rules and Orders.
3. Resolution passed at the monthly meeting on 14 September 1752.
4. Twentyseven approved by-laws for lodges. (These fourteen pages were removed and burned when the by-laws were superseded by those submitted by Laurence Dermott on 1 April 1752].
5. Black list, soon to be discontinued.
6. Register of members.
7. List of lodges.
8. Revised list of lodges.
9. Third list of lodges.
10. Minutes from 5 February 1752 to 27 December 1760.

RULES AND ORDERS

These were 'agreed and settled by a Committee appointed by a General Assembly Held at the Turk's Head in Greek Street Soho on Wednesday the 17th of July 1751 And in the Year of MASONRY 5751.' Apart from Rule 8 which dealt with the granting of Warrants and which has already been mentioned, three are particularly worth of note:

Rule 1 provided for a meeting to be held on the first Wednesday of each month 'for the better Regulation & Government of the Lodges.' These were the forerunners of the present-day Quarterly Communications of the United Grand Lodge of England.

Rule 9 stipulated that Masters and Wardens should be elected for six months only: 'THAT on St. John's day the 24th of June and St. Johns day the 27th of Decemr. the Master of every Lodge shall deliver into the Secretary of the Grand Lodge the Names of the Masters & Wardens that are appointed to serve for the Ensueing Half Year.'

There was no provision for re-election for a second term neither was there any stipulation against it nor, if it was permitted, any restriction as to the maximum period that could be served.

There were other meetings on 6 April and 1 July 1752 and at the latter, Rule 18 was added making the new Grand Lodge, in part, a funeral benefit society. It is one of the indications that in general the social status of its members was inferior to that of the members of the premier Grand Lodge and it reads as follows:

THAT upon the death of any of our Worthy Brethren whose names are or may be hereafter Recorded in the Grant Registry &c. the Master of such lodge as he then belonged to Shall immediately inform the Grand Secretary of his Death and the intended time for his funeral, and upon this notice the Grand Secretary shall summon all the lodges to attend the funeral in proper Order, and that Each Member shall pay One Shilling towards Defraying the expenses of Said funeral or Otherwise to his Widow or nearest friend, provided the

Deceased or his friends Realy want and Require the same otherwise the money so raised to be put to some other Charitable use, or as the Committee shall think proper &c.

RESOLUTION OF 14 SEPTEMBER 1752

A further meeting on 14 September is of far greater interest inasmuch as it reinforces the suggestion that there had been no previous central organization of Antient masons. The opening paragraph of the report is as follows:

> WHEREAS it is *highly expedient for the Universal Benefit of the Antient Craft* that a GRAND MASTER *and Grand Lodge shou'd govern and direct the proceedings of the several Ancient Lodges* held in and about the Cities of London and Westminster. And as the present low condition of the Ancient Society of Free and Accepted Masons renders the hope of Obtaining the honour a Noble Personage to preside over us at this time very precarious.
>
> In order *to preserve the present remains of the true Ancient Craft &c.* We the under Named being the present Masters and Wardens of the several Masonical meetings called Lodges of true Ancient Masonry aforesaid, do agree (pursuant to the powers vested in us by our Respective Brethren of the several lodges) *to form a Grand Committee (we mean such a Committee) as may supply the deficiency of a Grand Master* until an Opportunity offers for the Choice of a Noble Personage to govern our Ancient Fraternity: and that *We will, therein (by the Authority Aforesaid) make Statutes or laws* for the better government and well Ordering the said Fraternity Receive petitions, hear Appeals, and Transact Business (that is to say such Business as ought to be peculiar to a Grand Lodge) with Equity and Impartiality.

The italics, which are mine, surely indicate that it was thought expedient for a Grand Lodge to be formed, none having been in existence prior to that meeting. In the second place, and in a way this is even more significant, surely there was concern expressed for the state of 'the true Ancient Craft' at that time and that in an attempt to prevent it from falling into complete decay, a Grand Committee was to be formed to introduce 'Statutes or laws', a committee, by implication, the like of which had not existed previously. Had there been any governing body prior to this meeting, surely laws for the good government of the craft would have been drawn up? Everything in this rule and in all previous ones gives the impression of an entirely new organization passing resolutions that would normally be the concern of any embryo Grand committee or Grand Lodge. Further it should be noted that is was even considered necessary to define exactly what kind of committee was envisaged and what were to be its functions, also that the references were to 'the proceedings of the several Antient Lodges' and to 'the several Masonical meetings called Lodges' which, so it seems, had had no hand to guide them in the past. Nowhere in these rules nor in the subsequent Grand Lodge minutes is there even a single word that might refer to a previous body of any kind and indeed Rule 4 provided that no brother should be made a Master or Warden unless he was a mason of *six months* standing and a member of a regular lodge for that time. Again this suggests a body, and indeed lodges, of recent formation. A mason of six months' standing could be elected master of his lodge, without finding it necessary to go through the various junior offices as Laurence Dermott, for example, is reported as having done in his mother lodge in Ireland. Surely this

is another indication of a recently formed organization experiencing its birth-pangs?

The first reference to Warrants is also given in the minutes of this meeting but again it must be emphasized that this seems to refer to lodges that had been operating independently rather than under any central authority:

> And whereas several of the lodges have congregated and made Masons without any Warrant.... In order to rectify such irregular proceedings (as far as is in our power) It is hereby Order'd That the Grand Secretary shall write Warrants (on Parchment) for the Unwarranted Lodges, viz., The lodges known by the title of No. 2, 3, 4, 5, 6, and that all the said Warrants shall bare date July the seventeenth One thousand seven hundred fifty and One being the day on which the said lodges met (at the Turk's Head Tavern in Greek Street, Soho) to revive the Ancient Craft.
>
> That the Secretary shall leave proper Spaces for the Grand Master Deputy G.M. and Grand Wardens to sign all the said Warrants according to Ancient Custom.
>
> That as soon as we shall arrive at the Great happiness of installing proper Grand Officers the possessors of the Unsigned Warrants shall present them to the Grand Master for his Worship's Signature or Renewal, Until which time the said Warrants as well as those which have or may be ... granted in the like manner shall be deem'd good and lawful.

Even No. 2 Lodge, the first on the Register at that time, was to date from 17 July 1751 and, as mentioned previously, there were to be no 'Time Immemorial' lodges. Moreover, there is no record of any protest by the members of the lodge at this decision as might have been expected had they regarded their lodge as responsible, at least in part, for preserving 'the Ancient Craft'.

The minutes conclude: 'Lastly this our Regulation shall be Recorded in our Registry to show posterity how much we desire to revive the Ancient Craft upon true Masonical principles.' It has been held by some writers that the wording of this minute was responsible for the nickname 'Antients' being applied to the new Grand Lodge and consequently for the Premier Grand Lodge becoming referred to as the 'Moderns', but the terms are known to have been in use prior to this.

The Antients certainly regarded themselves as the true guardians of masonic tradition yet in truth they were probably guilty of more innovations than the Moderns, the most flagrant of which was the inclusion of the Royal Arch as an integral part of 'pure antient freemasonry'. Further, even if the Moderns did introduce alterations into the ceremonies, it has to be remembered that they were compiled originally for simple folk, workmen in the mason's trade who could neither read nor write, men brought up in the Roman Catholic faith whose only guide and mentor was the Church. Many of them would know nothing of any book other than the Holy Bible and their thoughts would automatically find expression in its language. As time went on and educated men having no con-nection with operative masonry came into the craft it was inevitable that changes would be made and this process was by no means complete at the time the premier Grand Lodge was founded in 1717.

When Anderson first issued his *Constitutions* in 1723 it was felt desirable to open the craft to men of all religions who believed in a Supreme Being, or, as Anderson put it, 't'is now thought more expedient only to oblige them to that Religion in which all men agree, leaving their particular Opinions to themselves.'

As a result it was inevitable that the ritual should be de-Christianized but obviously there were some, as is always the case with any change, who resented it. In addition, even at this late stage, when there is no evidence of any lodge under the jurisdiction of the premier Grand Lodge being of an operative nature, the Old Charges still bore the impression of having been drawn up for operative masons and many were patently absurd when addressed to non-operative masons.

The Rules and Orders adopted by the Antients are by no means complete and it seems likely, therefore, that the Antients looked upon Anderson's *Constitutions* for guidance and that these Rules and Orders related to matters peculiar to their own requirements. This suggestion receives support from Dermott himself who, when pointing out in 1784 that the Antients' Grand Lodge had been guilty of illegal acts, quoted (*inter alia*) Anderson's *Constitutions*. That Dermott should decide to make use of anything connected with the Moderns as his authority is indeed surprising, especially as it was such a very well-known and successful publication. This may also be why, so soon after his appointment as Grand Secretary, he set about the task of compiling his own constitutions though even so he obviously did not succeed in making Anderson entirely redundant.

BLACK LIST

This contains the names of the first twenty brethren excluded as being 'Persons Deem'd unworthy of the Society' and it is of interest to note that eight of them were excluded 'For making Masans Clandestinely'.

GENERAL REGISTER 1751

This is a register of members, the first seventy-nine entries relating to members of the five lodges that brought the Antients' Grand Lodge into existence. This has led some writers to state categorically that there were seventy-nine founding members but this is by no means certain as some may have been initiated subsequently. It is safer to say that they 'did not number more than eighty'. The last number is 1014 but there are several blanks and some duplication by reason of dual membership. One thing the list emphasizes is that many members were of Irish origin and came from the lower social strata, being shopkeepers and workmen, which no doubt is one of the reasons why many were excluded for non-payment of dues. Nowhere in this Register nor anywhere else is there even the remotest indication that any of the founders had ever owed allegiance to the Grand Lodge of the Moderns.

On 6 June 1752 there is recorded the first Modern mason, Thomas Floyd, to come over from the rival Grand Lodge and a further six are so registered up to August 1753 but none thereafter. No doubt there were other joining members who, even though they were not formerly members of Modern lodges, were members of independent lodges and has presumably been initiated in ancient form.

LIST OF LODGES

This is a list of fifteen lodges, numbered 2 to 16 inclusve, number 1 being reserved for the Grand Master's Lodge, now No. 1 on the register of the United Grand

Lodge of England and having seniority as from 2 September 1756, though its Warrant is dated 13 August 1759. However, it is possible that the Grand Committee may have regarded itself as being a kind of superior private lodge with the number 1 reserved for it. This seems to be indicated in the 1753 Engraved List of Lodges in which the Grand Committee, meeting at the Five Bells, is at the head. No number was shown against it originally but someone, perhaps Laurence Dermott himself, inserted the number 1 in ink. He certainly recorded his own lodge as being No. 1 as early as in the minutes of the Grand Lodge meeting of 2 September 1756 and it is possible that he may have held the Warrant in abeyance until it could be signed by a 'Noble Personage', an opportunity that did not present itself until William, 1st Earl of Blessington, was elected Grand Master. In any case the Warrant is in his handwriting and is the only one ornamented by him. There is no number shown on it.

REVISED LIST OF LODGES

This list, compiled for the Grand Lodge meeting on 27 December 1752 but added to later, indicates the expulsion of two lodges for disobedience of the rules of Grand Lodge and gives details of thirty-six lodges (Nos. 2–37) which constitute '... the true list and Numbers of all the Antient Regular Lodges in and about London', five being shown as founded on 17 July 1751 and the remainder on various dates from 29 January 1752 to 19 August 1754.

THIRD LIST OF LODGES

This list suggests that sixty-four lodges were in existence in 1755 but it is so obviously incomplete in details of them that it cannot be relied upon.

AHIMAN REZON

Undoubtedly one act for which Laurence Dermott will always be remembered is his publication of *Ahiman Rezon*. It was a private venture just as the 1723 *Constitutions* was a private publication of Dr. James Anderson and, just as the latter became the official constitutions of the Moderns so the former became the official constitutions of the Antients though there is no mention of its issue in the Grand Lodge minutes. Nevertheless it was an important factor in the evolution of the Antients and so must be considered in some detail. Why Dermott chose such a title is difficult to understand but it could have arisen from his private vendetta against the Moderns inasmuch as it represented his attempt to give tone to the constitutions of his Grand Lodge by providing them with a distinctive title and at the same time adding to his personal prestige. Much ink has been used without good purpose in trying to decide its meaning and it was for long a problem for Lodge Secretaries one of whom, the Secretary of Newstead Lodge No. 47, referred to it in his records as 'A.H. Iman's Reasons'. Dermott's own translation, or perhaps more correctly his alternative title, was 'A help to a Brother' and one Hebrew authority, the Rev. Morris Rosenbaum, translates it in somewhat similar words (*AQC 23* p. 162) as 'Faithfull Brother Secretary'. Bro Rosenbaum also pointed out that it was usual for Jewish writers to choose titles for their books so

that the numerical value of the letters in such titles equalled the numerical value of the letters in their names and apparently Dermott knew this. The numerical value of *Ahiman Rezon* is 372 and that of Dermott's name is 371. In numerical cryptography these would be regarded as equal.

The book has 238 pages measuring approximately 8 inches by 5 inches, so that it could be carried in the pocket, a great advantage over Anderson's much larger *Constitutions*. The first edition, published in 1756, was by subscription and 216 persons are shown as subscribers, including fifteen ladies. A peculiar circumstance about this first edition is that in the *Public Advertiser* of 16 November 1754 it was advertised as 'Now in the Press and speedily will be publish'd.' It is dedicated to the Earl of Blessington but there is no reference to him as Grand Master. As he was not appointed until 27 December 1756 it seems likely that Laurence Dermott delayed publication of his book for two years and until such time as it was certain they would have 'a Noble Personage' to preside over them. The original price in London was three shillings but apparently elsewhere it was different, though whether more or less is unknown. Later editions were far more expensive and indeed it became quite a profitable undertaking, far more so than Anderson's *Constitutions*. Although it was Dermott's personal property he did not retain for himself the full benefit of the demand for his book. On 29 September 1785 Grand Lodge expressed thanks to him for 'his Condisention in giving his property in *Ahiman Rezon* to the Charity', whilst his generosity prior to this included the gift of a Grand Master's Throne at a cost of £34 which was quite a considerable sum in those days.

Apart from the introduction, 'The Editor to the Reader', only a small portion of the book is Dermott's own work. He writes:

> I placed the following Works round about me, so as to be convenient to have Recourse to them as Occasion should require, *viz.* Doctor *Anderson* [Anderson's *Constitutions* (?1738 edition)] and Mr. *Spratt* [Spratt's Irish *Constitutions* (1756)] directly before me, Doctor *D'Assigny* [*A Serious and Impartial Enquiry into the cause of the present Decay of Free-Masonry in the Kingdom of Ireland* (1744)] and Mr. *Smith* [*Pocket Companion* (1735)] on my Right-hand, Doctor *Desagulier* [?1723 edition of Anderson's *Constitutions*] and Mr. *Pennell* [Book of *Constitutions* (Dublin) 1730] on my left-hand, and Mr. *Scott* and Mr. *Lyon* behind me. [?Councillor Schott and Jacob Jehuda Leon, each of whom wrote a description of King Solomon's Temple and had a model of it on exhibition in London].

He made most use of Spratt's *Irish Constitutions*, in fact it could be said that most of *Ahiman Rezon* is a rewrite of that book which, in turn, is largely a rewrite of Anderson. His interest in Spratt's book seems to have dated from the time he was still a Master Mason in Ireland for in the list of subscribers to the 1744 edition there is included the name Laurence McDermott which almost certainly refers to him. If so, it is the only masonic reference to him in Ireland. When he came to write his own book of constitutions, no doubt his intense dislike of the Moderns caused him to avoid making direct use, as far as possible, of any book connected with that body. Nevertheless he makes virtually no reference to the Moderns in the original edition and we have to wait for the second edition of 1764 for his opening offensive against them.

Apparently Dermott was in two minds about one thing. He felt that he should

begin with a history of masonry as others had done 'from the Creation to the Time of their writing' but he did not wish to copy or imitate what Dr. Anderson had written in his *Constitutions*. He therefore queried 'Whether such Histories are of any Use in the secret Mysteries of the Craft' but says, nevertheless, that he wrote 'the first Volume of the History of Masonry'. However, whilst he slept a young puppy entered the room and, so he relates, 'eat a great Part' of what he had written. This he regarded 'as a bad Omen' which caused him 'to deviate from the general Custom of my worthy Predecessors, otherwise I would have published a History of Masonry.' It is difficult to accept this as being the truth but that he did not do so can hardly be regretted as it might well have been even more fanciful than that of James Anderson though the real reason must surely have been that the Antients had no history for him to relate.

Following the custom of those days, the book opens with a subservient dedication 'To The Right Honourable William, Earl of Blessington', possibly because Dermott had him in mind as a suitable Grand master. He was originally a member of a Modern Lodge meeting at the 'Bear and Harrow' in Butcher's Row, London, had been Grand Master of Ireland (1738–40) and was living in London when *Ahiman Rezon* was published, though as yet he was probably not an Antient mason. The dedication is followed by a series of articles gathered from various sources relating to the duties and characters of masons and the value of Free-Masonry. After these comes a list of Old Charges copied from Spratt's *Irish Constitutions*, 'The Manner of constituting a new Lodge' and four prayers, the last of which is entitled *Ahabath Olam* [Eternal Love], a 'Prayer repeated in the Royal Arch Lodge at Jerusalem'. Next comes the main section of the book, the real reason for it being printed, in which Dermott relies heavily upon Spratt and D'Assigny. First there is printed, a list of twenty-seven General Regulations copied from Spratt's *Irish Constitutions*, but with such alterations as Dermott considered necessary for use by the Antients. They are printed just as Spratt took them from Anderson, with the Old and the New Regulations in parallel columns. At the end of these is a new Regulation (No. 28) divided into ten sections, all of which deal with procedure in Grand Lodge, followed by ten Regulations for Charity, the Irish Regulations and those for York Masons being given in parallel columns. There is an interesting footnote to this section, 'They [i.e. the Antients] are called York-masons, because the first grand lodge in England was congregated at York A.D.926 by Prince Edwin, who (at the same time) purchased a free charter from king Athelstan, for the use of the fraternity.' This is a fable that has caused a great deal of misunderstanding and confusion both here and abroad and has resulted in so many American brethren, especially those whose Grand Lodges are of Antient origin, claiming that their ancestors were the York masons of the tenth century and that they work the ancient York rite.

Finally there are the words of sixty masonic songs, three of which are by Dermott himself, several Prologues and Epilogues and the words of *Solomon's Temple*, an oratorio performed in Dublin for the benefit of distressed Free-Masons.

Eight years later (1764) the second edition appeared with certain alterations, mainly of a minor nature, but it seems that Dermott now regarded his Grand Lodge as being on a firmer basis as he did not hesitate to write scornfully of the

Moderns, referring in most derogatory terms to some of their practices. In the frontispiece there appears for the first time 'The Arms of ye most ancient & Honorable Fraternity, of Free and Accepted Masons'. On the shield is depicted a lion in the first quarter, an ox in the second, a man in the third and an eagle in the fourth, with the Ark of the Covenant as the crest and two cherubim as supporters. Underneath, in Hebrew and English, is the motto 'Holiness to the Lord', all features that have special significance for Royal Arch masons.

There is a new section in which the rival bodies are compared. It is here that he says 'I had the like curiosity myself, about sixteen or seventeen years ago [i.e. 1747 or 1748] when I was first introduced into that society.' Later he adds 'I have not the least antipathy against the gentlemen members of the modern society; but on the contrary, love and respect them, because I have found the generality of them to be hearty cocks and good fellows (as the bacchanalian phrase is) . . .' These two statements would seem to confirm the suggestion previously made that shortly after arriving in England Dermott joined a Modern lodge. There is no documentary proof of this but it must be remembered that records in those days were far from being complete and it is difficult to understand how Dermott could have acquired sufficient experience of Modern freemasonry to 'make such specific remarks both here and elsewhere if he had done no more than visit one of their lodges.

He is conciliatory in his attitude when he concludes this section by writing 'And hope, that I shall live to see a general conformity and universal unity between the worthy masons of all denominations. This is the most earnest wishes and ardent prayers of ... Laurence Dermott.' This unity was something that was being discussed amongst Freemasons in the latter part of the eighteenth century and it is most unfortunate that Dermott did not devote his undoubted talents and organizing ability to bringing about such an eminently desirable union. Had he done so it might well have become an accomplished fact during his lifetime rather than twenty-two years afterwards. Indeed he might have played an important and memorable role in establishing a United Grand Lodge of England and the debt that freemasonry owes to him would have been so much greater. Perhaps, however, he was only paying lip-service to the idea or perhaps he was willing to consider it only if the Moderns conformed to the practices of the Antients for, elsewhere in his book, he did not hesitate to pour scorn on them in words that he cannot possibly have intended should be taken seriously: 'Nor is it uncommon for a tyler to receive ten or twelve shillings for drawing two sign posts with chalk &c. and writing Jamaica rum upon one, and Barbadoes rum upon the other, and all this (I suppose) for no other use, than to distinguish where those liquors are to be placed in the lodge. There are many other unconstitutional proceedings, which (to avoid giving offence) I pass over in silence.'

He certainly did this but he returned to the attack in the next edition [1778] which was revised by him whilst he was Deputy Grand Master and is shown as having been printed for James Jones, Grand Secretary. He pours scorn on Anderson's history of masonry, he makes several accusations of deceit, declares the premier Grand Lodge to have been irregular in its foundation, accuses them of having usurped the arms of the London Company of Masons and their title of 'free-masons' which, he says, that Company alone had the right to bear and he

charges them with having initiated eunuchs and women. He also accuses them of having corrupted pure and ancient freemasonry: 'It is a truth beyond contradiction, that the free and accepted Masons in Ireland, Scotland and the ancient Masons in England, have one and the same customs, usages, and ceremonies: But this is not the case with the modern Masons in England, who differ materially not only from the above, but from most Masons under Heaven.'

In addition, be ridicules their ceremonies, as for example: 'After many years observations on those ingenious methods of walking up to a brother, &c. I conclude, that the first was invented by a Man grievously afflicted with the Sciatica. The Second by a Sailor, much accustomed to the rolling of a Ship. And the third by a man, who for recreation or through excess of strong liquors, was wont to dance the drunken Peasant.' All that from one who protested that his 'most earnest wishes and ardent prayers' were for 'a general conformity and universal unity between the worthy masons of all denominations.'!!

A strange outcome of this second edition of *Ahiman Rezon* was the publication of an anonymous pamphlet bearing the over-lengthy title of *A Defence of Free-Masonry, as practised in the Regular Lodges. Both Foreign and Domestic, Under the Constitution of the English Grand Master. In which is contained, a Refutation of Mr. Dermott's absurd and ridiculous Account of Free-Masonry, in his book, entitled Ahiman Rezon; and the several Queries therein, reflecting on the Regular Masons, briefly considered and answered.* All the vituperation was not on the side of the Antients for this was a most scurrilous pamphlet and certainly reflected no credit on the Moderns. Henry Sadler (*Masonic Facts and Fictions*) suggests that John Revis, Grand Secretary of the Moderns 1734–56 and Deputy Grand Master 1757–63 was the author, or possibly his successor, Samuel Spencer, Grand Secretary 1757–68.

A third edition of *Ahiman Rezon* was published in 1778 and a fourth in 1787, the last English edition to be issued during Dermott's lifetime. There were later editions in 1800, 1801, 1807, *c.* 1810 and 1813, all edited by Thomas Harper, Deputy Grand Master of the Antients (1801–13) who no doubt was responsible for the deletion of much of Dermott's fiction. There were twenty-one Irish editions between 1760 and 1858 and numerous American editions from 1783 onwards. It was, in fact, adopted as the basis of their constitutions by the Grand Lodge of Ireland, and by seven Grand Lodges in America that were of Antient origin viz. North and South Carolina, Georgia, Maryland, Nova Scotia, Pennsylvania and Virginia. It may seem strange, especially in view of the close connection between them and the fact of their ceremonies being identical for all practical purposes, that it was not also adopted by the Grand Lodge of Scotland, but there were no official constitutions issued by that body in the eighteenth century.

When the first edition was published in 1756 the Antients' Grand Lodge was small and virtually unknown, having possibly some 30-odd active lodges and probably less than 500 active members, precise figures being impossible to ascertain. It had no history and, as indicated earlier, Dermott felt obliged to invent a most bizarre excuse for not including one. By the time the union came in 1813 it was well established both here and abroad and this was due very largely to Laurence Dermott and to his propaganda in the various editions of *Ahiman Rezon*,

writings that illustrate quite clearly his amazing energy and dynamic personality. By the time of his death in 1791, its purpose had been served and much of what he had written was omitted from the 1800 and subsequent editions but nevertheless echoes of his writings survive even today in the constitutions of various Grand Lodges.

THE EARLY YEARS

As previously indicated, there was a meeting or 'General Assembly' in July 1751 about which nothing is known except that a committee was appointed to draw up a set of Rules and Orders 'to be observed By the Most Ancient and Honble. Society of Free and Accepted Masons.' The committee apparently consisted of Bros. Philip Mc.Laughlin, Samuel Quay, James Shee, Joseph Kelly and the Grand Secretary, John Morgan. No lodges are indicated against their names but it is known from the entries in the General Register that Quay was a member of No. 2 meeting at the Turk's Head, Greek Street, Soho; Shee of No. 4 meeting at the Cannon, Water Lane, Fleet Street; Mc.Laughlin, Kelly and Morgan of No. 6 meeting at the Globe, Bridge Street, Covent Garden. Mc.Laughlin left for Ireland twelve days later and Shee followed him soon afterwards. Whether John Morgan was, in fact, Grand Secretary at the time or whether the account of the meeting was written at a later date, after he had been so appointed, it is impossible to say.

It could also mean that no lodges of Irishmen were in existence in London on 17 July 1751 and certainly there are no traces of any in either the Irish or the English records. An Irish lodge (No.145) was founded in Norwich on 24 July 1745 whilst the only one in London (No. 247 – Middle Temple) was not founded until 8 May 1754 and neither seems to have had any connection with the Antients. Probably, therefore, it was a meeting of Irish and other freemasons living in London who owed no allegiance to the Moderns' Grand Lodge and that one of the decisions taken that day was to form lodges for the purpose of creating a rival Grand Lodge, lodges that subsequently received Warrants bearing that date, viz. 17 July 1751. Certainly there must have been other unrecorded decisions taken at that meeting for it is inconceivable that a General Assembly would be called for the sole purpose of appointing a committee to draw up a set of rules.

The first rule provided for regular committee meetings on the first Wednesday of each month at the Turk's Head so there could have been six such meetings between then and the first recorded meeting on 5 February 1752. On the other hand it is not known when these Rules were adopted and as it was agreed that the Master of Lodge No. 2 should take the Chair at the first meeting and the other Masters in turn subsequently, it could be that were only two such meetings as James Hagerty, who took the chair on 5 February 1752, was the Master of No. 4 and at the following meetings the Masters of Nos. 5, 6, 7, 8 and 9 took the Chair in that order. It seems that John Morgan omitted to make a record of whatever was discussed on these occasions which is most regrettable as if he had we should probably know far more about the origin of the Antients. It was fortunate that he resigned his office at the February meeting and it was fortunate also that Laurence Dermott was appointed to succeed him for Dermott wrote the minutes

of that and of later meetings. We might also know why, instead of meeting at the Turk's Head as specified in the Rules, meetings were held first of all at the Griffin Tavern in Holborn, then at the Temple in Shire Lane and at other hostelries. At the next meeting on 4 March 1752, complaints were considered: '... against Thomas Phealon and John Mackey, better known by the name of leg of Mutton Masons – In the course of the examination it appear'd that Phealon and Mackey had initiated many persons for the mean consideration of a leg of mutton for dinner or supper, to the disgrace of the Ancient Craft, that it was difficult to discover who assisted them if any as they seldom met in the same Alehouse. That Mackey was an Empric in Phsic; and both imposter in Masonry.' It was agreed that these two men should 'not be admitted into any Ancient Lodge during their natural lives.'

On 1 April 1752, the by-laws for private lodges drawn up by John Morgan and Philip Mc.Laughlin were compared with those submitted by Laurence Dermott of his mother lodge No. 26 (Dublin) and the latter were adopted as being more correct, though strangely enough, Dermott did not include them in the first edition of *Ahiman Rezon* (1756), which, in effect, was the book of Constitutions of the Antients. The by-laws of the Antient Lodge No. 20, meeting at the 'Hampshire Hog', Goswell Street, London and dating from this time (2 October 1753) appear in *AQC 32* pp. 115–8. They could well be identical with those submitted by Laurence Dermott, especially as they are virtually the same as those published by the Antients in 1771 for use by their lodges.

It was reported that there had been no success in finding a nobleman to accept an appointment as Grand Master and indeed Laurence Dermott begged the Committee to 'postpone the business until they had made choice of some proper place to receive and install his Lordship, the Temple Eating House being very unfit for that business.' This resulted in 'many altercations on both sides, not fit to be written' and the matter was therefore postponed.

At the meeting on St. John the Baptist's Day (24 June 1752):

> Having no Grand Master nor Grand Warden to Install the Grand Secretary was Reinstall'd according to the ancient Custom and manner of installing Grand Secretaries. And having gone through that ceremony he was proclaim'd and saluted accordingly. After which he repeated the whole Ceremony of Installing Grand &c in the manner which he had learn'd from Brother Edward Spratt Esqr. the Celebrated Grand Secretary of Ireland. The long Recital of this Solemn Ceremony gave great satisfaction to the Audience, many of which who never had an Opportunity of hearing the like before.

Minutes of other meetings at this time show the Grand Lodge concerned with day by day matters, even including petty squabbles in lodges. Some of them had an amusing twist, as for example:

> 1.7.1752   Moses Willoughby, who was ordered to refund nine shillings to John Robinson, was expelled because he declared that 'he would not conform to the Rules of any Society upon Earth by which he should lose nine shillings.'

Other typical entries are:

2.9.1752   It was agreed that every sick member 'shall receive one penny per week from every Registered mason in London & Westmister.'

14.9.1752   The Grand Committee was given power to 'grant Warrants and dispensation for forming and holding Lodges Otherwise the Ancient Craft, must dwindle into nothing.' Again, if an Antients' Committee had been in existence since the 1730s this says little for the efforts of its members.

6.12.1752   Upon a motion for the thanks of the General Committee to be given 'to the G.S. Dermott for the many pleasing Instructions which he had so often Administer'd to the Brethren,' four members protested that 'instead of being useful he had actually Sung & lectured the Brethren out of their senses'. Dermott replied that if the 'Grand Committee would allow him an hour's time . . . he would endeavour to sing them into their senses again.'

3.1.1753   It was resolved unanimously 'That every Member of a Regular Ancient Lodge in or about this Metropolis Shall Contribute the sum of four pence per month Towards raising a Charitable fund for the Relief of Indigent Free Masons.'
              [Note: There are many entries about this time dealing with applications for relief and with similar routine affairs.]

6.6.1753   'Heard – a petition from John Doughty and others praying to be Constituted into a regular lodge the petition was rejected.' No reason given.

13.7.1753   '. . . it appear'd that some persons of late had walked before the Corps in immitation of a Modern Lodge who had so done. It also appear'd that the Antient Masons had formerly walked in the following manner viz.,

Tylers
Corps
Mourners
Youngest Members of the Junior Lodge
Eldest Members of the Junior Lodge
Past Officers of the Junior Lodge
Deacons
Wardens
Master
The next youngest Lodge in the same manner &c.
The
Grand Officers (if attending) in the Rear
and
The whole procession revers'd in coming back.

5.9.1753   '. . . it Appear'd that . . . Gibbons, Bowen and Storer &c more guilty of misdemeanours and irregularities . . . in divesting the said Master without any Just Cause &c Agreed and Order'd that our worthy Brother John Smith aforesaid shall be reinstated in the Chair and Dignity.'

3.10.1753   The first provincial lodge (No. 24) was approved and warranted on 17 October 1753 to meet at the Edinburgh Castle, March Street, Bristol. It lapsed about 1765.

17.3.1754   'Open'd to hear a proposal for a play to be perform'd in the little Theatre in the Hay Market for the benefit of Indigent Free Masons.' Evidently this did not provide the hoped for benefit as:

3.4.1754   'Recd. Mr. Lauder's Bill and paid accordingly viz. for the expenses of a play for the Benefit of Indigent Masons Brother Lauder Charg'd four pounds Eight shillings and sixpence more than was Recd. at the Theatre or otherwise on Acct. of the play which Charge was immediately paid.'

6.11.1754	It was resolved that 'Grand Lodge cease meeting on the first Wednesday in every Kallendar month and instead thereof They shall (only) meet on the first Wednesdays in March, June, Sepr. and Decr. and on both St. Johns' days early Except in cases of emmergency this Regulation to Commence on the Twenty seventh day of December next'. This is the origin of the present Quarterly Communications of the United Grand Lodge of England, now held on the second Wednesdays in these months.
27.12.55	In a memorandum to these minutes Dermott could not resist an opportunity to pour scorn on the rival Grand Lodge. He wrote 'This year 1755. The Modern Masons began to make use of Certificates: Though the Ancient Masons had granted Certificates time immemorial.' This arose out of the minutes of the Moderns' Grand Lodge for 24 July 1755 which mentioned the issue of Grand Lodge certificates though there was no suggestion that it was an innovation.
	It is tempting to think that perhaps this caused Dermott to introduce into the certificates of the Antients a reference to the legendary meeting of masons at York in the year 926 for it was soon after this that the wording was altered to commence: 'We the Grand Lodge of the most Ancient and Honourable Fraternity of Free and Accepted Masons (according to the Old Constitutions granted by his Royal Highness Prince Edwin at York, Anno Domini Nine hundred twenty and six, and in the year of Masonry, Four thousand Nine hundred twenty and six) ...'
1.3.1758	William Welch was excluded for 'Attempting to Ravish two of the Brethren's Wives &c &c &c' whereupon he called upon 'the Women to make an Affidavit (before some Magistrate) of the crime they lay to his charge.'
	Received and considered a letter from the Grand Secretary in Dublin 'wherein he assured the Grand Lodge of Antient Masons in London that the Grand Lodge of Antient Masons in London that the Grand Lodge of Ireland did mutually concur in a strict Union with the Antient Grand Lodge in London and promised to keep a Constant Correspondence with them.'
6.12.1758	The first declaration that a lodge (No. 13) was 'vacant'. The offer of two guineas by Lodge No. 63 to purchase its Warrant and assume 'the Name Number and Rank of Lodge No. 13' was accepted.
5.9.1759	'Heard a petition (for a provincial Grand Warrant) from the Brethren at Philadelphia which petition was Seconded by the Officers of No. 2.'
5.12.1759	'The Grand Secretary made a long and labour'd speech against any victular being chosen a Grand Officer, which speech gave great Offence to some persons in the Grand Lodge.' A vote was therefore taken as to whether the speech merited applause or censure when there were 44 for applause against 4 for censure, whereupon the Deputy Master said '... by which it seems there are only 4 Publicans in the Room.'
5.12.1759	In the minutes of this meeting appeared the oft-quoted Memorandum: 'The private collection made for Carroll above mention'd [An Irish mason in need of assistance] amounted to five Guineas. It appeared that William Carroll a Certified freemason of Dublin petitioned the Modern Masons (not knowing any difference) and that Mr. Spencer then Secretary to the Modern Society sent out Answer to Carroll's petition in the following words viz. 'Your being an Ancient Mason you are not entitled to any of our Charity the Antient Masons have a lodge at the five Bells in the Strand &c their Secretary's name is Dermott. Our Society is neither Arch, Royal Arch or Antient so that you have no Right to partake of our Charity.' The petitioner

Carroll delivered the original paper Written by Mr. Spencer to Mr. Dermott G.S. in whose custody it remains.'

24.6.1760 ... The R.W.D.: G: M gave a Charge relative to the admission of visitors Concluded with the following Toasts viz.

1. The King & the Craft	9
2. The RWGM Earl Blessington	9
3. Deputy Osborn	7
4. G. Wardens	5
5. Lodges in General	9
6. The G Sec. Dermott	3

24.6.1761 Dermott was thanked 'for his unwearied diligence and Eminent Services to the Ancient Craft in General' and was saluted with five. He expressed the hope that in future he might be saluted with three but the Deputy Grand Master proposed that he should be saluted with the years of his age. He was then saluted with thirty-nine though in actual fact, he was in his forty-first year.

2.6.1762 It was agreed that 'a Constant Correspondence shall be kept with the G.L. of Ireland' ... 'And whereas the Grand Lodge of Ireland have agreed and firmly Resolved not to admit any Sojourner from England (as a Member or petitioner &c) without producing a Certificate (of his Good Behaviour) under the seal of the Ancient Grand Lodge in London. A like stipulation was agreed in respect of brethren from Ireland 'before he or they can be admitted as a Member or Receive any part of the General Charity.'

6.6.1764 Dermott was proposed as Treasurer but he obviously preferred to remain as Secretary and therefore declined.

12.6.1767 For the first time there is a record of Stewards being appointed for the 'Grand Feast'.

In view of the claims made by previous writers it must be emphasized once again that the impression gained from a study of the records of the Antients' Grand Lodge over the first ten years is that of a small and newly-created organization rather than of a body that had been in existence for some twenty years and had only suffered a change of name in 1751. Its first task had been to draw up a set of Rules and Orders, the obvious duty of any newly-created body. There is nowhere any suggestion that it was taking over, revising, or expanding the Rules and Orders of any Committee. Nowhere is there even the slightest hint of any previous administration. Nowhere is there reference to any brother who had previously served a committee of Antient masons in any capacity, nowhere are thanks expressed for former services. It seems impossible that there could have been a previous Committee but if there was it disappeared without leaving the slightest trace of its existence, just as though it had never been. In actual fact a new Grand Lodge came into existence doing precisely what a new Grand Lodge might be expected to do, concerned with securing its future, involved in day by day routine affairs but gradually, as it expanded, passing over more and more of these cases to the Stewards' Lodge.

The exact number of lodges, Antient and Modern, by 1760 is difficult to ascertain. The Antients had warranted 80 lodges and the Moderns 252, but the numbers of active lodges were possibly in the region of 50 and 200. Whatever may

be the truth of the matter the foundation of the Antient's Grand Lodge had been
well and truly laid.

THE LATER YEARS

By 1768 it can be said that the Grand Lodge of the Antients was firmly established
even though it had not as yet caused the Moderns any very great concern. As
previously indicated, this success was due in no small measure to the untiring
work of Laurence Dermott. But for him the antients might have faded away as,
later on, did the Grand Lodge of All England at York, the Grand Lodge of
England South of the River Trent and the Grand Lodge of Wigan, whilst at best
it might have degenerated into a Benefit Society and ultimately have suffered the
fate of most of those societies that sprang up in the eighteenth and early nineteenth
centuries. As it was, the organization of the Antient's Grand Lodge under Dermott's supervision was on a very efficient basis for those days and compared
favourable with that of the premier Grand Lodge which was often of a haphazard
or dilettante nature.

The one aspect in which Dermott had not been immediately successful was that
of securing a nobleman as Grand Master as had the Moderns from 1721 onwards.
Provision for a Grand Master had been made in the Rules and Orders of 1751
and 'the Rt. Honble. Lords George Sackville, Chesterfield, Ponsoby, Inchiquin
and Blesington' had all been approached without success though it seems doubtful
if some of them were Antient freemasons. Finally on 5 December 1753, 'it being
doubtful whether the Antient Craft cou'd be honour'd with a Noble GM at this
time' Robert Turner, the Master of Lodge No. 15 meeting at the Kings Head,
Mary le Bone Street, had been elected for a term of six months and installed as
their first Grand Master, with William Rankin as Deputy Grand Master and
Samuel Quay and Lachlan Mc.Intosh as Grand Wardens. The next meeting on
27 December 1753 was referred to for the first time as a meeting of Grand Lodge,
not of the Grand Committee, and was therefore opened 'in Ample form'. Robert
Turner had been re-elected for a further term of six months when he was succeeded
by the Hon. Edward Vaughan who served for two years and at the Grand Lodge
Meeting on 27 December 1756, Laurence Dermott had been able at last to
announce that he had persuaded a nobleman to accept nomination as Grand
Master. He was 'The Right Worshipll. and Right Honourable William Stuart,
Earl of Blesington, Viscount Mountjoy, Baron of Rawalton and Baronet' who
had been Grand Master of Ireland 1738–9. He was duly proclaimed Grand Master
of Masons even though he was not present and was therefore installed by proxy.
He remained Grand Master for four years but there is no record that he ever
attended a meeting of Grand Lodge though he signed warrants and dealt with
other matters.

He was followed by a succession of five Grand Masters, one of whom was also
Grand Master of Ireland and three of Scotland including the 3rd and 4th Dukes
of Atholl (1771–81 and 1791–1813) as a result of which the Grand Lodge became
known as 'The Atholl Grand Lodge'. Finally in November 1813, H.R.H. Edward
Duke of Kent succeeded John, 4th Duke of Atholl and thus officiated as Grand

Master of the Antients in the final arrangements that led up to the union with the Moderns and the foundation of the United Grand Lodge of England on 27 December 1813.

The second volume of minutes covering the period 31 January 1769 to 27 December 1773 shows the Grand Lodge still involved in domestic affairs as in the previous eighteen years, still concerned at intervals with the clandestine making of masons but showing increasing signs of responsibility as a governing body of freemasons not only in England but in countries overseas. Nevertheless, trivial and amusing affairs still occupied their attention from time to time as on 4 September 1782 when 'By desire of the D:G:M: all the Members present Solamly promised that they should not make use of any indecent languige against a Noble Grand Master & they Positively promised that they would Immadiatly give notice to the Grand Lodge Assembled of any one who for the future dare to make any Illiberal Speach against any Noble Grand Master that such person may be delt with accordingly.' Presumably, if he were not a nobleman it did not matter!

On 30 January 1771 'His Grace John Duke of Atholl was 'Unanimously Chosen Grand Master' and on 2 March 1771 was '(after the Manner of Gd. Masters of Israel) [sic] solemnly Installed in Soloman's Chair,' following which he invested Laurence Dermott as his Deputy. Dermott continued to act as Grand Secretary until the meeting on 6 March 1771 when William Dickey Junior was elected as his successor and he then signed as such for the last time: 'Here Ends the minutes taken by Lau. Dermott G S from the year 1751 to the year 1771.'

Later this same year is a record of what seems nowadays to be a peculiar practice of the Antients when a provincial lodge was to be consecrated, that of authorizing an experienced local freemason to perform the ceremony by appointing him Deputy Grand Master for three hours only.

The minute reads:

Grand Lodge opened at 11 O'Clo: in the Morning at the Castle Inn in the City of Exeter (Devonre:) Decemr: 23 1771.
Jno. Marsh (P:M: No: 74) in the Chair D:G:M: by an Authty: (for 3 hours only) from L. Dermott Esqr: D:G: Master.
    Installed Mr. Wm: Taylor   Master
               Jno. Waters   Sr. Warden:
               Saml: Page   Jr Warden:
    Prest: The Officers & Members of Lodge No. 74.
All matters relative to this Constitution being compleated Bro: Marsh by the Authority aforesaid Proclaimed the Lodge duly Constituted No. 170 Regested: in the Grand Lodge Vol. 7 letter G. – to be held in his Majesty's 3d. Regt. of Foot upon the 1st: Tuesday in each Kalender Month – Closed & Adjourn'd to the General Grand Lodge in London.

It is therefore of interest to note that this practice was not confined to England for there is a record of a similar meeting on 18 October 1781 in New York when the Rev. William Walter, Provincial Grand Master elect, was appointed Deputy Grand Master 'for three hours only' to consecrate Lodge No. 213 'to be held in the fourth Batallion Royal Regt, of Artillery'. Another such meeting was held on 21 February 1782, Bro the Rev. William Walter again officiating, to consecrate a lodge in 'the Second Regt. of Anspach Berauth', the minutes reading rather

quaintly 'Installed according to Ancient Usage – Maximilian De Strait, Master – the Rev. John Phillip Esq., S.W. vice David Schoeph, absent – George Daig, J.W. vice Ferd. Foerster, dead.' Even more strange is a third such meeting in the following month when all three of the principal officers of the new lodge 'to be held at the Royal Exchange in New York, North America,' were absent though no reasons were given.

That the Antients were seeking closer contact with other Grand Lodges and thereby isolating the Grand Lodge of the Moderns is shown in the minutes of their meeting on 2 September 1772 when it was resolved that 'It is the Opinion of this Grand Lodge, that a Brotherly Connexion and Correspondence with the Right W:G: Lodge of Ireland, has been, and will always be found productive of Honour and Advantage to the Craft in both Kingdoms'. It was also proposed 'that a Correspondence should be opened by this Grand Lodge with the Grand Lodge of Scotland'. This close liaison was soon to prove of value to the Antients as is shown in the minutes of the Grand Lodge meeting on 15 December 1773:

> Heard a letter from Lodge No. 148 at Gibraltar setting forth that in the month of Decemr. last they received a Summons for to Assemble with other lodges on St. John's Day the 27th: of said Month, in order to proceed in Procession to Church, which meeting they attended accordingly; that a set of People who had their authority from the Modern Grand Lodge thought proper to dispute the legality of said Warrant No. 148 &c. and proceeded to other Unwarrantable Measures; that in said Garrison there was also held the lodges, No. 11, 244, 290, 359, 420 and 466 on the Registry of Ireland and No. 58 on the Registry of Scotland that during these proceedings the lodges No. 290, 11, 244 and 466 on the Irish Registry supported the Lodge No. 148 as become Men & Masons as fully appeared in their letter sent the 3d. last May to the Deputy Grand Sectry. of Ireland; Also read the Answer of the R:W: Grand Lodge of Ireland to said letter.
>
> Order'd – That the thanks of his Grand Lodge be convey'd to the R:W: Grand Lodge of Ireland for their immediate Answer to the lodges No. 290, 11, 244 & 466.
>
> That the thanks of the R:W: Grand Lodge be conveyed to

Robt. Dowling	Master		
Michl. Clarke	S:W:	No. 290	
Peter Reid	Master		
Wm. Wilson	S:W:	No. 11	Upon the Registry
Thos. Surman	Master		of Ireland.
John Lowry	S:W:	No. 244	
Anthy. Brown	Master		
Willm. Apslin	S:W:	No. 466	

> for the noble stand they made in supporting the legality of Lodge No. 148 (under our Sanction) to the General Benefit of the Antient Craft.

Further evidence of the antagonism between the two Grand Lodges and of the uncertainty on the part of individual lodges appears on 1 June 1774 when it was reported that several Antient lodges both in England and abroad also held Warrants from the Moderns and that several had remitted money for charity to the Moderns under the impression that they were sending it to the Antients. It was decided to warn these lodges that unless they surrendered their Modern Warrants, their Antient Warrants would be cancelled. At the same time an inducement to Modern lodges to transfer their allegiance to the Antients was made by the offer

of a Warrant at a reduced fee. What effect this may have had is unknown but certainly the Antients were making considerable progress by this time as is shown in a letter sent by the Grand Master to the Grand Secretary in which he said 'It gives me pleasure to find that in all parts of the World the Ancient Craft *is regaining its ground* over the Moderns.' The words I have given in italics emphasize the contention of the Antients that when the Grand Lodge of the Moderns was founded in 1717 it began to corrupt the Craft and that they, the Antients, were restoring it to its true and proper form.

There is a further example of this on 6 September 1775 when letters exchanged with the Grand Lodge of Scotland are recorded in full. William Preston, founder of the Prestonian lectures, who had been initiated in an Antient lodge but had changed his allegiance to the Moderns and, with the fervour of a convert, had become a bitter opponent of the Antients, applied to the Grand Lodge of Scotland for a list of their Grand Officers and of the lodges under their jurisdiction. Before replying the Grand Secretary referred to the Antients' Grand Lodge and was promptly told its opinion of Bro Preston and informed that its lodges 'preserve the Universal Practice of the Royal Craft as appears by the Brethren now Assembled, several of whom were made in Scotland, Ireland, Asia & America' and that 'We so streniously Insist and most Religiously Declare that the Masonical Practice of the Gentlemen called Modern Masons (now under the sanction of Lord Petrie) is contrary to the Ancient & Universal Custom of the Royal Craft'. The latter concluded with the wish 'that our United Grand Lodges may ever be famed for handing down the Royal Art according to its Original Institution which is the only means for Masons of every Place and Language to be known to each other.' Bro Mason, Grand Secretary of the Grand Lodge of Scotland, then replied to Bro Preston and referred him to the Antients' Grand Secretary, Bro William Dickey, for the information he required. This brought forth a spirited reply in which Bro Preston regretted that the Grand Lodge of Scotland 'had been so grossly imposed upon, as to have establish'd a Correspondence with an irregular body of men who falsely assume the appallation of Antient Masons'. As proof of this he enclosed part of his *History of Masonry in England from the revival of the Grand Lodge in 1717* which explained 'the Origin of these irregular Masons'. He concluded with an expression of his desire 'to convince you that our Society is the only Antient and respectable Body of Masons, And that the other Masons here who falsely assume the Appellation have no such Vouchers to produce, and are of too recent a Date and of too unconstitutional an Origin to Merit the favour or patronage of either the Grand Lodge of Scotland or Ireland'.

In this wish he was entirely without success though Scotland did write to the Antients' Grand Lodge that 'We are by no means competent Judges of the differences subsisting between your Grand Lodge and that held under the Patronage of Lord Petrie. But since we have had the honor of opening a Correspondence with you, we have every reason to entertain the most Respectful opinion of your Grand Lodge.' This may indicate some doubt on their part as to whether they had chosen the right Grand Lodge in England but that having made the decision, they were going to stand by it. Had the Moderns had a Grand Secretary of Dermott's calibre and had they regarded the Grand Lodges of Ireland and Scotland

as partners rather than, in Anderson's words, as 'affecting Independency . . . under their own Grand Masters,' their standing in 1813 might have put them in a much more favourable state for negotiating the terms of a union. As it was the Antients strengthened their position by presenting gold medals to the Duke of Leinster, Past Grand Master of the Grand Lodge of Ireland, to Sir James Adolphus Oughton, Past Grand Master of the Grand Lodge of Scotland, for their 'attachment to the welfare and Dignity of the Ancient Rites of the Craft' and to Bro William Mason 'for the obliging and punctual manner in which he had conducted himself relative to the matter between our Grand Lodges.' One cannot help wondering if the hand of Laurence Dermott lay behind this. In expressing his appreciation of the honour, Bro Mason wrote that the Grand Clerk, Bro David Bolt was really entitled 'at least to the one half of it, as he co-operated with me in every Measure tending to bring that Affair to a Conclusion'. Grand Lodge took the hint and sent him a silver medal. Bro Corker, Grand Secretary of the Grand Lodge of Ireland, had to wait until June 1783 for his gold medal.

There were others who held views similar to those of Bro Preston even if they did not express them quite as forcibly. Lodge No. 174 at Southampton and Lodge No. 200 at Salisbury both reported that Bro Dunkerley, Provincial Grand Master of the Moderns, had queried the legality of their Warrants and subsequently in his reply to them, had queried the standing and authority of the Deputy Grand Master, Bro Dermott. Even the intervention of the Duke of Atholl did not cause Bro Dunkerley to alter his views as on 27 December 1777 the Grand Master advised Grand Lodge 'that Mr. Dunkerley had wrote him another letter relative to the affair at Salisbury, which he was determined to treat with the contempt it merited.'

The year 1784 saw problems of another nature as the former Grand Secretary, Bro Bearblock, failed to provide any accounts for the previous three years or to settle his indebtedness to the Grand Lodge, whatever it may have been, and was therefore excluded. Another matter that was not settled satisfactorily, at least for the two Grand Lodge employees concerned, was their application for increases in salary as the Grand Secretary 'was ordered to tell them to do their duty better and the Grand Lodge might take it into consideration.'

Dermott's health was beginning to fail by this time but that did not prevent his constant attention to masonic matters. Although too ill to attend Grand Lodge on 27 December 1784 he wrote a letter to be read at that meeting in which he stated that irregularities had occurred in the election of the Grand Officers. The following is an extract:

> I am not officially acquainted with the proceedings of the last meeting But by what I have learned they were Erroneous in attempting to recind the Confirmed Acts of a Grand Lodge in due form 1st Sept. – It is amazing!!! that amongst such a Number of Officers, Old Masons and even Candidates for the Secretaryship none shd be found to point out the Futility of such a measure or remember the difference between a Grand Lodge in form – A Grand Lodge in due form and a Grand Lodge in Ample form – Forms so materially significant Defined and useful in the Genl Govornmt of the Fraternity as to have been Constantly observed and Continued amongst the Craft in this Kingdom for upwd of 858 years. It requires but a Moderate share of Commen Sense to know that no

Act Law Regulation Order or Decree can be Reversed Rescinded nor repealed without a
power equal to that by which it was first made and Confirmed . . . for the truth of this see
Doctr. Anderson's Constitutions p. 162 . . .

It will be noticed that in stating 'upwd of 858 years', Dermott was referring to the
legendary assembly of Masons supposed to have been called by Prince Edwin at
York in AD 926.

It is not surprising to read a comment in the minutes to the effect that: 'The
Grand Lodge paused for some time after reading the above letter.' However, after
recovering from the shock, the members passed a vote of censure on the letter and
on the conduct of the Deputy Grand Master which they described as 'Arbitrary
if not altogether illegal'. As Dermott had written that Grand Lodge would not be
in order in proclaiming the Rt. Hon. the Earl of Antrim as Grand Master and in
installing the Grand Wardens, his action seems to have been tactless at the least
as he knew that a copy of the minutes would automatically be sent to the Grand
Master and there would seem to be reason for agreeing with the wording of the
vote of censure when it was contended that he had ample time to obtain any
documents from the Grand Master that might have been necessary. In a letter
submitting the minutes to the Grand Master and signed by the two Grand Wardens
and the Grand Secretary, a profound apology was included for what had transpired
and the hope was expressed that their conduct in the matter would be approved
by him.

At a Grand Lodge meeting on 31 January 1785 which was specially summoned
on authority of the Grand Master, Dermott read a letter from him in which he,
Dermott, was re-appointed Deputy Grand Master and the hope was expressed
that the matter 'might be buried in Oblivian'. Evidently Dermott was far from
satisfied as the minutes record not only that 'the said letter was read twice &
R.W.D. put the same into his pocket without any motion made thereupon by the
lodge,' but also that he then called upon the Grand Secretary for his accounts,
'insisting upon his right to see the same'. There was a long and undignified wrangle
between the two in which only the Grand Secretary, Bro Leslie, emerged with any
credit and after his accounts were approved, Dermott declared again that 'He
would not work with Secy. Leslie and recapitulated many old supposed grievances
between them upon which the Grand Lodge got into Confusion and Disorder for
some time.' However, as Bro Leslie had previously indicated that he would not
consider re-election, that problem was solved. At the following meeting, the vote
of censure passed on Dermott was rescinded, but only by a majority, whilst a
eulogistic vote of thanks to Bro Leslie for his 'faithful Diligent upright & Obliging
Conduct during his Secretaryship' was passed with only one dissenting voice. It
is not recorded if it was Dermott's voice.

What the Antients undoubtedly regarded as an important victory in their war
with the Moderns is reported in a letter dated 20 march 1786 sent by the Grand
Secretary to the Grand Master in which he informed him:

That the Ancient Craft under your Worship's Auspicious [Patronage(?)] is in a flourish-
ing State, daily increasing in wealth and Numbers: Amongst other pleasing matters too
tedious to relate – the Provincial Grand Lodge of Andalusia in Spain which has been
under the Government of the Modern Grand Lodge for upwards of 20 years past, have

lately petitioned for a new provincial Grand Warrant under your Lordship's Sanction. The prayer of which petition has been Granted by the Deputy Grand Master (Dermott) who has sent one of your Lordship's Warrant with an Order for a regular Installation &c.

This incident is much to the honour of the Ancient Craft As the Grand Lodge of Andalusia is Composed of General and subaltern Officers (none under the degree of an Ensign) in His Majesty's Service: and who have refused to act under the Authority of the Modern Masons; Though His Royal Highness the Duke of Cumberland is said to be their Grand Master!!!

They were also delighted to have evidence of a closer link with the Grand Lodge of Scotland as shown in a 'brotherly visitation of the Right Honourable and Most Worshipful Lord Elcho, Grand Master of Scotland' to their Grand Master's Lodge No. 1. In writing to express their appreciation the opportunity of firing a further salvo against the Moderns was too tempting to be missed:

> The Innovation which have of late crept into Masonry in the Kingdom, & which are happily unknown to the Lodges over which Your Lordship presides, as they tend to affect the integrity of the System, it is the duty of the Brotherhood to discountenance. We trust the time is not distant when sensible of the inconvenience as well as the ffault of the Deviation, they will come back within the Ancient landmarks of the Craft – when that Correction shall be Wrought, they will discover the nature & influence of pure Masonry, in the conciliatory Disposition which it gives to those, who feel and who practice its principles aright.

Lord Elcho replied saying that he, too, regretted the introduction of innovations which he considered to be highly improper and he expressed the hope that those who had deviated from pure masonry would soon return ' to that perfect model so properly exhibited in every Instance in the Grand Masters Lodge.'

On 6 June 1792 there is first mention of something that may have had a bearing on the subsequent negotiations leading up to the union of the two Grand Lodges and that was the appointment of H.R.H. Prince Edward as Provincial Grand Master for Lower Canada as on his return to England two years later he was presented with an address expressing 'the confident hope that under the conciliating influence of your Royal Highness, the Fraternity in general of Freemasons in His Majesty's dominions will soon be united' and His Royal Highness expressed himself as being in sympathy with such hope. Obviously the Antients had become well established by this time, not only in Canada but elsewhere overseas, for there is constant reference to correspondence with Nova Scotia, Gibralter [sic], Quebec, Pennsylvania, Maryland and elsewhere. Five years later, at the Grand Lodge meeting of 6 December 1797, there is the first mention of any action aimed at a union with the Moderns when: 'It was Moved by Brother Moreton of No. 63 and seconded by Gillevery Past Master of No. 3 That a Committee be Appointed by this R.W.Grand Lodge to meet one that may be appointed by the Grand Lodge of Modern Masonry and with them to Effect a Union. The Previous question was thereupon moved and Carried *almost* Unanimously.' [My italics]. There is no mention of any such committee being appointed and what was the outcome of this first tentative approach by the Antients towards a union is unknown.

There is an interesting discussion recorded on 6 June 1804 when consideration was given to the propriety or otherwise of initiating candidates who were not

perfect in body whereupon R.W. Bro Burwood P.S.G.W. stated that he had lately initiated a cripple but that 'after hearing the 3rd. & 4th Charges from the Constitutions of Masonry read from the Chair the impropriety of such proceedings touching upon the Ancient Land marks and tending to bring the Craft into Contempt and Disrepute' made him realize that he was in error. He promised not to do such a thing again but was nevertheless 'reprimanded from the Chair'. It was agreed that the initiate should be registered in the Grand Lodge books on the understanding that it should not be taken as a precedent but there is a laconic footnote reading 'Never was returned nor registered' so possibly he was quietly removed from the ranks of freemasonry. A somewhat similar problem was considered at the Grand Lodge meeting on 23 November 1808 when the Master and Wardens of Lodge No. 240 attended and admitted that 'they had *inadvertently* [my italics] Initiated and Crafted a Black Man, not free born, nor a fit person to be admitted to the Honor of Masonry and undertook to return his Money and not to proceed further in the Business.'

A very different matter was considered by the Stewards Lodge on 16 April 1806 when it was reported that 'Bros Tuffield and Allen of Lodge No. 264 and Bro Ward of Lodge No. 234 had taken upon themselves to address His Royal Highness the Duke of Kent and requested His Royal Highness to accept and take upon himself the Office of Grand Master and to which address his Royal Highness had been pleased to return an Answer under the Impression that the said address had been written by the Order of or under the Sanction of the Grand Lodge.' It would be most interesting to know precisely what the Duke said in reply but there is no record of this. Presumably he declined but had he accepted, Grand Lodge would have been in a most embarrassing position. The three brethren were summoned to appear before the next meeting of the Stewards Lodge when it was 'Resolved that such Conduct is highly reprehensible and Contrary to the Laws and Regulations of Masonry' and it was ordered that they 'be severely reprimanded from the Chair' and told 'that such like Conduct will in no Case be permitted to pass in future.' One can only say that the terms in which the members of the Stewards Lodge expressed themselves were very mild indeed and that the punishment was hardly made 'to fit the crime'.

By this time the Antients were showing signs of increasing stability and prosperity and of reaching parity with the Moderns, indeed they already exceeded their rivals numerically in Canada and America. Many of their members were still artisans of Irish nationality and, indeed, all nineteen founders of a lodge in Manchester in 1795 were muslin weavers and members of lodges on the register of the Grand Lodge of Ireland. However, they were also attracting persons of considerably higher social standing, as for example Sir Watkin Lewes, Knight, Alderman of and Member of Parliament for the City of London. The Grand Lodge minutes begin to take on a more stereotyped style but nevertheless give the impression of being those of a responsible body concerned rather less than in the past with routine affairs such as the relief of indigent brethren and payment of funeral fees, matters that were now dealt with by the Stewards Lodge. The minutes, in fact, tend to be tantalizingly brief at times as on 5 September 1804 when, after giving a list of the Grand Officers present there is the concise statement that 'All

business being over the Grand Lodge was closed.' Not until 1809 is there any further reference to the possibility of a union between the two Grand Lodges though obviously wiser counsels were beginning to prevail and no doubt many unofficial approaches and informal discussions took place behind the scenes.

TOWARDS A UNION

For a considerable time there remained bitter feelings on the part of some members of both Grand Lodges and certain private lodges, both Antient and Modern, were extreme in their attitudes but, especially in the provinces, there were indications of a gradual drawing together both as regards ritual and administration and inter-visiting undoubtedly increased. In particular it seems that many Modern brethren were beginning to show a preference for the ceremonies of the Antients and to accept them as representing the original and pure form of freemasonry, a tendency that resulted in some lodges obtaining warrants from both Grand Lodges. Thus it was that when a union eventually became possible, a spirit of toleration existed on both sides and although so many of the usages and customs of the Antients prevailed, it was not so much a matter of the Antients dictating terms but rather of the moderates on both sides agreeing on a common policy.

The first definite move on the part of the Antients was on 6 September 1809 when:

> Bror: Jeremy Cranfield P M of 255 again brought forward a Motion presented and afterwards withdrawn at the Meeting of Gd. Lodge 7th June last 'That a Committee be appointed from the Grand Lodge to consider of and adopt such prompt and Effectual Measures for accomplishing so desirable an Object as a Masonic Union'!! The R.W. Bro Charles Humphreys P.S.G.W. objected to the Motion being received as tending to annihilate the Ancient Craft, hereon a very long debate and Conversation ensued. The R.W. Deputy Grand Master in the Chair after Maturely Considering thereon and as at present advised and according with his Duty as Deputy Grand Master Conceived it incompatible with his Situation in the Absence of the Grand Master to receive such Motion.

Obviously there was still a certain amount of opposition to the proposed union, possibly on the grounds that it would result in some infringement of the ancient landmarks that the Antients had been so anxious to preserve and possibly because it was felt that the wording of the motion committed the Antients even before the basis on which a union might be possible was known to them.

This seems rather strange as the Moderns had already shown evidence not only that they considered a union desirable but also that they were prepared to make concessions to bring it about, for in April 1809 they had passed a resolution 'that it is not necessary any longer to continue those measures which were resorted to, in or about the year 1739, respecting irregular masons, and do therefore enjoin the several Lodges to revert to the Ancient Land Marks of the Society.'

In addition, six months later the Moderns founded the Lodge of Promulgation 'to promulgate the Ancient Landmarks and instruct their members in the consequent alterations to the ceremonies.'

However, at a meeting of the Antients' Grand Lodge Committee on 24 January

following a motion in much more cautious terms was carried in which the desirability of a union was expressed 'provided the Land Marks of the Craft were preserved.' Further, it was agreed that a copy of the resolution should be sent to the Grand Master for his consideration and also to the Earl of Moira, Acting Grand master of the Moderns. Even so, when the minutes came up for consideration at the Grand Lodge meeting on 7 March there was a prolonged discussion in which considerable opposition to the proposal was expressed until eventually confirmation 'of proceedings being loudly called for', the minutes were approved but again only by a majority.

The Moderns agreed that a union was desirable whereupon the Antients went into the fray, demanding to know if:

1. As the Grand Lodges of the United Kingdon, i.e. the Antients, Scotland and Ireland [*sic*] were all bound by the same Obligations, would the Moderns 'consent to work in the same terms' [This request could surely have been more tactfully expressed]
2. Would they agree to the proposed United Grand Lodge being composed of all the Grand Officers of both Grand Lodges, plus the Masters, Past Masters and Wardens of every lodge? [Past Masters of Antient lodges were automatically members of their Grand Lodge; Past Masters of Modern lodges were not.]
3. Would they agree to charity being distributed by a Lodge specially summoned for that purpose, as it now is' [i.e. as it now is by the Antients]

They further suggested a meeting of the two Committees after the Moderns had had an opportunity of considering these points. The Moderns replied by inviting the Antients to dinner at the Free Masons Tavern on Tuesday 31 July at 5.00 p.m. This did not satisfy the Antients who replied that they would accept the invitation to dinner if they could meet first of all at 3.00 p.m. to discuss the points they had put forward. This being agreed they 'proceeded in carriages to Free Masons Tavern', for some reason 'at $\frac{1}{2}$ past 3 O'clock'.

Various meetings were held after this at which some progress was undoubtedly made but there is no mention of them in the Antients' minutes until 9 February 1811 when it was reported that the Moderns had consented to the use of the same obligations and had confirmed that they would return to the Ancient Land marks, adding tactfully: 'when it should be ascertained what those Ancient Land Marks and Obligations were.' All through the negotiations constant stress was laid not only within Grand Lodge itself and the negotiating Committee it had formed, but also by the Grand Master, the Duke of Atholl in his correspondence 'that the root and main stem of Ancient Masonry entire and unimpaired' must be preserved. That may be the reason why, when the Moderns referred to the second of the demands of the Antients previously mentioned and suggested that it would result in the unequal representation of lodges, the Antients' Committee accepted the suggestion of the Moderns that there should be only one Past Master of each lodge but at the next meeting of the Antients' Grand Lodge, that suggestion was turned down. The Moderns had pointed out quite politely that they did not object to the demand on any point of principle or from any jealousy in comparative

numbers in representation but because there would not be a building big enough to hold them all. The Antients advised the Moderns of their rejection in a letter in which they admitted the practical difficulty but said that 'the exclusion of the existing Past Masters from the enjoyment of a right so long established they consider to be a point which cannot be surrendered. But the Committee still entertain the Hope that the Union may be affected on the basis of three propositions first submitted to your Grand Lodge.

This was an impossible position to take up and it is not surprising that William White, the Grand Secretary of the Moderns wrote that it seemed:

wholly unnecessary and nugatory that any further meeting between the two Committees should take place at present inasmuch as the Committee of the Grand Lodge under the Duke of Atholl is not furnished with any sufficient powers to enter into the discussion or arrangements of the various subjects necessary to the proposed Union, as is sufficiently manifest from the circumstance of the Grand Lodge under His Grace the Duke of Atholl having at different times negatived propositions which its Committee had acceded to, therby annulling & frustrating concessions which the Grand Lodge under the Prince Regent had proposed itself, upon certain points, willing to make.

He stated further that the Moderns' Committee would be pleased to meet the Antients' Committee when it had been vested with the necessary negotiating powers 'for effecting the Union of the two Societies upon terms honourable and equal to both.' The Antients promptly gave its Committee the necessary powers but even so, did not surrender its position entirely as it insisted: 'That the United Grand Lodge shall be composed of the present & past Grand Officers and the Past Masters of lodges under both the Constitutions, existing at the time of the Union, for their respective lives – and of the Masters Wardens and one Past Master of each Lodge that may become so after the period of the said Union'. It may seem that the Antients were proving unduly difficult on this point and indeed they declared that 'they could not consent to deprive a single existing Past Master of his established rights.' On the other hand, if they were genuine in their desire for a union, obviously they would not wish to run the risk of creating a body of opposition amongst the Past Masters in their own Grand Lodge who, if they thought they were to be deprived of this privilege, could easily raise sufficient numbers to veto any proposal for a union. At the subsequent joint meeting, the Moderns again stressed that it was only the impossibility of finding a hall large enough that had caused them to take their stand but the Antients felt they must refer the matter yet once again to their Grand Lodge. With a view to solving this difficulty the Antients subsequently produced a return of those they considered entitled to the privilege but emphasized that on no occasion had it ever been known for more than one-third of the Past Masters to be present:

Grand Officers Present and Past	16
Masters & Wardens (49 lodges)	147
Past Masters of same	375
	538

The discussion then centred on the first point made by the Antients and as to whether the Moderns were prepared to adopt 'the practice of the Grand Lodges of Scotland & Ireland, of America &c of the greatest part of the Continent which were in perfect unison with the practice of the Grand Lodge of England under the Duke of Atholl ... so as to give complete unity to the masonic World.' The Moderns replied that it was their wish to put an end to all diversity and 'to establish the one true system'. They pointed out that they had founded the Lodge of Promulgation for this purpose and had had the assistance of several Antient masons in their deliberations. Further, it was accepted that the uniformity of the Antients with the lodges of Scotland, Ireland and America was sufficient test of the Antients' working being the genuine one.

For more than a year there is no further reference to the negotiations in the minutes of the Antients though obviously there must have been many discussions and many moves made behind the scenes. A significant event occurred, however, at the Special Grand Lodge held on 18 May 1813 and presided over by His Grace the Duke of Atholl when H.R.H. the Duke of Kent attended by special invitation and in his speech expressed the opinion 'that however desirable an Union might be with the other fraternity of Masons, it could only be desireable if accomplished on the basis of the Ancient Institutions, and with the maintenance of all rights of the Ancient Craft. Another Special Grand Lodge meeting was called three months later to consider a letter received from the Moderns in which it was stated that H.R.H. the Duke of Sussex had expressed 'the fullest conviction that the Union so long contemplated of the two Societys of Masons in England would be of the greatest advantage to the Craft in general' and that he proposed taking 'such steps as may appear most proper for arranging and concluding so desireable an object upon terms that may be equal & honourable to both parties.' Behind the polite phrasing could possibly be seen the exasperation of one whose patience was becoming exhausted and in any case, a statement such as that coming from a son of the reigning monarch was almost a Royal Command. The letter was referred to the Duke of Atholl with a request that he should head a small deputation to meet the Duke of Sussex and representatives of the Moderns' Grand Lodge. Possibly prompted by higher authority the Duke replied regretting his inability to accede to the request but suggesting that 'our interest would be eminently guarded' if H.R.H. The Duke of Kent could be prevailed upon to act in his stead, which was duly arranged.

Things moved swiftly after that and at the Grand Lodge meeting on 8 November 1813 a letter from the Duke of Atholl was read in which he intimated his desire to resign in favour of H.R.H. The Duke of Kent, a request that was duly accepted with the hope expressed 'that he will be pleased to permit his Portrait to be taken by an artist of celebrity, that it may be placed conspicuously in the Grand Lodge, as a perpetual memorial of their love and reverence of his virtues, and of their gratitude for his services to the Craft.' This was one of those destroyed in the disastrous fire of 1883. There is, however, a full-length portrait of the Duke of Atholl in No.1 Lodge Room in Freemasons' Hall, painted in 1901 by T.R. Beaufort who was one of six artists engaged by Grand Lodge to replace the lost portraits. Sir James Stubbs (*AQC 79* p.15) states that it 'shows the Duke in his

Thistle robes, in contrast to the several Garter robes depicted elsewhere in the room. The picture is almost certainly developed from an oval head and shoulders of the Duke, the authorship and provenance of which are unknown; it includes the curious anachronism of a post-Union Grand Master's jewel.'

As the Duke of Kent had previously signified his acceptance of the office of Grand Master there was no problem about this and his Installation was arranged for the following 1 December. At that meeting H.R.H. The Duke of Sussex, Grand Master of the Moderns, and several of his Grand Officers 'were made Antient Masons in the Grand Master's Lodge No. 1, (in a room adjoining)' and they then entered Grand Lodge to witness the Installation of the Duke of Kent who had been their Provincial Grand Master for Gibraltar (1790–1800) during most of which time he had also been Provincial Grand Master of the Antients for Lower Canada (1792–7). The Duke of Kent presided over only one meeting of Grand Lodge, that held on the evening of his Installation when it was reported that the Articles of Union had been signed in duplicate at Kensington Palace the previous 25 November. These were ratified and confirmed and nine brethren were nominated as representatives of the Antients in the Lodge of Reconciliation which was formed to 'promulgate and enjoin the pure and unsullied system, that perfect reconciliation, unity of obligation, law, working, language and dress, may be happily restored to the English Craft.'

One further meeting was held on 23 December 1813 presided over by the Deputy Grand Master, R.W. Bro Thomas Harper, at which the Duke of Sussex, now an Antient mason, was present. Only routine business was transacted apart from a resolution of thanks to H.R.H. The Duke of Kent 'for the gracious condescension with which he came forward in a most interesting moment and yielded to our earnest and unanimous desire to take upon himself the truly important Task of negotiating a Union ... for the Zeal, ability & conciliation which he displayed in all the conferences that took place in the progress of the same – for the firm and brotherly determination with which he assisted maintained & secured the Ancient land marks of the Craft, as well as the rights & privileges of this Grand Lodge and all its Constituents. Thus the Antients were game to the last in their stand for pure and ancient freemasonry as they knew it. Moreover, they had kept in close touch with the Grand Lodges of Ireland and Scotland throughout, both of which had stressed the absolute necessity of preserving the ancient landmarks and both of which had elected representatives to co-operate with the Antients during the negotiations.

So it came about that at Freemasons' Hall, London, on St. John the Evangelist's Day, 27 December 1813, the long-desired union became an accomplished fact and the United Grand Lodge of England was born. A Grand Lodge of the Moderns was opened in one room and a Grand Lodge of the Antients in another after which they both entered the Grand Temple for the reading and ratification of the Articles of Union and for the proclamation by the Grand Chaplain, ending with the words '... and may T.G.A.O.T.U. make their Union eternal', a wish devoutly echoed by all who had the future of freemasonry at heart. H.R.H. The Duke of Kent, former Grand Master of the Antients, proposed his brother, H.R.H. The Duke of Sussex, former Grand Master of the Moderns, as the first Grand Master

of the new United Grand Lodge. He was probably the most autocratic Grand Master who has ever ruled the craft but it was in any case desirable to have a powerful personality in control as memories of the sixty-odd years of rivalry, often extremely bitter, were not obliterated in one day and there were elements that could have destroyed the union had there not been a firm hand at the helm.

According to Lane's *Masonic Records 1717–1894*, in the ninety-six years of their existence the Moderns had warranted 1085 lodges and in sixty-two years the Antients had warranted 521 but many of these disappeared early in their existence without even taking a number whilst others took over the number of a defunct lodge. The highest Modern lodge number at the time of the union was 640 and the highest Antient was 359, giving a total of 999, but many of these had ceased to work and only 648 were taken over by the United Grand Lodge of England, 140 in London, 404 in the Provinces and 104 abroad. Of these 260 formerly owed obedience to the Antients and 388 to the Moderns. In addition, as Bro John Hamill pointed out ('English Grand Lodge Warrants' *AQC 90* p. 129) the Antients issued Warrants to eleven provincial Grand Lodges and Lane has traced 106 lodges warranted by them:

Provincial Grand Lodge of Nova Scotia –	49 lodges
Provincial Grand Lodge of Lower Canada –	27 lodges
Provincial Grand Lodge of Upper Canada –	20 lodges
Provincial Grand Lodge of Andalucia (Gibraltar) –	8 lodges
Provincial Grand Lodge of New York (No. 210) –	2 lodges

An ordinary Warrant was issued to a lodge in Madras that subsequently acted as a Provincial Grand Lodge and warranted two lodges. The six other Provincial Grand Lodges that may possibly have warranted subordinate lodges without reporting them to London were Philadelphia; the Islands of Montserrat and Nevis; Minorca; York, Chester and Lancaster; New York (No. 219); Kingston, Jamaica.

Following the union it was, of course, necessary to renumber all the lodges and chance had it that the Antients were successful in the ballot to decide which Grand Lodge should head the list. Thus their Grand Master's lodge which was founded in 1759 became No. 1 and the Lodge of Antiquity, which was one of the founding lodges of the Moderns' Grand Lodge in 1717 and has 'Time Immemorial' status, became No. 2.

Thus comes to an end the story of the Grand Lodge of the Antients. Undoubtedly much went on in the years from 1809 to 1813 that is not recorded and certainly their Deputy Grand Master, Thomas Harper, played a major role in the unofficial negotiations leading up to the union but the greatest debt of all is owed to the Earl of Moira, Acting Grand Master of the Moderns (1790–1813) whose invaluable work behind the scenes was recognized and rewarded in January 1814 by the presentation of a handsome jewel valued at one thousand five hundred pounds, a very substantial sum indeed for those days.

APPENDIX

I – THE RITUAL OF THE ANTIENTS

Bro Chetwode Crawley was the first to emphasize that in the early days, English and Irish masonry were one and the same so that Dermott and other Irish masons moving to London found the ritual being worked in Antient lodges identical with that of their mother lodges. He wrote:

> There never had been any Freemasonry in Ireland, save that of England. To put it shortly, there were no edifices in Celtic Ireland calling for skilled labour. The Celts never took kindly to building. The ecclesiastical edifices, in which so much learning is said to have been preserved, seem to have been, for the most part, mere wattled booths. The Royal palaces, in which so much wealth is said to have been displayed, were little better than one-storeyed huts. The Round towers seem of extreme antiquity, only in consequence of the crudeness of their construction. It may well be doubted whether there existed in the whole of Celtic Ireland any building, church, abbey, castle, or palace, which could find occupation for a Mason's lodge . . . We have to await the advent of Anglo-Normans before we can find edifices that will justify us in ascribing their erection to the skilled Brotherhood of Masons . . .
>
> When the tide of Freemasonry, overspreading its former ebb with its new influx, absorbed the lodges of London and Westminster, its waves flowed into the English cities that happened to lie in Ireland. We find the same men at the head of the Fraternity on both sides of the Channel. In 1725, Sir Thomas Prendergast is Senior Grand Warden of Ireland and Junior Grand Warden of England at the same time. In 1729–30, Lord Kingston earns the title of International Grand Master by serving the office in both countries. In 1733 Lord Southwell, who had served as Grand Master of Ireland before 1730, presides in the Grand Lodge of England by virtue of his past rank. The Hon. James O'Brien and Springett Penn, respectively Grand Master and Deputy Grand Master of Munster before 1730, were members of London lodges. In 1723, an astute bookseller's hack thought it worthwhile to recommend his pamphlet by dedicating it "To the Grand Master, Masters, Wardens, and Brethren of the Most Antient and Most Honourable Fraternity of the Free Masons of Great Britain and Ireland." When the growing popularity of the revived Craft excited curiosity about its secret rites, the first of the Spurious Rituals was published in 1724. The attack in London drew forth a reply from Dublin. The scribes saw no difference between the systems.

The position in Scotland was by no means the same but nevertheless, it would seem that Scotland took its non-operative form of masonry from England, though this was in the form of borrowing for there was no question of unification as in the case of Ireland. An obvious example of this is the use of English Old Charges by Scottish operative lodges. Three Grand Masters of Scotland were also Grand Masters of the Antients and the third, John 4th Duke of Atholl, did not hesitate to express his opinion that the pure and ancient form of masonry was preserved in the Scottish lodges and those of the Antients. When in 1775 he accepted their invitation to become Grand Master he wrote to the Grand Lodge of the Antients that he 'imagined it might accrue to the advantage of Ancient Masonry in England by indubitably shewing the tenets to be the same' and throughout the negotiations leading up to the union, he constantly stressed the absolute necessity of preserving those tenets as practised in the lodges of those two Obediences. Thus, in the early days it would seem that, as far as was possible, bearing in mind that means of

communication were poor and had not improved to any considerable extent since the days of the Romans, masonry was similar in form throughout the length and breadth of the British Isles and a mason travelling around would not find any basic or substantial variations in the ceremonies when visiting a lodge elsewhere in these islands. Nevertheless, there were some differences for it was found necessary to call an Emergency Meeting of the Grand Lodge of the Antients on 13 March 1757 which was attended by 46 members of 25 lodges when Laurence Dermott 'Traced and Explained the 1st. 2d and 3d. part of the Antient Craft and settled many things (then disputed) to the intire satisfaction of all the brethren present who faithfully promised to adhere strictly to the Antient System and to cultivate the same in their several lodges.'

This had been the situation when the premier Grand Lodge of England was founded in 1717 and it was their members who made alterations not only to the ritual but also to the long-established usages of the masons though in some cases they may well have done no more than put into practice what had been tending to happen for some years past. To this extent, therefore, they justified the epithet 'moderns' and their rivals, who refused to accept these changes, the epithet 'antients'. What were these changes, however, it is virtually impossible to determine and it may well be that they were in procedure rather than in the ritual itself though it has to be remembered that Modern masons wishing to join an Antient lodge had to be re-made in the Antient manner and vice versa. Further, as had already been mentioned, even the Duke of Sussex himself, Grand Master of the Moderns at the time of the union, together with some of his Grand Officers, went through this process immediately prior to the union. Moreover, as they had to be re-made in all three degrees, it follows that there were important differences in all three and it was certainly not merely a question of reversing the means of recognition in the first two degrees as has been suggested by some writers. In fact, at a meeting of the Lodge of Promulgation on 28 December 1810 the Master referred to the differences ' – such as the form of the Lodge, the number and situation of the Officers – their different distinctions in the different Degrees – the restoration of the proper words to each Degree, and the making of the passwords between one Degree and another, – instead of in the Degree.' This is reinforced by the fact that at the Grand Lodge meeting of 28 August 1730 Dr. Desaguliers had 'recommended several things to the consideration of the Grand Lodge. Particularly the Resolution of the last Quarterly Communication for preventing any false Brethren being admitted into Regular Lodges ...' In this he had been supported by the Deputy Grand Master, Nathaniel Blackerby, who 'proposed several Rules to the Grand Lodge to be observed in their respective Lodges for their security against all open and secret enemies of the Craft.'

In defence of the Moderns it has to be admitted that the rules, regulations and ceremonies were originally formed for operative masons and although we have no detailed knowledge as to the nature of the early ceremonies nevertheless as men of education came into the craft there would automatically be an urge not only to disregard these, but more importantly to introduce innovations in keeping with their standard of learning. Unfortunately we have very little evidence to guide us as to the changes made by the Moderns and as to the differences in the rituals of

the two Grand Lodges. Several publications appeared in the latter part of the eighteenth century and the early part of the nineteenth that purported to show these differences but they are of doubtful value. In 1760 an exposure entitled *Three Distinct Knocks* appeared, which claimed to give the ritual of the Antients and two years later, *Jachin and Boaz* was published giving, in the main, the ritual of the Moderns, but this is both complicated and contradictory as it included the lectures of the Antients and indeed, has been described as 'shameless plagiarism' of *Three Distinct Knocks*. In addition, as they were exposures, they are bound to be suspect at least to some extent for they were written by Freemasons in violation of their oaths, either for financial reward or in a spirit of revenge for some imagined slight. On the other hand, they must have been reasonably accurate or they would not have met with such success, there being six editions of *Three Distinct Knocks* by the end of the century and more than thirty of *Jachin & Boaz*. Moreover, in the absence of printed rituals, they were used by freemasons as *aides-mémoire* and so, over the years, tended to standardize the ceremonies.

With such unsatisfactory material on which to work it is possible only to list the charges made by the Antients and suggest to what extent they appear to be justified. At the same time it must be borne in mind that in those days it was quite impossible for there to have been one uniform ritual for either body. Lack of any real contact or communication between lodges throughout the length and breadth of the land must have resulted in a considerable number of variations, in addition to which, no doubt some practices of the Antients came into use in Moderns' lodges and vice versa.

The charges levied against the Moderns were:

(i)   Preparing candidates incorrectly. It certainly seems that they did not prepare their candidates in the same way as the Antients inasmuch as it appears that the right knee was made bare and the left foot slipshod, also that no sharp instrument was presented when the candidate entered the lodge and that his breast was only made bare when he was about to take his obligation. Also, the Moderns removed the hoodwink before the candidate took his obligation, the Antients as is now the Custom. Further, some Modern lodges, as was the case in Old Dundee Lodge, did not prepare their candidates in any way whatsoever.

(ii)   Abbreviating the ceremonies. A comparison of the above-mentioned exposures certainly indicates that this may well have been so. Incidentally, *Three Distinct Knocks* was the first English exposure to include ritual openings and closings but it would be unwise to conclude from this that the Antients had such ceremonies and the Moderns did not.

(iii)   Omitting the lectures, i.e. the catechisms which were intended, by means of this system of question and answer, to give the candidate instruction in each degree. There was probably some truth in this as in *Jachin and Boaz* the Antients' lectures are included with a note: 'I give the whole of the Lectures, as delivered in the primitive time, but the modern Masons leave out *at least one half*.' [my italics]. The Antients regarded these virtually as a landmark. As the actual ceremonies were quite brief at this time and the candidates

would learn little about the craft other than by means of the lectures, the strictures of the Antients would appear to be justified and it would seem that as far as they were concerned, these lectures were the main feature of their meetings.

(iv) Omitting to read the Ancient Charges to Initiates. This may well have been so but many of them were outdated and certainly inapplicable to non-operative masons. As Bro Eric Ward has pointed out, some of the charges in Anderson's 1723 *Constitutions* that were to be read 'At the making of New Brethren or when the MASTER shall order it' were so absurd in a society not connected with the building trade 'that to read them to an initiate would only instil doubt in his mind as to the sanity of the organization he was about to join.' Nevertheless, the Antients regarded them as another landmark that was being violated.

(v) Omitting prayers. Again, according to *Jachin and Boaz* this may be so or if they did use prayer, it was only in the first degree. In this connection it is of interest to note that in some continental obediences that took freemasonry from the Moderns there is still a prayer only in the first degree.

(vi) Transposing the means of recognition of the First and Second Degrees. This was certainly true and was regarded by the Antients as a violent and inexcusable violation of a landmark. Again, some continental obediences that derive from the Moderns have retained them in this way. It is ironic that in altering the columns so that, to a person approaching the Temple, B was on the right and J on the left, the Moderns were putting them, as we now know, in their correct positions.

(vii) Using an incorrect word for a Master Mason. It differed from the word used by the Antients and obviously they thought theirs was correct. Agreement on this could not be reached at the union which is why there are two words today.

(viii) Including the passgrips and passwords in the actual ceremonies instead of as a preliminary to them. This would seem to be proved.

(ix) De-christianizing the ritual. This is certainly true. Originally the ceremonies were definitely Christian and, indeed, Roman Catholic in phrasing. Anderson's 1723 *Constitutions* declared 'But though in ancient Times Masons were charg'd in every Country to be of the Religion of that Country or Nation, whatever it was, yet 'tis now thought more expedient only to oblige them to that Religion in which all Men agree, leaving their particular Opinions to themselves.'

(x) Ignoring the Saint's Days, especially those of St. John the Baptist (24 June) and St. John the Evangelist (27 December). The obervance of these was certainly regarded as important by operative masons but had probably been neglected, especially following the Reformation, before the Moderns came into existence. The Antients almost invariably chose one of these festivals for their installations and other ceremonial occasions whereas in the eighteen years prior to the foundation of the Antients' Grand Lodge, the Moderns had not once installed a Grand Master on such a day.

(xi) Arranging the lodge incorrectly. There certainly were differences. The Three

Great Lights were possibly arranged differently, the Three Lesser Lights certainly were. Both Antients and Moderns had a Candle in the S. but whereas the former had Candles in the E. and W. the latter had them in the N.E. and N.W. In a Moderns' lodge the Jnr.W. was originally in the S.W. but seems to have moved to the S. by the middle of the eighteenth century. The Snr. W. was in the N.W. and in some lodges apparently remained in this position instead of moving to the W.

(xii) Not having Deacons. In the main this was probably true as the two Wardens 'or their assistants' took charge of the candidate but certainly some Modern lodges had Deacons.

(xiii) Neglecting the esoteric ceremony of Installing the Master. This was true inasmuch as the Moderns installed a Master following the consecration of a lodge but largely neglected it thereafter. Not until after the formation of the Lodge of Promulgation in October 1809 did it admit that the ceremony was an essential part of freemasonry. In the minutes of its meeting on 19 October 1810 it was 'Resolved that it appears to the Lodge, that the ceremony of Installation of Masters of Lodges is one of the two [presumably a mistake for 'true'] Landmarks of the Craft, and ought to be observed.' On the other hand, the Antients also neglected the ceremony in their early days as their Grand Lodge minutes of 24 June 1756 record that many of their Masters were incapable of performing the ceremony.

Whilst any conclusions drawn from the above can only be tentative nevertheless it is obvious that we owe a considerable ritual debt to the Antients and, in another way, also to the Moderns, for, in the words of Henry Sadler, 'their readiness to revert to the Ancient forms and ceremonies is much to their credit, and speaks volumes for their intelligence and genuine Masonic spirit.' Thus it was that Bro Heron Lepper could write in his Prestonian Lecture '. . . many of the finest portions of the ceremonies we practise today have been preserved for us by the tenacity of the Antients and their stubborn resistance to innovation . . .' However, one matter concerning which they were not successful in imposing their will involved the Royal Arch. They had always contended, quite incorrectly, that 'Antient Freemasonry consists of Four Degrees' of which the Royal Arch was the fourth, a degree that was 'certainly more august, sublime and important than those which precede it, and is the summit and perfection of Antient Masonry.' The Moderns, on the other hand, repudiated it most emphatically contending, in the words of their Grand Secretary, Samuel Spencer, 'The Royal Arch is a society which we do not acknowledge and which we hold to be an invention to introduce innovation and to seduce the brethren.'

It must have been obvious that the Antients would not contemplate a union if the Royal Arch was not to be recognized and as early as 10 December 1811 the First Grand Principal of the Moderns announced that they would do so. Nevertheless the Moderns were still not prepared to accept it as a fourth degree and as 'the summit and perfection of Antient Masonry'. A compromise was therefore reached and in the Articles of Union, it was declared and pronounced that 'pure Ancient Masonry consists of three degrees and no more, viz., those of

the Entered Apprentice, the Fellow Craft, and the Master Mason, including the Supreme Order of the Holy Royal Arch.' Thus the Royal Arch instead of being the fourth degree became the completion of the third. This was a substantial concession on the part of the Moderns as well as on the part of the Antients. Possibly the Antients felt that they were by no means on firm ground. In the first place they must have known, in spite of their protestations, that the Royal Arch degree was actually of comparatively recent introduction and not a part of ancient masonry. Secondly, they had pressed for recognition by the Moderns of the pure form of ancient masonry as practised by them and by the Grand Lodges of Ireland and Scotland yet Ireland and Scotland regarded the Royal Arch in exactly the same way as the Moderns and for many years refused to recognize it.

Clause II of the Articles of Union concluded, 'But this article is not intended to prevent any Lodge or Chapter from holding a meeting in any of the degrees of the Orders of Chivalry, according to the constitutions of the said Orders.' Was this another concession to the Antients who contended that their Warrants entitled their lodges to work not only the Knight Templar and Rose Croix degrees but any other of the accepted degrees of freemasonry and that no further authority was necessary? If so, it was a substantial victory for them but on the other hand an empty one, for the Duke of Sussex successfully kept these additional degrees in abeyance and thus protected the new United Grand Lodge against the dangers that would have arisen from a conflict between those members who were enthusiasts for the additional degrees and those who were bitterly opposed to them.

There may, however, be two things we have inherited from the Moderns. In the 1764 edition of *Ahiman Rezon*, as mentioned previously, Laurence Dermott poured scorn on the fact that there were two columns in Moderns' lodges, one marked J and the other B, whilst in the 1779 edition, he ridiculed the way their candidates were instructed to take their steps. Certainly, in an exposure (*Three Distinct Knocks* 1760) purporting to disclose the working of the Antients, there is reference to two columns at the entrance to the Temple but no indication that they were in any way included in the furniture of the lodge whereas in another exposure (*Jachin and Boaz* 1762) supposedly giving the working of the Moderns, there is an emblematical diagram that includes them. Further, the steps indicated in the former are quite simple ones, the candidate taking one step in the first degree, two in the second and three in the third. However, as with so much else in the eighteenth century, this can be no more than guesswork.

II – GRAND MASTERS

1753	Robert Turner
1754–6	Hon. Edward Vaughan
1756–9	William, 1st. Earl of Blesington (G.M. Ireland 1738–9)
1760–5	Thomas Alexander, 6th. Earl of Kellie (G.M. Scotland 1763–5)
1766–70	Hon. Thomas Mathew
1771–4	John, 3rd. Duke of Atholl (G.M. Scotland 1773)
1775–81	John, 4th. Duke of Atholl (G.M. Scotland 1778–9)
1783–91	Randall William, 6th. Earl and 2nd. Marquess of Antrim (G.M. Ireland 1773 and 1779)

1791–1813   John, 4th. Duke of Atholl
1813   H.R.H. Edward, Duke of Kent

III – GRAND SECRETARIES

1751–2	John Morgan
1752–71	Laurence Dermott
1771–7	William Dickey
1777–9	James Jones
1779–83	Charles Bearblock
1783–5	Robert Leslie
1785–90	John McCormick
1790–2	Robert Leslie
	Robert Leslie
1792–1800	Thomas Harper
	Robert Leslie
1801–13	Edwards Harper

IV – EXISTING LODGES OF ANTIENT ORIGIN

No.	Lodge	Constituted	Original (a)	1813	1814	1832
			Previous Numbers			
1	Grand Master's, London	1756		1	1	1
3	Lodge of Fidelity, London	1754	32	2	3	3
5(b)	St. George's and Corner Stone, London	(1756)	55	3	5	5
7(c)	Royal York Lodge of Perseverance, London	1751		4	7	7
9(d)	Albion, London	1762		5	9	9
11(e)	Enoch, London	1754	37	6	11	11
13(l)	Union Waterloo, Eltham	1761	86	7	13	13
15	Kent, London	1752	9	8	15	15
19(g)	Royal Athelstan, London	1769	159	10	19	19
22(h)	Neptune, London	1757	64	13	22	22
24(j)	Newcastle-upon-Tyne, Newcastle-upon-Tyne	1766	131	15	26	24
25(j)	Robert Burns, London	1810		16	27	25
27(j)	Egyptian, London	1811		21	33	29
30(j)	United Mariners, London	1753		23	36	33
31(j)	United Industrious, Canterbury	1776		24	37	34
32(j)	St. George's Lodge of Harmony, Liverpool	1755		25	38	35
34(j)	Mount Moriah, London	1754		31	47	40
36(j)	Glamorgan, Cardiff	1808		33	50	43
38(j)	Lodge of Union, Chichester	1812		35	52	45
40(j)	Derwent, St. Leonards	1813		36	54	47
44(j)	Lodge of Friendship, Manchester	1803		39	59	52
47	Newstead, Nottingham	1763		44	63	55
49(j)	Gihon, London	1810		46	65	57
50(j)	Knights of Malta, Hinckley	1803		47	66	58
53(j)	Royal Sussex, Bath	1812		49	69	61
54(j)	Lodge of Hope, Rochdale	1813		50	70	62
57(j)	Humber, Hull	1775		53	73	65
62(j)	Social, Manchester	1811		62	85	75
63	St. Mary's London	1757		63	86	76
65(j)	Lodge of Prosperity, London	1810		68	91	78
68(j)	Royal Clarence, Bristol	1807		72	95	81

No.	Lodge	Constituted	Previous Numbers			
			Original (a)	1813	1814	1832
70	St. John's, Plymouth	1759		74	98	83
72(j)	Royal Jubilee, London	1810		77	100	85
73	Mount Lebanon, London	1760		81	104	87
74(j)	Athol, Birmingham	1811		83	105	88
79(j)	Pythagorean, London	1813		93	116	93
80(j)	St. John's, Sunderland	1805		94	118	95
81(j)	Doric, Woodbridge	1812		96	120	96
84(k)	Doyle's Lodge of Fellowship, Guernsey	1806	336	98	123	99
87(j)	Vitruvian, London	1810		104	128	103
90(j)	St. John's, London	1763		113	138	107
95(j)	Eastern Star, London	1802		128	151	112
98(j)	St. Martin's, Stoke-on-Trent	1805		130	154	115
101(j)	Temple, London	1813		136	163	118
104(j)	Lodge of St. John, Stockport	1806		139	168	121
107(j)	Philanthropic, Kings Lynn	1810		142	172	124
110(j)	Loyal Cumbrian, Merthyr Tydfil	1810		144	175	127
115	Lodge of St. John, Gibraltar	1767		148	181	132
117(j)	Salopian Lodge of Charity, Shrewsbury	1810		153	186	135
119(l)	Sun, Square and Compasses, Whitehaven	1768		157	190	138
121(j)	Mount Sinai, Penzance	1813		163	200	142
125(j)	Prince Edwin's, Hythe	1807		168	205	147
128(j)	Prince Edwin's, Bury	1803		209	150	128
130	Royal Gloucester, Southampton	1772		174	212	152
131	Lodge of Fortitude, Truro	1772		175	213	131
141	Lodge of Faith, London	1774		192	235	165
142	St. Thomas's, London	1775		193	237	166
143	Middlesex, London	1775		194	239	167
145	Lodge of Prudent Brethren, London	1775		195	241	169
146	Lodge of Antiquity, Bolton	1776		196	242	170
147(j)	Lodge of Justice, London	1801		198	245	172
151(j)	Albany, Newport, I. of W.	1801		200	249	176
152(j)	Lodge of Virtue, Manchester	1796		201	250	177
153	Inhabitants, Gibraltar	1776		202	251	178
156(j)	Harmony, Plymouth	1804		205	256	182
158(j)	Adam's, Sheerness	1797		207	259	184
159(j)	Brunswick, Plymouth	1802		208	260	185
164(j)	Lodge of Perseverance, Sidmouth	1813		213	268	190
168	Mariner's Guernsey	1784		222	279	197
169	Lodge of Temperance, London	1784		225	281	198
171	Lodge of Amity, London	1784		227	284	200
173	Phoenix, London	1785		231	289	202
175(j)	East Medina, Ryde	1813		232	291	204
177	Domatic, London	1786		234	293	206
178	Lodge of Antiquity, Wigan	1786		235	294	207
180	St. James's Union, London	1787		239	299	211
184	Gillingham Lodge of Benevolence, Gillingham	1787		243	306	216
185	Lodge of Tranquillity, London	1787		244	308	218
186	Lodge of Industry, London	1788		245	309	219
188	Lodge of Joppa, London	1789		253	319	223
190	Oak, London	1789		255	321	225
193	Lodge of Confidence, London	1790		259	327	228
194	St. Paul's, Southgate	1790		261	329	229
196	Albion, Barbados, W.1.	1790		263	333	232
198	Percy, London	1791		264	335	234
199(j)	Lodge of Peace and Harmony, Dover	1801		266	336	235
200	Old Globe, Scarborough	1788		267	337	236
201(j)	Jordan, London	1810		268	338	237
203	Ancient Union, Garston	1792		276	348	245
204(j)	Caledonian, Manchester	1802		278	351	246
205	Lodge of Israel, London	1793		280	353	247
207	Royal Kingston, Jamaica	1794		283	357	250
209(j)	Etonian Lodge of St. John, Windsor	1813		284	359	252
210	Duke of Athol, Ashton-under-Lyne	1795		289	366	254

No.	Lodge	Constituted	Previous Numbers			
			Original (a)	1813	1814	1832
211	St. Michael's, London	1795		290	367	255
212(j)	Euphrates, London	1812		292	370	257
213	Lodge of Perseverance, Norwich	1795		294	374	258
214	Lodge of Hope and Unity, Hutton	1795		295	375	259
215	Lodge of Commerce, Haslingden	1796		297	378	261
216	Harmonic, Liverpool	1796		299	380	263
217	Lodge of Stability, London	1797		300	381	264
218(m)	Lodge of True Friendship, Stapleton	1797		315	383	265
220	Lodge of Harmony, Garston	1796		302	385	267
221	St. John's, Bolton	1797		303	386	268
222	St. Andrew's, London	1797		305	388	269
223(j)	Lodge of Charity, Plymouth	1797		306	389	270
224	Atlantic Phoenix, Bermuda	1797		307	390	271
225(j)	St. Luke's, Ipswich	1804		309	393	272
226	Lodge of Benevolence, Rochdale	1797		310	394	273
227(j)	Ionic, London	1810		312	397	275
228	Lodge of United Strength, London	1798		314	399	276
230(j)	Lodge of Fidelity, Plymouth	1810		320	405	280
232	Marine, Portishead	1801		323	410	282
233	Prince Alfred, Bermuda	1801		324	411	283
239	Friendly, Kingston, Jamaica	1797		342	438	291
243	Loyalty, Guernsey	1810		349	448	299
244	Yarborough, Jersey	1812		352	452	302
245	Duke of Normandy, Jersey	1813		355	457	306
246	Royal Union, Cheltenham	1813		357	461	307
254	Trinity, Coventry	1755	471	382	476	316

NOTES

(a) If different from 1813 number.
(b) St. George's Lodge No. 55 (A) purchased No. 3(A) on 6 June 1759 for £4.14.6 and on 6 December 1843 amalgamated with Corner Stone Lodge No. 63(M) constituted 1730. It is now regarded as of Modern origin.
(c) Lapsed about 1765 but revived in 1769.
(d) Laurence Dermott purchased No. 5 in 1769 for £5.5.-.
(e) Purchased No. 6 on 2 october 1754 for £1.1.-.
(f) Purchased No. 7 on 4 June 1788 for £5.5.-.
(g) Purchased No. 10 on 7 March 1792 for £5.5.-.
(h) Purchased No. 13 on 6 December 1758 for £2.2.-.
(i) Warrant exchanged for Warrant of No. 15 on 2 April 1813.
(j) Issued with Warrant of lapsed lodge.
(k) Purchased No. 98 on 14 September 1807 for £21.-.-.
(l) Issued with Warrant of lapsed lodge of same name.
(m) Issued with Warrant of lapsed lodge at Lisbon, Portugal.

THE GOVERNMENT OF THE CRAFT

THE PRESTONIAN LECTURE FOR 1982

SIR JAMES STUBBS, K.C.V.O.

Many Prestonian Lectures have started with a description of William Preston's life and works and a well-deserved eulogy: as however, with four exceptions, the first twenty-seven have been collected and reprinted – and I would here urge that the series be brought up to date with a second volume of reprints – there is little point in doing this once more. As an alternative, I am going at once to acknowledge my indebtedness to Plato's *Republic* and to two other equally non-Masonic works written by eminent historians of the last century: the *English Constitution* by Walter Bagehot which I first read as a schoolboy, and the *Constitutional History of England* by my grandfather, Bishop Stubbs of Oxford C.G., D.D., under the shadow of which I grew up.

My grandfather drew out the long thread of continuity in the development of our political institutions from the Dark Ages to the Wars of the Roses: it was an exposition of government as it developed rather than of the governed, and little would be gained by bringing his views to bear upon our private Lodges or even the higher organisations, but I would commend to close attention Bagehot's classic demonstration of the various elements of government, and in particular, his essay on checks and balances of power. I owe a debt, incurred unwillingly at the time, to Plato whose *Republic* Books 8 and 9, contain what is still the best and clearest analysis of the different types of government and leaders, of his own time and indeed of ours. But we should ask ourselves scrupulously whether Plato's classic definitions of artistocracy, oligarchy, democracy and tyranny can still be fruitfully applied: I think that they can, provided that we clear our minds of the cant definitions in vogue nowadays of these forms and relate to any consideration of Masonic Government only their original senses within the city state.

It would have been tempting to entitle this lecture 'The Constitution of Freemasonry at home and abroad ', but I was deterred on two grounds: first, I can speak only at secondhand – good secondhand having been corresponding with other Grand Lodges consistently over the last thirty years and more – of their theory and practice; secondly 'Constitution' and its derivatives are terms of art in the Craft not bearing the same connotations as in the works I have quoted: our rules, the act of establishment associated with the ceremony of consecration of new Lodges and, in the more distant past, the actual physical authority, by which power was conveyed to an individual Freemason or to a group desirous of working corporately, i.e. as a Lodge, have all pre-empted that title. However the

172

'Government of the Craft' is a title that all should be able to understand even if, as I suspect, it does not rate very high in terms of popular interest.

Looked at from the constitutional or governmental point of view Freemasonry consists of three tiers in England, Ireland and Scotland, and in a few other parts of the world which would have copied the grand originals: – these tiers are the private Lodges, the Provinces or Districts, and the Grand Lodge, I propose as far as circumstances permit to deal with them in that order.

THE PRIVATE LODGES

The Lodge is the basic, as indeed it is the oldest, organisation in Freemasonry, and it should not be forgotten when we come to consider the power and authority of the higher bodies that at least up to 1717, and probably in remoter areas till a good deal later, Lodges were entirely self-governing. We can have no certainty (and mere speculation is of little use) how the pre-1717 Lodges governed themselves: it will be rather more profitable to move on to the mid-18th century and to consider briefly the differences between those holding from the Premier Grand Lodge and those from the Antients. The latter tended to be at least on the surface more democratic bodies as all officers instead of only Master, Treasurer and Tyler were elected. This is something which has substantially been handed down to us in our Royal Arch Chapters, and preserved in many bodies overseas that derive from the Antients. On the other hand, in the Premier Grand Lodge's constituent bodies the appointment of officers lay for the much greater part in the hands of the Master, a practice which prevailed at the Union in 1813.

The election of Master by the members is, I believe, universal practice: once elected and installed, he is responsible for his Lodge's behaviour and still more for its good name. But how does he stand in actual power? He still has the last word in the appointment of officers other than the Treasurer and the Tyler: it would however be a foolhardy Master Elect who did not go through some process of consultation with senior members, particularly if changes are envisaged. The surest route to an unhappy, and generally an unproductive year, is to disregard, and to show that this is done intentionally, the advice of the Lodge's elder statesmen. But this said, we must ask ourselves what power and authority these elders have. It is not obligatory[1] to have a Lodge Committee: its primary function, if authorised and appointed at all, is to consider and report on proposals for membership. Other matters may be specifically referred to it for consideration and report and, within defined limits, action: but no Committees can be invested with any general executive powers. even however with this shaky basis, we all know that the Lodge Committee almost invariably guides the Lodge, and does it very well: from time to time one hears of agitation from less senior and probably less experienced members, more often than not members of the Lodge of Instruction who meet, particularly in London, very much more often than the Lodge or the Lodge Committee.[2]

Having doubts as to these two being absolute sources of constitutional power, and being aware that votes in open Lodge are infrequently split down the middle of the membership, we should examine the powers of the Master in the light of the

limitations imposed on him; we have already seen that his power of appointment of officers, though theoretically absolute, is in fact limited by the need to carry the Past Masters and the Lodge Committee with him: it may well be, as some rituals announce, that all offices are declared vacant when the installation begins, but in practice some officers will remain where they are and others almost automatically take a step forward. Through the Secretary the Master summons Lodge regular meetings but he is not a free agent as there is no power to cancel a meeting,[3] nor is he any longer permitted to summon an emergency meeting without authority from above. (This limitation was imposed soon after World War II when it was clear that if they were not controlled in some way Lodges would take in far more candidates than they could absorb) R. 180 *B. of C.* lays upon the Master the requirement to admonish unharmonious behaviour in the Lodge, and if persisted in, to censure it, or even exclude the brother causing the disharmony for the remainder of the meeting, but only if the majority of the members agree. It is undoubtedly his prerogative to decide what is to be the business transacted at each Lodge meeting, but much of this is governed by the by-laws of the Lodge and the *Book of Constitutions*. As regards degree work as often as not a pattern has evolved over the years, and he will do well to fall in with this: he has, however, more freedom in seeking assistance or in deciding to 'go it alone' with the actual ceremonies. Here too, there is a good deal of variation of established practice: to generalize, it would seem that the further one goes from London the less ritual work is undertaken by the Master and the more is usurped by Past Masters. So it would appear the Master's absolute power is strictly limited both in extent and in the way it can be usefully be practised – in extent because the *Book of Constitutions* generally the Lodge by-laws in particular hedge him round, and in practice because he will have seen on his way up the Lodge that there is a considerable brake put upon his own impulses – if indeed he has any – by the elder statesmen of the Lodge.

From the point of view of legislation, neither Master nor Lodge has any absolute authority, since no by-laws or amendment can be effective until it has been approved by a higher authority: in any case the Grand Master's approval would not be given to any by-law or amendment which was repugnant to the *Book of Constitutions*.

In the matter of internal discipline, a Lodge is free to exclude one of its members 'for sufficient cause', provided that it goes the right constitutional way about it; and I cannot recall a case where an appeal against such action on the grounds that the cause was insufficient has succeeded. Indeed, unless the cause is thoroughly frivolous the members are held to be in much the best position to decide whose company they would sooner be without. It must be borne in mind that one Lodge's meat may be another Lodge's poison: I well remember a case where a previous Grand Master refused to exercise his powers under R. 182(a) *B. of C.* as it now is and order the reinstatement of a member of a Lodge that had excluded him, precisely when he was appointing him to London Grand Rank following another Lodge's recommendation.

Argument often arises, generally from disgruntled members who have lost an argument on the floor of the Lodge, as to the full meaning of R. 155 *B. of C.*

which states that the members *present at any Lodge duly summoned* have an undoubted right to regulate their own proceedings ... In many cases the words are taken out of their context and used in a far wider sense to claim that Lodge affairs generally, and not just their handling in Lodge itself, are the business of the members only, and that no interference from outside is permissible.

A Lodge has indeed much of the semblance of a democracy with one man one vote on all matters of domestic concern, but it is the shadow rather than the substance, since it is governed not only by its by-laws, which as we have seen are subject to outside control, but also by the *Book of Constitutions* itself and by the abundance of case law arising from decisions of Grand Lodge itself, which we shall be considering in some detail later.

THE PROVINCIAL AND DISTRICT GRAND LODGES

What has been expressed so far may be taken as applying with but little variation to all Lodges, but when we pass on to the second tier of government, that of Provincial and District Grand Lodges, it would be rash to treat them all as if cast in one mould (For the sake of brevity it is proposed to use 'Provincial' only, and at the end of this section some minor differences between Provinces and Districts will be discussed.) Provincial Grand Masters have been appointed from the earliest days of organised English Masonry, often indeed before there was anything for them to be Masters of: we can also pass quickly by those early stages when a Provincial Grand Lodge may have consisted of little more than the Provincial Grand Master's own private Lodge, and arrive at the point where there was really something to guide and control – in the words of a Grand Superintendent's patent 'advise, instruct and where neccesary admonish'. It is obvious that with strengths varying from over five hundred to single figures there must be great varieties in the methods of internal administration and government, but there are some basic principals which apply to both great and small. The Provinicial Grand Master is appointed by the Grand Master, like all other Grand Officers, except for the anachronistic Grand Treasurer and he has his prescribed place in the Grand Officers' table of precedure.[4] After his installation (for till then as Provincial Grand Master designate he has no power except to summon a Provincial Grand Lodge meeting for his installation) he is in full control: he will have been asked to appoint or confirm the existing appointment of officers to the scale laid down in R. 68 *B. of C.* and to confirm with his approval the by-laws of his Province. Henceforward he is in a position of great power and responsibility: he is the fountain of honour within his Province, and to a numerically lesser, but practically more important extent, it will be only by his recommendation that members of his Province as such have their names submitted to the Grand Master for the ultimate honour of Grand Rank. He has very considerable powers of Masonic discipline subject only to the right of appeal from his decision to the Grand Lodge: his effective power however lies in his largely unwritten '*auctoritas*': this is not quite the same as 'authority' and has no precise equivalent in English: it means that, because they trust him, his brethren will do what they believe that he wants them to do, will follow his lead, and take his personal advice much as if it had constitutional force.

In the great majority of cases Provincial Grand Officers are appointed for a year only, and their ranks are honours conferred for work done or to be expected. Some offices, however, varying from Province to Province, are semi-permanent, and it is on the holders of such offices that the Provincial Grand Master will rely for the day-to-day government of his Province. Such government has, as elsewhere, increased greatly in complexity, and a full-time Provincial Grand Secretary is no longer the rarity he was in 1930. It was recognised by the Grand Master, as long ago as 1919, that a Provincial Grand Master needed more than a Deputy to help him discharge his duties, and the introduction of Assistant Provincial Grand Masters has done much to bring a closer relationship between the private Lodges and the government of the Province: indeed so useful have they proved that the scale permitting their appointing has been adjusted twice in the last thirty years till there may now be one for every forty Lodges. How they are actually deployed varies from Province to Province: the most comprehensive, and probably the most efficient, method is geographical. Although this is not always possible, it is desirable somehow to give some kind of group responsibility, not only to ease the burden on the Provincial Grand Master and his Deputy but also to give the Assistant(s) additional experience by taking charge of a number of Lodges.

Generations ago when many Provincial Grand Masters were local magnates, or absentees, or both, it was not unusual for a Province to be effectually ruled by the Deputy in the name of his Provincial Grand Master, and many Provinces were none the worse for an oligarchy of the Deputy, and the Provincial Grand Secretary acting for their rather nominal Master. Such a Deputy would probably have had little or no thought of succeeding in due time to the Provincial Grand Mastership, nor inclination either, and when a vacancy arose and a new appointment was made he was there to supply valuable continuity: the position also gave him a great deal more authority than was strictly his, and there is a well attested story of a Deputy Provincial Grand Master of not so long ago who declined the offer of appointment to Provincial Grand Master with the comment 'If I accepted I would lose all my power'.

Inevitably, however, where a Province has increased beyond the size where it is the case that everybody knows everybody of any masonic consequence some form of representative body, or bodies, will need to be set up. What form they take varies a good deal, as also do the frequency of their meetings and the degree to which they are brought into lively discussion of the Province's affairs. In general it may be said that there will be a Committee for charitable purposes, itself two headed, for the relief of distress within the Province and for the organisation of major collections for the Central Charities when that Province's turn comes round: the other will have to deal with such routine matters of administration as are referred to it by the Provincial Grand Master and the Provincial Grand Secretary. It should be emphasised that its function is mainly consultative, and, if it does recommend some course of action to the Provincial Grand Lodge, it is more than likely that it is echoing the views of others.

It will be well to be clear as to the composition of a Provincial Grand Lodge: it is essentially a body of qualified individuals, who are not in the strict sense representatives or delegates of their Lodges: the ordinary Master Mason, though

encouraged to be present, is there as a courtesy and has neither voice nor vote in its proceedings. The membership is clearly defined by the *Book of Constitutions*[5] and is virtually the same as that of Grand Lodge localised to the Province. Each Lodge may have some of its members attending such meetings, but there is in no sense an equality of voting strength between one Lodge and another, and one can easily visualise a meeting packed by determined members of a Lodge, or group of Lodges, pushing through or blocking resolutions where feelings run strongly; the rest of the Province would have no remedy – except to try again next time.

We should next ask ourselves what then is the function of Provincial Grand Lodge: in most cases it meets annually and the main, or at any rate the longest, item of business is the appointment and investiture of officers.[6] The actual form of the meeting is based, from start to finish, on the procedure at the Annual Investiture and Quarterly Communications of Grand Lodge: the formal entry and recession, the ritual opening and closing, the presentation of reports are all to be found at both levels. Provincial Grand Lodge no doubt has the power to refuse to accept a report downright, or to ask its proponents to think again: it alone can pass resolutions to amend its own by-laws, and this includes the rate of annual dues and fees generally. In respect of conferment of honours the power of the Provincial Grand Master is limited, but in this case by a comprehensive set of Rules in the Book of Constitutions, designed to apply with the least possible inequity to Provinces both large and small.

It would appear, therefore, that of the powers which exist at this intermediate level there lie with the Provincial Grand Master discipline with which Provincial Grand Lodge has nothing to do, conferment of honours, and presiding over meetings which he alone summons.[7] The Provincial Grand Lodge decides what taxation to impose, and what by-laws to lay down. Neither of them can establish a new Lodge or bring to final conclusion the activities of an existing one. Neither, therefore, can claim absolute or unfettered power: the *Book of Constitutions* controls the actions of both, while within the meetings of the Provincial Grand Lodge those present as members could, if feelings were sufficiently aroused or predilections antagonised, vot down any recommendations put to it.

A Provincial Grand Lodge can hardly be described as a democratic organization since it consists of perhaps only a fifth (i.e. Past Masters, Master and Wardens) of the whole body which it taxes, and for which it legislates, while the other four fifths can only in a vague and farfetched sense be said to be represented by them, and are certainly not for the much greater part (i.e. Past Members and Wardens) chosen by them. On the other hand, it is by no means an oligarchy in the accepted sense of the word, and it would be unjust so to describe it; nor by any stretch of the imagination can a Provincial Grand Master be equated with Plato's typical tyrant. Plato's concept of aristocracy, as government by those best qualified by nature and improved by training, could without overstraining the truth be applied to the membership of such a body as we have been considering. For it should be an article of faith that the members of the Craft are good men, and it is at least to be hoped that in the years between initiation and wardenship they will have acquired something of the principles of Masonry as well as its ritual.

It remains briefly to consider such differences as there still are between Provinces

at home and Districts overseas, a distinction in name dating from 1865: in the era of slower and even more unreliable mails it was desirable to give Masonic authorities (of whom it should be remembered that there were proportionately far more than now)[8] a greater degree of independence. This took various forms. First, there is the power of the District Grand Master to issue provisional warrants for new Lodges[9]: it should be noted that this provision is a time-saver pure and simple, and does not in any real sense enhance the District Grand Master's powers. Secondly, where a Province has one or more Committees, a small District may, and a larger one must, have a District Board of General Purposes, which is a small edition of Grand Lodge's Board of General Purposes and has wide but defined functions:[10] there may also be a District Board of Benevolence, something of an anomaly now that the Board of Benevolence has put an end to itself. Thirdly, the Rules governing changes of dues are made more easy for isolated Lodges whose members would find it difficult to get to a District Grand Lodge meeting to express their views. Fourthly, District Grand Secretaries are sent blank Grand Lodge certificates of a very slightly different pattern which they issue to the members of their Lodges and account for quarter by quarter to the Grand Secretary: this is a matter of two way convenience as also is the practice in Districts of collecting all annual returns and sending them in bulk to London.[11]

It will be seen that, as indicated earlier, there are no basic differences in the powers of Provinces and Districts and their respective rulers: such differences as exist were created for convenience, speed and ease of administration.

LODGES DIRECTLY ADMINISTERED FROM FREEMASON'S HALL

No specific reference has been made to the Masonic government of 34 scattered Lodges, some of which are loosely put together under a Grand Inspector[12] whose patent from the Grand Master quotes in detail the powers delegated to him: these make him almost a one-man District Grand Lodge. A slightly larger number is controlled directly from Freemasons' Hall. Last but in no way least, nearly one-fifth of Lodges in England and Wales are directly under the jurisdiction of Grand Lodge: these include three out of four that formed the premier Grand Lodge in 1717 (the fourth has perished) and a very high proportion of Lodges already in their second and third centuries of existence. Their honours derive from the Grand Master directly, their problems and discipline are dealt with by the Board of General Purposes through the Grand Secretary and his office, and about one third of them recognise Freemasons' Hall as their Masonic home. While they are described as London Lodges for purposes of jurisdiction it would be as unrealistic to state that they are composed of Londoners as to claim that every Freeman of the City of London lives within the 'square mile'. They are, in fact, composed of brethren who find central London the most convenient gathering place from all parts of the country: there is no homogeneity about them like 'friends around the Wrekin', 'Red Rose', 'White Rose' or 'Men of Kent', but there is great pride in one and all being London Masons, the descendants of those who formed Grand Lodge and gave the pattern to Freemasonry all over the world. Attempts are made from time to time to diffuse this pride by inserting arbitrarily in the same kind of

Masonic government as has sprung up naturally in the geographical limits of the Provinces: an attempt by Lord Ampthill so to do was frustrated by the outbreak of war in 1914, from which he returned a wiser man.

The carrot hopefully dangled before the Masonic donkey includes the likelihood of a larger proportion of Masonic honours and more supervision by Masonic visitations: to continue the homely metaphor, the ass however is an intelligent animal and can see the disadvantages too – higher dues because somehow such visitations and their administration will have to be paid for, less liberty of action than they presently enjoy, loss of direct contact with the central government of the Craft and the straitjacket of charitable activities, into which Provinces[13] are fitted every ten years or so, instead of their own methods which, even if haphazard, are less forced and therefore more truly charitable.

It is at least arguable that London Lodges are more independent than those in the Provinces, and have therefore a greater aptitude for inculcating their own lessons of character building – indeed a wider experience of self government which the authorities at Freemason's Hall do nothing to diminish.

THE GRAND LODGE

Having now considered the Private Lodges and various forms of intermediate control we proceed logically to the heart of government: but before doing so must again look back in the history of English Masonry and recall that two bodies came together in 1813 in an act of reconciliation which had been none the easier to achieve for its being common sense.[14] Their differences at Lodge level have already been outlined: when we come to the two sovereign bodies, it is not too much of an over-simplification to state that the strength of the Premier Grand Lodge was its administrative machinery, and of the Antients' its enthusiasms for Masonic ritual and 'tradition'. At home the Antients had neither a headquarters nor a Provincial organisation (nor one would suspect any more control over their Provinces abroad than the Premier Grand Lodge). Their rivals had had for generations a well tried, if laxly administered, system deriving from the Committee of Charity, as well as a long established headquarters. This system was expanded after the Union into a complex organisation, the details of which are given in the Appendix.

THE BOARD OF GENERAL PURPOSES

It will be seen that over the generations since 1813 the Board of General Purposes has gradually absorbed administrative control over the affairs of Grand Lodge, and, while doing so, has at the same time become a less unrepresentative body: the most notable step in this direction was taken in 1917, when it became possible for the Provincial members of Grand Lodge to have some say in the choice of Board membership. The complicated procedure[15] is eased by the arbitrary but self imposed division of the forty seven Provinces into twelve groups, each of which by courtesy supplies one member: it must be emphasised, however, that these twelve are primarily members of the Board and only very secondarily

delegates from, or representatives of, the Provinces which have nominated them and organised their election. Other constituent elements of the Board are (*i*) twelve elected members from London Lodges, who often are coincidentally members of Provincial Lodges also, (*ii*) eight nominated each year by the Grand Master and more often than not reappointed from year to year, (*iii*) the occupants of certain defined offices in the Grand Lodge, at present fourteen in all: the Grand Secretary is very properly not a member of the Board, but is the channel of communication to and from it. He may even come to be considered its guide, philosopher and friend.

In much greater detail than for Provincial Grand Lodge Committees or those of Private Lodges the functions of the Board are laid down in the *Book of Constitutions*: it has the administration and control of the property and finances of the Grand Lodge and the regulation of all its affairs. 'Generally the Board shall take cognizance of all matters in any way relating to the Craft'.[16] Thus it conducts correspondence with other Grand Lodges and with Private Lodges, and, most important, may recommend or report to the Grand Lodge or to the Craft (an interesting distinction to which we will return) whatever it may deem conducive to the welfare and good government of the Craft. Any such references when adopted by the Grand Lodge are treated as its edicts, that is to say become part of the Masonic case law. Case law used to derive also from decisions by Grand Lodge when deciding appeals or expulsion, but there is little now of new principle to be found from this source, and the much more practical method of conducting such business through Appeals Court has virtually brought it to an end. As a Court of First Instance the Board also acts as a kind of corporate Provincial Grand Master in judicial matters affecting London Lodges or members, or elsewhere where there are not Provincial or District Grand Masters: it has just the same powers as they do, and there is a similar right of appeal from its decisions.

With all these powers and duties and with a wealth of experience at its disposals, it might be thought that the Board would indeed be supreme: this however is not the case, for numerous examples could be turned up where the Grand Lodge has not been in agreement with the Board, and its proposals have had to be amended or abandoned. Much will depend on the care with which its reports are drafted, and still more on the tact with which they are submitted by its President: but most of all it is vital that the Board should have the confidence of the Craft that it is working for the benefit of the Craft as a whole and not for itself or any single section of the Craft. Fortunately this is much more the case now than it was at the beginning of the century, when rows and arguments in Quarterly Communications proliferated. Sir Alfred Robbins, who in his earlier years had been a thorn in the flesh of the Masonic establishment, became a great, if overbearing, President. He was a classic example of poacher turned gamekeeper; but too little thought perhaps is given to how such conversion is regarded by other poachers, and he probably never quite lived down his past. The story is told – I have it from one of those who voted – of how in some fairly trivial dispute, which provoked one of his long winded speeches, word was passed among the Grand Stewards 'Come on, let's vote the old man down' – and they did.

Later Presidents, by their personalities and by their self-evident disinterestedness

and ability, have gained the confidence of the Grand Lodge, which seems now to take the sensible view that the matters laid before it have been considered by Board members who collectively have a wealth of experience denied to the individual mason. A good example is the difference of attitude between 1930 when a suggestion of adding six pence to annual dues provoked a descent from the north in a special train – and a subsequent Especial Grand Lodge – and the present era when the Grand Lodge is now content to accept annual recommendations from the Board as to the dues required two years ahead.

THE BOARD OF BENEVOLENCE

I will not attempt an obituary notice of the Board of Benevolence, that oldest of the offshoots of the Grand Lodge and the direct progenitor of the various useful Boards and Committees which Grand Lodge has formed and through which it has worked. It may have been necessary to remove so venerable a feature (one hesitates to use the word 'landmark') in order to maintain the illusion that the Bagnall Report is going to be faithfully and totally implemented, but it is much to the credit of Grand Lodge that, unlike the independent Institutions, it rapidly adjusted itself to the Bagnall framework.

It has already been stated that the Board of General Purposes' parameters (no essay in this day and age would be complete without the use of this newest substitute for functions)[17] are clearly defined in the *Book of Constitutions*: so too are the functions of the Grand Lodge, and though it would be a tidy piece of politicial theorization to compare them to Cabinet and a Parliament, with the whole Craft as the *mobile vulgus* or electorate, it is not so easy to see how exactly the Craft is able to act as such, apart from the fact that each Masonic tier is composed of members of the larger one below it. Again applying the argument that the Craft is composed of persons of good report, and of increasingly sound judgement and experience as they rise in importance through their Lodges, we hope to find that members of Grand Lodge's functioning Boards or special committees combine good reputation and widened experience with a determination to work for Freemasonry, but little hope of self-advancement within the Craft and none outside it.

THE GRAND LODGE AND THE CRAFT

The distinction, to which allusion has already been made, between the Grand Lodge and the Craft underlines that they are two separate entities, just as at Lodge level a meeting of Past Masters differs from the Lodge itself in session. Appeals such as the Duke of Connaught's at the start of the Masonic Million Memorial Fund may be, and were, issued to the Craft as a whole through Grand Lodge, but thereafter Grand Lodge had really very little to do with it: nor indeed had the Board for almost all the detail was carried out by the Peace Commemoration Building Committee which reported regularly to Grand Lodge till it was wound up, *functus officii*, in 1938. The Lodges were used as the vehicle for raising money, and the Grand Secretary's office collected it and generally serviced the Committee:

but Grand Lodge's own contribution financially was a minor one, and was more than repaid when the building was handed over in 1938. It is not easy to provide other examples of positive action by the Craft, though when Grand Lodge expels a mason it expels him from the Craft. While such a brother does not cease to be a Freemason, as the ceremonies performed over him and the secrets communicated to him cannot be reversed, he does cease to be a member of the Craft losing his membership of that shadowy but corporate body.

THE GRAND MASTERSHIP

It only remains now, respectfully, to consider the summit of this Masonic pyramid, the Grand Mastership. From the earliest days of the Grand Lodges the office has been elective, none the less so for its having very often and fortunately been repetitive: there has not been any sign of a contested election since 1844, following the death of the Duke of Sussex, and a rather crackpot attempt at opposition some twenty years later by a brother who thought that the system of honours was unsatisfactory:[18] although once, when presiding over his own re-election, the late Earl of Scarborough jokingly referred to Grand Lodge playing its little democratic game election is no figment. Once elected a Grand Master takes office forthwith and does not have to wait for formal and ceremonial installation[19] like a Provincial Grand Master.

This will be a logical starting point for the consideration of his powers and prerogatives which, unlike the functions of other leading Grand Officers, are not defined in a single place. On a very much wider scale than is the case with Lodges and Provinces, he is the fountain of Masonic honour for London, and in respect of Past Grand Ranks and Promotions his authority is unfettered. He has power to form any specified area into a Province, District, or Inspectorate, and to rearrange existing boundaries: and with this naturally goes the power to appoint Provincial and District Grand masters and Grand Inspectors to give effect to his actions. Warrants for new Lodges are granted by him and remain his property, though curiously enough he cannot either erase a Lodge or revoke an appointment to Grand Rank: in each case reference has to be made to the Grand Lodge whose decision is final. Dispensations are issued in his name, though contrary to almost universal belief there is no general power of dispensation: it is only for those cases specifically referred to in the *Book of Constitutions* (a dozen or so in all) that a dispensation can be obtained. He alone can approve the pattern and use of jewels, this being in practice extended to Lodge badges generally and banners when they include the Lodge badge.

In addition to appointing to Grand Rank, the Grand Master has also powers of appointing scrutineers for the elections of Grand Treasurer,[20] and members of the Board of General Purposes, and of direction, through the Grand Stewards, of the Grand Festival: also he may direct how admission to meetings of the Grand Lodge is to be arranged, i.e. when tickets need for one reason or another to be issued. In addition to Grand Officers, he also appoints Brethren of other Constitutions, with which the Grand Lodge is in amity, as Representatives and makes suggestions for similar appointments in reverse: these should be, and mostly

are, purely honorific, but the appointments are highly prized and much care and consideration goes into the selection of their holders.

Whether these powers are held to be great or small, too great or not great enough, will be largely a subjective judgement or will depend on theoretical comparisons with other jurisdictions: what stands out however is that in the English system of long-lasting tenure of the Grand Mastership a considerably greater degree of experience will mature, and equally important, there will not be a posse of Past Grand Masters ready and anxious to advise. It would seem therefore that in the English system much more depends on the Grand Master as the apex of its pyramid, and on his relations with the Board of General Purposes and with the massed body of Provincial and District Grand masters. Sir Alfred Robbins, again, was apt to describe himself as the Prime Minister of English Freemasonry, with the implication that the Board was the Cabinet: he did not, so far as I know, ever proceed to a comparison between the Grand Master and the Crown, or between the Grand Lodge and the House of Commons though he might very well have carried his analogy upwards and downwards and, for good measure, have worked in a comparison of Provincial and District Grand Masters with Lords Lieutenant or Colonial Governors, of whom in his day there were plenty enough. What he *definitely* did not do was to refer to himself as Lord President of the Council, or designate any Privy Council, yet it is manifest that however long a Grand Master may remain in office he will require advisers in the actual exercise of those prerogative powers already outlined, which are not within the purview of the Board. Hence it is that in the last hundred and forty years the practice has grown up informally and almost imperceptibly of having a Grand Master's Council, all the more useful in that its membership and its meetings are alike unfettered by rules and by-laws. It is however[21] customarily composed of the major dignitaries of Grand Lodge with a sprinkling of Provincial Grand Masters, of experts on the affairs of English Freemasonry overseas, and of Brethren too with an intimate knowledge of problems of the Masonic Chairities, on which, as he is their Grand President, the Grand Master stands in need of disinterested advice. Though it is the normal practice not to refer to the Council as such, and even when referring to the members as the Grand Master's advisers to use a small 'a' to avoid any implication of official status, it is pretty widely known that it exists, and there really seems to be no reason why it should not be known: indeed if it were to be abolished something very like it would undoubtedly grow up in its place. Comparison might usefully be drawn to the stages of devolution of power in English History from the Great Council to Parliament, from Parliament via the Privy Council to Cabinet, from Cabinet to Parliament and back to the Privy Council, particularly as so much present day legislation is put into effect by Orders in Council. It must remain clear that in Masonry too there will always be an inner circle of personal advisers, whose advice on matters of Masonic prerogative needs to be sought, and whom it would be unwise to disregard or take for granted.

Students of Plato's *Republic* will have observed that till now there has been no reference to what he considered the lowest form of political life, tyranny. This aspect is covered neatly by R.15 *B. of C.*, which states the position in quaint but explicit terms. 'If the Grand Master should abuse his power and render himself

unworthy of the obedience of the Lodges, he shall be subjected to some new regulation, to be dictated by the occasion; because, hitherto, the Antient Fraternity have had no reason to provide for an event which they have presumed would never happen.' Within the velvet glove there is at least an implied threat, and we should not forget that when Grand Lodge was founded in 1717 it was less than a generation after James II was toppled off the throne following the trial of the Seven Bishops, and then bundled out of Ireland by the tune of Lilliburlero: moreover, the successful 'putsch' by which the Whig Grandees had bought in the Hanoverians was only three years back, while the unsuccessful 1715 rising must have been a very fresh memory. Grand Lodge was born into a Whig Oligarchy, and despite what happened abroad it continued along Whig rather than Tory lines.[22]

THE PRO GRAND MASTERSHIP

It would be leaving a large gap if nothing were said about the Pro Grand Mastership, which stands in a peculiarly personal relationship to the Grand Mastership. Our Masonic ancestors saw clearly that the other commitments of a Royal Grand Master would prevent his giving the detailed care and attention to the office that a lesser man might be expected to give: also it is quite possible that they wished to prevent him being exposed to the pressures normally attendant on the office. Hence originated the office of Pro Grand Master, designed to carry out the day to day functions of government,[23] leaving the Grand Master himself unembroiled. The Pro Grand Master is to the Craft as a whole the outward and visible form of the Grand Mastership in action, and just as he will have the confidences of the Grand Master so must he justify the confidence of the Craft in the choice that is made of him by the Grand Master after consultation with his Council. It is reasonable to hold this out as the theory of the matter: to make it work effectively it is essential that the Grand Master remains outside the usual run of events, approached only the Pro Grand Master[24] or through him. Any breach of this protocol is likely to lead to the potentially dangerous situation of the Grand Master and Pro Grand Master being given conflicting briefs on the same matter.

THE DEPUTY AND ASSISTANT GRAND MASTERSHIP

I have purposely left out reference to the specific functions of the Deputy Grand Master and the Assistant Grand Master(s) which remain the same whether or not there is a Pro Grand Master. Their appointments derive from the prerogative of the Grand Master, and they may be conveniently looked upon both as manifestations of himself in his absence and as the most senior and responsible of his advisers. It is worthy of note that most formal documents have the Deputy Grand Master's signature on them, and that in the ritual of Grand Lodge he has to answer both for himself and for the Grand Master. (If the Grand Master and the Pro Grand Master are both present it is still the Deputy Grand Master who answers).

Ideally this little knot of rulers of the Craft, advised by the Board or by the Council in matters of high policy and by the Grand Secretary in routine affairs, will give their directions with one voice, and the Craft as a whole will follow them with unimpaired respect and affection. If however it ever becomes clear that such counsels are divided, as in the case particularly of the Masonic Charities, very deep and lasting divisions will develop in the Craft as a whole; nor will they easily be healed.

THE MASONIC CIVIL SERVANT

Practically nothing hitherto has been said about the Masonic Civil Service: it exists to serve the Craft, whether it be at the Provincial or Grand Lodge level. At the latter it has passed through periods of considerable unpopularity: references to John Hervey and his staff in the Proceedings of Grand Lodge are remarkable for their virulence, even by the uninhibited standards of those days. Since then it seems that the image has improved, and though from time to time there have been objections from one quarter or another to various aspects of the Grand Secretaries' work,[25] by and large we have been accepted, if sometimes grudgingly, as doing our best. The staff itself, ever since there has been one of appreciable size, has known its job and done its best to function without fear or favour: its members acquire a very real expertise in Masonic administration, and in many cases in Masonic ceremonial too – the run up to annual investitures and even great occasions such as Albert Hall meetings are taken in their stride. The Grand Secretary himself can rely with confidence on someone in the office, male or female, being able to produce an answer or precedent, which may have slipped his memory or antedated his experience. For almost any problem or question it is then for him to channel it, and the appropriate answer to it, in the right direction for the Grand Master and his advisers or to the Board of General Purposes, often he has to use his own judgment or give the unpalatable answer that it has nothing to do with Freemasonry and its administration, and should be addressed elsewhither.

The Grand Secretary's office is thus the nodal point in the communication system; without having powers in himself but simply by experience and not least by always being available for consultation, he soon acquires the *auctoritas* that will encourage those whom he meets in person or by correspondence to accept what he tells them as authentic and unbiased.

CONCLUSION

Thus we find at the Grand Lodge level rather more similarity with our British principles of government including the distinction between legislative, administrative and judicial. Bishop Stubbs' insistence on the continuity of development of constitutional organisations helps us to understand that almost everything of significance in our system derives from our Masonic ancestors. Plato gives us invaluable guide lines of definition between, in his vocabulary, aristocracy, oligarchy and democracy: Bagehot guides us to a clearer conception of the different tiers of government in the Craft as a whole.

What must not be lost sight of is that a framework which suits the English Masonic temperament will not necessarily suit others – hence in any consideration of other Masonic Jurisidictions we must be careful not to equate 'different' with 'wrong'. No doubt this lecture could be rewritten on the foundation of American, Latin, Germanic or Scandinavian systems: it is probably true that just as apt a series of comparisons of their forms of government could be made out. It can never be stressed enough that, while Masonic governments may differ, the true principles of Freemasonry do not, whatever may be the temperament of governors and governed.

It was for the furtherance of knowledge of the Principles of Freemasonry that William Preston, who in his time had been an archrebel against the administration of the Craft, established his lectures: but it is my belief that, if he had ever turned his mind to the Government of the Craft, he would have reached empirically the same kind of conclusions as have been laid before you.

NOTES

1. R. 154 *B. of C.*
2. They may be not uncharitably compared to the 'Young Turks' in the last years of the Sultan Abdul in Istanbul, useful at producing evidence of feelings that might not otherwise find expression, but do not necessarily merit acceptance.
3. R. 137 *B. of C.*
4. R. 5 *B. of C.*
5. R. 65 *B. of C.*
6. This has become in very large Provinces so lengthy that it is spread over two meetings.
7. A Provincial Grand Master shares with certain other distinguished Masons the right to demand admission to any Lodge within his jurisdiction and preside over it: in this respect it could be argued that he 'overtrumps' the right of the Master of a private Lodge, but in practice it is unlikely that this power will often be invoked for more than purely formal purposes.
8. In 1863 there were 64 Provinces and Districts for 1000 Lodges. Now the figures are 72 and over 8000.
9. This still exists in Rule 95 but is now virtually a dead letter: any holdup nowadays is more likely to be due to (*i*) petitioners who fail to produce all the necessary information when forwarding their petitions or for inclusion in the warrant; (*ii*) the actual writing of the warrant which is largely obviated by its main text being massproduced and (*iii*) the recurrent difficulty of obtaining the necessary signatures.
10. R. 81 (b) *B. of C.*
11. With the curious proviso that the District Grand Master is himself responsible personally for the remittance of dues.
12. Any comparison between such Grand Inspectors and the Inspectors General that are an integral part of the whole organisation of the Ancient and Accepted Rite is pure fantasy: they are a modern (1927) introduction into the Craft's system of government and having been primarily intended to obviate postal delays, have ceased with the prevalence of air facilities to perform that function: except as a stepping stone to the formation of a new District in a developing area such as Trinidad, Cyprus or the Bahamas, or conversely, as a step down where a District is in process of dissolution (Northern China) their continued necessity is debatable.
13. A very senior Provincial Grand Master of the recent past is on record as having said that even in his highly organised Province he reckoned that never more than 50% of his members supported a festival which he was sponsoring – and that only once in ten years.
14. It would be ungrateful not to refer with appreciation to the valuable help I have received from my immediate predecessor's lecture on the Antients.
15. R. 219 *B. of C.*
16. So says Rule 227, and one is sometimes tempted to ask by what kind of self-denying ordinance or sophistry does it consistently decline to deal with ritual and charitable matters.

17. 'Guide lines' are already out of fashion.
18. He was not a Grand Officer himself.
19. R. 14 *B. of C*. The last three such installations (which have taken place at the Royal Albert Hall) did not in any way increase the Grand Master's power or remove any limitations upon it.
20. There has not been a contested election for his sinecure since 1912.
21. Membership is at the personal invitation of the Grand Master and lapses with a change of Grand Master.
22. A close study of John Locke's 'Essay of Civil Government' might well be illuminating; I have not undertaken it.
23. It is significant that the earliest holders of such appointments were described as *Acting* Grand Masters.
24. Logically, if not verbally, R. 17 *B. of C*. applies equally to the Pro Grand Masters.
25. Some trivial minds in high places have quoted Dunning's condemnation of the power of the Crown: – 'has increased, is increasing and ought to be diminished'. Such fatuity can safely be disregarded: he has plenty to do without looking for more.

APPENDIX

THE DEVELOPMENT OF THE BOARD OF GENERAL PURPOSES AND ITS COMMITTEES

1. Prior to the union of the two Grand Lodges in 1813 there had been no Boards as such, but administration was carried out by the Committee of Charity for the Premier Grand Lodge and its Stewards' Lodge for the Antients. No useful purpose seems likely to be served by going into details of pre-Union administration, and it will be best to start with the new situation as it emerged on 27th December, 1813.

2. Resolutions by the Grand Assembly for the Union established five separate Boards, all of whose functions were prescribed in the 1818 Book of Constitutions: they were:–

> General Purposes
> Finance
> Works
> Schools
> Benevolence

In addition it should be mentioned that there was to be a 'General Committee' and an 'Audit Committee'. With this plethora of administration (and two Grand Secretaries) the re-united Craft proceeded to business.

3. It is however only fair to mention that the Board of Benevolence, which is referred to from time to time as the Committee or Lodge of Benevolence, was restricted from the start to charitable activities and never impinged upon administration as its predecessor in the Premier Grand Lodge had done. It does not appear ever to have had any control even over the administration of the Fund of Benevolence, except in the matter of distribution to those qualified to be relieved. Its activities and constitution are therefore irrelevant to this review.

4. As the Boards of Works and Schools disappeared with the 1818 revision of the Books of Constitutions, it is tempting to suppose that they had never been intended to go on longer than was needed to sort out the problems of the two Schools, one a Premier and the other an Antient foundation, and to organize

something agreeable to both parties in the matter of Freemasons' Hall, which was a purely Premier Grand Lodge building. This however would be an over-simplification. The Schools Board's function was to certify to Grand Lodge whether the money Grand Lodge voted was being applied to its object, and to report generally on the needs of the Institutions and on the sums of money required for their support or expansion: it was not however 'in any way to interfere with the privileges of the governors and subscribers thereto in the management and control of such establishment'. It had no regular dates of meeting.

Similarly the Board of Works was to have the direction of everything relating to the buildings and furniture of Grand Lodge, to suggest improvements, to make preparations for meetings in Freemasons' Hall, and to see that the Master of Tavern made adquate arrangements for meetings held there. The Board was to control normal expenditure but to obtain the sanction of Grand Lodge for extraordinary expenses.

5. The Board of Finance was designed to see that no unnecessary or improvident expenditure took place: it was to check bills and order the Grand Treasurer to pay them – the order then as now being signed by the President and Grand Secretary, the Grand Treasurer being simply Grand Lodge's banker. Before each Quarterly Communication a balance was to be struck and reported to Grand Lodge, and the list of Lodge Contributions printed and published (this went on till 1940). Annually the Board was to prepare the accounts for the audit committee and circulate the accounts for the past year. At first it met monthly, but by 1819 had reverted to quarterly meetings: it disappeared in 1838 by a mutually agreed amalgamation with the Board of General Purposes, when Grand Secretary Harper (formerly of the Antients) retired and a general reorganization ensued.

Reference has been made to the Audit Committee which consisted of the Grand Officers of the year and twenty-four Masters of London Lodges. Its functions seems to have been identical with that of the Grand Lodge Auditor, who does not appear till 1859, when he is appointed by the Grand Master: by 1881 the Auditor is elected by Grand Lodge as he now is. The Committee fades out of existence between 1859 and 1881, having indeed been found, as large Audit Committees generally are, quite unsuited to its task.

6. The functions of the early casualties have now been dealt with, but it may be useful to look at their pattern of membership: each of the four had a President and Vice-President. In the case of the Board of Works, it was automatically the Grand Superintendent of Works (for many years Sir John Soane). The Grand Master, Deputy Grand Master and Grand Wardens were *ex officio* members together with twelve others (twenty in the case of General Purposes). Half were appointed by the Grand Master, and half were elected by Grand Lodge from among the actual Masters: at least one third of the members went out of office each year. This must have ensured a regular turnover, accentuated by the fact that among the elected members it would be unlikely that an 'actual Master' would be so for more than two years at the most. Meetings were mostly monthly (but see Finance and Schools above).

7. Apart from the Board of General Purposes and what has sprung from it, only the General Committee now remains to be considered. This body had a long existence though it must be admitted that with the increase in the Craft, the introduction of penny postage and the better circulation of Papers of Business, its usefulness diminished: it served a useful purpose at first, but when it was finally abolished in 1918 it died almost unnoticed. Its function was to go through the Paper of Business a few weeks before Grand Lodge and 'vet' any motions that might be proposed from the floor, so that those attending Grand Lodge might not be caught unawares. Its membership consisted of all Grand Officers and all Masters of Lodges or their accredited representatives: as in this respect it was at the time practically identical with the Board of Benevolence and met on the same date, that Board seems in effect to have run the Committee. When it was laid down in 1858 and 1871 that the Paper of Business was to be circulated to all Lodges (and to Grand Officers) before Quarterly Communications, the Craft obtained prior cognizance of all official business, and it was felt by the Board of General Purposes that it was itself the body which should be made aware formally, and not by the accident of the General Committee's review, of any other motions. In December, 1918, after a long debate this view prevailed and to all intents and purposes the Board took over the functions of the General Committee.

8. During the long Grand Mastership of Lord Zetland (1844–1870) we find the first stirrings of Masonic independence overseas: it started with Canada and there is little doubt that money was at the back of it: the Lodges thought they were being overcharged for registration and certificates (no dues were payable for administration or benevolence). When Grand Lodge at last tried to assuage their resentment by reducing the fee it was too late, and there was no hope of persuading them to remain under Grand Lodge. Correspondence with Lodges overseas had always been fraught with difficulty: both sides complained justly of lack of attention, and even if a letter arrived safely at either end and was answered, the time lag was so long that it had probably lost its relevance. Besides there was no particular body in Grand Lodge that was directly responsible for supervising such correspondence. It is significant that in 1857, very soon after the Grand Lodge of Canada (now restricted geographically to Ontario), had won its independence, the Colonial Board started work. (This was the year too when Grand Secretary White at last resigned: he had served since 1809, his father having first come on the scene in 1781, no less than 76 years earlier: before the end of such a long tenure was in sight it may well have been difficult to introduce such an innovation). The Board was established to review all overseas correspondence, whatever its nature. It met monthly though not infrequently failing to produce a quorum, with a Chairman, a Vice-Chairman, and eight other members. Much of its work was concerned with quarrels in and between overseas Lodges, especially those that were not under any local organization, but it was also concerned with problems arising from the establishment of other Grand Lodges in the Colonies. Eventually the Board was wound up and its functions were absorbed by the Board of General Purposes, which produced a further Committee with the full title of

the Colonial, Indian and Foreign Committee. A good deal of argument occurred as to its membership, since it was felt that it should have adequate representation from overseas: it was eventually decided that as far as possible it should be composed of members of the Board who were Past Masters of Lodges abroad, but no provision was made to ensure that such qualified Brethren were elected to the Board. The Rule was thus anomalous, and must have remained something of a dead letter till authority was given a good many years later to the Committee to invite to its deliberations Brethren who had overseas experience: the last of them was R. W. Bro. Sir Henry McMahon, since whose death no further advantage has been taken of the permission.

After the establishment of the Committee under this cumbersome title its work embraced all the relations of Grand Lodge with other Masonic powers including even Ireland and Scotland. Colonial however soon became an opprobrious word (particularly to a Canadian President) and general satisfaction ensued when in 1954 its name was changed to External Relations, without any alteration of its function.

9. The dissolution of the Board of Finance, to which reference has been made, was followed at once by the establishment of the *Finance Committee*. It is not clear that this change was the direct result of Harper's resignation, but there seems to be little doubt that there was a good deal of financial confusion brought about by his unbusinesslike methods: one item in the consequent reorganization lasted unchanged until 1960, as Grand Lodge's contribution to the educational Institutions of £150 a year in lieu of a percentage of the Registration Fees remained unaffected by either the growth of the Craft or the fall in the purchasing power of the pound.

While in many organizations the equivalent to the Finance Committee has gradually accumulated additional powers and control, this has never been the case in the government of the Craft, since the Board has consistently refused to delegate its authority in any general sense to any of its Committees; all six stand in an equal relationship to the Board. Similarly the Board has never granted powers of general application to a Committee specially brought into existence for that purpose. From time to time this type of predominance has been suggested, but no evidence is forthcoming that it has been more than a suggestion, the nearest to actuality being a Committee of Chairmen of the 'Spending Committees' (presumably Finance, Premises, Officers and Clerks and Library, Art and Publications). This body, which met a few times in 1917–1918, was mainly concerned with estimating the future expenditure of its various Committees in order to obtain a forecast of the General Purposes bank balance with a view to advising on investments, a far cry from real control. In very recent times the investments of the two funds of Grand Lodge ceased to be solely gilt edged, and under the exhilarating influence of R. W. Bros. Sir Frank Newson-Smith and F. W. R. Douglas an attack was made on equities. It became obvious that it was not practiable for the best effects of such a policy to be achieved through the monthly meetings of the Finance Committee, and an Investment Sub-Committee was formed in 1951: its work was so conspicuously successful that it is surprising that it took a decade to

realize that Grand Lodge's real estate was just as much an investment as its stocks and shares, and needed to be similarly treated. Eventually, however, in 1971 the two sources of revenue were put on a comparable basis, and the Finance Committee established a Property Sub-Committee which took over the functions hitherto exercised by the Premises Committee in respect of properties other than Freemasons' Hall.

10. While these two Committees have existed without interruption since their establishment, even if the name and scope of one of them has altered, the same is not quite the case with the *Premises Committee* which first came into being in 1845. It is reasonable to assume that the Board assigned to it functions similar to those with which the old Board of Works had been invested in 1813, but when the almost complete rebuilding of Freemason's Hall was contemplated in 1862 a special Building Committee was set up, not by the Board but by Grand Lodge itself, with full authority to pay bills in connection with the rebuilding without even reference to the Board. A similar procedure followed sixty years later with the Masonic Peace Memorial, whose Special Committee operated from 1919 to 1938.

When the 19th century rebuilding was completed in 1869 the Building Committee was wound up. It appears that the Premises Committee came back into activity; it has continued uninterrupted ever since and, by a curious chain of circumstances, assumed, or was assigned, a responsibility for Grand Lodge's other properties too. There is no need to go in detail into the gradual acquisition of properties which were not directly used by the Craft, as were Freemasons' Hall, the Tavern (now the Connaught Rooms), and Bacon's Hotel (later Mark Masons' Hall now part of the Connaught Rooms). What happened however was that at the peak of the purchasing movement the Chairman of the Premises Committee (R. W. Bro. Blay), a builder himself and a dabbler in the property market, came to the rescue of the Grand Secretary, who at that time had no Deputy or Assistant and was moreover heavily committed in running the basement of Freemasons' Hall as an air-raid shelter. Bro. Blay virtually took control of that part of the Board's affairs and the system continued till 1971, when as indicated above it was recognized that property as much as investments were income producing, and should be under the control of the Finance Committee.

11. A *Library Committee* appears in 1837 very soon after the decision to establish a Library. Over the next generation the Board Minutes refer on several occasions to the Library: there were rules for its use in 1848: in the next year evening opening was terminated as insufficient use was made of the facility. By 1860 at the latest it had become the Calendar Committee, and the Calendar or Year Book in fact seems to have been its principal function for many years: this is hardly surprising when one considers how little there was by way of Library or Museum, for only in 1898 did a new phase of building produce them a permanent home. In 1881 the double title Calendar and Library appears for the first time and persisted till 1911 when Publications took the place of Calendar: two years later the existing title appears in the Masonic Year Book.

In this title Library, it need hardly be said, includes the Museum: Publications over and above the Year Book now includes ordering and price-fixing for the Book of Constitutions, other printed matter, and latterly the very popular transparencies of the building and its contents. Art as part of the title is almost inexplicable, since outside the Library and Museum Grand Lodge's art treasures amount to forty portraits of dead and living Masons, half a dozen busts and the massive statue of the Duke of Sussex.

12. The first reference to the *Officers' and Clerks' Committee* is in 1894. By 1911, when the earliest extant Committee Book begins, the Committee interested itself in matters so diverse as typewriters and addressographs on the one hand, and on the other the selection of a Chief Clerk (*alias* Assistant Grand Secretary) and the wages of the stoker. In 1913, at the same time as negotiations were going on with the Commercial Union to effect a pension scheme, the Committee turned down a recommendation from the Chairman of the Finance Committee that the Cashier's salary should be increased (i.e. without reference to those enjoyed by the older clerks). During the first war the Committee, rather surprisingly, dealt with the preparation of a Library Catalogue. Appointments were put forward to the Board from time to time for the Library on the recommendation of the Library, Art and Publications Committee, and for the Porters' Staff at the Committee's own initiative. In general it has throughout its existence been primarily concerned with salaries and pensions, and only comparatively seldom have other matters, e.g. holidays and five day week, come its way. In 1975 it was more appropriately renamed the *Staff Committee*, as by then it covered the whole workforce of Freemasons' Hall.

13. The *Procedure Committee* as such came into existence only in 1917, but on various occasions before then special committees had been formed to deal with the subjects which thereafter fell naturally within its scope: the Committee almost at once found itself dealing with such thorny subjects as music in Lodges, full dress regalia, proposal forms, and women Masons. A great deal of what the Committee considered and recommended to the Board was included in the revisions of the Book of Constitutions of 1926 and 1940, while other points of procedure were printed in the Masonic Year Book, and more recently in the booklet Information for the Guidance of Members of the Craft. Hence it follows that at the present time meetings are less frequent and agendas shorter than in its early days. In the main the Committee took care to avoid involvement in ritual matters, particularly after the episode of the extended installation ceremony.

14. All six of the 'statutory' committees have now been touched upon, but the Board from early times has had the power, and used it, to appoint committees for specific purposes: though sometimes wrongly referred to as Sub-Committees, a title which belongs to bodies appointed by one or other of the six committees, they are in fact in the same relationship to the Board as those Committees, i.e. they make recommendations which the Board proceeds to consider.

The most frequent is the Committee on Committees, which started in 1914. It is set up each year and normally consists of all six Chairmen, the Vice-

President and two other members, representing the Provinces and London: the President takes the Chair. Its sole function is to allocate membership of the six Committees equitably among the Board Members.

Perhaps the longest lived and best known of such Committees was the one formed to deal with the question of the Loyal Order of Moose: it did so in such masterly fashion that subsequent questions about para-Masonic bodies have been dealt with in the light of its findings.

Special Committees have from time to time considered appeals procedure, vocal music, precedence of Grand Officers, and have reported their findings in due course to the Board which has taken such action as it has thought fit.

15. From time to time a Judicial Committee was suggested, but nothing came of it following doubts expressed by the Grand Registrar of the time as to its constitutional propriety. Eventually however, and in stages, sufficiently recent to need no recapitulation, the judicial aspect of Grand Lodge was put on to an effective basis without involving the Board as such or any Committee emerging from it: this preserved the tradition of Grand Lodge as the ultimate Court of Appeal, while doing away with the ineffectual method of hearing appeals in circumstances where the weighing of evidence by an informed jury of 1500 was impossible and an appellant could, if he tried, win the sympathy of Grand Lodge by calling upon their compassion at the expense of their comprehension.

Looked at purely as a matter of political theory, the solution finally reached was much sounder than it would have been to have had a Committee of the Board acting as judge, jury and prosecutor.

16. The Board has never fettered itself with standing orders, or if it has outlined them they have quickly passed into oblivion. The nearest equivalent is perhaps the three or four line descriptions issued each year about the duties of the six Committees for the benefit of new members, which might very unofficially be described as their charters.

It does not appear that the absence of standing orders has in anyway impaired the efficiency of the Board's machinery. For the most part, the Board respects the judgement of the various Committees which tend to remain much the same from year to year, and to gain thereby considerable experience in the matters that come before them.

THE PRE-EMINENCE OF THE GREAT ARCHITECT IN FREEMASONRY

THE PRESTONIAN LECTURE FOR 1983

RICHARD H. S. ROTTENBURY, M.A. (Cantab.)

1. THE NAMES OF THE GREAT ARCHITECT IN THE CRAFT DEGREES

A sad-looking, crumpled figure of a man stands hesitantly at the bolted door, unkempt, dishevelled, ill-shod and blind. He seeks admittance to the warmth and friendship which the cold world outside cannot purvey. To attain those privileges, the help of mere man is impotent. Only by the help of God can that door be opened and the greater Truth revealed. Such is the familiar opening to the ceremony of initiation. It is no coincidence that the first utterances of the candidate, in a lodge, invoke the name of the Great Architect twice. To the first question to test his maturity and his responsibility as a man of full age, he replies, 'I am', unaware that 'I am' is one of the names of the Great Architect. In the Book *Exodus* is related the remarkable occasion when the great leader Moses was first confronted by the Almighty at the foot of Mount Horeb, in the form of a burning bush, with the words, 'Thus shalt thou say unto the Children, of Israel, "I AM hath sent me unto you".' Then, before the candidate is faced with the second question, he is aware of a powerful invocation, and being blind, his focus of attention is sharpened. The chaplain pronounces the titles 'Almighty Father' and 'Supreme Governor of the Universe', which indicate a supreme eminence and an absolute pre-requisite of acceptance of implications, before the ceremony can proceed further. The candidate is to unfold the beauties of true godliness not just for his own edification or benefit but primarily to the honour and glory of the Holy Name. Then comes the second question: 'In Whom do you put your trust?' 'In God', he replies.

Thus, in the first three minutes of the reception of a candidate, five names of the Great Architect emerge:

> I AM
> ALMIGHTY FATHER
> SUPREME GOVERNOR
> THE HOLY NAME
> and GOD

The sixth does not occur until the Obligation, when the candidate repeats that he is in the presence of the GREAT ARCHITECT. Finally, in the Charge after Initiation, the seventh name, CREATOR, is invoked, with the firm injunction of

194

'never mentioning His name but with that awe and reverence which are due from the creature to his Creator'.

In the Second Degree, He is called LORD, and in the Obligation, the GRAND GEOMETRICIAN. In the Third Degree, He is the RULER OF THE UNIVERSE; in the Obligation, THE MOST HIGH, and in the Charge, THE LORD OF LIFE. These twelve names of the Divine Being each describe a point of view, but nowhere does freemasonry offer a definition of the nature or attributes of God. It leaves such matters to each individual to fashion as best he can.

2. THE VERACITY OF THE GREAT ARCHITECT TO A FREEMASON

Freemasonry asks of a man only that he believes that God is. It was what every candidate in the old days of operative masonry had to affirm. The 'Charges of a Freemason' which preface the early Constitutions of the United Grand Lodge, and have a strong medieval background, say in their very first paragraph:

> A Mason is obliged, by his tenure, to obey the moral law; and if he rightly understand the art he will never be a stupid atheist nor an irreligious libertine. He, of all men, should best understand that God seeth not as man seeth; for man looketh at the outward appearance, but God looketh at the heart. A Mason is, therefore, particularly bound never to act against the dictates of his conscience. Let a man's religion or mode of worship be what it may, he is not excluded from the Order, provided he believe in the glorious Architect of heaven and earth, and practice the sacred duties of morality. Masons unite with the virtuous of every persuasion in the firm and pleasing bond of fraternal love; they are taught to view the errors of mankind with compassion, and to strive, by the purity of their own conduct, to demonstrate the superior excellence of the faith they may profess. Thus masonry is the centre of union between good men and true, and the happy means of conciliating friendship amongst those who must otherwise have remained at a perpetual distance'.

Freemasonry, therefore, does not even try to prove the existence of God. It assumes that Candidates already have that belief in their hearts. Yet, while freemasonry does not define its conception of God, certain attributes are assumed by the masonic system and taken for granted – such as the Fatherhood of God which it specifically names. For by its pattern masonry rests on God, lives in God, and seeks to lead men to God. Everything in masonry, every lesson, every lecture from the first step to the last degree, assumes the pre-eminence of God. Without God it has no meaning and no mission among men.

3. THE TITLE G.A., IN EARLY FREEMASONRY

Masonry rarely uses the name God. It uses alternatives like The Great Architect of the Universe. Of course such a phrase fits into the symbolism of the Craft, but the concept of the Creator as the Great Architect is much older than speculative masonry. The second oldest version of the manuscript Constitutions of Masonry (the *Cooke Manuscript* of 1410) is prefaced by a prayer which begins:

Thanked be God our Glorious Father and Founder and Former of Heaven and all things that in them is....

Another early reference to the Great Architect comes in a book written by J. V. Andreae in 1623: (translation by F. F. Schnilger and G. W. Speth)

> The best logician is our God
> Whom the conclusion never fails;
> He speaks – it is; He wills – it stands;
> He blows – it falls; He breathes – it lives.
> His words are true – e'en without proof,
> His counsel rules without command,
> Therefore can none foresee his end
> Unless in God he has his building
> And if we here below would learn
> By Compass, Needle, Square and Plumb,
> We never must o'erlook the mete
> Wherewith our God hath measured us.

Andreae took the symbols of the working tools from the Steinmetzen, the German masons, and he uses them in the sense that they were used in the early eighteenth century rituals, which he anticipated by a hundred years.

The first use of the expression 'Great Architect of the Universe' occurs in *Anderson's Constitutions* of 1723. Prichard's *Masonry Dissected* (1730) speaks of The Grand Architect and Contriver of the Universe. There is no doubt that the expression was current in freemasonry by the second half of the eighteenth century more usually in the form of Grand Architect rather than 'Great'. The Charter of Compact which set up the first Grand Chapter in 1766 is headed 'In the Name of the Grand Architect of the Universe'.

The expansion of the concept of the Almighty into separate designations for the three craft degrees, seems to have been a fairly late development. The terms Great Architect of a Universe, the Grand Geometrician of the Universe and The Most High, do not appear in the later English exposures such as the *Three Distinct Knocks*, of 1760, or the book *Jachin and Boaz*, published in 1762. In 1802, John Browne published, *The Masonic Master Key through the three degrees*. This was not an exposure but was a ritual written in cipher. Browne uses, 'In the Name of the Grand Architect of the Universe', in the Opening and Closing of the Lodge; the prayer for the First Degree Candidate has 'Grand Architect and Contriver of the Universe', and in the Third Degree, Hiram Abif is said to have gone into the Temple to pay his adoration to 'The Almighty God, the Grand Architect of the Universe'.

It seems most likely that the three designations now known to us were evolved when separate extended formal openings and closings were developed for the second and third degrees round about 1810. They appear thus in Preston's Lectures dating from about that time, but they probably became standard usage, throughout the craft as a result of the work of the Lodge of Reconciliation between 1813 and 1816. This was the lodge which was set up when the two Grand Lodges united in 1813, for the purpose of reconciling the two systems of working. One of the

results of this was that Christian elements and references were removed from the ritual so bringing it on to a border theistic basis, where it has remained.

We must bear in mind that the use of different names to describe the Creator has always been associated with a sense of awe and great mystery which goes back to the threshold of recorded history. From the writing of the Rev. C. J. Ball, a scholar of Asiatic literature, we learn that mysterious names, which it is unlawful for a man to utter, have played a great part in the sphere of religion, and we may trace the existence of such names from the earliest times. *Tradition says that the forefathers of the Hebrew Tribes were emigrants from Ur Casdim or Ur of the Chaldees. Many religious ideas and customs of the Jews had their origin in Babylonia. After their return from the Exile, a practice gradually prevailed of avoiding all utterance of the personal name of the God of Israel – Jahweh or Jehovah. Among the later substitutes for the name we find 'Adonai' (Lord) and 'Elohim' (God). In the Septuagint (the Greek Translation of the Old Testament, of which the oldest portion dates from the 3rd century B.C), the ineffable Name is always translated by the Greek word for LORD.

4.   THE LETTER 'G'

Whilst discussing words, a comment should be made about the letter 'G' which in most English lodges is found in the centre of the ceiling and is on every second degree tracing board. The absence of the letter 'G' in the appointments of most foreign lodges, is a key to much of the misunderstanding surrounding the symbol. In the English alphabet it is the seventh letter. In Greek and Coptic it occupies third place. It was associated with the third sacred name of God in Hebrew – GHADOL. In Syriac we have GAD, in Swedish GAD, in German GOTT and in English GOD – all derived from the Persian pronoun Goda – meaning 'HIM-SELF'.

It is reasonably certain that the letter 'G' was not used in English lodges as meaning GOD until late in the eighteenth-century, although the letter itself was certainly there in the early 1700's if not in the 1600's. William Hutchinson, in his *Spirit of Masonry* published in 1775, with the special sanction of Grand Lodge, wrote that the name of God is only part of the masonic import of the letter. 'It denotes Geometry, which to Artificers in the science by which all their labours are calculated and formed, and to Masons, contains the determination, definition and proof of the order, beauty and wonderful wisdom of the power of God in His Creation'.

A Masonic Catechism of 1730 ran as follows:

Q.   Why were you made a Fellowcraft?
A.   For the sake of the letter G.
Q.   What does G denote?
A.   Geometry, or the Fifth Science.

Thirty-six years later in 1766, in another Catechism, there was a clear reference to God:

Q.   Why was (sic) you made a Fellow Craft?
A.   For the sake of the letter G which is enclosed in a great light.
Q.   What does G denote?

* A.Q.C. Vol. V.

A.   Glory for God, Grandeur for the Master of the Lodge, and Geometry for the brothers.

A wise view is that God Himself and Geometry have much in common, and that today we may regard the symbol as standing for each and both of them. Then we shall not be far wrong when we teach the Fellow Craft that the letter G denotes God who is the Grand Geometrician of the Universe.

We can quote great authorities:

Plato, in the 4th century B.C., said that God was a Geometer – one versed in Geometry, a Geometrician.

Sir Thomas Browne in his *Religio Medici* of 1643, wrote that 'God is like a skilful geometrician'.

Milton in his *Paradise Lost* Book VII, clearly saw God as the Supreme Geometer:

> Then stayed the fervid wheels, and in his hand
> He took the Golden Compasses, prepared
> In God's Eternal store, to circumscribe
> This universe, and all created things.
> One foot he centred, and the other turned
> Round through the vast profundity obscure,
> And said, 'Thus far extend, thus far they bounds,
> This be thy just circumference, O World!'

5.   THE GREAT ARCHITECT AND TRACING BOARDS

Another symbol which directly links the freemason with the Great Architect is found on first degree tracing boards. Jacob's ladder represents the ladder which Jacob saw in his dreams when he beheld 'a ladder set up on the earth, and the top of it reached to Heaven; and behold angels of God ascending and descending on it'. It is not the only ladder known as a symbol of moral, intellectual and spiritual progress. There have been many, for the belief in the existence of a ladder leading from earth of Heaven was common at one time throughout the world. Many ancient mysteries such as the Persian, Brahmin and Scandinavian, used this symbol. A ladder is associated with the name of St. Augustine, and a ladder of Perfection is known in one of the additional degrees. Jacob's ladder was a prominent symbol in the early days of speculative masonry, and it is found on many breast jewels of the 1760 period. The number of rungs or steps in the various ladders was generally seven, which has been a mystic or sacred number for thousands of years. There were for example seven sacred planets, seven days in Creation, seven ages of Man, the seventh son of a seventh son was notable, among the Hebrews every seventh year was Sabbatical. The stories of Biblical characters like Pharaoh, Jacob and Samson, often turn on the number seven.

The number of steps in Jacob's ladder in freemasonry should apparently be seven: Temperance, Fortitude, Prudence, Justice, Faith, Hope and Charity. But often it is only three, for at some time or other an artist found he had not room for seven rungs on the tracing board he was painting, so he reduced the number. It will not surprise you perhaps that in an Irish ritual of the year 1796, the ladder is shown with eleven rungs! As might well be expected, the emblem has been found

capable of varied and elaborate explanations. It was supposed to lead the thoughts of the brethren to heaven; its rungs represented a moral and religious duty; if there were three rungs they represented Faith, Hope and Charity, with which the whole earth could be encircled. But for the purposes of our study, Jacob's ladder in freemasonry seems to point to the connection between earth and Heaven, man and God, and to represent Faith in God, Charity towards all men, and Hope in immortality.*

6. THE ATTITUDE OF THE FREEMASON TO THE GREAT ARCHITECT

In nothing is masonry more deep-seeing than in the way in which it deals with our attitude towards God, who is both the meaning and the mystery of life. It does not intrude, much less drive, in the intimate and delicate things of the inner life. Theologians will say that there are three aspects of the reverence due from the creature to his Creator: the reaching out of the mind to him in wonder, as elijah did at the month of the cave; the attempt to know Him in personal encounter as Job made it; or we may seek direction like Jeremiah or Jonah in fear and trembling. All these aspects are laid down as duties for us as freemasons but the gift of faith, the spiritual power, the very will to obey, are assumed as essential. The religious attitude is taken as already developed in every candidate and to seek further light without the previous preparation is like building walls without foundations.

All that masonry asks is that we confess our faith in a Supreme Being. It does not require that we analyse or define in detail any thought of God. Few men have formulated their profoundest faith. It goes deeper than the intellect, down into instincts and feelings. Life and love, joy and sorrow, pity and pain and death, the blood in the veins of men, the laughter of little children, the coming and going of days, all the old sweet, sad things that make up our mortal life – these are the basis of our faith in God. Older than argument, it is deeper than debate.

Two implicit suggestions however remain; that we continue to pray and that we continue to think about the pre-eminence of the Great Architect not only in masonry but in our lives. For to live in His World without becoming aware of the meaning of that world, is like wandering about in a great library without touching the books. And the response of the individual to the calls of masonry is quickened by the use of illustrative symbols: the Grand Design; the settlement of accounts without scruple or diffidence; rendering to neighbours every kind office that justice or mercy may required.

Of course this is nothing new. Men lived and died by faith in God long before philosophy was born. Ages before Theology had learned its letters. Vedic poets and penitential psalmists were praising God beyond the pyramids. In Egypt, 5,000 years ago, a poet king sang of the unity, purity and beauty of God, celebrating His presence revealed yet also concealed in the order of life.

---

* Rev. A. F. A. Woodford in *Kennings Masonic Cyclopaedia* 1878.

7. *FREEMASONRY AND DOGMA*

No man can put such things into words, much less into a hard and fast dogma. Masonry does not ask him to do so. All that it asks is that he tells, simply and humbly, in whom he puts his trust in life and in death, as the source of moral life and spiritual faith; and that is as far as it seeks to go.

One thinks of the talk of the old mason Alexeyevich Bazdeyev with the young nobleman Count Petrovich Bezuhov who was an atheist, in the Tolstoi story 'War and Peace'. When the young Count said with a sneer that he did not believe in God, the old mason smiled, as a mother might smile at the silly sayings of a child. Then he said, 'Yes, you do not know Him, Sir, you do not know Him, that is why you are unhappy. But He is here. He is within me. He is in you, even in those impious words you have just uttered. If He is not, we should not be speaking of Him, Sir. Whom hast thou denied? Who invented Him if He does not exist'. There was silence for a space. Something in the old man touched the young Count deeply, and stirred in him a longing to see what the old man saw and know what he knew. His eyes betrayed his longing to know God and the old man read his face and answered his unasked questions: 'Yes, He exists, but to know Him is hard. It is not the mind that compehends Him, it is life that makes us understand. Supreme wisdom and truth are like the purest dew. Only by inner purification can we know God'.

And in knowing Him, freemasonry warns us not to be dogmatic. It shows us that there are more facets for our vision of God than in the most curiously cut and largest diamond known to man. To focus merely on one facet, to have too rigid a conformation to any exclusive dogma can have its shortcomings and dangers. A touching story of a humble and ignorant worshipper was told about 750 years ago by the great Sufi poet of Persia, Jallalu d'Din. Moses, in his wanderings in the wilderness came upon a shepherd who was praying to God in the fervour of his soul, and saying, 'O my Master, my Lord, would that I knew where I might find Thee and become Thy servant. Would that I might tie Thy shoe-laces and comb Thy hair, and wash Thy robe and kiss Thy beautiful feet, and sweep Thy chamber and serve the milk of my goats to Thee, for whom my heart crieth out'. And the anger of Moses was kindled and he said to the shepherd, 'Thou blasphemer! The Most High has no body, and no need of clothing nor of nourishment, nor of a chamber, nor of a domestic. Thou art an infidel!' And the heart of the shepherd was darkened, for he could make to himself no image of one without bodily form and corporeal wants; and he gave himself up to despair and ceased to serve God. And God spake to Moses and said, 'Why hast thou driven my servant away from me? Every man received from me his mode of living, his way of speech. What is evil in thee is good in another. What is poison to thee is honey to him. Words are nothing to me. I read the heart. The compass serves only to direct the prayers of those who are without the Ka'ba. Within, no one has need of it'.

So, avoiding dogmatic interpretations of the Great Architect, masonry enables, on the floor of a lodge, men of all races and creeds to meet on common ground and make their devotions to a Creator who is neither God nor Allah nor Brahma nor Adi-Buddha nor Jehovah – but who is yet each and all of these.

8. THE MORALITY OF FREEMASONRY IN THE MODERN WORLD

Still, on the floor of the lodge, as men and as masons, we are aware of our human frailty. We are aware that although our mould is in the likeness of the Creator, yet we have imperfections which magnify our inadequacy before the throne of Grace. And in this space age of microtechnology, lasers and a pandora's box of scientific tricks which most of try with varying lack of success to comprehend, it is difficult to find the link between the morality of our masonry and the dubious morality of a bustling modern world. The link of course is the Great Architect Himself, who stands in timeless perfection as the Great Light, the Great Truth, the Great Reality.

9. THE INCOMPREHENSIBLE DIMENSION OF THE GREAT ARCHITECT

Yet even here our human inadequacy veils our understanding. in contemplating the miracle of Creation, we think of ourselves, of man, as having a very special place. Yet our judgements are made puny by our inability to appreciate the infinite. We are slaves of measurement and time. 'What time is it?' 'How long before ...' 'When does ...' 'How far is it to ...' 'How long is that?' 'How you've grown!' 'What a long way!'. We measure our minutes our hours, our years; we relate our location; we are fettered by dimension. These weaknesses continue as we look out into space. We feel so clever that man has been to the moon and has managed to push sophisticated lumps of staggeringly expensive machinery into orbit around the planet Venus, yet we still cannot comprehend that space is not only infinite, its curved; that in it there is no yesterday and no tomorrow.

10. THE HUMILITY ESSENTIAL IN ALL FREEMASONS

The more we learn of our world, our universe, the more we learn of the composition of matter, of atoms and their particles, then the more awe-inspiring becomes the perfection of the Divine Creator. Yet, bound as we are by the conventions of time and dimension, our humility is rarely as abject as it should be. We fall so easily into the humanistic trap that man is supremely important. We lose sight of our insignificance in the wonder of Creation.

Let me illustrate this by the light-heartened but far-fetched story of three intrepid entered apprentices, who were instructed to do an unusual thing. Early one summer's morning when everyone was fast asleep, obeying their written instructions, they arrived in Trafalgar Square with a huge crane, an enormous articulated aircraft fuselage container and a compressed-air engine. With commendable speed and using the power engine, they unscrewed the lions at the foot of Nelson's column, and, using the crane lifted off the column with Nelson on the top and laid it carefully on the fuselage transporter. Then, without delay they left London, reached the M2 and sped on to Dover where 'Free Enterprise X' was waiting to take them to Calais. Thence on through France to the Alps, to the great Mont Blanc, where with the considerable diligence expected of eager young masons they

proceeded to the top of the mountain where they erected the column. Carefully placing a ladder against the side, they climbed to the top and on the top of Nelson's hat they placed a ten-penny piece, and on the top of the ten-penny piece they placed a 15p postage stamp. They climbed down, well pleased with their work well done.

This preposterous story is less futile than at first it may seem, for using its imagery we can pamper our yearnings for dimensions in finding out more about ourselves. Let us refresh our minds of the picture: Mont Blanc, with Nelson's column on top, with a ten-penny piece on the top of Nelson's hat, and a postage stamp on top of that.

Now the height of Mont Blanc represents the time it took for the planet Earth to form, cool and take its shape. The height of Nelson's column represents the time it took for very early life forms to develop – lichens and amoeba. The thickness of the ten-penny piece represents the time it took for the development of mammals; and the thickness of the postage stamp represents the time it took for the development of us – man. And the thickness of the paint on the top of the postage stamp represents the time of masonic history since the building of the first Temple at Jerusalem – a time in which we play a tiny and recent part. A sobering thought!

It is sometimes useful to reflect on how significant we are in this pattern of Creation and how magnificent is the Creator of it all. In many ways we are at a stage in our culture not unlike that of three centuries ago, when speculative masonry was sorting itself out. The world has struck its tents and is on the move again. Changes are taking place in public opinion as violent as nuclear reactions. Vast regions are becoming as unified as present day towns. Races, long uncivilised, are turning into more prosperous industrial nations. Organisational man is in control and he is not specifically white, black, brown or yellow.* As the aristocracy of blood, family, caste, race, culture, religion and even political skill die around us, what is still needed is a way of talking about love and justice which will put searching questions to 20th Century independent man.† Will brotherly love, relief and truth be capable of solving man's problems? Only, I suggest, if the pre-eminence of the Great Architect is a reality and is seen to be a reality. And this relies on a triangle of intent so neatly expressed by a contemporary continental mason, Robert Amadou:

> Croyez en Dieu, au Dieu que vous voudrez, mais croyez en Dieu. Priez Dieu, de la prière que vous voudrez, mais priez Dieu. Travaillez à la gloire de Dieu, du travail que vous voudrez, mais travaillez à la gloire de Dieu.

Believe in God, pray to God; build to the glory of God.‡

I close with a gem which I found when prowling around the shelves of the little masonic library in Canterbury. It comes from a magazine – *Boldino Masonico* – Masonic Bulletin, published in Mexico in 1892. Even in translation it carries something of the beauty which, for each mason, is the pre-eminent relationship between him as a private individual and his God:

* V.Rev. H. G. M. Clarke in *Grand Lodge 1717–1967*
† Ian McKenzie in *The Times*, 6.8.66.
‡ Robert Amadou. MS *Le Grand Architecte de l'Univers*.

The God of Masonry is the benign and compassionate Creator, who is felt in all that smiles and all that sighs; where there is suffering and where there is love; where we hear the songs of the children and see the tears of the aged; in the rainbow that changes its colours; in the luminous bodies in the heavens; in all that has wings and perfumes, essences and balsam, music and prayers, intuition and smiles, linked to the immense veneration that exists in our hearts.

APPENDIX A

SOURCES

Of the many sources consulted, the following short list represents those which were most helpful:

AMADOU, Robert: *Le Grand Architecte de l'Univers*, MS.
ANDERSON, J.: *Constitutions*.
BALL, Rev. C.: *The Proper Names of Masonic Tradition*.
CARR, H.: *The Freemason at Work* and *The Early Masonic Catechisms'*. (ed.).
CLARKE, V. Rev. H. G. M.: *Freemasonry and Religion*.
COCKBURN: *Freemasonry*.
GRIFFITHS: *The Great Architect of the Universe*, in the *Masonic Record* 1924.
HALL, M. P.: *Freemasonry and Philosophy*.
HAUNCH, T. O.: *The Great Architect, A.Q.C.*, Vol. 86 (1973).
JOHNSON: *The Great Architect*, Boston 1915.
JONES, B. E.: *Freemasons Guide and Compendium*. *The Freemasons Book of the Royal Arch*.
STUART, N.: *The Long Search*.
THORPE: *The Religion and Ethics of Freemasonry*, in Transactions: Leicester Lodge of Research 1916–17.
TYDEMAN, Rev. R.: *Freemasonry and the Church*.

APPENDIX B

THE RELATIONSHIP OF FREEMASONRY AND RELIGION

Statement adopted by Grand Lodge on 12th Sepember 1962 and re-issued in the Extracts from the proceedings of the Quarterly Communications of Grand Lodge of 9th December, 1981:

It cannot be too strongly asserted that Masonry is neither a religion nor a substitute for religion. Masonry seeks to inculcate in its members a standard of conduct and behaviour which it believes to be acceptable to all creeds, but studiously refrains from intervening in the field of dogma or theology. Masonry, therefore, is not a competitor with religion though in the sphere of human conduct it may be hoped that its teaching will be complementary to that of religion. On the other hand its basic requirement that every member of the Order shall believe in a Supreme Being and the stress laid upon his duty towards Him should be sufficient evidence to all but the wilfully prejudiced that Masonry is an upholder of religion since it both requires a man to have some form of religious belief before he can be admitted as a Mason, and expects him when admitted to go on practising his religion.

GETTING AND GIVING MASONIC KNOWLEDGE

'... and be always ready to give or to receive instruction...'

THE PRESTONIAN LECTURE FOR 1984

HARRY MENDOZA

Immediately following the Sanction of the *Book of Constitutions* comes the 'Summary of the ANTIENT CHARGES AND REGULATIONS to be read ... to the MASTER ELECT, prior to his Installation into the Chair of a Lodge'. The ninth clause in this summary includes;

'You agree to ... propagate the knowledge of the Mystic Art as far as your influence and ability can extend.'

It was Preston who, in the 1775 edition of his *Illustrations of Masonry*, first published such a précis for this purpose. The one we know is substantially the same as his. One difference is in the clause just quoted. Preston said '... and be always ready to give or to receive instruction.' It is these words that I have chosen as a sub-title to this Prestonian Lecture.

It has been said that Preston was not an innovator of ritual. He did not compose new material; what he did was to weld together the words of others to suit a particular purpose. His Lectures and Consecration Ceremony are good examples. But he was also what I would call a masonic educator, one who uses a process or method of imparting knowledge on subjects relating to Freemasonry.

In Preston's day masonic instruction was conveyed in a series of Lectures in question and answer form. Today we have other methods but the Lectures are still occasionally heard.

My purpose is to outline briefly the ways of obtaining and imparting masonic knowledge practised in our own and some other Constitutions, and then to suggest possible alternatives. What I hope to achieve is

(a) to inculcate the *desire* amongst brethren to get and be willing to give more masonic knowledge;

(b) to satisfy that desire to some extent by showing how a modest masonic knowledge can be obtained or given, and

(c) to encourage the more enthusiastic mason to seek further enlightènment.

Although I shall throughout refer to the Craft, my remarks will also apply (*mutatis mutandis*) to the Royal Arch. I would remind you of the 'Preliminary Declaration' in our *Book of Constitutions* that in England pure Antient Masonry *includes* the Royal Arch while emphasising that different views are held elsewhere.

A TYPICAL 'CASE-HISTORY'

Let us start by asking ourselves what masonic knowledge a freemason is likely to have by the time he reaches the Chair of his lodge. Much, of course, will depend on the individual, his curiosity, his willingness and ability to learn, his enthusiasm and his fortune in having brethren who can guide him and can answer his questions correctly. What follows is, I believe, a fairly typical example.

The candidate for initiation will have been told that he will be taking part in a ceremony and given a friendly pat on the back accompanied by the words 'Don't worry, we've all been through the same ceremony. You'll probably be a little bewildered when it is all over, but you'll soon learn all about it!' I wish I had as much faith in the last few words as I have in the phrase which precedes them! He almost certainly *will* be bewildered by the time the ceremony is over but, regrettably, it is unlikely that he will soon know all about it.

He will not have time to recover from his bewilderment when he is given the *Book of Constitutions* and the By-Laws of the lodge, both of which he is advised to read. He should also be given a copy of the booklet *Information for the Guidance of Members of the Craft*, but this does not always happen. More's the pity, because at this stage of his masonic career this is the best of the three for him to read! In addition some lodges give the new brother a copy of *The Constitutions and Regulations of the Grand Charity*.

Some relaxation will follow at the 'after-proceedings', and provided that he is not too worried about the response he knows he has to give to the Toast to himself, he will enjoy them. But some of his bewilderment will return when (as so often happens) the brother who proposes this Toast proceeds to explain the significance of parts of the ceremony barely remembered by the candidate. He is already confused, and confusion becomes worse confounded by his attempts to master the masonic 'fire' for which he may be given three or four different explanations.

He will soon have heard about the Lodge of Instruction and may even have been encouraged to attend on suitable occasions.

When he has taken his second degree he will probably have learnt a little about the masonic Charities. He will also know that there is a 'Headquarters' known as Grand Lodge and may even take some notice of the snippets of information from the Quarterly Communications read by the Secretary towards the end of the lodge meeting when some of the brethren are becoming restless and want the formal proceedings to end and the informal to begin.

In time he becomes a Master Mason. He begins to appreciate that if he wants to master the ritual he will have to attend the Lodge of Instruction on a more regular basis. He does so and, showing some aptitude, he progresses through the various offices and even takes the chair to perform the ceremonies. Thus by the time he takes office in the Lodge he may well have acquired a measure of competency. But questions he raises on matters other than ritual are often brushed aside with the comment that he should concentrate on learning the ritual by heart before worrying about anything else! There are times when he feels positively discouraged in his efforts to extend his masonic knowledge beyond the ritual he has learnt.

When he becomes Junior Warden he decides to attend the next Quarterly

Communication. When he arrives he is told that he cannot be admitted because he hasn't brought his collar with him; nobody had told him he should do so. Indeed, his lodge's Tyler will have collected it from him after each meeting. With luck, one of the attendants at the Grand Temple will lend him one so that he can be admitted.

As Senior Warden he is encouraged to give the 'long working' at the presentation of the apron. At the same meeting there is a talk by a visiting brother on English Craft aprons and he is surprised to find that what he has been taught, and what he sincerely believes, as the reason for its shape and adornments, and to which he has himself just referred in his address, are without foundation; they are just someone's idea of the symbolism which could be attached to our badge.

And so to the chair, where he agrees to propagate the knowledge of the Mystic Art so far as his influence and ability can extend. On the way home from his Installation he reflects on this and begins to realize that perhaps he is not as adequately prepared for the task as he should be. But the Secretary is always to hand and with his assistance, and that of the Preceptor of the Lodge of Instruction (who is also the Director of Ceremonies), he copes reasonably well and at the end of his year of office feels that he hasn't let the lodge down after all.

It may be that perhaps I have been unfair in this typical 'case-history', but I really do not think so. A remark made nearly twenty years ago by R. W Bro Sir Lionel Brett is still apposite. He said; 'Most (brethren) would ... regard the purpose of masonic teaching for the ordinary brother as being correctly summed up in the words "secrecy, morality and good fellowship." '

The amount of masonic knowledge the newly-Installed Master possesses is, regrettably, fairly limited. I must acknowledge, however, that there are always exceptions. Some brethren are not satisfied with the answers they get to the questions they ask and they take the trouble to find someone who is willing and able to give them correct information. Others are lucky enough to find themselves in the company of knowledgeable masons who are only too willing to encourage the brother who evinces a general desire for knowledge.

THE REASONS FOR LIMITED MASONIC KNOWLEDGE

The reasons for limited masonic knowledge put forward by a brother can be summarized as follows:

(a) his family commitments must come first;
(b) he hasn't the time because of business commitments;
(c) he is either reluctant to ask or feels discouraged from asking questions;
(d) he doesn't know where to get information;
(e) he is too busy learning the ritual, and
(f) he has lost interest.

One also hears that there is no time to spare in lodge for talks and the like because, firstly, there must be candidates as finances depend of their fees. Secondly, the progression of the candidates must not be held back, and thirdly the lodge programme is too full for anything but the three degrees and Installation.

A few words on each of these. It is surely far better for the Craft in general and the member in particular that he should possess a limited knowledge of Freemasonry and have a happy and contented wife than be a knowledgeable freemason and have a wife who is resentful about the length of time he spends on masonic affairs! So the pressure of family and business commitments are valid reasons why it is difficult (but not impossible) for a brother to acquire a good standard of masonic knowledge.

One can readily understand that a brother may feel reluctant to ask questions or is intimidated from asking them because he does not want to give the impression of seeking information that he should not have or of appearing to go beyond the boundaries that have been set. This reluctance should not apply with the same force once he has been raised. Another reason for his reluctance may be that he has gained the impression that those who are asked the questions *cannot* answer them correctly.

It is difficult to argue with the next reason given, that he is too busy learning the ritual. But, if the ritual *is* being well and truly learnt, the brother *is* gaining masonic knowledge.

As for loss of interest, I suggest that something could and should be done by the Lodge Committee. Boredom may arise from the repetitious nature of the work; first degree; second degree; third degree; Installation; repeated *ad infinitum*.

As to the lack of time for talks and the like I suggest that the first reason given should be rejected out of hand. It surely cannot be right for the finances of the lodge to be dependent on candidates' fees. One can appreciate the other two reasons given though a careful look at the programme could result in improvements. The giving of masonic knowledge other than in the degree ceremonies need take only a few moments. A forty-minute talk is not necessary; a brief session at each meeting could be very useful. For example it only takes about three minutes to read out one of the questions and answers printed in the Quatuor Coronati Lodge summons. I am sure members would rather hear something like that than some of the 'long-workings' that creep in. A careful study of how lodge time is apportioned (a kind of 'time and motion' study) might well show that there is more than enough space for a short talk or demonstration.

Not knowing where to get information can easily be overcome as will hereafter be explained.

So we can see that there *are* some very good reasons why brethren have a limited amount of masonic knowledge, and that there are areas where some improvement could and should be made to stimulate interest and encourage pursuit of that knowledge.

WHOSE RESPONSIBILITY?

Who has (or should have) the responsibility for giving masonic knowledge? A lot of useful information is published, particularly by Grand Lodge, which if read and digested would assist any brother in his 'daily advancement'.

One important thing is missing – a recommended plan. As will hereafter be seen, some Grand Lodges have Masonic Education Committees; our Grand Lodge

does not. Should it have one? Should a Grand Lodge be responsible for ensuring that masonic knowledge is obtainable in an orderly and recognized manner? Or should this be the responsibility of the Preceptor of the Lodge of Instruction or the Master of the Lodge, or the candidate's sponsors? Should the candidate accept that the responsibility for learning about Freemasonry is *his*? If so, who should guide him?

Let's start with the candidate and his sponsors. The candidate agrees in open lodge that he has 'a general desire for knowledge'. But, at least in the early stages of his masonic career, he cannot get it on his own; he must have some guidance. Surely both his sponsors have a duty to guide him in this matter. Many do so, at least so far as the ritual is concerned. But there is usually little help beyond that.

The Preceptor of the Lodge of Instruction certainly has a duty to impart masonic knowledge; after all he is in charge of the proceedings at the Lodge of *Instruction*. But too often (and for very good reasons) it is only the ritual work that is practised and guidance on other masonic matters is rarely given. Indeed not every lodge has a Lodge of Instruction.

The Master also has a responsibility. On the night of his Installation he agreed to propagate the knowledge of Freemasonry as far as his influence and ability can extend. That responsibility doesn't end when he leaves the chair; it applies to every *Past* Master. In addition the Master is also told that it is within his province to impart light and instruction to the brethren of his lodge.

Many Past Masters, including Grand Officers, have told me that the responsibility of giving masonic knowledge should be that of Grand Lodge. They were not always too happy when I pointed out that this meant the responsibility was *theirs*. The members of Grand Lodge include not only Grand Officers, but also the Master and suitably qualified Past Masters and Wardens of every regular private lodge. Perhaps what they really meant was that the Board of General Purposes should make a recommendation about masonic education and that this should be adopted by Grand Lodge. This could be done under Rule 229 of the *Book of Constitutions*:- 'The Board may recommend or report to the Grand Lodge … whatever it may deem conducive to the welfare and good government of the Craft.' The furtherance of masonic education must, I think, be deemed to be 'conductive to the welfare and good government of the Craft.' Once adopted by Grand Lodge, the recommendation must be treated as an Edict in accordance with the terms of the Rule.

WHERE CAN ONE GET MASONIC KNOWLEDGE

The following sources are suggested;

(a) the Preceptor of the Lodge of Instruction
(b) the Past Masters and officers of one's own lodge
(c) talks and demonstrations
(d) Lodges of Installed Masters
(e) Lodges of Research and their publications
(f) masonic libraries and museums
(g) books; a list of recommended reading can be obtained from Grand Lodge,

Quatuor Coronati Lodge, the London Grand Rank Association and from most Provincial Grand Lodges

(h) Grand Lodge publications:
  (i) THE BOOK OF CONSTITUTIONS (current edition)
  (ii) INFORMATION FOR THE GUIDANCE OF MEMBERS OF THE CRAFT (current edition)
  (iii) GRAND LODGE 1717–1967 (1967)
  liv) MASONIC YEAR BOOK (annual)
  (v) MASONIC YEAR BOOK HISTORICAL SUPPLEMENT (2nd ed., 1969; Supplement, 1977)
  (vi) Proceedings of the Quarterly Communications of Grand Lodge
  (vii) THE REPORT OF THE GRAND MASTER'S COMMITTEE OF INQUIRY ON MASONIC CHARITY (The Bagnall Report, 1973)

Questions on the Charities and about other masonic Orders and degrees can be put to the relevant headquarters, the addresses of which can normally be obtained from Grand or Provincial Grand Lodge. It is important to emphasize that correspondence with sister Grand Lodges of the Craft must be initiated through our own Grand Secretary.

Masonic libraries and museums are valuable sources of knowledge. The measure of their usefulness will largely depend on whether the librarians and their staffs take active or passive roles, and inevitably on the funds available to them.

There are many masonic libraries in England, some combined with museums. The encouragement and help given by the staff of the library and museum at Freemasons' Hall, London, are of a high order. I have found that the information which they provide often extends my masonic knowledge well beyond the boundaries of my original question.

Lodge Secretaries should regularly remind brethren (as Grand Lodge Proceedings recommends) of the notice in the *Masonic Year Book* about the Grand Lodge library and museum. A visit cannot fail to arouse interest and so lead to the extension of one's masonic knowledge.

A REASONABLE AMOUNT OF MASONIC KNOWLEDGE

I am not suggesting that all Installed Masters should be 'learned masons', but they should have a *reasonable* amount of masonic knowledge. Let me be more specific by making comments under selected headings. What follows is not meant to be a 'curriculum', nor does it set an upper limit to the extent of research. Indeed it is hoped that Masters-to-be will so enjoy getting masonic knowledge that as Past Masters they will continue to seek it and that they will be encouraged to pass to others the benefit of their studies.

Ritual matters.   Here is where most of us begin. Before taking office a brother should be able to satisfy himself and his Preceptor (or Director of Ceremonies) that he is fully capable of discharging his duties in a satisfactory manner. He should not only know the *words*; he should also have a good idea of their meaning and the moral lessons that they are intended to convey. This will help him to

deliver the ritual effectively and with understanding, thus enabling the candidate to both appreciate and enjoy the ceremony.

It is to be hoped that the brother will have learnt that the ritual has *not* been handed down from the days of Solomon, that there is no 'authorised version' of the ritual in England (things may be different under other Constitutions) and that there are many recognized 'workings'. Whilst he does not need to know much about the Lodges of Promulgation and Reconciliation, he should at least know why and when they were set up.

Some knowledge should also be had of the 'permissive' variations of the penalties mentioned in our Obligations.

Not many lodges work the Lectures of the degrees, but I would strongly recommend every brother to read them as soon as he can and certainly before he reaches the Master's chair. They can help considerably his understanding of the ritual.

The history of Freemasonry.   Despite what we say about 'time immemorial' and despite the fact that our ritual and Lectures make many references to Biblical events and personalities, Freemasonry does *not* go back that far. It is not essential that a brother should be aware of all the arguments put forward by masonic historians as to when Freemasonry *did* start, but he should have a general idea of its growth.

He should certainly be aware that the first Grand Lodge was formed in England in 1717; that another Grand Lodge came into being about 1751; why the earlier Grand Lodge was called 'the Moderns' and the latter 'the Antients'; that there was discord between the two Grand Lodges but that they were happily 'united in December 1813 and that this is the reason why our present-day Grand Lodge is called 'the *United* Grand Lodge'.

A brother should also have some knowledge of the growth of the three degrees as well as knowing something of the history of the lodge furniture, the regalia worn and the custom of giving 'fire' at the after-proceedings. With such knowledge he will enjoy his Freemasonry much more.

Symbolism.   Freemasonry, we are taught, is 'a peculiar system of morality, veiled in allegory and illustrated by symbols.' We can understand the ritual much better if we appreciate the allegory and can interpret the symbols.

A symbol (according to *The Shorter Oxford English Dictionary*) is 'something that stands for, represents, or denotes something else (not by exact resemblance, but by vague suggestion, or by some accidental or conventional relation)'.

There is not much difficulty in understanding the symbolism when the ritual working or Lecture tells us what the word, act or object is meant to symbolize. It is when no such explanation is given that we find great difficulty. Symbolism is subjective; it has its source in the mind. Hence, since we do not all think alike, the interpretation of a symbol may well be different from man to man. Some early masonic writers have given us their ideas of the symbolic nature of much that is found in our ceremonies. Amongst the foremost of these are Wellins Calcott, William Hutchinson, William Preston and Dr. George Oliver.

Whilst we may be guided by our masonic ancestors, each of us should try to find his own interpretation. I suggest that the keynote should be simplicity, and not some abstruse theory comprehensible to only a few. Nor should a dogmatic attitude be adopted. This is one aspect of Freemasonry where imagination occasionally runs wild. In a paper read to Quatuor Coronati Lodge some years ago Bro T. O. Haunch wrote; 'Symbolism is a fertile field in which equally fertile minds have in the past reaped an exotic harvest'. Bro Harry Carr has referred to 'a paralytic harvest'.

The ethics and dogma of Freemasonry. By 'ethics' I mean the virtues we are charged to uphold; Brotherly Love, Relief and Truth, the three Grand Principles of the Order; the three moral virtues of Faith, Hope and Charity, and the four cardinal virtues of Temperance, Fortitude, Prudence and Justice. Every brother has heard them referred to in the ritual, but I wonder how often he stops to think about them! These virtues and the moral lessons we learn from the ritual may be said to be the ethics of Freemasonry.

The word 'dogma' usually tends to be associated with religion, but this is not necessarily so. The word also means 'a philosophical tenet' or 'a decree'. *The Shorter Oxford English Dictionary* also gives 'the body of opinion formulated and authoritatively stated'.

I suggest that the dogma of Freemasonry is principally represented by the Landmarks and the principles and tenets of the Order. For explanation of these terms I can do no better than direct your attention to the book by Bro Harry Carr, *The Freemason at Work*.

Two important statements issued by Grand Lodge, 'Basic Principles for Grand Lodge Recognition' and 'Aims and Relationships of the Craft' (both of which are included in the booklet *Information for the Guidance of Members of the Craft*) represent part of the dogma of Freemasonry and, like the Landmarks, and tenets and principles of the Order, should be part of every brother's masonic knowledge.

The government of the Craft. Most brethren have a general idea of how the Craft is governed. They know that the affairs of the lodge are usually looked after by a committee, guided by the Secretary. Many brethren would say that, although the Master is said to 'rule and direct' the lodge, it is quite often the Secretary who is 'the boss'. Occasionally one hears that it is the Preceptor or Director of Ceremonies, or perhaps the 'Father of the lodge' who takes the lead in discussion.

Some brethren will also tell you that 'orders' or 'instructions' emanate from Grand Lodge, though there is some vagueness in answer to the question 'What is Grand Lodge?'. I get the impression at times that, using a large business concern as an analogy, some brethren think that the Grand Master is president, the Pro Grand Master the non-executive chairman, the Deputy Grand Master, the Assistant Grand Master and some other Grand Officers the executive board of directors and the Grand Secretary the managing director, other Grand Officers holding a kind of honorary membership. There is often some surprise when I have told the newly-invested Junior Warden that he is now a full member of Grand Lodge and that he has the same right to vote as the Assistant Grand Master!

It is not necessary for the brethren to know much about the government of the Craft, but surely it can only be to everyone's advantage if they know the broad details; the relationship between their lodge and (where appropriate, Provincial Grand and) Grand Lodge; the existence and functions of the Board of General Purposes and the Secretariat.

The Charities.   Whilst it may not be necessary for brethren to know the details of the Bagnall Committee Report, they should at least be broadly aware of what is happening as a result of that Report. The most up-to-date information (at June 1983) can be found in Appendix B to the Minutes of the General Meeting of the Grand Charity held on 9 March 1983.

The Masonic Foundation for the Aged and Sick was set up in 1979. This is concerned with the care of the aged and sick, work at present being done by the Royal Masonic Benevolent Institution and the Royal Masonic Hospital.

The Masonic Trust for Girls and Boys was established on 8 September 1982. It will lead to a complete amalgamation of the present two separate Institutions on or soon after 1 January 1986.

A greater understanding of the good work done by our Charities should help every freemason to know more about one of the three Grand Principles on which our Order is founded, namely Relief. Hopefully such knowledge will encourage those who can afford it to be more generous in their donations.

Talking to non-freemasons.   It would be helpful to many members of the Craft to have some guidance on discussing Freemasonry other than with their brethren. Some take the view that no-one outside their immediate family should know that they are freemasons. When questions are asked they change the subject as adroitly as they can. If they can not they are at a loss, fearing to divulge something that ought not to be known by non-freemasons. They may have read and remembered the Antient Charge found at the beginning of the *Book of Constitutions* which says 'You shall be cautious in your words ... that the most penetrating stranger shall not be able to discover or find out what is not proper to be intimated; and sometimes you shall divert a discourse ...'

Whilst due caution should be taken it must surely be right when the occasion demands to say something about the Craft. This is especially so with regard to possible candidates.

In an Address to Grand Lodge on 28 April 1982 the Grand Master said 'Misconceptions about Freemasonry die hard and I am not convinced that we in the Craft are always as active in dispelling them as we might be ... it may now be worth exploring why people become freemasons ... doing so may help us clear our minds for the next time we encounter a potential candidate for initiation, or when we meet a sceptic about the Craft who is prepared to be open-minded'.

An announcement made in Grand Lodge on 9 December 1981 is also relevant. It advised that there could be no objection to a neutrally-worded approach being made to a man who is considered a suitable candidate for Freemasonry. He could be reminded once but then left to make his own decision without further solicitation.

I wonder how many of us could, without guidance, discuss Freemasonry with a potential candiate or a critic of the Craft who is prepared to be open-minded. I am sure many could. I am equally sure that many could not and it seems to me therefore that this is an item worthy of consideration under the heading 'Getting and giving masonic knowledge.' I might add that some years ago Bro Dashwood, a Past Master and Secretary of Quatuor Coronati Lodge, wrote a very helpful article entitled 'What shall we tell the candidate?' copies of which are still available from Quatuor Coronati Lodge or the London Grand Rank Association.

OTHER CONSTITUTIONS

General. Our Grand Secretary was kind enough to write on my behalf to his counterpart in the following Grand Lodges (selected by him) asking them to give me what information they could on the subject of masonic education in their jurisdictions. They are here listed in order of seniority:

The Grand Lodge of Ireland	(c. 1725)
The Grand Lodge of Scotland	(1736)
The Grand Lodge of the State of New York	(1781)
The Grand Lodge of Texas	(1837)
The Grand Lodge of Canada in the Province of Ontario	(1855)
The Grand Lodge of South Australia	(1884)
The United Grand Lodge of New South Wales	(1888)
The United Grand Lodge of Victoria	(1889)
The Grand Lodge of New Zealand	(1890)
The Grand Lodge of Western Australia	(1900)
The Grand Lodge of Alberta	(1905)

It is not claimed, nor is it intended to give the impression, that these eleven Grand Lodges are representative of the whole. They govern barely ten per cent the regular Craft, though it should be pointed out that some of them acknowledge the help they have had from other Grand Lodges in devising their masonic education programmes. In passing, however, one might mention that some well-known public opinion polls have been shown to be fairly accurate in their findings on such a sample!

A great deal of information has been received from these Grand Lodges, all of which was full of interest but only a part can here be incorporated.

A positive attitude. The general impression gained is that in all but two cases the Grand Lodges showed a great concern for getting and giving masonic knowledge in its widest sense. The two exceptions were Ireland and Scotland. This concern manifested itself in four areas:

(a) in statements made by the Grand Master or other senior Grand Officers;
(b) in the formation of Masonic Education Committees and the like;
(c) in the active part played by senior Grand Officers, including the Grand Master, in giving masonic knowledge, and
(d) in the efforts made to gain the interest of the wife and family of the candidate.

Authoritative educational bodies.   The majority of the Grand Lodges contacted have Masonic Education Committees. Some have been formed fairly recently; others have a history of up to half a century. Each is responsible to its Grand Lodge either directly or through the Board of General Purposes. Their responsibilities may generally be described as being similar to those laid down in the Canada/Ontario *Book of Constitutions*, namely 'To stimulate, supplement and support lodge and district programs about matters relating to the history, philosophy and symbolism of Masonry; to arrange for the preparation and distribution of masonic literature and information; to encourage the participation of members in education and information programs on lodge and district levels, and to provide assistance and counsel, when requested, in the organisation of education programs on lodge and district levels'.

The Masonic Education Committees do not usually deal with ritual matters, especially where there is an official ritual, other committees existing for this purpose.

Information booklets for candidates.   All the Grand Lodges referred to issue booklets or pamphlets to the prospective candidate, the Entered Apprentice, the Fellow Craft and the Master Mason. These usually contain information on Freemasonry in general and the appropriate Grand Lodge in particular, some details regarding the relevant degree and its symbols and allegories, and some philosophical matter.

Lodge System of Education.   In some jurisdictions this is known as 'The Mentor System of Education'. An experienced member of the lodge is appointed to act as a companion to each candidate accepted for initiation and to guide him through each of the degrees. His task is to educate the candidate, thus supplementing the information contained in the booklets already mentioned and to ensure that the candidate and his wife are made welcome.

Leadership Courses.   These are special courses run by some Grand Lodges, usually for officers of the lodge. They cover such subjects as planning the year as Master, planning the meeting, planning the work programme, training the lodge team, communication, planning the social programme, lodge business procedure, finance, getting the best from lodge ceremonies, monthly meeting agenda items, the festive board, proposing Toasts, fraternals, the Tyler, examination of visitors, investigation of candidates and masonic funeral service. In some cases a course is specifically designed for Wardens to equip themselves for Mastership of their respective lodges.

Study Courses.   A few Grand Lodges run special correspondence study courses. These cover a wide variety of masonic subjects and their objective is to ensure that the student really does have a comprehensive masonic education. One such course consists of a four-year programme of eight monthly assignments in each year. Each assignment contains explanations, readings and illustrations and should take up to about five hours work. Brethren are under no compulsion to complete the

four-year course, though a successful completion of each stage is necessary before any attempt can be made on the next stage.

Special publications. Some Grand Lodges authorize special publications. For example, Canada/Ontario issue four particularly interesting books, *Beyond the Pillars, Meeting the Challenge, Whence Come We?* and *A Functional Glossary of the Work.* The first three received commendatory reviews in *Ars Quatuor Coronatorum* (vols. 86, 90 and 94 respectively). The fourth contains something like 250 words and names and gives a clear indication of how they should be pronounced. The purpose of this book is stated to be 'to assist in producing uniformity' in the communication of the ritual.

Alberta issues a four-page monthly *Grand Lodge Bulletin.* Each issue contains articles, local masonic news, photographs and reviews. There are occasional editorials and messages from the Grand Master. The *Bulletin* is printed as a service to masons in Alberta under the guidance of a Bulletin Committee.

Other features of interest. At least one Grand Lodge (Western Australia) holds talks for presentation within the lodge room at a function for ladies and their guests. These talks comprise a brief history of Freemasonry in general and of that in Western Australia in particular, some details about the charitable work undertaken by the Grand Lodge and some general comments on the lay-out of the lodge.

This same Grand Lodge holds an Entered Apprentices' function every quarter. Recently initiated brethren and their ladies are invited and the Grand Master and Senior Grand Officers address them, describing Freemasonry from its beginnings to the present day.

SUGGESTIONS

It is tempting to suggest that because a particular plan of action has proved worthwhile under other Constitutions, the same plan would prove worthwhile in England, but that isn't necessarily so. Many factors have to be considered before embarking on any masonic education programme, amongst which are:

(a) the attitude of Grand Lodge;
(b) the necessity for taking any action;
(c) whether or not there is an official ritual working;
(d) the problems of communication;
(e) financial aspects, and
(f) how the programme is going to be maintained.

Perhaps the most important aspect is whether it is necessary to take any action at all. So far as England is concerned, I am quite certain that some brethren will say 'We've managed well enough without a masonic education programme for over 250 years. Why start one now? What we do is surely enough'.

I believe that our facilities for getting and giving masonic knowledge *are* reasonably good, though perhaps they are not always used as effectively as they might be. I also feel that some improvements could be made.

In England we can, I suggest, very roughly split the Craft into three classes so far as the acquisition of masonic knowledge is concerned. First we have those who do not *want* to acquire any further masonic knowledge. They are quite content to attend meetings, make their contributions to the Charities and above all else, to enjoy the social side of Freemasonry. They may not have been forcibly impressed by the dignity and high importance of Freemasonry, they almost certainly do not disgrace it and, in their own way, they probably practise out of the lodge those excellent precepts they are taught within it. But they have no desire to extend their limited masonic knowledge. Although there are plenty of facilities and maybe plenty of opportunities for them to do so, they are unwilling to take what is there for the asking; rather like the proverbial horse who, when led to water, refuses to drink.

We must recognize this and not be despondent about it. Such members derive their own satisfaction from the Craft. Their contribution to the Craft is that they provide the 'audience' for the 'actors'; more often than not they are the 'Centre of Union' so far as the social aspect of Freemasonry is concerned. Above all, they are usually very good supporters of the Charities. We must not alienate their affection for the Craft by giving them the impression that they are 'truants' from school. But that doesn't mean that we should not try to help.

It may be that the reason for their attitude is that they have become bored by the repetitious nature of the workings in the lodge. If this is so then an attempt should be made to put this right. Further, a discussion may show that their interest lies more in the Charities than in the ritual or historic side, and with proper encouragement they might make that their speciality, so that they can give the benefit of such special knowledge to others.

Next we have those who *are* anxious for more masonic knowledge. They are, or will become, members of study circles, Installed Masters' lodges or lodges of masonic research. Some are willing and able to help others by giving correct answers to the questions they have been asked. All of them question others and are not easily fobbed off by false information.

This group needs encouragement and guidance; the will is there and they will certainly make progress. These brethren are the future *givers* of masonic knowledge (if they do not do so already), and it is guidance and encouragement towards that aspect that will bring the greatest reward here. Every effort should be made to ensure that they get the right material to enable them to become proficient in the subject matter they have chosen. An equally important feature is to ensure that they become effective communicators.

The third group is those that would like to know more, but for a variety of reasons (listed earlier) either cannot or do not get the required information. How can we help them?

Every effort should be made to find a way round the obstacle that prevents them from making the progress they want to make; for example, by encouraging them to ask questions; by doing everything possible to ensure that they get an authoritative answer to those questions; by finding time for talks, lectures or question-and-answer sessions within the lodge; possibly by giving demonstrations, some of which can only be given when the lodge is 'called-off'; by ensuring that

information from Grand Lodge *is* disseminated; by encouraging them to make use of masonic libraries and to read recommended books. All or any of this can be done without special approval from Grand Lodge.

But what about some other ideas? Let me 'float' some suggestions for discussion. Some of them would need the approval of the Board of General Purposes or Grand Lodge itself, and obviously **until that approval is given they cannot be adopted.** The 'numbering' of the ideas that follow has no special significance.

1. Adopt the system of giving booklets to the prospective candidate, the Entered Apprentice, the Fellow Craft, the Master Mason (and in the Royal Arch, the newly-admitted Companion). Each booklet should contain information relevant to the masonic grade, plus other general information on such matters as the moral lessons of each grade, the tenets of the Craft, the 'landmarks of the Order' and religion and Freemasonry.

Some would argue that giving the candidate yet another book after his Initiation would not be a good idea. He already gets a copy of the *Book of Constitutions*, the By-laws of the lodge, the booklet *Information for the Guidance of Members of the Craft* and in some cases, the *Constitutions and Regulations of the Grand Charity*. The gift of yet another book might well discourage him from reading any! I think this is a valid argument.

Why not withhold the *Book of Constitutions* until a later date, such as that on which he is presented with his Grand Lodge Certificate and told that his name has been entered in the books of Grand Lodge? It is true that when the candidate has been initiated he has joined an organization that legislates for him and therefore he is fully entitled to know how the organization works, what his financial commitments are and some of what might be called the important 'do's and don'ts'. Perhaps this difficulty can be overcome by incorporating in the booklet issued after the first degree a synopsis of the rules in the *Book of Constitutions* of which every brother should from the outset be aware; his duties and responsibilities, the 'hierarchy', subscriptions, certificates, regalia, elections in the lodge and visiting other lodges both at home and abroad. He should also be told that a copy of the *Book of Constitutions* will be presented to him later but that, if in the meantime he wants to consult a copy, he should ask the Secretary.

The candidate's booklet should of course be made available to him upon election; the other booklets should be presented after the relevant ceremony.

I envisage informative, readable and authoritative booklets that, when the set is complete, will provide the foundation of a good masonic knowledge.

2. A further series of booklets could be made available to cover subjects such as the history of the Craft, the development of the ritual, regalia and lodge furniture and fittings, the government and administration of the Craft and symbolism. (The Grand Charity is already preparing a booklet containing extended particulars of the Masonic Charities.) Authors with the necessary skills would, I am sure, be forthcoming.

The booklets should, I suggest, be issued under the general authority of the Board of General Purposes and match in format the five previously mentioned. Whereas those five should be issued free to members (after purchase by the lodge in the same way as the *Book of Constitutions* is now bought), a charge should be

made for these further publications. The whole set would make a very informative collection.

3. Set up a Masonic Education Committee whose responsibilities would include arrangements for the writing of all the booklets referred to above and advice to the Board of General Purposes on other suggestions pertaining to the getting and giving of masonic knowledge (such as those which are herein made).

4. The Lodge of Instruction, where there is one, has long since supplanted the old Scottish practice of the candidate choosing his 'intenders' (or instructors) to assist him in memorizing the ritual. But it is almost always wholly concerned with helping the brethren to learn words and movements. As I have already complained, questions on other matters are often brushed aside with the comment that the brother should concentrate on learning the ritual before worrying about anything else. The Preceptor is far too busy with ceremonial to be bothered by other matters.

It is, however, at lodge level that the encouragement for getting and giving masonic knowledge is most needed. Why not then consider the appointment of an additional lodge officer to be responsible for this, to whom the brethren can put their questions? Quite obviously it is unlikely that he will have all the information at his command, but it would be his duty to get the correct answer and convey it to the lodge in general and to the enquirer in particular. And why not call him the 'Lodge Intender'? This would make use of the old Scottish name. An early meaning of the word Intender was 'one who directs the mind or attention'. As for his jewel of office, why not use a flaming torch, an emblem long associated with enlightenment and the spreading of knowledge?

5. Some lodges occasionally work the Lectures. These are a series of questions and answers dealing with the ceremonies, the symbolism and the moral explanations of the three degrees. A knowledge of them would certainly help brethren enjoy their ritual more. Let me quote M W Bro Lord Ampthill, when he was Pro Grand Master (*AQC*79, p. 165). On the lectures he said: 'Learn the questions and answers and then teach the novice . . . If you will try this I can promise you that you will be astonished by the keen interest and enthusiasm that will be aroused. Your older brethren will realise at once how much there is they have forgotten or never learnt, and your younger brethren will be animated with a wild thirst for information.'

But in addition to the lectures, why not a series of questions and answers on other masonic matters? There are very many questions that brethren have put to Past Masters which have not been satisfactorily answered, possibly because the Past Master doesn't know the answer himself. There are many other questions that *should* be put but are not, because the enquirer fears that he may be considered foolish for asking the question. Not long ago Bro Harry Carr published *The Freemason at Work*. It contained 200 questions and answers, the latter being given in a clear, informative manner by an acknowledged expert. The frequent reprinting of the book clearly demonstrates the need for authoritative information.

The Masonic Education Committee suggested could devise a series of questions and answers to be used either in lodge or at the Lodge of Instruction. The questions could be put by junior brethren and the answers given by Past Masters, It would be better if both were learnt by heart, but they could be read from a book. There

is of course always the danger that some may regard the use of books in lodges as an unwelcome precedent. If this be so, then 'call-off' before beginning this item on the agenda.

The questions should be of a general nature so that all freemasons can be present. Separate sections could contain questions relating to specific degrees and the Order of the Royal Arch. Such sections would have to be restricted to those in the appropriate masonic grade. Who knows, perhaps Lord Ampthill's comment may prove just as true in relation to this suggestion as to its connection with the Craft Lectures.

6. Reference to masonic libraries and museums has already been made, with particular emphasis on Freemasons' Hall, London. Could more help be given? Perhaps the answer is 'Yes, if only we had more money, staff and time'. It is a fact that for some years past much reorganization has taken place in the library and museum in London, thus cutting down the time that could have been spent on arranging special displays. I am sure many brethren would welcome exhibitions on such things as masonic personalities, the development of the tracing boards, successive Grand Masters and the development of the Royal Arch.

There are many brethren who cannot get to London and there may not be a masonic library or museum near their home. Why can't some of the items from the museum in London be taken round the Provinces for display? I believe that this question has been very carefully considered in the past and the idea rejected on practical grounds. Would the same answer be given today?

Is there any reason why our Grand Lodge library and museum cannot follow the practice of most of our national museums and galleries and publish coloured booklets with a suitable text? This would give brethren, wherever they live, the opportunity of seeing photographs of many of the items of interest, thereby encouraging them to extend their masonic knowledge. Well-produced books on specific subjects such as portraits, regalia, jewels, silver, china, ceramics and special exhibitions, all illustrated in colour and with informative texts, would surely be readily sold and the proceeds used to recover the costs. Such a move would do much to stimulate the brethren to make an effort to extend their masonic knowledge. Some Provincial libraries and museums may find that they could follow a similar practice.

CONCLUSION

What advantages would accrue if brethren in general had a higher standard of masonic education? Put very simply, I would suggest that the work in the lodge would improve and that there would be a greater appreciation and understanding of the ceremonies. Possible 'spin-offs' might include greater familiarity with the Volume of the Sacred Law. And, because of a greater desire to carry out the principles and tenets of the Craft, an improvement in our efforts to help one another. Another facet would be that more brethren would be able to convince non-masons of the value of our society. This in turn may encourage more suitable candidates. A breadth of understanding might lead more brethren to the Royal Arch to participate to the full in 'pure Antient Masonry'.

Surely all this is worth striving for! There is much that each of us can do now. Every Master and Past Master should ask himself if he *is* 'always ready to give or to receive instruction' and whether any of the suggestions here put forward (not needing official approval) can be implemented by him or given greater emphasis. And this applies even more to every Principal and Past Principal of a Royal Arch chapter, for there is no doubt that more work could be done here.

I believe that more could be done to improve the general standard of masonic knowledge if approval were given by Grand Lodge for some (if not all!) of the suggestions outlined above.

To the best of my knowledge our Grand Lodge has never debated the subject of getting and giving masonic knowledge; nor has it been considered by the Board of General Purposes (although a Masonic College was proposed in 1809, *AQC* 63, pp. 43 *et seq*). Other Grand Lodges put much emphasis on the subject of masonic education. I notice that in the celebrations to mark the completion of their first seven years, the Grand Lodge of India released 'an excellent handbook on masonic education' (Bro Sir James Stubbs, *The Four Corners*, p. 72). I have already suggested the setting up of a Masonic Education Committee to consider and advise the Board of General Purposes on suggestions pertaining to the subject of getting and giving masonic knowledge. This I suggest is the first step to be taken. I hope that this Lecture prompts such action and that a healthy debate on the subject will follow.

ACKNOWLEDGEMENTS

There are many brethren who have helped me in the preparation of this Lecture, and to all of them I say a very sincere 'thank-you'. In particular I would like to mention V W Bro Cdr. M. B. S. Higham, Grand Secretary and his predecessor R W Bro Sir James Stubbs; the Grand Secretaries of the Constitutions mentioned in this Lecture; the librarian, W Bro John Hamill and his predecessor, W Bro T. O. Haunch; R W Bro Wallace McLeod of the Grand Lodge of Canada in the Province on Ontario and Immediate Past Master of Quatuor Coronati Lodge No. 2076; W Bro Harry Carr; W Bro F. Smyth and W Bro Eric Nabarro, J.P.

Let me also publicly thank my wife for being so patient with me whilst I have been engaged on this Lecture – and indeed in *all* my masonic activities! Without her understanding and forbearance I could not have given the time and effort to the ancient fraternity to which I am so proud to belong.

'… not only Ancient but useful and necessary Officers …'
THE DEACONS

THE PRESTONIAN LECTURE FOR 1985

SINCLAIR BRUCE

When I was first approached with a view to my preparing a paper for possible presentation as a Prestonian Lecture, the choice of subject was a great problem.

So many facets of the Craft had been dealt with in these Lectures and it appeared that all avenues of investigation had already been explored by many very eminent and acknowledged masonic scholars.

My masonic 'delving' had hitherto been mainly concerned with Freemasonry in the Province of Durham, but a Prestonian Lecture needs to be of general rather than local interest. For some years I had been interested and intrigued by the 'Sun and Moon' jewels worn by the Deacons in a few lodges in this area; a path pursued, but with limited success, by the late Brother William Waples, and, being a member of various lodges which severally employed these 'Sun and Moon' jewels, the 'Winged Mercury' or the 'Dove' I realised that 'The Deacons' could be a suitable subject for consideration.

Although we are all familiar with the Deacons, as officers in our lodges, where we admire, or criticise, their performance, and tend to take them for granted, very little seems to have been written about them.

There was considerable doubt as to whether there was sufficient information available on which to base a satisfactory lecture.

What material is available is scattered very thinly over a wide field, and by collecting these 'bits and pieces', putting them together and using a certain amount of imagination and a little conjecture, I trust that I have been able to give a reasonable and acceptable account of the derivation, history and development of the office of Deacon.

The primary aim was to make the paper interesting and informative to all members of the craft, but in particular to those ordinary Masons to whom William Preston directed his Lectures.

THE ORIGIN OF THE WORD 'DEACON'

The word is derived from the Greek, *'diakonos'* and the Latin *'diaconus'*, meaning *Servant, Waiting-man, Helper* or *Messenger*.

DEACONS IN THE CHURCH

Among the treasures of Durham Cathedral is a *maniple* which was found in the coffin of St. Cuthbert, (635–687) whose tomb is in the Cathedral, and it was probably given to the shrine by King *Athelstan* when he visited nearby Chester-le-Street in the year 934.

This vestment bears the representations of St. Peter, St. Lawrence, St. John the Baptist and St. John the Evangelist, who are shown as:–

PETRVS DIACONVS . . . . Peter the Deacon
LAURENTIVS DIACONVS . . . . Lawrence the Deacon
JOHANNES B. . . . . John the Baptist
JOHANNES EVG . . . . John the Evangelist

(Truly masonic names!)

The inscriptions on the end panels inform us that this maniple was made at the command of Queen AELFLAED (d.916), for Frithstan, Bishop of Winchester from 909.

The maniple is a Eucharistic vestment worn over the left arm of a priest or *deacon* when assisting at Mass. Thus we have evidence of Deacons as early as c.900 A.D. and that on my 'own doorstep' which is only 12 miles from Durham!

But, of course, this was not the beginning of the term 'Deacon' or of the duties that these officers perform. It occurs in the New Testament, in Acts. 6:1–6, Philippians 1:1, and 1 Timothy 3:8–13.

The 'Acts of the Apostles' passage tells of the Greeks, in Jerusalem, c.62 A.D., complaining of the partiality displayed in the care of the poor 'because their widows were neglected in the daily ministration'. The apostles appointed seven *helpers* to serve under them and attend to the material needs of the community.

The Epistle to the Philippians is addressed to 'the *bishops* and *deacons* which were at Philippi', and chapter 3 of 1 Timothy gives 'charges' for the conduct of the *Deacons*, that 'they that have used the office of deacon well [will] purchase to themselves a good degree'. Thus we have the beginning of the relationship between the Bishops (apostles) and the Deacons (helpers).

The duties of the Deacons in the early church were to *assist* the priest and to baptise when no priest was available: the modern Roman Catholic church defines the role of Deacons as *assistants* to the priest and as a substitute (proxy) in certain functions.

Part of the early Deacon's duty when assisting the priest was to administer the chalice at Mass; today the officiating priest is assisted by the Deacon who carries a *maniple* over his left arm, (*cf* the modern waiter and his napkin!).

In the Anglican church the Deacon is the lowest office in the threefold ministry – Bishop – Priest – Deacon; in the Craft we have – Master – Warden – Deacon. A man who aspires to the priesthood must serve a year as a Deacon before being ordained as priest, and his duties include the *instruction* of the young and reporting illness and necessities to the priest.

So we have the Deacon as:–

Servant, Waiting-man, Helper, (as well as proxy) but not yet as *Messenger*.

DEACON IN FREEMASONRY

Having outlined the origin and evolution of the office of Deacon in the Church we now come to these officers in Masonry.

In many of the early masonic catechisms there are several references to the 'Lodge of St. John', 'the Holy Lodge of St. John', then we have the term 'St. John's masons', and there are 'St. John's' lodges today, including my Mother-lodge, St. John's No. 80. There has been much conjecture, discussion and argument among masonic students, for many years, as to which of the many Saints John we are dedicated; one school of thought, supported by Henry Sadler, Chetwode Crawley and others is that our 'patron saint' was St. John the Almoner, St. John of Jerusalem. This St. John was the son of the King of Cyprus, born in the late 6th century who, about the year 600 A.D., founded a charitable fraternity and a hospital in Jerusalem to care for the sick and wounded pilgrims who visited the Holy Sepulchre. He was adopted as the patron saint of the later order of the Hospitallers. The present-day masonic order known as the 'Knights of Malta' is officially named the 'Order of St. John of Jerusalem, Palestine, Rhodes and Malta'.

When referring to this 7th century fraternity Bro. Chetwode Crawley said

> ... the serving-brethren (Diaconi) played a prominent, though subordinate part, which seems to have been without an exact correlative in the medieval guilds of Freemasons. Be this as it may, – and it is little better than pure conjecture – the appointment of Deacons served, in later days, as a distinction between Irish and English work for the Lodges under the Constitution of the Antients naturally followed the Irish use.

Leaving aside the reference to Irish and Antients masonry, which will be discussed later in the paper, this appears to be a reasonable explanation of the use of Deacons, and of the name, in Freemasonry as *junior officers* whose main duties are to assist senior brethren.

'ANTIENT' AND 'MODERN' FREEMASONS

Before dealing with the appointment of Deacons and with their duties let us briefly consider the history of the Craft in the 18th century.

The premier Grand Lodge of England

The first or premier Grand Lodge of England was established in 1717; originally intended to serve the cities of London and Westminster, it soon began to gain support and allegiance from other areas. The 'Four Old Lodges' which formed the Grand Lodge were not the only lodges in London nor was London the only place with lodges. There are records which indicate that many lodges were working in several parts of the country in the 17th and 18th centuries; some of these, and many new lodges, affiliated with the new Grand Lodge and others remained independent as unattached lodges of what were termed 'St. John's masons' or 'Lodges of St. John', – owing no allegiance to any higher authority than themselves.

The organisation of Grand Lodge was slow in starting, but in 1723 the first *'Constitutions'* was published, the first Minutes were recorded and the Grand Lodge began to be aware of the need to give guidance to its member lodges. The

pre-1717 concept of purely Christian Masonry began to be widened, and other developments, away from old established practices, were inevitable, but the major changes introduced in the fourth decade of the century had far-reaching, if not disastrous, effects on the whole future of Masonry.

In and about the year 1730 there were published several 'exposures' purporting to disclose the whole of the secrets and ceremonies of the Craft; the most notable of these was *'Masonry Dissected'* by Samuel Prichard, a publication which had an enormous popularity and, together with some others, threatened to undermine the very basis of the Order. Grand Lodge was naturally alarmed and 'some variations were made in the established forms' in order to keep out imposters. The actual changes are not recorded nor is the date of their introduction, but we now know that, included in these measures, was the transposition of the 'words' and other modes of recognition in the first and second degrees.

These alterations were, of course, not welcomed by some of the old-established lodges who were jealous of their traditional practices and who, although maintaining unswerving allegiance to the Grand Lodge, continued to work in the ancient manner. Also the means of communication in those days being so very difficult, the changes were extremely slow in reaching the more remote parts of the Craft.

The Antient Grand Lodge
Another Grand Lodge was formed in 1751, mainly by Irish Masons, who found that the masonry in England was, in many essential parts, different from that which they knew at home. This new organisation called themselves 'The Grand Lodge of England according to the Old Institutions' with the avowed intention 'to show posterity how much we desire to revive the Ancient Craft upon true masonical principles'. Their use of the words 'Ancient' or 'Antient' led to these Brethren being known as the 'Antients' and the 'Antients' Grand Lodge, and conversely, the premier body, founded 34 years earlier became the 'Moderns'.

The 1751 body was also referred to as the Atholl Grand Lodge as the 3rd and 4th Dukes of Atholl were Grand Masters for 31 of the 62 years of its existence.

(Throughout this paper the Grand Lodge of 1717 will be referred to as the premier or the Moderns Grand Lodge, and that of 1751 as the Antient. The word 'ancient', with a 'c', will be reserved for the description of old, long-standing and traditional usages not appertaining to any specific organisation).

The majority of the Antients brethren were of the lower-middle and working classes of artisans and shopkeepers, whereas the Moderns consisted mainly of the 'gentry' and fashionable section of the community. The Antients were principally concerned with the preservation of old traditional workings, the long lectures and catechisms in which the essence of masonry was taught, and in the universality of the Craft. On the other hand the Moderns were more intent on introducing into the Society 'men of quality', to preserve and enhance the respectability of the Order, even to the point of curtailing the ceremonies if they should prove irksome.

With these totally opposed philosophies of the Craft and the general difference in social standing of the two Grand Lodges, it is not surprising that there was much rivalry, bad feeling and downright animosity between 'Brother Masons' on

the two sides, particularly in London and nearby towns, although in the more distant areas the feeling was, on the whole, more 'fraternal'.

Towards the end of the 18th century there was a growing feeling, in both 'camps', that a union of the two factions was desirable, and this was brought to fruition on 27th December 1813 when the United Grand Lodge of England was formed, under H.R.H. the Duke of Sussex as Grand Master.

Much of the preparation for this bringing together of all masons in England, was done in 'The Special Lodge of Promulgation'.

THE SPECIAL LODGE OF PROMULGATION

The situation, in 1809, which brought about the need for the Lodge of Promulgation is best described by quoting from Bro Henry Sadler's comments on Bro Hextall's paper on the Lodge, in *AQC.23*. (*Transactions of Quatuor Coronati Lodge, No. 2076*), he says.

> ... there were two rival Grand Lodges in London; one of these bodies known as the 'Moderns', had made, many years before, certain alterations in the Ritual and Ceremonies, but it was not clear to all of their members, in 1809, what the alterations were, nor when they were made. The other body, briefly described as 'Ancients', professed to have made no alterations. It was with a view to harmonizing the differences between the two systems and bringing the rival factions more into line – paving the way, in fact, to a friendly alliance – that the Lodge of Promulgation was warranted. It answered its purpose fairly well, for in about two years after the termination of its labours the long desired union was formally cemented.

The 'trigger' which instigated the formation of the Lodge of Promulgation was a resolution at a meeting of the premier Grand Lodge, on 12th April 1809, in which it was 'Resolved that this Grand Lodge do agree ... that it is not necessary any longer to continue in force those measures which resorted to *in or about the year 1739 respecting Irregular masons and do therefore enjoin the several lodges to revert to the Ancient land Marks of the Society*'.

The 'measures resorted to' refers to the decisions made in Grand Lodge, in 1730, and included the transposition of the 'words'.

Here was an admission on the part of the Moderns Grand Lodge that they had deviated from the Ancient landmarks and practices, (how? or when? – they were not quite sure!) and we must give them every credit for admitting it and for going to great lengths to correct their errors.

A Warrant was issued by the Acting Grand Master, the Earl of Moira, on 26th October 1809, for the establishment of a Lodge *'for the purpose of ascertaining and promulgating the Ancient Land marks of the Craft'*. The first meeting of the Lodge was on 21st November 1809 when it was decided that it should be named 'The Special Lodge of Promulgation'.

At the second meeting, Bro Charles Bonnor was invested as Secretary. He was the Senior Warden of the Lodge of Antiquity No. 1, and had a great influence on the deliberations of the Lodge of Promulgation. Bro Bayford, another member of 'Antiquity', directed the attention of the Lodge *'to the ascertaining what were the Ancient Landmarks which they were required to restore'* Bro. Bonnor gave an

'accurate description and recitation of the Ancient Practices (*as adhered to in the Lodge of which he was a member*) . . . which constitute the Ancient Landmarks in Question'. There followed an '. . . animated discussion, which was protracted till half past twelve o'clock . . .'.

The Brethren evidently had much to say and to think about! Many items were discussed but the first matter which, according to the Minutes of the Lodge, merited a *resolution,* was that appertaining to Deacons, and which forms the title of this paper:–

> Wednesday 13th December 1809 . . . 'Resolved that Deacons (being proved on due investigation to be not only Ancient but useful and necessary Officers) be recommended.

Thus we see that the office of Deacon was considered to be of great importance, even of prime importance, a *landmark* and part of ancient practice. It is unfortunate that there is no account of the discussion which led to the resolution on Deacons, consequently we have no record of the *reasons* for the decision.

It seems that, although, officially, Deacons were not appointed in Moderns lodges, there were important duties being performed which could not be abandoned, and that therefore there should be officers appointed to perform them. These duties were probably already being done by some members of the lodges, maybe by Stewards, or an untitled brother and certainly several lodges of the Moderns had appointed Deacons many years before 1809, as will be seen later. Thus it is clear that the Lodge of Promulgation was giving tacit approval to *existing practices.*

Following the resolution on the necessity of Deacons there were other decisions made in that matter, e.g. they determined the situation of the Deacons, the Senior to be at the right of the master; the position of the Junior Deacon is not mentioned in the Minutes of the Lodge but at the same meeting Bro Joyce was appointed as Senior Deacon and Bro Carr as Junior.

The Masters of 33 *London* lodges attended the meeting on 26th January 1810 when they were informed that the Junior warden was now to be in the South, (in many Moderns lodges both Wardens were in the West); that Deacons were useful and Ancient officers, and of their duties, as well as those of the Stewards, 'not as Officers but as appendages'. They also learned that the candidate

> is then received by the *Junior Deacon* and after the Invocation, the *Senior Deacon* takes charge of the Candidate, and conducts him through the ceremony of Initiation.

This is the first and only time that any of the duties of the Deacons are defined in the Minutes.

At the end of the meeting the Masters were told that –

> they were not to receive the Communication of the Evening as the result of dictatorial dispositions on the part of the Lodge of Promulgation whose prescribed province it was first to ascertain what were the landmarks and the Ancient practice: and then to communicate them to the Craft at large . . .

Although the Warrant of the Lodge laid down that notice of such meetings was to be given to all Masters of Regular Lodges – '. . . (that they) may have an opportunity of attending the same', the meetings that were called for instruction

were for 'the Masters of the *Town* Lodges'. No attempt appears to have been made at this time to promulgate the new forms outside London.

The Lodge of Promulgation was a purely Moderns affair, warranted by the premier Grand Lodge, but as the membership included some ten or eleven members of the Lodge of Antiquity, together with others who have never entertained the modern practice and at least three with Antients experience or background, it seems that, as Bro Wonnacott wrote in *A.Q.C.*23 in 1910, the true object was to make the Lodges of the Moderns fall into line with those of the Antients.

They seem to have attained this objective and made many concessions to the working of the Antients lodges, particularly in relation to:–

(a)   the appointment of Deacons, and
(b)   the ceremony of the Installation of the Master.

Thus emphasizing the relative importance of the Deacons and smoothing the way for agreement between the two opposing factions.

The Lodge of Promulgation ceased operation in February 1811 and the union of the two Grand Lodges and the formation of the United Grand Lodge of England was effected on St. John the Evangelist's Day. December 27th 1813.

THE APPOINTMENT OF DEACONS

Deacons may be appointed or elected, according to the Laws of each jurisdiction, but the method of the appointment is of no import in our present enquiry.

It has been stated on many occasions that whilst Deacons were regular officers in the lodges of the Antients there were none, or very few of these officers in the Moderns lodges; and that the presence or absence of Deacons was an indication of Antients or Moderns affiliation, respectively. However, the dividing line between Moderns and Antients was not so well-drawn, especially outside of London. There were many lodges of the Moderns, who, although giving unswerving allegiance to their Grand Lodge, but lacking information and guidance, worked in their own, traditional way.

Several lodges of the Moderns had Deacons long before the Union of 1813, some prior to the advent of the Antients in 1751.

But let us first go to Ireland where, in the earliest Minute book of the Grand Lodge of Munster, which also contains, intermixed with the records of the Grand Lodge, the Minutes of 'the subordinate lodge', (now Cork No 1 I.C.), we read that:–

> Att a monthly meeting of ye worshipful Society of Freemasons at the House of Mr. Herbert Phaire Thursday ye 2nd of Febr. 1726 [1727 New Style] Mr. Herbert Phaire was appointed to act with Mr. William Lane as Wardens of this Lodge and Mr. Septimus Peacock and Mr. Adam Newman to act as *Deacons* in ye said Lodge.
>
> Springett Penne
> D.G.M.

Thus we have a lodge with two Wardens, two deacons, and, we presume, a Master, although it is quite likely that the Grand Master filled that office and that the Grand Lodge and 'the subordinate lodge' were, at times, indistinguishable,

particularly as the Minute is signed by the Deputy Grand Master, evidently as presiding officer.

The Grand Lodge of Ireland did not appoint Grand Deacons until 1859, if required, they selected from the Deacons of private lodges brethren to act for each meeting. The first appearance of these temporary Grand Deacons was at the meeting of that Grand Lodge on Nov. 7th 1811, when it was decided that 'The Deacons to collect the Charity of the night which will prevent the grand wardens' chairs being vacant during the sitting of Grand Lodge'.

There are several other references to Deacons in Irish lodges in those early days, for example Bro Bernard Jones, in his *'Compendium'* refers to Deacons, spelt 'Dacken', in the records of another County Cork Lodge, at Youghall in 1733. There is also the well-known account of the procession at Youghall, on St. John the Evangelist's Day, 27th December 1743, when listed in that gathering were:–

'Seventhly – two Deacons with their Rods gilt'.

Two Deacons were in the funeral procession at the burial of Dr. Fifield D'Assigny in 1745 and Laurence Dermott, Grand Secretary and inspirer of the Grand Lodge of the Antients, acted as Deacon in his mother-lodge, No. 26. Dublin, in about 1743.

Thus we see that Deacons were an established part of Irish Masonry in the first few decades of the eighteenth century, and Bro Heron Lepper said that 'Deacons, I consider to belong to that older Freemasonry that settled in Ireland long prior to 1717; how long? that is a question I cannot answer'.

Bro Chetwode Crawley, another great Irish masonic scholar, was of the opinion that 'up to the time when the Grand Lodge of Munster and the Grand Lodge of Ireland were merged, that is until 1730, there is no reason to suspect that there was the least difference between modes of working in Ireland and in England'. In their *Early Masonic Catechisms,* Knoop, Jones and Hamer expressed the same sentiments.

The Grand Lodge of Munster decreed in 1728, that every lodge should have in their possession a copy of the 1723 English *Book of Constitutions,* which gives credence to these opinions that Irish and English masonry were identical at that time.

Further cause for speculation is provided in the first Irish *Constitutions,* published by John Pennell (G. Sec. I.C. 1732–39) in 1730, where, in Charge IV it stated that 'No Brother can be a Master, Warden or Deacon of a Lodge until he has passed the Part of a Fellow-Craft'. This charge, together with most of the book was taken from James Anderson's English *Constitutions* of 1723, but in the latter, the charge does not include 'Deacon'.

Add to this evidence the fact that Lord Kingston, a resident land-owner in County Cork, was Grand Master of England in 1728, of Munster in 1729 and of Ireland in 1730 and we have another indication of the affinity of Irish and English masonry.

So we have the very early records of Deacons in Ireland, and if the two jurisdictions were identical there may also have been these officers in England.

Indeed the earliest known record of the office in England is in the Minutes of

the 'Lodge at Swalwell,' now the Lodge of Industry No. 48, at Gateshead, Province of Durham.

The Minute consists of a list of officers and reads:–

June ye 25: 1733
Joseph Clark Master Mason
Jn°. Robinson Senr Warden
Edwd. Alport Junr. Warden
Matt. Armstrong Senr. Decon (*sic*) or Steward
Matt. Lee Junr. Decon Deputy Steward

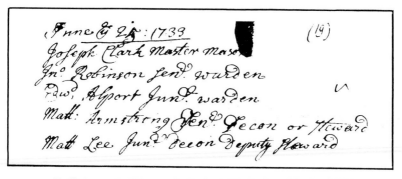

Earliest record of Deacons in England. The Lodge of Swalwell 1733.

The next year, 1734, other Brethren were appointed to these same offices, but in 1735, also on St. John the Baptist's Day, 24th June, the record says:–

At a lodge held at Brother Thompson's at Swalwell, when the Lodge was constituted by Mr. Joseph Laycock, Provincile (*sic*) Grand Master:–

Kendrick Jones – Master

| Wm. Hawdon | Wardens |
| John Armstrong | |

| Matthew Lee | Stewards |
| Alex Turner | |

The Lodge had become 'regular', the 'Master Mason' had become 'Master' and the title 'Deacon' has disappeared, but 'Stewards' have survived.

This 'Lodge at Swalwell' was an unattached lodge of operative masons together with two 'Gentleman Masons' who had been made 'free of the Lodge'. One of these was Joseph Laycock, manager of the local ironworks, who had been appointed the first Provincial Grand Master for Durham in 1734 whilst he was Senior Warden of the Lodge.

The question of whence these operative masons got the title 'Deacon' is confusing. Some writers say that it was Scottish influence, since Swalwell is only 45 miles from the border with Scotland, but in that country the 'Deacon' was the *senior* officer and often ruled the lodge, whilst at Swalwell they were the *junior* officers.

It may be pertinent, bearing in mind the opinions of Brothers Lepper and Crawley, that the officers of this lodge in 1733–4, are the same as those in Lodge No. 1, Cork, in 1727 – Master (?), two Wardens and two Deacons. Another factor in the choice of the word may have been that William Smith, author of *'The Freemason's Pocket Companion'*, (Dublin 1735) and *'Book M'* published in Newcastle upon Tyne (1736) was also made 'free of the Lodge' in 1735. Smith was familiar with the office of Deacon from his time in Ireland and from his avowed knowledge of Pennell's Irish *'Constitutions'*.

The removal of the Style 'Deacon' may have been at the insistence of the new Provincial Grand Master who, quite possibly, may have had experience of 'regular' lodges, who had 'Stewards' rather than Deacons before he came to Swalwell in 1731, and at the constitution of the Lodge 'regularised' the offices.

From the north east of England let us now go to the west, to Chester, where, in the records of the Lodge at the 'Royal Oak' we find that on St. John the Evangelist's Day, 27th December 1743, there were elected, among others:–

Ambrose Orme – Master's Deacon
John Matthews – Warden's Deacon

and these officers were elected annually until 1758 when they became 'Senior and Junior Stewards', just as at Swalwell in 1735.

When Bro Jacob Rogers was elected master of the Lodge at the 'Crown' in Bristol in 1758, he appointed two Wardens, two Deacons and a Secretary.

Returning to N.E. England, the by-laws of an unattached lodge at Newcastle were signed – 'John Miller, Senior Deacon' in 1759. There were Deacons also in the lodge at Darlington, now Restoration Lodge No. 111, in 1769, and in the Lodge of Concord, Barnard Castle, also in Durham, in 1771.

One of my own lodges, Phoenix No. 94, Sunderland, already had Deacons when the earliest extant Minute book began in 1778.

In the same year, in the Lodge of Antiquity, then No. 1, now No. 2, William Preston's Lodge, Bro Sealy and Bro Nantes, previously listed as Stewards, are named in the Minutes as 'Senior and Junior Deacons'. This was the election meeting, 16th December, when Brother Sealy was elected as Secretary, Bro Nantes as Junior Warden, and *they* appointed their successors as Senior and Junior *Stewards*.

It appears that the title 'Deacon' may have been a mistake on the part of the writer of these Minutes, as it was not used again until 1787, after the return of Bro Preston, who had resigned in 1781.

It is interesting that in the by-laws of the Lodge of Antiquity of 1788 it is laid down that the Deputy Master, Wardens, Treasurer and Secretary must have previously served as Deacon.

The Deacons had 'arrived' in the Moderns, as in Ireland in 1727!

All the above lodges, with the exception of the Irish, were of the Moderns grand Lodge and there were many more who had Deacons before the Lodge of Promulgation recommended their appointment in 1809.

Deacons in the Antients Lodges
It is not surprising that we hear of Deacons under the Antient Grand Lodge from the beginning of their organisation, since the majority of their founders were Irishmen.

We have seen that John Pennell included Deacons in Charge IV of his Irish *Book of Constitutions* of 1730, and that Laurence Dermott, Grand Secretary, 1752–1771, had been a Deacon in Ireland before coming to England.

In 1752, Dermott introduced the by-laws of his former Irish lodge for the use of the Antients private lodges, and a number of copies of these, in Dermott's own hand, are still in possession of lodges. These regulations state that each lodge shall '... consist of One Master, two Wardens, two *deacons* and a Tyler with as many Members as the Master and majority shall think proper.

As early as 1753, the officer is referred to in the Minutes of the Antient Grand Lodge, where the order of procession at funerals is given as 'formerly' observed by 'Antient Masons', and this list includes Deacons immediately preceding the Wardens.

At the Constitution of Lodge No. 37, (now Enoch No. 11), on 19th August 1754, the officers appointed were Master, Wardens, Deacons and Secretary, in that order. Thus it is evident that Deacons were a regular part of the structure of the Antients lodges from their inception.

Deacons in the Moderns Lodges
Since Deacons were not, officially, part of the premier Grand lodge system, what was it that induced so many Moderns lodges to introduce the office?

In those lodges that made the appointments before 1750, for example, at Swalwell and at Chester, they may have been influenced by their succession from lodges of St. John's Masons, part of that Masonry in England that Bro Lepper, and others, considered was identical with that in Ireland where there were Deacons from at least 1727.

It may have been through more or less direct contact with Irish masons, such as Lord Kingston, Grand Master, in official circles, or itinerant Irishmen in the private lodges, or with military lodges stationed in the garrison towns such as at Barnard Castle, Darlington, Newcastle and Sunderland. Most military lodges were of the Irish Constitution or Antients, and even if they had a Moderns warrant, their constant contact with Irish and Antient masons almost guaranteed that their working would be influenced in that direction.

In towns like Bristol and Chester, doing regular business by sea with Ireland, some influence from that country's masons was a certainty.

With the advent of the Antients lodges, with their Deacons, it was inevitable that the Moderns lodges would become aware of the office through their contact, regular and clandestine, with Antients masons, for example, in the Lodge of Antiquity where William Preston was so active – he was initiated in an Antients lodge which, although changing its allegiance to the Moderns, continued to work in the same way.

Many Moderns lodges possessed a copy of Dermott's *Ahiman Rezon,* the book

of constitutions of the Antients, possibly to the exclusion of that of their own Grand Lodge, and were therefore quite receptive to Antients influence.

The wide use of the exposures, *T.D.K.* and *J. & B.*, in the second half of the 18th century, would be a great factor in the introduction of Deacons into many Moderns lodges. (see Dalziel's letter, p. 24).

Once the Lodge of Promulgation had made their recommendation of Deacons as '. . . useful and necessary officers . . .', several lodges appointed them for the first time. Two examples are the Old Dundee Lodge, at Wapping, now No. 18, and Lodge of Love and Honour, now No. 75, at Falmouth.

The minutes of Old Dundee Lodge, then No. 9, dated 8th February 1810 read as follows:–

> The Master reported that two new officers are necessary to carry the new alterations into effect, and they are to be named 'Deacons' and the R. W. Master then appointed . . . Bro. Nathl. Lavers as Senior Deacon, and Bro. John Pickett as Junior Deacon'.

These new officers were later supplied with Black Rods and Silver jewels. The R.W. Master was Bro John Walton who was a member of the Lodge of Promulgation, hence the early compliance with that Lodge's resolution which is used in the title of this paper.

The Lodge of Love and Honour had a visit, in September 1812, from Bro 'Wm. Ernshaw' (*sic*) who had been Master of the Lodge of Promulgation, and in consequence of the visit, Deacons were appointed.

The United Grand Lodge of England

The necessity and usefulness of Deacons having been established by the Lodge of Promulgation, it was incumbent upon the newly-formed United Grand Lodge to implement the recommendation. However, at the 'Grand Assembly of Freemasons' held on St. John the Evangelist's Day, 27th December 1813, to celebrate the 'Union', there were no Deacons listed as being in the processions, nor are they included among the new Grand Officers nominated by H.R.H. the Duke of Sussex, Grand Master, for investiture at the Installation Meeting that was to be held on St. George's Day, 23rd April 1814. This meeting actually took place on 1st May and among those present were:–

W. Rev. G. A. Browne, S.G. Deacon,
W. Humphrey Donaldson, J.G. Deacon

and 'The Grand Deacons' were included in the procession.

It seems that the Grand Deacons were neither nominated nor invested, but in the list of Grand Officers in the *'Historical Supplement'* to the *Grand Lodge Year Book*, Bros Browne and Donaldson are listed as Senior and Junior Deacons in 1814, together with two other brethren appointed to those offices in that year. The office of Deacon being an innovation it is possible that they were overlooked, in error, in 1813, and the matter put right in the following year.

Also at this meeting the 'Masonic Clothing' and 'Insignia' to be worn was laid down, including 'A Dove with an Olive Branch . . .' for the Deacons.

Having considered the Deacons in Ireland, the Moderns and the Antients, and

seen them regularly established in the United Grand Lodge of England, let us now turn north to Scotland.

Scotland

That there were well-established lodges of operative stone-masons in Scotland before the end of the 17th century is proved by the existence of actual Minutes of several such lodges dating from 1598. But the style and title 'Deacon' occurs 150 years earlier, in 1424. In that year the Scottish Parliament, meeting at Perth, enacted that each craft or trade was empowered to choose a 'Dekyn or Maisterman' to 'govern and assay' all work produced by their particular trade. This was to protect the community against frauds by the craftsmen.

In the Schaw Statutes of 1598 and 1599, which were codes of rules and regulations for the Scottish masons, drawn up by William Schaw, the King's master mason, the craftsmen were charged to be obedient to 'thar wardenis, dekynis and maisteris in all thingis concernying thar craft'.

Under the 1424 legislation 'Seals of Cause' were issued to individual crafts and trades; these documents gave the consent of the Provost of the town, and others, to statutes and rules, made by the tradesmen, for the regular government of their separate crafts. The bodies thus organised were known as 'Incorporations', and at the head of each was the *Deacon*.

In 1475 such a Seal of Cause was granted for the establishment of 'The Incorporation of Wrights and Masons of Edinburgh'. The Incorporation was the means of communication between the masons and the community, but the internal affairs of the mason trade were governed by the Lodge, the Lodge of Edinburgh (Mary's Chapel) No. 1, and at its head was a *Warden*.

Thus there was the 'Deacon' of the Incorporation and the 'Warden' of the Lodge, two individual offices. The Deacon was appointed by the Town Council and the Warden by the Lodge.

At the Quarterly Communications of the Lodge it was the Deacon who presided, the Warden acting as Treasurer. If the Deacon was not present, the Warden did not fill his place, another was chosen to preside and conduct the affairs of the Lodge. The Incorporation and the Lodge, were thus two separate but interconnected bodies with the Deacon of the Incorporation being the Senior Officer. In 1708 the Deacon became known as 'Preces' and in 1727 – 'Master'.

At Kilwinning, where there was no Incorporation or Town Council, the Lodge was under the direction of a Deacon and the Warden was the Treasurer. In 1735, when the titles of the officers were changed, it was the Deacon who became 'Master of the Freemasons', later 'Right Worshipful Master' and then 'The Right Worshipful the Grand Master'.

R. F. Gould said that:

> We meet with the titles Deacons and Wardens in the records of the Kilwinning (1643), the Aitchison's Haven (1700) and the Peebles (1716) Lodges though there they are used disjunctively and apart.
>
> In each of these intances the Deacons was the chief official. Such was the case of the Haddington Lodge in 1607 where, apparently there was no Warden, whilst on the other

hand the Lodge of Glasgow, in 1613, was ruled by a Warden and there was no such officer as Deacon.

Thus we see that in Scotland the Deacon was a senior officer if not *the* senior, rather than a 'Servant' as indicated in the Latin 'diaconus', and this gives credence to the opinion of Bro Lionel Vibert that the term was possibly derived from the Roman *'decanus'*, which meant, literally, 'a ruler of ten', which was, in all probability, a most suitable description of the status of the 'Dekyn or Maisterman' of 1424. It also reinforces the writer's opinion that the office of 'Decon or Steward' in the Lodge at Swalwell, in 1733, was not of Scottish origin.

Deacons as junior officers, in the English sense, began to appear in the Scottish lodges in the 1730s when the officers were Master, two Wardens, two Deacons, two Stewards and an Officer (Tyler). In the lodge Holyrood House (St. Lukes) No. 44 S.C., Senior and Junior Deacons were appointed in 1744 and probably up to seven years previously (i.e. from 1737) for which period no records are available.

So we see that two Deacons were being introduced into Scottish speculative lodges at about the same time as they were appearing in the English system.

THE DUTIES OF THE DEACONS

Having shown that Deacons are indeed ancient (rather than Antient) having existed in our lodges for over 250 years, let us now consider how they became 'useful and necessary officers'.

The Minutes of lodges that have given us the records of the appointment of Deacons afford little help as to their duties. No doubt the over-zealous observance of an oath of secrecy prevented the early secretaries from giving any information on their ceremonies. Consequently we are dependent upon the various manuscripts, pamphlets and printed exposures for guidance.

We have already mentioned Samuel Prichard's *'Masonry Dissected'* (M.D.)* which caused a furore in grand Lodge in 1730. It was the earliest popular publication to give a well-detailed description of the ceremonies, and the first to give the three separate degrees.

There was a gap of thirty years during which nothing further of any real importance appeared in England. Then in 1760, came *'Three Distinct Knocks'* (T.D.K.)* which purported to give the ceremonies of the Antients lodges, and it included Deacons in the 'opening' ceremony.

Next we have *'Jachin and Boaz'* (J.&B.)* (1762) which claimed to give the procedure of both Moderns and Antients, but was, in fact, a plagiarized version of *T.D.K.* together with narrative material taken, almost word for word, from a French 'exposure', *'L'Ordre des Francs-Macons Trahi'* of 1745.

The earliest French publications were based on *M.D.* and since France received its Masonry from England before 1740, the French system, like *M.D.*, had no Deacons.

Up to recent years these exposures had been very suspect as to their veracity, being, by their very nature, breaches of an obligation of secrecy by some of our members, and published either for profit or from spite; but it is now generally

* These publications will be subsequently shown as:– *M.D.*, *T.D.K.* and *J. & B.* respectively.

accepted that they do give us a good picture of the form that our ceremonies took in the 18th century.

Although the exposures were meant mainly to interest and titillate a curious public, and to enable the 'profane' to gain irregular admission into our assemblies, there can be no doubt that a considerable proportion of the sales, and they were enormous, was to our own members. It must be remembered that there was no 'little blue book' available at that time, not until George Claret's 'ritual' of 1838. consequently, *T.D.K.* and particularly *J. & B.*, with its narrative description of the ceremonies, were a great boon to the brethren as 'aides-mémoire'. Indeed their popularity in this respect did a great deal to produce a certain degree of uniformity in our ritual and ceremonial, there being no other form of instruction.

The position in 1815 is well illustrated by a letter from Alexander Dalziel, a P.M. of All Saints Lodge, at Wooler, Northumberland, to Edwards Harper, Grand Secretary, part of which reads:–

> ... I can find little better in general practice in the North of England than what is contained in that [book] called J. & B. ... and so corrupted is the science in many parts, that a Brother of ours who now resides in Glasgow, and has visited many lodges in the North, informed me that immediately after their initiation in those parts, they were advised to purchase J. & B. for their instructions.

We must take notice however, that although these exposures probably reflected the general practices of their day, they may have given an accurate description of the ceremonies in some lodges, but did not correspond with those in others; the procedure would vary from area to area, and lodge to lodge, as it does today!

With the aid of these exposures and the earlier catechisms we are able to study the early lodges from Prichard's time and observe the gradual process of development in the ceremonies and see how the multifarious duties of today's Deacons arose, at the same time bearing in mind the duties of the Deacons as expressed by Preston and in our present lodges.

In the investiture address to the Deacons given in Preston's *Illustrations* of 1792 they are informed that:–

> It is your Province to attend on the Master and Wardens, and to act as their proxies in the active duties of the lodge; such as in the reception of candidates into the different degrees of masonry, and in the immediate practice of our rites ...

And in the English rituals of today the recital of the duties of each Deacon includes:–

> ... to bear all messages and commands ... of the Master and ... to attend on candidates during the ceremonies ...

The early 18th century lodges would meet in the 'long room' above a coffee-house, tavern or inn; there would be probably only twelve or fifteen brethren present and they would sit at a long table. The Master sitting at the East end, his Wardens opposite to him, both in the West, and the brethren in between. The lighting would be by wax candles and there would also be 'three large candles placed on high candlesticks' (*M.D.*), our 'Lesser-Lights'.

The lodge would be opened with some formality, the Master would ask the

Senior Warden 'the first care' and he would reply that it was to see that 'none but Masons are present', he would ascertain this by going to each brother in turn, taking from him the G. and W., this being satisfactory he would then report that 'all is safe within'. The next duty was to see that all was 'safe without' and the Junior Warden would go to the door and knock which would be answered from outside, the Junior Warden would open the door, see who was there, close the door and report that 'a faithful brother, properly armed protects the Lodge from intrusion'.

At this period the only officers in the lodge were the Master, and the Senior and Junior Wardens, Prichard mentions no others, unless we include 'an Enter'd 'Prentice' who brought the candidate to the outside of the door, a duty later done by the Junior Warden, and today, in some jurisdictions, by a Deacon.

The Entered Apprentice also, at times, took the G. and W. from the brethren in the lodge, acting for the Senior Warden.

Today, particularly in America, Canada and probably elsewhere, the Deacons perform this duty called 'purging the lodge', that is, freeing it from any person who is not entitled to be there. The procedure is that the Senior Warden is ordered to collect the G. and W. (or the P.G. and P.W.) from the brethren present and he delegates that duty to the Deacons. Both Deacons make their way to the East end of the lodge, and, the Senior Deacon taking the South side and the Junior the North, they proceed to examine each brother. Meeting before the Senior Warden they pass the G. and W. to him, he approves and the Senior Deacon takes it to the Master. The Senior Deacon is a *'messenger'* from the Senior Warden to the Master, both are acting as 'proxies' for the Senior Warden.

At the opening of the lodge the Junior Warden attended at the door to see that the lodge was properly tyled, a duty that was later done by an Entered Apprentice, the 'Inner Tyler', 'Inner Guard' or the Junior Deacon; all of whom were acting, individually, as 'proxies' for the Junior Warden, whose responsibility it still is.

In the Antients lodges, up to the 'Union' in 1813, the youngest Entered Apprentice was invested, by the Master, with his apron, and with a small silver trowel on a narrow white ribbon round his neck, and he attended to 'the door on the inside', and this jewel served as the 'S . . . p i . . . . t' which he presented to the candidates' 'n . . . d l . . t b . . . . t'. A number of these beautiful 'Trowel' jewels are still to be seen in masonic museums and, in a few lodges, worn by the Inner Guard.

In the 'ORDERS' (c. 1765) of the Marquis of Granby lodge, No. 124, at Durham, (a Moderns lodge of pre-1738) we find:–

> 21. It is likewise ordered, that there shall be always two Entered Apprentices belonging to this Lodge; Each to have a White Rodd (*sic*) in his hand. The Senior to sit in the North, next to the Pass Master to carry Messuages (*sic*) from the Master to the Senior Warden. The Junior to stand at the door on the inside, to welcome strange Bretheren (*sic*), and to carry Messuages (*sic*) from the Right Worshipful to the Tyler.

Thus the Senior Entered Apprentice occupied the same position as our Senior Deacon, in approximately the north-east corner of the lodge, and the Junior acted as the English Inner Guard, or American Junior Deacon.

This lodge did not sanction the appointment of Deacons until 1807, and that

at the instigation of the Secretary who had been a member of the Lodge of Antiquity No. 1, but no regular appointment was made until 1817, probably to agree with the Lodge of Reconciliation.

These situations of the Entered Apprentices in the Marquis of Granby Lodge do not agree with those indicated in *M.D.* but they do illustrate the need for officers other than the Wardens. In the Catechism in *M.D.* we have:–

Q. Where stands the Senior Enter'd 'Prentice?
A. In the South.

Q. What is his business?
A. To hear and receive instructions, and welcome strange
   Brothers.

Q. Where stands the Junior Enter'd 'Prentice.
A. In the North.

Q. What is his business?
A. To keep out all Cowans and Eves-droppers. (*sic*)

From this we see that the youngest brethren, the Entered apprentices, were carrying-out the duties that really belonged to the Junior Warden, and later, were performed by the Deacons.

When we come to *T.D.K.* and *J. & B.* the places of the Entered apprentices have been filled by the Deacons.

In the 'opening' ceremonies in both these exposures,(the words are identical) we read:–

'Master to the Junior Deacon. What is the chief care of a Mason?
Ans. To see that the Lodge is tyled.
Mas. Pray do your duty.
N.B. The Junior Deacon goes and gives Three Knocks at the door; and if there is nobody nigh, the Tyler without answereth with Three Knocks: The Junior Deacon tells the Master, and says, Worshipful, the lodge is tyl'd.
Mas. to jun. Dea.. The junior Deacon's place, in the Lodge?
Deacon's Ans., At the back of the Senior Warden, or at his Right hand if he permits him.
Mas. Your business?
Deacon's Ans. To carry Messages from the senior to the junior Warden, so that they may be dispersed round the Lodge.
Mas. to Sen. Dea. The Senior Deacon's place in the Lodge?
Sen. Deacon's Ans. At the Back of the master, or at his Right hand if he permits him.
Mas. Your business there?
Sen. Dea. Ans. To carry Messages from the Master to the senior Warden'.

So we have both Deacons acting as *Messengers,* a duty that is so seldom seen in today's lodges but is very well illustrated in the ceremony of 'Calling off' as given in these publications. *T.D.K.* gives the procedure thus:–

The Master whispers to the Senior Deacon at his Right-hand, and says, 'tis my will and Pleasure that this lodge is called off from Work to Refreshment during Pleasure, then the Senior deacon carries it to the Junior (*sic*) Warden, and whispers the same words in his

Ear, and he whispers it in the Ear of the junior Deacon at his Right-hand and he carries it to the Junior Warden and whispers the same to him, who declares it with a loud Voice, and says it is our Master's Will and Pleasure, that this Lodge is called from Work to Refreshment, during Pleasure; then he sets up his Column, and the Senior lays his down; for the Care of the Lodge is in the Hands of the junior Warden while they are at Refreshment.

There are some lodges in England where the Deacons still act as messengers in this way when the Minutes are taken by the Senior Deacon to the Master, for signing, then to the Senior Warden, the Junior Deacon carries the book to the Junior warden and back to the Senior Deacon who has been waiting by the Senior Warden, and so back to the Secretary.

We now go back to that old lodge in the tavern. The lodge has been opened and the brethren, seated at the table, talk business which may include a proposal of a candidate for initiation. If he is to be accepted, the sponsor of the candidate is sent out of the room to prepare him.

'Masonry Dissected' indicates that it was the Entered Apprentice who prepared the candidate, in *J. & B.* it was both Wardens. Today, in most English lodges, this is done by the Tyler, but in some, in the north of England, Bristol and possibly elsewhere, the Deacons prepare him and the Junior Warden goes out to see that it is properly done. In America, it may be done by a Steward, or a Master of Ceremony, but invariably under the supervision of the Senior Deacon. Again, Deacons acting for the Junior Warden.

While the candidate is out of the lodge, the room is being made ready for the ceremony of 'making' (initiation). A design, representing the form of the lodge, is drawn on the floor, 'at the far end', with chalk or charcoal, and on it will be placed the V.S.L., the Square and Compasses, the three 'high candlesticks', and possibly other emblems such as pillars etc. For the ceremony the brethren stand round this drawing, 'the lodge', in the same positions that they occupied at the table, that is the Master in the East etc.

The candidate is brought to the door of the lodge and is received by the Junior Warden; and this, as given in *M.D., T.D.K.* and *J. & B.* to have been the practice until this duty was allocated to the Junior deacon, by the Lodge of Promulgation, in 1810.

After he was received by the Junior Warden, the candidate was taken to the Master for a prayer and after asserting his belief in G. he was told to follow his 'leader'. He was then led three times round the lodge, and *T.D.K.* goes on:–

Mas. Where did you meet with the first opposition?
Ans. At the back of the Junior Warden in the South where I gave the same three knocks as at the Door . . .

The second opposition was at the back of the Senior Warden and the third at the Master. Therefore it could not have been either of the Wardens, or the Master, who was conducting the candidate – it must have been someone else!

Was this how another officer was introduced into the ceremonies, he who came to be known as the 'Deacon,' or the 'Steward?'

After these three perambulations, the candidate is taken 'to the Senior Warden

in the West, to receive instructions', and he shows him how to advance to take his 'Oath'.

The new Mason then retires to restore himself to his personal comforts and is then brought back to return thanks to the 'Master, Senior and Junior Wardens, Senior and Junior Deacons'. The Master invests him with his apron and he joins the others at the table for the Lecture.

The remainder of both *T.D.K.* and *J. & B.* is taken up with the catechisms, 'reasons' (explanation of the symbolism of the degrees), songs and a description of the customs at the table, such as the toasts and 'firing'.

In the ceremony just given we see that the Reception, Conducting and Instruction of the candidate were all carried out by the Wardens, all are now, in the majority of lodges, performed by the Deacons – as proxies for the Wardens.

Included in *J. & B.* but not in *T.D.K.*, is a ceremony for Masonic funerals, and the form of the procession does not include Deacons, indeed the only places in which *J. & B.* mentions these officers are in parts that were copied from *T.D.K.* which seems to indicate that Deacons were not part of the Moderns system, at least not by that name or title. It is reasonably certain that those parts of the ceremonies that, in the Antients working, were performed by Deacons, or by that 'someone' who conducted the candidate after the prayer, were also performed in the Moderns lodges, but by a brother without a title or by a 'Steward'.

We have seen the introduction of new officers into our lodges, the Deacons. They emerge in the ceremony of opening the lodge, in place of the Entered Apprentices, and their duties there are to act as 'messengers'.

However, they do not appear in the degree ceremonies, – why?

There was that 'someone' who conducted the candidate to 'the back of the Junior Warden', a duty, on the floor of the lodge, that must have been performed for some time previously by brethren other than the Wardens; but this function had not yet been allocated to a titled officer, there were none!

We saw in the section on 'Appointments' that 'Deacons' were reported, perhaps in error, to be present in the Lodge of Antiquity in 1778. Error or not, it indicates that the title 'Deacon' had 'taken root' in that Lodge, although Deacons were not officially appointed until 1787, and from then annually to the present day.

In 1790, the duties of the Deacons were specified in the Bye-laws of this Lodge:–

> The Senior Deacon shall attend at the Senior Warden's Right Hand for the more regular communication between that Officer and the Master; the Junior Deacon shall attend at the Right Hand of the Junior Warden for the more regular communication between that Officer and the Senior Warden; and these Deacons shall take care of Candidates for Initiation into the different Degrees and conduct them to the respective Officers in antient Form.

The Deacons were to '. . . take care of Candidates . . . and conduct them . . .'. Brother 'Someone' had been given a title and an office in the Lodge, together with definite duties in addition to that of 'messenger'. They had been stationed near the Wardens, (not the Master and Senior Warden), and were to act as their proxies.

In 1810 the Lodge of Promulgation, which included in its membership many brethren of the Lodge of Antiquity, made their only pronouncement on the *duties* of the Deacons, – to receive and conduct the candidates. This, together with the

resolution as to the Deacons being '... useful and necessary Officers ...', made their appointment in the lodges 'official'.

Deacons and Stewards
The offices of Deacon and Steward, in pre-union lodges, are difficult to differentiate, and can produce some confusion and lack of understanding, as they did in contemporary lodges; they were, in many cases, different names for the same officer, under different Grand Lodges. The officer that we are at present describing was usually 'Steward' in the Moderns, and 'Deacon' in the Antients.

Stewards were first mooted on the masonic scene in James Anderson's *'Constitutions'* of 1723 where regulation XXIII runs:–

> If ... the Grand-Master agree[s] to hold a Grand Feast according to the ancient laudable Customs of Masons, then the Grand-Wardens shall have the care of the Tickets ... and of every other thing that concerns the Entertainments.
>
> But that the work may not be too burthensome to the two Grand-Wardens, ... the Grand-Master, or his Deputy, shall have power to nominate and appoint a certain Number of Stewards ...'
>
> 'XXIV ... The Grand-Wardens and the Stewards are to account for all the money they receive, or expend.'

Thus we see that provision was made for the appointment of Stewards as 'Assistants' to the Grand-Wardens.

Under the date of Lady Day (March 25th) 1721, Anderson records, in his 1738 *'Constitutions'*, that:–

> ... the General Assembly requir'd more room, [and] proposed the next Assembly and Feast to be held at Stationers-Hall, Ludgate-Street; which was agreed to.
>
> Then the Grand Wardens were order'd as usual, to prepare the Feast, and to take some Stewards to their assistance ...

This was in preparation for the Festival of St. John the Baptist to be held on 24th June following, and at which the first noble Grand Master, John 2nd Duke of Montagu, was to be installed.

Thus introduced in 1721, and regularized in 1723, the Stewards were to be responsible for everything appertaining to the Festive Board, and William Preston, in the first edition of his *'Illustrations'*, 1772, gives the following in the Charge to the Stewards on their appointment:–

> ... The duties of your office are to introduce visitors, and to see that they are properly accommodated; to collect the quarterage and other fees, and to keep an account of the lodge expenses ...

The two junior officers in the Lodge at Swalwell, in 1733, were entitled 'Decon or Steward', two titles for the same person. Up to that time the Lodge had been purely 'operative' and were just beginning to accept 'Gentleman Masons', and, having no Secretary or treasurer, it is possible that the title 'Steward' was the more appropriate for the brother who was probably introduced for the purpose of looking-after the financial and domestic affairs of the Lodge. It is likely that both titles were intended to mean 'Assistant to the Wardens'. When the Lodge was constituted under the Grand Lodge of England in 1735, these officers were listed

as 'Stewards' and the name 'Deacon' disappeared from that Lodge for a period of some forty years.

We have seen that the 'Deacons' listed in the Lodge of Antiquity in 1778, Brother Sealy and Brother Nantes, were previously shown as Stewards, as were their immediate successors. Bro C. W. Firebrace in *'Records of the Lodge of Antiquity No. 2., Vol. II'*, when commenting on the 'regular' appointment of Deacons in 1787 says that '... from this date until the re-union of the two Lodges of Antiquity in 1790, the word "Deacons" takes the places of "Stewards"...' and when talking about the re-union, he points out that one section of the Lodge (Preston's) had had 'Deacons', whilst the other (Noorthouck's) had 'Stewards' and that 'The difference in their duties would appear to be nominal'.

In the section on 'Appointments', those at Chester, in 1743, were:–

'Master's Deacon and Warden's Deacon'

And in 1765, there were appointed in St. George's Lodge, at Taunton, (erased 1783):–

'Master's Steward and Warden's Steward'

These appointments were continued in this form until the Lodge faded out in 1778, and I'm sure that each pair of these were appointments to the same offices, to perform the same duties.

There also seemed to be some confusion, or changes of mind, in the Lodge of Antiquity, as to where the Stewards, later 'Deacons', should sit.

In 1777, before they became known as 'Deacons', the Stewards were on the Left of the Wardens (in the South and West), in 1790 the Senior Deacon was on the Right of the Senior Warden, and the Junior on the Right of the Junior Warden; they reverted to the Left of the Wardens in 1798, and in 1811 the Deacons were on the Right and the Stewards on the Left of their respective Officers. this despite the Lodge of Promulgation's recommendation that the Senior Deacon should be at the Right of the Master and the Junior at the Right of the Senior Warden.

It appears, therefore, that the Deacons, (and the Stewards), in the Lodge of Antiquity, were 'attached' to the Wardens, rather than to the Master and Senior Warden. This is also in agreement with Preston's note in his *'Illustrations'* of 1812 (p. 89) that 'The Deacons are the acting Deputies of the Wardens ...'

Richard Verstegan in his 'A Restitution of Decayed Intelligence ...'. 1634, gives an early meaning of the word 'Steward' as 'one who supplies or fills the place of a superior officer'. A definition that describes our 'Deacon or Steward' admirably.

In general, before 1814, the brother who conducted the candidate (as proxy for the Warden) whom we call 'Deacon', was 'Steward' in the Moderns. When both officers were appointed the Steward was usually the senior but in the Antients the Deacon took precedence. But, as in all generalities there were many exceptions.

Deacons and Stewards, like the Entered apprentices before them, were the deputies and assistants to superior officers, and were frequently referred to merely as 'The Assistants'.

In the narrative portion of *J. & B.,* the candidate is received at the door of the lodge by '... the Senior and Junior Wardens, or their assistants...'.

Another note in Preston's *'Illustrations'* of 1812 says 'The Stewards are assistants to the Deacons'.

And in the *'Constitutions'* of 1815, the first of the United Grand Lodge, we find '... the Wardens and their assistants, the two Deacons ...'. This is repeated in each subsequent edition up to 1873, but from 1896 the 'Deacons' appear in the list under their own style and title.

The lowest estimation of the standing of the Stewards appears to be that given in the Lodge of Promulgation when, on January 23rd 1810, an explanation was given with regard to the '... Stewards and their Duties, not as Officers but as appendages' – an opinion that is, unfortunately, still held in many areas to-day, despite the fact that, according to the English *'Constitutions'*, the Stewards are, nevertheless, officers of the Lodge.

It seems that having allocated the duties of the Moderns 'Stewards' to the newly approved 'Deacons', the Lodge of Promulgations did not know what to do with the Stewards!

In those lodges with both officers, the duties that had been performed by the 'Deacon or Steward', tended to be split between the two officers; the Deacons took part in the ceremonies in the lodge-room, and the Stewards attended to the refreshments and finances of the Festive Board.

Here are some extracts from lodge records, showing how the financial arrangements for the refreshments were part of the duties of the Junior Warden and are now performed, mainly by the Stewards, on behalf of another relatively new officer – the Treasurer.

1740	The Lodge of Antiquity. '... the Tyler to collect visitors' supper fees at the door ... to save the trouble of the Junior Warden and Secretary'.
c. 1740–50	An unattached lodge at Newcastle upon Tyne. 'By-law XVII ... the Junior Warden shall take care of the shot [the Tavern bill] and receive every Brother's dividend'.
1755	Phoenix Lodge, Sunderland. By-laws '... the Junior Warden ... shall at the hour of Ten in each Lodge-night, call in the Bill of Expenses and collect the reckoning'. The above was altered, in 1778, in that 'Junior Warden' was deleted and 'one of the Deacons' substituted.
1765	The Great Lodge, at Swaffham. By-laws '... the Junior Warden shall see the Bill upon the Table at TEN o'clock ...'.
1772	Lodge of Loyalty, Truro. The Junior Warden collected the Supper fees (1/-).

Here we have ample justification for the investing of the Junior Warden as 'the ostensible Steward of the Lodge'.

In *T.D.K.*, (1760) there is a section on the toasts and 'firing' at the table and there:–

... the Senior Deacon charges (as they call it) in the North and East, and the Junior Deacon in the South and West, for it is their duty so to do (i.e. to fill all the glasses).

Before the toasts, the Master enquires whether 'all are charged' in the South and West, to which the Wardens reply that 'all are charged'. This custom still obtains in many lodges before the toasts and 'taking wine'.

When one considers the large number of toasts that are listed in the masonic publications of the 18th century, it is not surprising that arrangements had to be made for supplying liquid refreshment, ale, spirits, punch or wine – to see that it was paid for, and that over-indulgence was kept to a minimum. These objects were attained to some degree, by the imposition of fines for brethren being 'disguised in liquor', or for ordering without the Warden's permission. Again in the Lodge of Antiquity a by-law of 1788 reads 'No liquor to be ordered by the Deacon after the Master leaves the chair', and in the by-laws of the Marquis of Granby Lodge, at Durham, it was stated that 'The Stewards are appointed for economical arrangements'. In the same Lodge in 1786 they appointed a Steward as 'GOVN^r. of the LIQUORS'.

Before leaving the subject of the Festive Board it would not be inappropriate to remind the reader that 'at table' in English lodges, and possibly elsewhere, it is the custom for the Senior Warden to sit at the head of the 'sprig' on the Master's far Right, that is, in the North-West, and the Junior Warden in the corresponding position on the Master's Left, in the South-West, – the same positions that were occupied by their predecessors in the early 18th century, when both Wardens were in the West.

This account of how our Deacons evolved does not, however, tell the whole story. There are several other duties performed by these officers with which most English masons are familiar but which may be of interest, particularly to brethren of other jurisdictions.

Apart from accompanying the candidate throughout the ceremonies, the Deacons, in many English lodges lead the procession of the Master and his Officers entering the room for the opening of the lodge, and also when they leave. They light the candles, (the three Lesser Lights), at the opening of the lodge, and, in some workings, extinguish them, in progression in the various degrees.

This little ceremony is carried out in a very impressive way in Pilgrim Lodge, No. 238, London, who work a very old form of ritual, in the German language. The procedure is described in the *Transactions of Quatuor Coronati Lodge No. 2076, vol. 76.*

Before anyone enters the Lodge room, a small candle is lit on the Master's pedestal. The S.D., at the appropriate moment, hands the Master a taper and the Master lights it from his candle, which is then extinguished. The S.D. then takes the taper and proceeds to light each candle in turn, saying:–
At the W.M.'s pillar.....'Wisdom guide our Building'.
At the S.W.'s pillar.......'Strength erect it'.
At the J.W.'s pillar.......'Beauty adorn it'.

In the second degree the perambulations are 'particularly attractive, because the S.D. leads the 'procession' and walks, [backwards], facing the candidates all the way, strewing their path with cut-flowers, of which he carries a large basket-full.

A truly impressive sight.

'The History of Two Hundred Years of Pilgrim Lodge No. 238, published in 1979, records that at the Festival of St. John, June 1881 'the Wardens sat in the West with the Deacons beside them'.

The Tracing Boards, (modern versions of the 'drawing' on the floor) in our lodges are arranged, in each degree, by one of the Deacons.

The Ballot, for new members and for the Officers at the annual election, is supervised by the Deacons, a procedure which varies from lodge to lodge. In the Great Lodge at Swaffham (erased 1791), in 1765 the 'Junior Warden carried the ballot-box to the Master and to the Secretary, who counted the papers'. Another example of the Junior Warden's duty passing to the Deacons.

We have followed the evolution of the Deacons from the Entered Apprentices in Prichard's *'Masonry Dissected',* through the mid-eighteenth century, with *T.D.K.* and *J. & B.,* to the time of the Lodge of Promulgation in 1809–11. On Dec. 7th 1813, a few weeks before the 'Union', the Lodge of Reconciliation was set-up to effect a uniformity of working, based on the recommendations of the Lodge of Promulgation, throughout the English Craft. It completed its task in 1816 and our present-day working, in all its variations, is based on those findings.

The early degree ceremonies that have been described were of relatively short duration, of maybe ten to fifteen minutes, and the remainder of the evening was taken up at the 'table' with the catechisms and 'reasons' (the lectures) for the instruction of the brethren, particularly the new initiate.

Today's meetings are quite different. Most of the teaching in the lectures and catechisms at the 'table', has now been absorbed and incorporated into the 'floor' ceremonies, so that the degree-work takes longer and there is, unfortunately, no time available for further teaching. Consequently the Lectures, for which William Preston was largely responsible, are far too infrequently performed.

However there are compensations. Our present meeting-places are a great improvement on the taverns and inns of Prichard's day. The rooms of today are large, elegant Temples. The 'table' has been removed to a dining-room, and the Master's and the Wardens' chairs have moved away from the centre of the floor to the East, South and West sides of the room. Each of these Officers has a pedestal before him, on which the Master places the three Great Lights, and the Wardens, their Columns. The Lesser Lights, the 'three large candlesticks' of Prichard, are placed near these three pedestals. The brethren are seated along the North and South sides, and Past Masters on either side of the Master on the dais in the East.

These arrangements have now given a large area in the centre of the floor, most of which is occupied by a chequered carpet, the 'squared pavement'.

On the carpet is placed the tracing Board and in lodges where the Master's pedestal is not used for the V.S.L., there is an altar for that purpose.

There is now ample room in which the Deacons can conduct the perambulations with, of course, 'squaring' the chequered carpet, so as not to disturb the 'drawing' that was once there!

The solemn dignified atmosphere that should always pervade our ceremonies is greatly enhanced, or destroyed, according to the manner in which the Deacons perform their duties, – they are very important officers.

INSIGNIA

The definition of the word 'Insignia' is given in the Oxford English Dictionary as 'Badges or distinguishing marks of office or honour'.

In our present context the term includes Jewels, Collars, Rods or Wands and Columns.

One of the earliest references to masonic jewels of office is in the Minutes of the Grand Lodge of England, where it is recorded that, at the meeting held on 24th June 1727 it was resolved.

> ... that in all private lodges ... the Ma^{rs}. and Wardens do wear the Jewells of Masonry hanging to a White Ribbon (Viz^t.) that the Ma^r. wear the Square the Senr. Warden the Levell and the Junr. Warden the Plumb rule.

It is probable that this resolution was necessary because of the variety of badges and jewels being worn at that time and so brought some order out of confusion.

The first official specification for the jewels of the Officers of Grand Lodge and of private lodges was given at the meeting of the then new United Grand Lodge, held on 2nd May 1814, and the list was included in the first *'Constitutions'* of that Grand Lodge in 1815. This list included the jewels for Deacons which were to be the 'Dove with an Olive Branch' and it has remained so to the present time.

These regulations also stated that the jewels of Grand Officers and Provincial Grand Officers shall be of Gold or Gilt, and that those in private lodges should be of Silver.

It has been understood, but, as far as I know, never enacted, that lodges which up to that time had employed jewels of other designs, could continue to use their old jewels. Consequently we find lodges in which the Deacons wear the 'Winged Mercury' or the 'Sun' or the 'Moon' or the Inner Guard has a silver 'Trowel', and this according to, shall we say, 'time immemorial practice' or 'inherent right'.

Let us now consider the various emblems that are, or have been, worn by our Deacons.

The Compasses.
J. & B. says that 'The Senior and Junior Deacons have each a black rod, with the compass hanging round their necks ...'.

I can find no record of the compass having been worn in a lodge, but there are at least two versions of an engraving 'The Ceremony of Making a FREE-MASON', one, dated 1764 and appearing in the exposure *'HIRAM'*, shows brethren standing round a large table, the Master in the East, (his jewel appears to be the square but it is very indistinct), the Senior Warden in the North-West with the level, the Junior Warden on the South side with the plumb rule, and a brother with a rod or wand, at the Master's right hand, he is evidently a Deacon, wearing the Compasses. The other Deacon, also with his rod, is at the South-West corner of the table but his back is turned so that his jewel cannot be seen.

The Winged Mercury.
These jewels are representations of the Roman god Mercurius (or the Greek Hermes), with a winged helmet (Petasus) and winged shoes, carrying a Caduceus,

which is a rod, also with wings, and with two serpents twined around it. The Caduceus is believed to have been originally an olive branch, a symbol of Peace, carried by the heralds.

Mercury of St. John's Lodge No. 80
Thomas Harper 1805.

Dove with Olive branch
Deacons' Jewels. Introduced 1813.

Hermes, or Mercury, appears as a god in Greek and Roman mythology, the son of Zeus (or Jupiter) and he was the herald and messenger of the gods. He was the patron of merchants and of the thieves who preyed on them. He was also the god and guide of travellers, including those on their way to Hades. The serpents on the Caduceus are thought to have been the streamers or ribbons on the white wand of the herald, and, in consequence of Hermes' association with Hell, the streamers were transformed into serpents to symbolise his dealing with that place.

Altogether, Mercury appears to have been a very appropriate choice as the emblem of the 'messengers' in our lodges, – the Deacons.

A few eminent and erudite Masonic writers have said that the Mercury was the 'original;, or 'earliest' jewel of the Deacons, but they give no evidence of its early use. It was adopted, but not 'officially', by the Antients and most of the examples still in existence come from those lodges, or from Ireland, whence one assumes the Antients obtained the emblem.

There is a record of a procession in Lodge No. 25, Cork, Ireland, in 1751 which included Deacons – '... and every officer wearing his proper Jewel'. – but what the Deacons' jewel was, it does not say!

Enoch Lodge No. 11, one of the oldest of the Antient lodges (1754), have Mercuries for their Deacons; two such jewels were supplied by Bro John McCormack in 1771. That Mercuries were being worn by the Deacons in Ireland in about 1777, is indicated by a note, in a copy of *J. & B.*, by Emanuel Zimmerman at that time.

Most of these jewels that I have been able to trace are from the last quarter of the 18th century or the first decades of the 19th. Many of them were made by

Thomas Harper, a well-known London silversmith, who was a prominent officer under both the Antients (Dep. G. Master) and the Moderns (G. Steward). There are records of some Antients lodges paying various sums to Bro Robert Leslie, grand Secretary, for 'the constitution and jewels', the fact that Thomas Harper was Deputy Grand Master, and, at one time, joint secretary to Leslie may, of course, have nothing to do with the matter! Such was probably the case with my Mother-Lodge, St. John's No. 80, constituted 4th January 1806, and we still use our 'Thomas Harper' Mercury jewels.

Several of the Moderns lodges which appointed Deacons before 1814 adopted the Mercury as their jewel, probably because it was the only design available. The Lodge of Antiquity's Deacons' jewels are Mercuries by Thomas Harper (hall-marked 1783–4), and together with their other officers' jewels are gilt, rather than silver, by special permission of Grand Lodge. Another of the 'Four Old Lodges' of 1717, Royal Somerset House and Inverness, No. 4. also have Mercury jewels, and they are probably those presented to the Lodge by the first Deacons on their appointment in 1813. Old Dundee Lodge No. 18, (see under 'Appointments') have Mercuries that they obtained in 1810.

There seems to have been some misapprehension in the 18th century as to the provenance of the figure represented in these jewels.

In 1769 Wellins Calcott in his *'Candid Disquisition ...'*, describes, 'Jupiter with Petasus and Caduceus' and in his 1786 edition this is amended to 'Jupiter Mercury'.

An inventory, dated 1865, of the Lodge of Probity, No. 61, Bury, Lancashire, gives – '2 columns, S.D. and J.D.' and this is corrected to '2 Jupiters' and presumably refers to the Deacons' wands surmounted by Mercuries, which the Lodge still possesses.

Another inventory, this time of Lodge Holyrood House, (St. Luke's) No. 44, S.C., Edinburgh, lists 'An Esculapian (*sic*) Rod', which was carried before the 'Lodge' in public processions. Aesculapius was the Roman god of medicine and is often represented in medical literature by a rod with a serpent twined around it – one serpent! Maybe this 'Esculapian Rod' was a Caduceus. Another Edinburgh lodge, Roman Eagle No. 160 had an office-bearer assigned to the 'Aesculapian Rod'.

Several newspapers have been named 'Mercury', (e.g. the Scarborough Mercury) presumably meaning the same as 'Courier' and 'Messenger' in the same field.

In the 'Mark' degree the Mercury is the emblem of the Deacon, having been allocated to that Officer in 1886, in place of the Dove, which latter is still used in a few old 'Mark' lodges.

The Sun and Moon.
There are a few lodges in the north-east of England which have Deacons' jewels in the shape of a 'Meridian Sun' and a 'Crescent Moon.' They are all between $2\frac{1}{2}$ and 4 inches in diameter and are of sheet silver. The 'Sun' has a full-face' design with irradiations, and the 'Moon' shows a profile 'face'.

I know of seven sets of these unusual jewels, five belonging to lodges in the Province of Durham and two in Yorkshire.

Deacons' Jewels. Sun and Moon of Phoenix Lodge No. 94.

The lodges are:–

The Lodge of Industry No. 48 (1735)	Gateshead
Phoenix Lodge No. 94 (1755)	Sunderland
The Marquis of Granby Lodge No. 124 (1763)	Durham
Union Lodge No. 456 (1772 erased 1827)	Gateshead
St. Bede's Lodge No. 308 (1774 erased 1828)	South Shields
Minerva Lodge No. 250 (1783)	Hull, Yorkshire
Constitutional Lodge No. 294 (1793)	Beverley, Yorkshire

Unfortunately only two sets can be dated, those at the Lodge of Industry are hall-marked as being made by Thomas Watson, at Newcastle upon Tyne, but bear no date-letter, however the maker's mark indicates that the date of marking must have been between 1793 and 1803, together with other jewels in the Lodge with the same markings. Those at Beverley are also hall-marked, 1793. This latter hall-mark is important.

I have been unable to find evidence in any of these lodges that their 'Sun and Moon' jewels were intended for use by the Deacons, but, in Beverley, all the jewels of the Officers appointed at the constitution of the Lodge bear the same hall-mark, 1793, the year in which the Lodge was formed, they are those of the Master, Senior and Junior Wardens, Treasurer, Secretary and Tyler, and the 'Sun and Moon'. There were no other officers appointed, except the Deacons, therefore the 'Sun and Moon' must have been for those officers.

The Lodge of Industry, previously the 'Lodge at Swalwell', obtained new 'Dove' jewels for the Deacons in the 1850s and now the 'Sun and Moon' are worn by the Senior and Junior Stewards to commemorate the 'Deacon or Steward' of 1733. The Phoenix Lodge No. 94, Sunderland, of 1755, the Marquis of Granby Lodge No. 124, Durham, of 1763 and the lodge at Beverley still use these jewels for the Deacons. Those at Hull are now museum pieces and are exactly the same as those

at Beverley, which are not 'plate' jewels, as the others, but *repoussé* work. The 'Sun and Moon' of Union Lodge No. 456 are now with the Borough Lodge No. 424, also at Gateshead.

St. Bede's Lodge No. 308, of 1774, at South Shields, Co. Durham, moved to Morpeth, Northumberland, in 1789 and their 'Sun and Moon' are now with their successors, Lodge de Ogle No. 636 at Morpeth. Neither of these lodges, Borough, or de Ogle, can wear these jewels, not having done so before the 'Union'.

The reason for these lodges, all in the north-east Provinces, having chosen Sun and Moon for their Deacons is obscure, and any explanation must be conjecture.

The Sun and Moon are, of course, centuries-old symbols and, at times, objects of worship. They appear in almost all forms of masonic decorative art of the 18th century; on engraved plate jewels, pierced jewels, as decoration on some Masters' Squares, on Levels and Plumb-rules of the Wardens, and on banners and aprons, indeed they still appear on the apron of the Grand Master Mason of Scotland.

They are usually two of a group of three emblems, the third being either the 'Blazing Star', or the 'All-seeing Eye', (symbols of the Deity) indicating the 'rule of three' one of the oldest phrases in the Craft.

We have, in a printed catechism of 1725, *'The Whole Institutions of Free-Masons Opened'*, several examples, Father, Son, and Holy Ghost; Sun, Moon and Master Mason; Square, Level and Plumb; and from *'Masonry Dissected'* to the present day, 'The Sun, Moon and Master ...'. Of particular importance in our study of the lodges of the north-east of England, is a passage in William Hutchinson's *'The Spirit of Masonry'* of 1775 – '... the SUN and MOON are messengers of His Will and all His Law is CONCORD'. Hutchinson was Master of the Lodge of Concord, Barnard Castle, Durham, and a very prominent Orator and Masonic teacher in that area, at the time. The same passage appears, almost verbatim, in the explanation of the First Degree Tracing Board in many modern rituals.

So much for the symbolism and provenance of the Sun and Moon, but why should they be used for Deacons?

Bro Lionel Vibert said in a letter to Bro William Waples, in 1934, that he thought that, at one time, the 'Sun and Moon' had belonged to the Wardens. He did not say on what he based his opinion, but he may have obtained the idea from the Sword of State of the Grand Lodge of England, which is housed in the Museum at Freemasons' Hall, Great Queen Street, London.

In the William Waples Museum, in Sunderland, we have a tinted engraving by John Pine, of 1730; it shows this sword, and was to mark its presentation to Grand Lodge by the Duke of Norfolk, Grand Master, in that year. The sword had belonged to Gustavus Adolphus, the warrior King of Sweden, who was killed in battle in 1632, and it was refurbished, and given a new scabbard, by Bro George Moody, the King's Sword-maker. Both the scabbard and the engraving are of 1730.

One of the medallions, which decorate the scabbard, shows a Mason with his apron, and the compasses on a ribbon round his neck. In the background is a representation of Arundel Castle, and a 'Blazing Sun'. This is evidently the Duke of Norfolk, Grand Master, whose home was Arundel Castle.

Another similar medallion shows two Masons, with aprons, one wearing the

Medallions on the Sword of State of Grand Lodge, 1730. Thomas 8th Duke of Norfolk, G.M.   Geo Carpenter S.G.W.   Thos. Batson J.G.W.

Level and, above and behind him, – the 'Crescent Moon'; the other figure wears the Plumb-rule and has the 'Meridian Sun' on his left. These brethren are obviously the Senior and Junior Grand Wardens, Col. George Carpenter, and Thomas Batson, respectively. This is confirmed in another design on the engraving showing three hands clasped together, with the initials:–

'N.B'. (Nathaniel Blackerby, D.G.M.),
'G.C'. (George Carpenter) and
'T.B.' (Thomas Batson).

Again, the 'rule of three'.

So we know that in 1730 the Moon was identified, or associated, with the Senior warden, and the Meridian Sun with the Junior Warden. Now the conjecture.

As we have seen, the Level and Plumb-rule were made obligatory for the Wardens in 1727, only three years before the medallions were made. Were the Sun and the Moon placed beside the Wardens to commemorate the jewels that may have been worn by the Wardens before 1727 – the Sun and Moon?

There was a 'Meridian Sun' on the South Wall and a 'Crescent Moon' on the West wall, in each case above the Warden's chair, in the Masons' Hall, Vine Street, Sunderland, in 1778, (demolished 1936). In the present Hall of Phoenix Lodge, built as a replica and replacement of the earlier building, which was severely damaged by fire in 1783, these emblems occupy the same positions and there are records to show that they were placed there at the erection of the building in 1785. The same emblems appear also on the Wardens' chairs, (dated about 1770). Again the Moon for the Senior Warden and the Sun for the Junior Warden.

These same emblems are also incorporated in the designs on the ceiling-cove in

the Grand Temple, in Freemasons' Hall, London; the Sun in the South and the Moon in the West.

As we have seen earlier, the Deacons were the Deputies and assistants to the Wardens and therefore, what more natural than to choose their emblems for the new officers – the Deacons?

It may be very pertinent to our argument that all the lodges possessing these 'Sun and Moon' jewels were Moderns; also that we know that six practised the old north-east Harodim. The predecessor of the seventh, at Beverley, was St. George's East York Militia Lodge which was constituted in Newcastle upon Tyne, in 1782, by St. Nicholas Lodge, another body that had the Harodim! The Sun and Moon played a very important part in this order. This 'conjecture' could provide a starting point for further research into these most unusual 'Sun and Moon' jewels.

There are two peculiar jewels in the Lodge of Perseverance No. 213, Norwich, which are basically 'Dove' jewels, but each has another smaller emblem added on the circular body of the jewel, a Sun on one and a Moon on the other. Unfortunately their is no information whatever as to their origin.

The Sun and Moon are used in the majority of the lodges in the United States of America, those in Pennsylvania excepted, as jewels for the Deacons, but in this case the Sun or the Moon, is enclosed within the Square and Compasses. I have not been able to glean any information on the reason for their choice of Sun and Moon except that the two emblems serve to distinguish between the Senior Deacon, who has the Sun, and his colleague who has the Moon.

The Marquis of Granby Lodge use the same system, Sun for Senior and Moon for Junior, but in Phoenix Lodge it is the reverse, the Senior Deacon wearing the Moon as deputy, or assistant, to the Senior Warden, and the Junior Deacon has the Sun as acting for, or with, the Junior Warden. If we consider the Deacons as acting as messengers, (rather than deputies or assistants) to the Master and Senior Warden, then the Durham and American brethren are right, or more logical; but I am on the side of Phoenix Lodge as our Deacons act much more on behalf of the Wardens than as 'messengers'.

The Dove carrying an Olive Branch

I have already mentioned that the official jewel of the Deacon in the English Constitution is the 'Dove and Olive Branch' which was introduced at the formation of the United Grand Lodge of England.

The reason for the choice is a subject of much speculation, and many theories have been advanced. Some writers suggest that it is a survival or a resurrection of ancient Irish practice. The Dove was not officially adopted as the jewel of the Deacons in the Grand Lodge of Ireland until 1859, and when commenting upon this, in his *'History of the Grand Lodge of Ireland, VOL II'*, Bro. P. R. Parkinson regrets the passing of 'the handsome old "Mercuries".'

But Bro Bernard Jones, in his *'Compendium'* says that '... the Irish Masons had this emblem long before it was adopted in England', and he was probably referring to a seal of Lodge No. 134, Lurgan (1734) showing 'a dove carrying a sprig of

olive' mentioned by Heron Lepper in his '50 years of Freemasonry in Antrim' published in *A.Q.C.* vol. 35.

This of course only indicates that the Irish had the emblem, but does not necessarily associate it with the Deacons.

A similar situation is illustrated in John Cunningham's popular masonic poem, 'Let Masonry from Pole to Pole . . .', the last verse of which runs:–

> Peace adds to olive boughs, entwined
> An emblematic dove,
> As stamped upon the Mason's mind
> Are unity and love.

Bro Cunningham was born in Dublin in 1729, died and was buried in Newcastle in 1773.

Under the Grand Lodge of Pennsylvania, a body said to have been derived from Cork, Ireland, in 1731, the jewel of the Deacons is still the 'Dove'. There is little doubt that this emblem was well-known in Ireland in the early 18th century.

Noah sent out a Dove from the Ark and it returned with an Olive Branch – a 'messenger' and a 'herald'. The Caduceus was supposed to have been originally an olive branch, and Mercury – a herald, and both are symbols of Peace.

The change from 'Mercury' to the 'Dove' may have been a way of changing from a pagan god to an Old testament biblical symbol of Peace, – the Peace in Freemasonry which had just been achieved by the Union of the two Grand Lodges, or maybe, the temporary lull in the Napoleonic wars.

It is generally supposed that this change was largely brought about under the influence, or at the insistence of the Duke of Sussex. This is given support in a suggestion from Bro P. J. Dawson when he points out that in the Coat of Arms of the Chevalier Ruspini, the Crest is a 'Dove carrying an Olive Branch', and Bro Ruspini was a great friend of the Duke of Sussex, he was his dentist. He was also an influential member of several very important Moderns lodges, joined No. 1 of the Antients, 'The Grand Masters Lodge', and worked very hard preparing the way for the Union, which unfortunately he never saw as he died a short time before the actual event.

Thus the choice of the Dove for the new Deacons could, quite possibly, have been influenced by the Grand Master's affection for a departed friend.

The Compasses, the Mercury and the Dove were emblems for both Deacons, Senior and Junior, the Sun and Moon were used to distinguish one from another, and in the Scottish jurisdiction also, different jewels are used for each Office-bearer:–

The Trowel and the Mallet

The youngest Entered apprentice, in the Antients Lodges, (and some others), wore the trowel, he attended 'at the door of the lodge on the inside', a duty later performed by the Junior Deacon and is still his duty in American lodges, now the Scottish Junior Deacon wears the Trowel.

The Senior Deacon is distinguished by the Mallet (maul-ette) indicating his connection with the Master of the Lodge whose messages and commands he carries.

It may be of interest, here, to note that in another exposure *'The Grand Mystery Laid Open';* of 1726, the candidate for initiation is said to hold a Trowel in his right hand and a Hammer (maul) in his left when taking his obligation.

Collars

Collars, or 'ribbons', on which the jewels of office are suspended, are referred to many times in the Minutes of Grand Lodge and other bodies. They are a very distinctive part of the regalia, but it must be remembered that the sole purpose of the collar is to carry the jewel, the collar has no other purpose.

The Square, Level and Plumb-rule were ordered, in Grand Lodge in 1727, to be hung from a White ribbon, in 1731 the ribbon was to be Blue for Grand Officers and Red for Stewards. Today the collars of the officers of private lodges in the English Constitution are, with one or two exceptions, light blue and four inches wide.

There is a very interesting record in the Minutes of Enoch Lodge No. 11, dated June 1777, where it is ordered that:–

> ... alteration be made to the Hangings belonging to this Lodge, viz:– the Linings to be Blue and the Middle Crimson, with three rows of Silver Lace on two Hangings viz: – on the Master's and Past-Master's Hangings. The same linings and the same middle with two rows of the same lace as above on three Hangings viz:– the Senior and Junior Warden's and Secretary's Hangings, and the same lining and the same middle with two rows of Silver lace but narrower on the two Deacons' Hangings.
> Paid for 7 hangings – £7.

Rods or Wands

From ancient times the Rod, Wand, or Staff, has been a symbol of power and authority, and has appeared in many forms and for many offices. There are the sceptre, mace, beadle's staff and the Caduceus and many others.

A Rod or Wand is now universally recognized in the British Isles, in the United States, and elsewhere, as the Deacon's badge of office.

Wands have never, I believe, been the subject of regulation in the English Craft and their form and colour have varied enormously.

We had the Wardens' batons in some old lodges, then the Warden's columns that they carried in lodge and in processions, the Director of Ceremonies' baton, and, of course, the Deacons' Wands.

In *T.D.K.* 'The Master and his two Deacons have each a Black Rod in their hands about 7 foot high, when they open the Lodge and close it'. The Master's rod signifies his power in the lodge and those of the Deacons, the authority deputed to them.

James Anderson in his 1738 *'Constitutions'* gives an order of procession including:– 'The Stewards 2 and 2 a breast with white Rods'. We saw the Entered Apprentices with white 'Rodds', in the Granby Lodge by-laws.

At various times and places, the Deacons' and Stewards' rods have been blue, black, white, gilt and 'tipped with gold'. On festive occasions they have been decorated with ribbons, and at the funeral of Bro George Washington, President of the United States of America, on February 11th 1800, the Deacons and Stewards in the procession had 'mourning staves', (? decked with black crêpe).

The Bye-laws of Royal Somerset House and Inverness Lodge, No. 4, in 1776, made provision for the appointment of two Stewards '. . . one to officiate as Master of Ceremonies, to examine, introduce and place VISITORS [? Deacon] and the other to have the ordering and care of the Supper and Liquors'. The former officer was equipped with a gold stick and the brother holding the office of Master of Ceremonies became known as 'Gold Stick'.

The Deacons, and Stewards, in many of today's lodges, in England and abroad still carry plain white rods. The sight of the Stewards in Grand Lodge, some twenty or more, each with his white wand, is most impressive and adds greatly to the overall air of dignity that pervades the Temple.

In private lodges many Deacons' wands are surmounted with silver replicas of the collar-jewels of the office, most often it is the Dove, more unusually the Mercury and very rarely, the Meridian Sun or the Crescent Moon.

In the United States of America the majority of the Grand Lodges favour the Square and Compasses enclosing the Sun or the Moon for the Deacon's staves.

Pennsylvania have the Dove, and there were, at one time, several examples of rods being tipped with a Pine-cone or an Acorn; and I believe that, in the past, the Texas wands bore the 'Lone Star'.

Columns

The last items of Insignia to consider with respect to the Deacons are the Columns.

Columns, as insignia of office, are usually associated with the Wardens, as the symbol of their authority in the lodge; *T.D.K.* 1760, says:–

> The senior and junior Warden have each of them a Column in their hand, about twenty inches long, which represents the Two Columns of the Porch at Solomon's Temple, BOAZ and JACHIN,

But William Preston, in his 1792 *'Illustrations'* allocates them to the Deacons during the address to them at the investiture, part of which has already been quoted under 'Duties', the address concludes:–

> . . . Those columns, as badges of your office, I entrust to your care, not doubting your vigilance and attention.

This is repeated in subsequent editions of the book and in the 1812 edition there is a foot-note to p. 90 which reads:–

> When the work of Masonry in the lodge is carrying on, the column of the Senior Deacon is raised; when the lodge is at refreshment the column of the Junior Deacon is raised,

which is the same procedure as 'Calling Off' given in *T.D.K.* (when the columns belonged to the Wardens).

The Minutes of the Lodge of Promulgation, 26th January 1810, show that the Lodge considered 'the arrangement of the Wardens' Columns'. It seems therefore, that Preston's allocation of the Columns to the Deacons was not accepted, and the question arises as to whether he was describing the practice in his Lodge of Antiquity, or was he trying to make innovation?

An inventory of the Lodge of Peace and Unity, No. 314, Preston, Lancashire, founded in 1797, includes – '2 Deacons Columns'.

These are still in possession of the Lodge and are two mahogany pillars approximately 24 inches high, each surmounted by a vertical metal disc, some 6 inches in diameter. The discs are painted blue and on one is a gold 'Meridian Sun', and on the other a 'Crescent Moon', also gold.

How they were employed in the lodge is a mystery; they are too short to have been used as floor pillars, but could have been used as columns on pedestals, possibly for the Wardens, the Sun for the Junior Warden in the South and the Moon for the Senior Warden in the West; or for the Deacons?

The lodge at Beverley, 'Constitutional' No. 294, has a set of three Columns, one on each pedestal. These are all Doric columns some 22 to 24 inches high, beautifully carved and inlaid with different woods. On the sides of the pedestals of the columns are the following designs, one emblem on each side:–

Master's column – The Square, V.S.L., R.A., and K.T. emblems.
Senior Warden's – The Level, the Crescent Moon, emblems of other degrees.
Junior Warden's – The Plumb-rule, the Sun, emblems of other degrees.

Each column is surmounted by a short-cylinder, or thick disc, each enclosing an emblem:–
Master's – the head of a man – (The Master?)
Senior Warden's – the Moon
Junior Warden's – the Sun.
Thus we have:– 'the Sun, the Moon and the Master of the Lodge'.

CONCLUSION

Our lodges of today, with their fine furniture in elegant temples, and formalized ceremonies performed by brethren in splendid regalia, appear to bear very little resemblance to the tavern lodges of Prichard's day, but the basic essentials remain.

The lodge is still ruled by the Master and his two Wardens, the candidate is admitted with the same due caution, he is received and conducted round the lodge, brought to the Master for his obligation, and he is entrusted and invested. The fundamentals of the ceremony continue but whereas most of these duties were carried out by the Wardens, they have now been allocated to the '... *Deacons, being proved on due examination to be not only Ancient, but useful and necessary Officers ...*'

Brethren, I hope that I have given sufficient information on the derivation, development and importance of the Deacons, to interest you and encourage you to continue to make a Daily Advancement in Masonic Knowledge.

Appendix

(a) THE DEACON IN AMERICAN FREEMASONRY

America received its Masonry in the late 1600s and early 1700s, brought from the British isles by the immigrant settlers. The first Freemason in America is generally considered to have been John Skene, 'made' in the Lodge at Aberdeen, Scotland, who settled in Burlington, New Jersey in 1682. The second was Jonathan Belcher, born in Boston, Mass. in 1681 and made a mason during a visit to England in 1704; and there must have been many others of whom we have no record. These brethren came together in various locations, and formed themselves into lodges, as it was their 'immemorial right' to do, that is, unattached lodges owing allegiance to no higher authority than themselves. These first American masons learned their Craft before 1730, some before 1717, and thus were not influenced by the great changes that took place in English Masonry in those first decades of the 18th century, consequently there are many early practices and customs still preserved in America which disappeared from English Masonry generations ago.

'Regular' Freemasonry came to the American colonies in the 1730s with the appointment, by the premier Grand Lodge of England, of Provincial Grand Masters for several areas, and, of course, private lodges were formed under that and other Grand Lodges.

There were also several regiments of British soldiers in the American Colonies and they, too, had their Masonic Lodges. There was an Irish Military lodge working in Cape Breton Island in 1746, No. 85 I.C., in the 30th Regiment of Foot.

Several more regiments of the British Army arrived in America for the war against the French (1754–1763), and most of these had their regimental lodges, mainly Irish and Antients. These in turn, established new lodges among the civilian population, and no doubt, also influenced those lodges already existing and introduced Irish customs. Although the Antient Grand Lodge did not set up Provincial Grand Lodges in England, several were created for America, for Nova Scotia in 1757, Pennsylvania 1761, South Carolina 1787.

Thus there were, in the American colonies, three types of masonic lodges, the unattached 'time-immemorial' bodies, those under the authority of the Grand Lodge of England, (the Moderns), and those of the Antients. As pointed out in the section on 'Antient and Modern Freemasons' the members of these bodies had different concepts of the Craft and came from different social backgrounds. The position in America in the mid-1700s is very well described in *'Whence Come We? Freemasonry in Ontario 1764–1980'*.

> This distinction was carried over to America. Here the Moderns were made up largely of government officials or leaders of the business world – in short, the members of 'The Establishment'. The members of an early Ancients lodge on the other hand are described as 'very poor mechanicks (though honest men).' When the Revolution broke out, the Moderns naturally tended to side with the British while the Ancients more often joined the Revolutionaries. The Provincial Grand Masters for the Moderns in Massachusetts, New York, Pennsylvania, and South Carolina were all Loyalists, and two of them left the colonies.
>
> In New York the lodges of the Moderns were left rudderless, and those that survived

were taken over by a P.G.L. of the Ancients. In Pennsylvania the Moderns vanished altogether, leaving the way clear for the Ancients.

There are now 50 separate, independent Grand Lodges in the United States of America, one in each State, except Hawaii, and there is one in the District of Columbia, serving the Federal Capital, Washington D.C. Each jurisdiction has its own 'standard' ritual which is rigidly controlled by its Grand Lodge. The majority of these workings are based on Thomas Smith Webb's *'Freemason's Monitor, or Illustrations of Masonry'*, first published in 1797, which was taken, in great part, from William Preston's *'Illustrations of Masonry'*, of 1792. This edition of 'Preston' was the first in which Deacons were mentioned as officers and, in due course, they appeared in 'Webb'.

The office was, however, not unknown in America at that time, for New York had a Deacon in 1771. This was under the jurisdiction of a Provincial Grand Lodge of the Moderns, which Grand Lodge did not recognise the office.

There were undoubtedly many other such appointments at, or even before that time, and when one considers the presence of large numbers of British soldiers, with their Antient and Irish working, and their Deacons, and with the natural fraternisation between the military and civilian lodges, the interchange of customs and practices was inevitable.

Having given the background to the emergence of Deacons let us now turn to these officers in today's American lodges.

Every lodge has a Senior and Junior Deacon; both may be elected, or appointed by the Master, in some jurisdictions the Senior Deacon is appointed by the master, and the Junior by the Senior Warden.

Under the English jurisdiction the two Deacons in the private lodges, although differentiated by the titles of 'Senior' and 'Junior' are almost of equal standing and wear, and carry, identical emblems, but in American lodges the Senior Deacon is very much the more important officer, some writers consider him to be 'the most important' after the Master.

One feature of the lodge rooms in the United States, which is not found in the majority of those in England, is the use of two doors placed in the West end of the room, to the left and right of the Senior Warden. One door, usually that in the south-west, is for the reception of members and visiting brethren, and is referred to as the 'outer door'.

The other, in the north-west is for the admission of candidates for the degrees and is termed the 'inner door'. The 'outer door' is guarded on the outside by the Tyler and, on the inside, is attended by the Junior Deacon. There is no Inner Guard as in other constitutions, and the Junior Deacon is responsible for the security of that door and for everyone who passes through it.

The Senior Deacon is seated at the right of the Master, but on a lower level, and his duties are many and varied, both outside and inside the lodge-room.

Outside, the Senior Deacon receives the visitors, examines them as to their qualifications for entry and sees that they are properly clothed. He puts the necessary questions to the candidate for initiation, and receives from him the declaration of his motives and beliefs. He sees that the candidate is properly

prepared, this latter usually being done by a Steward or Master of Ceremony, but under the direction of the Senior Deacon.

Inside, the visitors whom the Senior Deacon has already seen outside the door, are introduced by him and he, acting as host, (as proxy for the Master), sees that they are properly accommodated according to their rank.

He attends to the Altar, the Great Lights and the Lesser Lights, and, together with the Junior Deacon, carries out the 'purging' of the lodge, under the direction of the Senior Warden.

One very important function of the Senior Deacon is the delivery of the so-called 'Middle Chamber' lecture in the Fellowcraft Degree, which is one of the longest and most involved lectures in American workings.

The greater part of the duties of Senior Deacon is that of conducting the candidate in each degree, he is with him from the preparation room until he retires after the ceremony.

Thus the Senior Deacon has more floorwork than any other officer of the lodge, with the exception of the Master. He is the connecting link between the Master and all candidates and visitors, and the smooth running of the ceremonies relies almost wholly upon whether he does, or does not do, his work as it should be done.

The Junior Deacon is stationed on the right of the Senior Warden, his duties are to supervise the outer door, attend to alarms from the Tyler, report to the Master, and to permit none to pass, in either direction, without the necessary permission. Except for his part in the 'purging' of the lodge at the opening, the Junior Deacon has no other duty inside the lodge, and takes no part in the conducting of the candidate in any degree.

However, there is one area in which both Deacons play a very important, although unseen part, – the instructions of candidates. In American Masonry there are many questions that have to be answered, by candidates for the different degrees, many more than under the English system, and these have to be answered from memory and without prompting.

The importance, therefore, of careful, patient and thorough instruction, cannot be overstressed and the responsibility for this teaching, and for the candidate's performance, devolves upon the two Deacons. Within recent times, however, this role has usually been delegated to either a committee, an Intender (a beautiful Scottish term), or a coach.

The emblem on the Deacon's wand, his badge of office, is in most jurisdictions, the Square and Compasses, sometimes enclosing the 'Blazing Sun' or 'Crescent Moon' to indicate the Senior and Junior Deacon respectively. The Grand Lodge of Pennsylvania employ the 'Dove carrying an Olive Branch' as in the English and Irish Constitutions. In any description of general American practice, the words – 'Pennsylvania excepted' – should be included, since by 1785, after the 'War of Independence', Pennsylvania Masonry had become entirely 'Antient', and they are now the proud custodians of many old customs of that jurisdiction. Many 18th century lodges in England still use the Antient Mercury and there is some evidence that it was in use in some of the eastern seaboard lodges of the United States up to about the end of the 19th century.

(b) MODERNS LODGES WITH DEACONS BEFORE THE 'UNION'

Lodge	No.	Location	Constit.	Deacons	Notes
Industry	48	Gateshead	1735	1733	Before constitution
'Royal Oak'	71	Chester	1739	1743	Master's Deacon and Warden's Deacon
'The Crown'	220	Bristol	1757	1758	Antients lodges in the city
St. Nicholas	261	Newcastle	1766	1759	Before constit. – merged with Athol No. 131 (A) in 1814, now No. 24
Probity	61	Halifax, Yorks.	1738	1763	
Moderns No. 1	197	Jersey	1765	1765	First Master was Antient working Erased 1812
Anchor & Hope	37	Bolton, Lancs.	1732	1765	
Unanimity	154	Wakefield	1766	1766	
Brittania	139	Sheffield	1765	1768	Predecessors were Antients
Restoration	111	Darlington	1761	1769	
Concord	231	Barnard Castle	1770	1771	Erased 1838
Antiquity	2	London	T.I.	1778	Stewards entitled 'Deacons' Have gilt Mercury jewels
Phoenix	94	Sunderland	1755	pre 1778	Have 'Sun & Moon' jewels
Old Unanimity	328	Penrith	1776	1781	Erased 1811
Pilgrim	238	London	1779	1784	Had three Deacons 1817–18
Tyrian	253	Derby	1785	1785	In procession for constitution
Whitchurch No. 1	388	Whitchurch, Shropshire	1785	1785	Had the same first Master as Moderns No. 1, Jersey
Palatine	97	Sunderland	1757	1785	Present at dedication of Phoenix Hall. 5th April 1785
Salopian	262	Shrewsbury	1788	1788	Adopted 'Moderns' practice 1791 and changed title to 'Stewards'
Lodge of Lights	148	Warrington	1765	1791	
St. George's	355	North Shields	1792	1792	Erased 1834
Constitutional	294	Beverley, Yorks	1793	1793	Have 'Sun & Moon' jewels
Minerva	250	Hull	1783	1798	Have 'Sun & Moon' jewels
Silent Temple	126	Burnley, Lancs	1762	1803	
Three Grand Principles	208	Dewsbury, Yorks	1804	1804	
Unanimity	89	Dukinfield, Ches.	1807	1807	
Marquis of Granby	124	Durham	1763	1807	By-law re. E.A. ca. 1765 Have 'Sun & Moon' jewels
Relief	42	Bury, Lancs	1733	1809	Have 'Mercury' jewels
Old Dundee	18	London (Wapping)	1722	1810	Have 'Mercury' jewels
Fortitude & Old Cumberland	12	London	T.I.	1812	As L. of Fortitude before union with Old Cumberland in 1818
British	334	South Africa	1811	1812	Have 'Mercury' jewels
Love & Honour	75	Falmouth	1751	1812	Had 'Mercury' jewels, now lost
Lennox	123	Richmond, Yorks	1763	1813	

The Number of the lodge is the present number, unless the lodge has been erased, when the last number is given.
This list is not exhaustive.

THE OLD CHARGES

THE PRESTONIAN LECTURE FOR 1986

WALLACE McLEOD

(*In quotations from early texts the spelling and punctuation have usually been moderated.*)

'The Charges of a Free-Mason'

The 'Old Charges' have kindled the imagination of Freemasons for centuries, and hundreds of pages have been written about them. We might therefore imagine that the topic was by now exhausted. Even so, the younger brethren may need to be reminded of these remarkable relics, which one student, half a century ago, used to call the 'Title Deeds' of the Craft. And (who knows?) perhaps after all we shall be able to say something new about them. If it turns out that I can see somewhat farther than my predecessors, it is largely because I stand upon their shoulders. In particular there are three giants of an earlier age to whom I am indebted: William James Hughan (1841–1911), Wilhelm Begemann (1843–1914), and Herbert Poole (1885–1951). They all died before I became a Mason, and I know them only through their writings. As well, of course, I must express my thanks to those who have helped me personally – particularly the late Bro. Harry Carr; Bro J. M. Hamill, the Librarian and Curator of Freemasons' Hall; and the former Librarian and Curator, Bro T. O. Haunch.

If you open your Book of *Constitutions of the Antient Fraternity of Free and Accepted Masons under the United Grand Lodge of England* at the very beginning right after the 'Summary of the Antient Charges and Regulations' you will find ten pages entitled, 'The Charges of a Free-Mason.' Virtually the same pages occur in *The Book of Constitution* of the Grand Lodge under which I was initiated.

Thirty-four years ago, when I became a Mason, I read through these pages. Because they came near the beginning, it seemed natural to assume that they were important. Some parts sounded a little like the ritual. 'The persons made masons or admitted members of a lodge must be good and true men, free-born, and of mature and discreet age and sound judgment, no bondmen, no women, no immoral or scandalous men, but of good report' (III) 'A man ... is not excluded from the order, provided he believe in the glorious architect of heaven and earth' (I).

Other parts seemed perfectly true, and beautifully expressed in the kind of English that we have forgotten how to write. 'Masonry is the centre of union between good men and true, and the happy means of conciliating friendship amongst those who must otherwise have remained at a perpetual distance' (I). This much could be related to the Craft as I understood it, and it lent credence to the remainder.

I remember being upset when I was urged to stay for the festive board, because I felt I should go home and attend to my studies. Didn't my breathren know their Masonic jurisprudence' There it was in black and white. 'You may enjoy yourselves with innocent mirth, treating one another according to ability, but avoid all excess, or forcing any brother to eat or drink beyond his inclination, or hindering him from going when his occasions call him …' (VI.2). My occasions were calling me, and they were hindering me from going.

But what was one to make of other portions? 'No master should take an apprentice unless he has sufficient employment for him' (IV). 'The master, knowing himself to be able of cunning, shall undertake the lord's work as reasonably as possible, and truly dispend his goods as if they were his own; nor to give more wages to any brother or apprentice than he really may deserve.' 'All the tools used in working shall be approved by the grand lodge' (V).

Such rules as these cannot apply in any literal sense to most of us. Why then are they printed for every Mason? The reason is historical. In its present form more than 99% of the working goes back two hundred and fifty years. This is not the occasion to rehearse the tale of how the Premier Grand Lodge of England was instituted on 24 June 1717; or to tell the full story of the learned but undisciplined Presbyterian clergyman, the Reverend James Anderson, late Grand Warden. We note simply that in 1723, Anderson, with the approval of the Grand Lodge, published the most influential work on Masonry ever printed, the first book of *The Constitution of the Free-Masons.* Suffice it to say that he included a section entitled 'The Charges of a Free-Mason, extracted from The ancient Records of Lodges beyond Sea, and of those in *England, Scotland,* and *Ireland,* for the Use of the *Lodges* in London: to be read At the making of New Brethren, or when the Master shall order it.' Apart from a dozen or so tiny changes, the modern wording is identical.

Anderson's Sources for 'The Charges or a Free-Mason'

Where did Anderson find this material?' The second edition of his *Constitutions,* printed in 1738, has a historical section that reveals a bit more. (Strictly speaking, we ought to say that it *would* reveal more if we could take it seriously. Elsewhere much of Anderson's narrative can be shown to be imaginative and fantastical; in this portion of the story we can neither refute him nor confirm him.) He reports that at the Annual Festival on 24 June 1718, when the Grand Lodge was one year old, the new Grand Master, George Payne, 'desired any Brethren to bring to the Grand Lodge any old *Writings* and *Records* concerning *Masons* and *Masonry* in other to shew the Usages of antient Times; And this Year several old Copies of the *Gothic Constitutions* were produced and collated.'

Even in those early days there were reticent Masons who did not choose to risk disclosure. In his narrative of 1720, Anderson says, 'This Year, at some *private* Lodges, several very valuable *Manuscripts* … concerning the Fraternity, their Lodges, Regulations, Charges, Secrets, and Usages … were too hastily burnt by some scrupulous Brothers, that those Papers might not fall into strange Hands.'

The next year, at the Quarterly Communications of 29 September 1721, the

Grand Master, His Grace the Duke of Montagu, and the Grand Lodge, 'finding Fault with all the Copies of the *old Gothic Constitutions*, order'd Brother *James Anderson*, A.M., to digest the same in a new and better Method.' The end result of these labours was the first book of *Constitutions*, which was duly approved by the Grand Lodge, and printed in 1723. Even as he asserted, James Anderson did make use of the old manuscripts which he termed 'the Old Gothic Constitutions,' and which today are usually known as the 'Old Charges' or 'Old Manuscript Constitutions.' We can tell from the wording of his text that by the time of his second edition, in 1738, he had obtained access to at least six of them, and that he quoted and paraphrased them quite extensively.

The Old Charges: Number, Date, Location, Form, Names, Masonic Affinities

Despite the destruction wrought by zealous brethren in 1720, the texts of 113 copies of these Old Charges have come down to us, and there are references to fourteen more that are now lost. Nearly two-thirds of them are earlier than the first Grand Lodge of 1717 – at least 63, perhaps as many as 75. Fifty-five go back before 1700. Four were written about 1600, one is dated Christmas Day 1583, one is about 1400 or 1410, and one goes all the way back to 1390.

Most are located in England; London alone has fifty-two. Eleven are in Scotland – none of them earlier that 1650; four are in the United States; one was last heard of in Germany; and one has wandered to Canada – the Scarborough Manuscript of about 1700, which is kept in the offices of my mother Grand Lodge.

The Old Charges present various aspects. Some fourteen are known only from printed transcripts. A few are handwritten on separate sheets of paper or vellum; about thirty-three are written on sheets that are fastened together in book form; but the typical shape, represented by more than fifty versions, is a scroll or roll of paper or parchment, between three and fourteen inches wide, and anything up to fourteen and a half feet in length.

The copies are known by various conventional titles. Sometimes they are named for the present owner (Antiquity, Supreme Council); or sometimes for a former owner (Fisher, Wood); or the scribe (Crane, Foxcroft); or a name written on the manuscript (Chadwicke, Scarborough); or the place of discovery (Wakefield); or the printer (Briscoe, Roberts); or the first man to publish a transcription (Cooke, Dowland); or a friend or benefactor of the owner (Cama, Strachan); or a notable Mason at the time of discovery (Devonshire, King George VI); or the similarity to another text (Harris No. 2); or a combination or two of these reasons (Bolt-Coleraine, Levander-York).

Their connection with operative lodges is guaranteed by the contents; but their association with speculative Freemasonry is also well attested. Nearly a quarter (24) have been owned for over 200 years by private lodges in England or Scotland. Another 20 have some traceable connection with lodge meetings or lodge officers; for example, one, as we can tell by the handwriting, was copied by the man who was Clerk of the lodge at Edinburgh from 1675 to 1678 (Kilwinning); three are by the Clerk to the London Masons' Company in 1677/78 (Bain, Phillipps No 1, Phillipps No 2); one is by the Clerk to the London Society of Freemasons in 1686

(Antiquity); another five are by the Secretary to Grand Lodge from 1727 to 1733 (Fisher, Songhurst, Spencer, Supreme Council, Woodford).

The Old Charges: Contents

The strangest thing about these one hundred and thirteen texts is that they all say basically the same thing. The only possible explanation is that they are all related, and go back to a single original, now lost. Evidently it was edited and reedited dozens of times, and copied and recopied hundreds of times in the years between 1350 and 1717, all over England and Scotland. The versions that survive represent only a small fraction of the ones actually penned. The text is relatively short, and in its most common form runs to about 3500 words. For facility of reference, the basic text has been arbitarily divided into numbered chapters and sections.

Let us summarize the contents, with a few typical examples of the wording.

(1) They all begin with an Invocation: 'The might of the Father of Heaven, with the wisdom of the glorious Son, through the grace and goodness of the Holy Ghost, that be three persons in one Godhead, be with us at our beginning, and give us grace so to govern us here in our living that we may come to His Bliss that never shall have ending. Amen' (Chapter 1).

(2) Then comes an announcement of the purpose and contents (Chapter 2), followed by a brief description of the seven liberal sciences (Chapter 3); one of them is Geometry, which is synonymous with Masonry. Then we have a proof of the fundamental nature of Geometry (Chapter 4). 'For it teacheth mete and measure, ponderation and weight, of all manner of things on earth. And there is no man that worketh any craft, but he worketh by some mete or measure; nor no man that buyeth or selleth, but by measure or weight, and all this is Geometry. And these merchants and craftsmen find all other of the seven sciences; and especially the ploughmen, and tillers of all manner of grain (both corn and seeds), vine-planters, and setters of other fruits. For Grammar nor Rhetoric, nor Astronomy nor none of all the other sciences, can find a man measure or mete without Geometry. Wherefore methinketh that science is most worthy that findeth all other.'

(3) Then there is an extended Traditional History of Geometry, Masonry, and Architecture, taking up over half of the text. It is based in the first instance on the Bible, the only book that most people ever saw or heard in the Middle Ages. The art of building was invented, we are told, before Noah's Flood, by Jabal; and metal-founding was discovered by his brother Tubal-cain. They knew that God would send destruction for sin, so they wrote their arts on two great pillars, that were found after the Flood (Chapters 5, 6). Then we hear about Nimrod, and the Tower of Babel (Chapter 7); and how Abraham went to Egypt, and taught the liberal arts and sciences to the Egyptians; and how he had a student Euclid (Chapters 8, 9, 10; this brings together two men who lived 1600 years apart); how King David loved Masons well (Chapter 11); how Solomon built the Temple, with the help of King Hiram and his Master Builder – whose name is not what we would expect (Chapter 12). One man who worked at Solomon's Temple later went to France, and taught the art to Charles Martel – who in reality came 1700 years

later (Chapter 13); subsequently the Craft was brought to England, in the time of Saint Alban – a leap backwards of 500 years (Chapter 14); and finally about the year 930, Prince Edwin called a great assembly of Masons in the city of York, and established the regulations used 'from that day until this time' (Chapters 15, 16).

(4) Then we have the manner of taking the oath; usually, for some reason, given in Latin; a literal translation runs, 'Then let one of the elders hold the Book, so that he or they may place their hands upon the Book, and then the rules ought to be read' (Chapter 17).

(5) Next comes the admonition: 'Every man that is a Mason take right good heed to these charges, if that you find yourselves guilty in any of these, that you may amend you against God. And especially ye that are to be charged, take good heed that ye may keep these charges, for it is a great peril for a man to foreswear himself upon a Book' (Chapter 18).

(6) Next come the regulations or Charges proper. Some are to administer the trade: 'No Master shall take upon him no lord's work, nor no other man's work, but that he know himself able and cunning to perform the same ...' (20.2). 'Also that no Master take no work but that he take it reasonably ...' (20.3). These are the ones that are still quoted almost *verbatim* in 'The Charges of a Free-Mason.' Others do not concern trade matters at all, but are intended to regulate behaviour. No doubt they were essential in a community of tradesmen who were thrown together in close proximity for twenty-four hours a day. Still, they are unexpected, and serve to mark the masons' lodge as different from most other draft organizations. 'Ye shall be true liege men to the King without treason or falsehood ...' (19.2). 'And also that every Mason keep true counsel of lodge and of chamber (19.4). 'You shall not take your Fellow's wife in villainy, nor desire ungodly his daughter nor his servant' (19.7). 'And also that no Fellow slander another behind his back, to make him lose his good name or his wordly goods' (20.9). 'And that no Fellow go into the town in the night time there as is a lodge of Fellows, without a Fellow with him, that may bear him witness that he was in honest places' (20.14). 'And also that every Mason shall receive and cherish strange Fellows when they come over the country, and set them to work; ... and if he have no stones for him, he shall refresh him with money to the next lodge' (20.19). Chapters 19.20).

(7) Finally comes the Oath: 'These charges that we have rehearsed, and all other that belong to Masonry, ye shall keep, so help you God and Halidom, and by this Book to your power. Amen' (Chapter 21).

The Old Charges: Purpose and Function

It is fair to ask what the Old Charges were used for. To begin with, the rules and orders served a practical purpose. They clearly were intended to regulate the Craft. Twenty-five of the copies actually bear the heading 'Constitution' or 'Constitutions;' two more (Gateshead, Levander-York) are hand-written on extra sheets of paper bound in with the printed text of the *Constitutions*; four (Aitchison's Haven, Alnwick, Kilwinning, Thistle) were written in lodge minute books, and one (Aberdeen) in the lodge's mark book.

We also know that occasionally they were treated like a Warrant of Constitution.

The old Scottish lodge at Stirling had a copy of the Old Charges, written on a single sheet of parchment; it had been mounted and framed, and the members believed that their meetings would not be legal unless the manuscript was exhibited in the lodge room. Another text, the Aberdeen Manuscript, has the heading 'The Mason Charter.' In former days the Lodge of Hope, in Bradford, regarded its scroll as the authority for conferring the Mark Degree.

In a sense, the Old Charges also served as The Work, because they described certain procedures that were to be followed when any man was made a Mason, and they included little bits of ritual, such as the Invocation, and the Obligation. It is clear that some of them were actually used at lodge meetings. One (the one in Canada) bears an endorsement, describing a gathering at Scarborough in Yorkshire, in 1705. Another (Sloane No 3848) was written on 16 October 1646, at Warrington, expressly for the initiation of the antiquary Elias Ashmole. Yet another (York No 4), dated 1693, includes a list of the members of the lodge.

We see then that they provided ordinance, authority, and ritual, three practical matters. But as well they must have had a psychological effect. They inculcated in masons a sense of respect and reverence for their craft. They told how it went back to antediluvian times, how it was connected with famous buildings in the Sacred Writings, and how it could number among its votaries even monarchs themselves. This was no servile trade of recent devising, but an ancient and honourable institution.

Textual Criticism and its Rôle

The next question is, what do you do with 113 texts, all nearly identical? Do you copy each of them as accurately as you can, and then publish your transcription? Well, you may. In fact, this is what has been done with the Old Charges. Exactly one hundred of them have been published. But there is another way of approaching them, and that requires a digression.

The craft of printing from movable type reached Europe at some time about 1450. Before that date, all literary works, all legal documents, all political propaganda, had to be transcribed by hand. Copies were few in number, and no two were identical. Each one was unique, laboriously written one at a time by an individual scribe. If you have ever had to copy out an extensive text, you will realize that mistakes were inevitable. So far as books by ancient authors are concerned, someone has said that the transmitted text 'in physical terms means a monk whose knowledge of Latin hovers between insufficient and non-existent, copying in a bad light from a manuscript in an unfamiliar hand, feeling miserably cold and looking forward to his dinner' (James Willis, *Phoenix* 20 [1966] 319–320). No doubt much the same could be said of those who copied out the words of the Old Charges.

The introduction of the printing press had two wonderful effects. It meant that a large number of identical copies could be made. And it introduced a standard of accuracy previously undreamt of. Before publication the editor now could read proof and correct his type as often as he wanted. When we come to consider

literary works written since 1500, we can normally assume that almost every word of the printed page accurately reflects the intent of the author.

For older works the case is far otherwise. We do not in most instances have the author's own handwritten text. What we do have are transcripts, at an unknown number of removes. Sometimes there are a very few copies, or even only one (for example, Aristotle's *Constitution of Athens*, and the Anglo-Saxon poem *Beowulf*). At other times a great many copies exist (thus, *The Bible*, and Virgil's *Aeneid*). In either event, if we want to recover the author's actual words, we cannot simply transcribe the text of a single manuscript, for, as we have seen, scribes are prone to error. We must make use of a discipline known as 'Textual Criticism.' 'The business of textual criticism,' in the words of one authority, 'is to produce a text as close as possible to the original' (Paul Maas, *Textual Criticism* [Oxford, 1958], 1).

An example or two may serve to establish the utility of the process. In the Greek text of the Old Testament, in the Book of *Ecclesiastes*, chapter 12, verse 6, some manuscripts read, 'or the pitcher be broken at the fountain' (*epi tēn pēgēn*), but Tischendorf's great *Codex Sinaiticus* has, 'or the pitcher be broken on the ground' (*epi tēn gēn*). When we print our authoritative text, how do we choose between them? Again, do you recall the Four Horsemen of the Apocalypse? Is the second one riding on a red horse (*hippos pyrrhos*) or a horse of fire (*hippos pyros*)? Both readings occur in manuscripts of *The Revelation of St John the Divine*, chapter 6, verse 4. Or to take a third example, in Chaucer's *Troilus and Cressida*, Book 1, line 949, some versions have, 'The rose waxeth swoote and smothe and softe.' Others have, 'The lilie wexith white, smothe and soft.' Presumably *both* cannot be correct. We must choose. But on what basis?

Or again, consider Shakespeare's *Richard III*; towards the end of Act 4, when William Catesby enters with news of the fugitive traitor, the first Quarto edition of 1597 has him announce:

> My liege, the Duke of Buckingham is taken,
> That's the best newes; that the Earle of Richmond
> Is with a mightie power landed at Milford,
> Is colder tidings, yet they must be told.

An edition published in London in 1700 lets Catesby say,
>   My liege, The Duke of Buckingham is taken,
and then has Richard interrupt him with the words,
>   Off with his head. So much for Buckingham.
A very good line! So good in fact that Sir Lawrence Olivier kept it in his film version of the play (1956)! But how do we decide whether it really belongs there?

'A hundred years ago it was [the] rule to count the MSS and trust the majority.' But we now know that 'MSS must be weighed, not counted,' and one good one outweighs forty bad ones (A. E. Housman, *Juvenalis Saturae* [corrected edition, Cambridge, 1931], xiii). Should we then follow the best one, correcting it here and there from other sources when it falls into manifest error? This procedure attracted the scorn of one of the masters of invective, who commented as follows.

To believe that wherever a best MS gives possible readings it gives true readings, and that only when it gives impossible readings does it give false readings, is to believe that an incompetent editor is the darling of Providence, which has given its angels charge over him lest at any time his sloth and folly should produce their natural results and incur their appropriate penalty. Chance and the common course of nature will not bring it to pass that the readings of a MS are right wherever they are possible and impossible wherever they are wrong: that needs divine intervention; and when one considers the history of man and the spectacle of the universe I hope one may say without impiety that divine intervention might have been better employed elsewhere. How the world is managed, and why it was created, I cannot tell; but it is no feather-bed for the repose of sluggards (A. E. Houseman, *Manilii Astronomicon* 1 [London, 1903], xxxii).

Well, then, we can guess, on the strength of our understanding of the author's practice, or the sense demanded by the context. If we are well-trained and sensible, we shall be right some of the time. But there is another way, which minimizes the guesswork. It involves determining the family relationships of the various manuscripts, and then inferring what must have stood in the ancestor of all the extant versions. That is the way in which the text of ancient authors is normally recovered. That is 'textual criticism.' Though many of the manuscripts of the Old Charges postdate the introduction of printing, they behave much like earlier manuscripts, and they may be approached in exactly the same way.

The Families of the Old Charges

The manuscripts of the Old Charges exhibit a basic similarity, but they fall readily into 'families,' each of which displays a large measure of textual uniformity. This classification was first worked out by the great Masonic scholar Dr Wilhelm Begemann in 1888. There are eight families, each indicated by a name and a code letter.

A	Regius Manuscript	(1 text);
B	Cooke Family	(3 texts);
C	Plot Family	(6 texts);
T	Tew Family	(9 texts);
D	Grand Lodge Family	(53 texts);
E	Sloane Family	(21 texts);
F	Roberts Family	(6 texts);
G	Spencer Family	(6 texts); and then
H	a residue of sundry versions	(8 texts).

In addition there are 14 'missing manuscripts,' which are known only from passing allusions; they are labeled with the letter **X**. Each of the 127 versions is designated by a code or abbreviation, which consists of a letter (to mark the family) and a serial number. In the two larger families a second letter is used as well, to point to a particular branch.

Actually, apart from **A**, which is in a class by itself, the families fall into two great groups. One (which is made up of Families **B** and **C**) clearly stems from an original composed before 1400; it was verbose and leisurely, in short 'Mediaeval.' At some date in the sixteenth century it was completely revised; a lot of the excess

verbiage was pruned away, and the whole thing was made much crisper and easier to read. This new text, which is called the 'Standard Original' Version, does not survive, but was the ancestor of Families **T**, **D**, **E**, **F** and **G**.

What needs to be done is to recover the original text of the 'Mediaeval' version and of the 'Standard Original.' This can be done with a fair measure of certainty. The Mediaeval Version is not hard to reconstruct. The Standard Original is somewhat more laborious, but in an Appendix to this paper, we present a tentative text of it. Before we turn to consider it, we may appropriately explain how it was reconstructed.

Working out the Relationships

First we must work out some of the relationships of the various copies. We do this by making detailed comparisons of the readings of individual passages. We take a portion of the text in which we are reasonably sure what the original said, and then we note which manuscripts diverge from it. We shall generally find that a certain group of texts will share a whole series of these new readings, and we may safely assume that they are all descended from a common ancestor. Sometimes the new reading will arise from a misunderstanding; sometimes it will be a modernization of an old word; sometimes it will be an expansion of the text, or an abbreviation of it. Let us cite a few examples.

20.18, in the regulations: 'And also that no Master nor Fellow set no layer, within the lodge nor without, to hew mould stones with no mould of his own making.' The final phase, 'with no mould of his own making,' is omitted in over fifty texts, all belonging to the Grand Lodge Family.

7.4, when Nimrod's stonemasons were helping to build the city of Nineveh; the original reading was, 'When he sent them forth.' Some thirty-five manuscripts read this as 'When they went forth;' this helps to define the Tew, Sloane, and Roberts Families.

I, the Invocation begins, 'The might of the Father of Heaven.' Apparently in one copy the first three words were illegible or torn away, and the transcriber filled in the gap by writing in their place, 'O Lord God the Father of Heaven.' There are eight descendants, all in the Tew Family.

8.3, talking of Egypt in the time of Abraham: 'And in his days it befell that the lords and estates of the realm had so many sons that they had gotten, some by their wives and some by other ladies of the realm, for that land is a hot land, and plenteous of generation.' Someone had trouble with the writing, and converted the passage into nonsense: 'for that land is a holy land and plenished generation.' Fifteen manuscripts have this or something like it. They belong to the Sloane Family.

In chapter 7.4 we are told that when Nimrod sent his Masons forth, 'he gave them a charge on this manner.' Some thirty or forty lines further on, when Euclid had finished teaching his students, we are likewise told in chapter 10.1 that 'he gave them a charge on this manner.' Apparently on one occasion a copyist was interrupted in his work when he had written the first passage. On his return he wrongly took it up with the identical words in the second passage, leaving out the

intervening two and a half chapters. There are five descendants exhibiting this peculiarity – the Landsdowne Branch of the Grand Lodge Family.

2.1, the address 'Good brethren and Fellows' was corrected or misread as 'Good Deacons and Fellows;' this reading is shared by two copies, which make up the Stirling Branch of the Grand Lodge Family.

13.7, the text explains how Charles Martel was elected King of France. 'And when he was in his estate,' says the usual version, 'he took many Masons.' But one copyist misread the word 'estate' (or actually 'state'), and wrote, 'when he was in his stall.' There are five descendants, all in the Thorp Branch of the Sloane Family.

By proceeding in this fashion, it is possible eventually to draw up a full table of the relationships of all the manuscripts in the branch. Then we can use the table to reconstruct the ancestor of the branch.

Scribal Personalities

A study of the individual copies confirms that each writer has his own personality, and some of them are quite strongly marked. Most of them try conscientiously to copy exactly what is before them. If the words they imagine they see don't make sense, well, so be it! They still transcribe them. Thus, in 2.1, the writer of the Embleton Manuscript (**E.d.7**) read 'craft' as 'ghost.' In 10.6 the Boyden Manuscript (**D.e.44**) copies 'lineage' as 'learage.' In 14.1 the Lansdowne Manuscript (**D.d.2**) converted 'for any' – an alternative reading for 'of any' – into 'Foragine' (and later members of the branch, **D.d.15, 42, 48,** inevitably 'corrected' this into 'foreign'). In 14.5 the Phillipps Manuscript No 3 (**D.b.31**) has 'nurses' instead of 'nuncheons.' Two members of the York Branch (**D.c.17. 37**) wrote 'evill any' for 'villainy' in 19.7. And three members of the Hope Branch (**E.c.5, 8, 18**), in 20.19, transcribed 'stones' as 'sconder' or 'scounder.' Some of these corruptions would be utterly unintelligible if we did not have other texts to provide the correct reading.

Unfamiliar names are particularly vulnerable, and so frequently we meet such monstrosities as 'Harmonise' instead of 'Hermarines' (**D.b.41**), 'Mirth' for 'Nimrod' (**D.h.55**), 'Nimmorah' for 'Nineveh' (**D.e.49**), 'Evesidde' for 'Euclid' (**T.7**), 'Fireland' for 'Jerusalem' (**D.i.11**), 'Brenithmen' for 'Frenchmen' (**E.d.13**), or 'Hoderine' in place of 'Edwin' (**E.c.5, 8**).

Some scribes, if they come to a passage they cannot read at all, will leave a space just the right length. Thus, the writer of the Antiquity Manuscript (**D.d.15**) could not read the word 'paynim' or 'pagan' in 14.2, and left a blank. (Of course, if in turn a later copy is made, then sometimes the blank is closed up, or filled in by guesswork, and we lose all indication that anything is awry. So two younger relatives of the Antiquity Manuscript, **D.d.42 and 48,** filled in the gap for the word 'pagan' by guessing 'mason.') Again, in 13.2, some scribe could not read the full name of 'Naymus Grecus,' and so he transcribed '[*space*] Grecus' (**D.a.4, 5. 39**); later members of the family were less punctilious, and closed up the gap, writing simply 'Grecus,' with no hint that anything was missing (**D.a.8, 29, 43**).

Occasionally we encounter someone with a bit of initiative, someone who is not afraid to rewrite a phrase or two in the interest of clarity, or what he takes to be

clarity. Such a one was the man who wrote the Huddleston Manuscript (**D.e.49**). The text he was copying defined Music by saying, 'it teacheth voice of tongue, harp or organ' (3.7). He embellished this and wrote that it 'teacheth to sing and play on harp and organ and other instruments.'

Again, when Mark Kypling in 1693 copied out his version of the Old Charges (York Manuscript No 4, **E.c.9**), he apparently decided that the historical section concluded too abruptly. He therefore inserted a retrospect at the end of Chapter 16: 'Now you have heard in particular how this noble and famous Craft of Masonry was first invented; and how miraculously it was preserved; and, since, how it hath been loved and cherished both by kings and potentates, from its first beginning to this very day, and how it should and ought still to be loved and kept in high repute and estimation by all manner of persons whatsoever.'

From time to time a studious type intervenes. A few of them made a habit of checking assertions against their Bible, and sometimes they would substitute a scriptural quotation for the original version. Thus, in 5.9 the original told how Tubal-cain 'found smith's craft, of gold, silver, copper, iron and steel.' One group of copies (**D.a.29** and Family **G**) carries instead the statement that Tubal-cain was the 'instructor of every artificer in brass and iron' – words which come from Genesis 4:22.

Only rarely do we find a creative editor, one who works over the whole text thoroughly, bringing the language up to date and introducing new material. Such men were responsible for the Harris Branch, the Roberts Family, the Spencer Family, and above all the Raymond Manuscript. Estimable people, I'm sure, but my only comment as a student of the text is, thank Heaven there weren't more of them.

The Reconstituted Text

The text that we finally recover (printed in the Appendix to this paper) does not hold any real surprises. It is close in wording to many of its offspring, though it does not coincide with any of them. It is certainly more authoritive and readable than its earliest surviving descendant, the Grand Lodge Manuscript No 1. In hundreds of places the readings differ. In most, to be sure, the difference is not substantive; but in several dozen there is a real distinction; to cite but a single example, in 20.4 an indispensable negative is omitted.

Its exact date is uncertain, but we can determine the limits within which it was composed. The Grand Lodge Manuscript No 1 (**D.a.1**) was written in 1583. We know as well of two earlier descendants that are no longer extant. The Melrose Manuscript No 2 (**D.sundry.12**) is certified to be transcribed from a lost original of 1581, and the Levander-York Manuscript (**D.b.41**) purports to be copied from a text of 1560. All of these versions, as we can tell from the text, are not copied directly from the Standard Original, but stand at several removes distant. It follows that the Standard Original must have been written somewhere before 1560. Likewise, it must postdate 1470, because it clearly derives from the Plot Family, which mentions 'our late sovereign lord King Henry the Sixth.' The extreme limits then seem to be 1470 and 1560. Those who knew about such things say that 'the

language and style hardly suggest a date before the first half of the sixteenth century' (Douglas Knoop and G. P. Jones, *The Genesis of Freemasonry* [Manchester, 1947], 76). Perhaps Poole's pronouncement, 'some such date as 1520–40,' is as good as any (*Gould's History of Freemasonry*, revised by Herbert Poole [London, 1951], 1.36).

The text has a distinct flavour of Middle English. Words that were current 450 years ago, but are now obsolete or changed in meaning, occur regularly:

'an' (= if);
'behest' (= promise);
'clerk' (= scholar);
'cry' (= proclaim or proclamation);
'cunning' (= skill or skilful);
'curious' (= skilful);
'depart' (= divide or share);
'deserve' (= serve);
'drew to' (= came to);
'fere' (= companion);
'find' (= support or provide for);
'get' (= beget);
'Halidom' (= that which you regard as sacred);
'hight' (= called);
'journey' (= day's work);
'mete' (= measure);
'mo' (= more in number);
'nuncheons' (= light refreshments);
'paynim' (= pagan);
'practic' (= practice);
'sithen' (= thereupon);
'take' (= hand over or give);
'travel' (= exertion);
'tree' (= timber);
'wit' (= know);
'worship' (= honour);

and so on.

Biblical names are used in the Latin forms which were familiar in the Vulgate, rather than in the Hebrew ones that became current after the Reformation; thus, Ada for Adah, Jabel for Jabal, Nemrod for Nimrod, Ninive for Nineveh, Noe for Noah, Salomon in place of Solomon, Sara for Sarah, Sella for Zillah, and Sem instead of Shem.

Why Bother?

There are many reasons why the effort of reconstructing a lost manuscript is worth while. Not least is the sheer intellectual satisfaction of bringing order out of chaos. There are practical benefits as well. If you are concerned with the contents of the Old Charges, the material you need to consider is reduced to manageable bulk.

You no longer have to worry about 113 distinct texts, all of equal evidential value. And you can be sure that you are dealing with the author's original intention, rather than with a casual misreading.

Now, instead of arguing about which variant reading we should follow, we have a single text. Let us take a passage where there is a wide range of variants. In 14.5 we are told that St Alban raised the wages of masons from a penny a day, and made it right good. But what did he raise it to? Some versions say two shillings a week, others two and six, yet others three, or three and six, or even four or four and six. What was the original figure? Textual criticism enables us to say that the Standard Original and the Mediaeval Original both had two shillings and sixpence. It is at least possible that this figure may have some implications for dating the original composition of the Mediaeval Version. If it represents the actual wage that was then current, it points to the mid-fourteenth century. The average pay for masons was fivepence a day (or 2/6 a week) at Oxford during the decade 1351–1360 (Douglas Knoop and G. P. Jones, *The Mediaeval Mason* [3rd edition, Manchester, 1967], 211). On other grounds the date of the original (known as the 'New Long History') had been set between 1350 and 1390 (Douglas Knoop, G. P. Jones, and Douglas Hamer, *The Two Earliest Masonic MSS.* [Manchester, 1938], 59).

Or again, consider the name of the architect of Solomon's Temple. In modern Masonry of course he is called Hiram Abif, a form which goes back ultimately to the Bible, 2 Chronicles 2:13 and 4:16. You will see it hinted from time to time that the name of Hiram was a Masonic secret, transmitted by word of mouth through the middle ages, while written texts carried instead the 'substitute name' Aymon; this (we are told) is a corruption of the Hebrew word meaning 'master workman.' In two texts (**D.e.13, 14**) the architect is called 'Apleo,' which (we are assured) is another Hebrew 'substitute name,' meaning 'the secret.' Speaking for myself, I do not believe *any* of this. Aymon, or more probably Aynon, was certainly the form in the Standard Original. Where other names appear instead, they arise from one of two causes. One is a simple misunderstanding, of the sort that we have noted elsewhere. Aymō (in which the suprascript stroke represents a final N) as written in a script of about 1600 could easily have been misread as Apleo. The second is conscious correction. The name Hiram begins to appear about 1675, and it occurs in eighteen copies. And we can *prove* that in each of these texts the new name was introduced by one of those scribes who consulted their Bibles, and found the name Hiram there; we can prove it because in *every* instance he gives a Biblical reference or allusion. Probably at least some of these scribes checked their Bible because the name before them was illegible or unfamiliar. In short, there is no evidence for any 'secret doctrine' here.

Once the details of relationship are worked out, we can proceed to make inferences about where and when the lost intermediaries were made. This will tell us a great deal about the building masons of the period before the first Grand Lodge: where they were located, how they communicated, how often they moved on to a new job, and how far they moved. We may also be able to say that a certain manuscript was *not* in such-and-such a place at such-and-such a time. For example, in a recent issue of *AQC*, it was asserted that in 1665 the Grand Lodge

Manuscript No 1 was in Edinburgh, and that a copy of it was made for the use of Lodge Kilwinning. I can now challenge this assertion, for the Kilwinning Manuscript is not a copy of the Grand Lodge Manuscript.

Or again, in recent years there has been an effort to push the introduction of 'Speculative Masonry' back into the sixteenth century, and to suggest that all the versions of the Old Charges except for the two oldest, the Regius (**A**) and the Cooke (**B.1**), are in fact speculative. According to this hypothesis, the older text, which belonged to the operative masons, was revised for some non-operative organization not too long before 1580. To be sure, there is no evidence whatsoever for non-operative Masons in England before 1600; but even beyond that, we now see that the Grand Lodge Manuscript No 1 is not an isolated phenomenon, but is really part of a continuing tradition that is considerably older.

Dividends

As you browse among the Old Charges, from time to time you reap dividends – little extra bits added in a single copy, or a set of manuscripts. Sixteen versions have a further body of regulations, apparently added about 1650, headed 'The Apprentice Charge,' including: 'And that he shall not purloin nor steal the goods of his master or dame, nor absent himself from their service, nor go from them about his own pleasure by day or by night without license of one of them.' This is clearly operative.

Another special group of rules, called 'The New Articles,' is found in four members of the Roberts Family. They are said to have been adopted in 1663. They include: 'That no person shall be accepted a free mason unless he be one and twenty years old or more.' This probably concerns the non-operative Craft.

Particularly interesting are the small additional texts, or 'fillers,' added in a very few copies. Some are injunctions to govern behaviour: 'Do all as you would be done unto' and 'Pray heartily for all Christians' (**D.h.18**); 'Provoke nobody; mock nobody; swear not; dispraise nobody; be against nobody; nothing is long lasting' (**D.c.37**); 'Man, do not foreswear yourself; fear God, honour the King' (both in Latin, **D.d. 48**); 'Praise God always' (in Latin, **D.e.49**); 'Fear God and keep his commandments: for this is the whole duty of man' (Ecclesiastes 12:13; **D.d.15, 42, 48**); scriptural exhortations to live in brotherly harmony (1 Corinthians 1:10; **H.7**); and to dwell in the house of learning (Ecclesiasticus 51:23; **E.a. 10, H.7**).

Some of the additions are specifically Masonic. As many as fifteen versions include either a rendering or a description of the arms of the Masons' Company, which serves to acknowledge the connection with the operative craft. There are scriptural tags that allude to the craft of building (Psalm 127:1; **D.sundry.6**), and to craftsmen (Ecclesiasticus 9:17; **E.a.10**), to the works and wisdom of God (Psalm 104:24; **E.D.22**), and to the raging of the heathen (Psalm 2:1; in Hebrew, **D.sundry. 54**); the traditional verses that commence, 'In the beginning' (Genesis 1:1; in Hebrew, **D.sundry.54**; John 1:1; **D.a.1**). There are texts on scorning the profane (in Latin, from the Roman poet Horace; **T.6**), and on the virtues of the mathematical sciences (in Latin and Greek, again in **T.6**). There are notes on the size of the stones in Solomon's Temple (**D.b.41**); on the date at which the Company of

Masons was incorporated (**D.e.19**); a list of the eleven metals (in badly garbled Latin; **E.d.13**; the architect of the temple was a metal-founder). Five versions have a brief Latin summary of the seven liberal arts and sciences, which runs like this (I translate): 'Grammar speaks; Logic teaches truth; Rhetoric colours words; Music sings; Arithmetic counts; Geometry weighs; Astronomy cultivates the stars.'

In three copies a section of the traditional text is found combined with a series of 'Orders' that are clearly operative ('That no Mason shall take any work by task or by day, other than the King's work, but that at the least he shall make three or four of his Fellows acquainted therewith . . .'); fines are assessed on the members for infraction (**E.a.10**), signed by the members; **E.a.19**, **H.2**).

One copy (**D.g.34**), clearly speculative, is written on some pages inserted into a copy of the *Freemason's Calendar* for 1781; in addition to the Old Charges we find several pages copied here from Preston's *Illustrations of Masonry* (second edition, 1775; pages 50–56, 132–136).

There are sometimes brief hints of ritual or procedure beyond what we already know. The Dumfries Manuscript No 4 (**H.1**), of about 1710, has a whole series of questions and answers, of the sort that we know were used in early lodges ('Where lies the key of your lodge? In a bone box . . .'). The Carmick Manuscript (**H.7**) of 1727 has a drawing of the lodge – a precursor of the Tracing Board. Four texts in the Harris Branch have the following instructions: 'Then let the person that is to be made a Mason choose out of the lodge any one Mason who is to instruct him in those secrets which must never be committed to writing; which Mason he must call his tutor. Then let the tutor take him into another room and show him all the whole mystery, that at his return he may exercise with the rest of his fellow Masons.' Two other manuscripts, closely related, have something similar. This must be at least as old as 1650. And six out of this same group have an oath of secrecy, again going back at least to 1650.

There are occasional personal notes that make us feel we know these unknown brethren better. One writer, of 1693, has added a subscription explaining why he copied the text: 'These for my cousin John Kipling, with my kind love to him presented' (**E.c.8**). Or again, 'Your Master, George Webster, 1722, being 27 years old, March the 25' (**F.5**).

Retrospect and Prospect

In this paper I have tried to do several things: (1) to introduce you to the Old Charges; (2) to explain how we can work out the relationships of the various copies; (3) to recover a text which is older than any surviving copies; (4) to argue that this is worth doing.

Incidentally, I hope that you have learned a bit more about the men who wrote our manuscripts. We have seen the constant tension between fidelity and utility. Some scribes regarded the texts they were copying almost as sacred relics; they transcribed what was before them with as much accuracy as they could muster, even when it had gaps in the text, or did not make sense. Others treated the Old Charges as working documents, which had to be intelligible; they modernized the

language, filled the gaps, corrected the errors. But most of their alterations were casual surface changes, and had little fundamental effect on the contents.

What now remains to be done? Well, we can attempt to improve the text of the Standard Original Version. We can continue to study the text in detail, and see what it tells us about the Craft in the first half of the sixteenth century – a period from which this sort of evidence has hitherto been lacking. We can set out the evidence for the affinities of the various families of the Old Charges; then it will be easy to describe the peculiarities of each new descendant, and to set forth its relationships. And we can proceed to trace the paths by which this text spread across England and even into Scotland.

Conclusion

There is one other class of dividend that I reglected to mention in its proper place, and it might be an appropriate note on which to close. From time to time the manuscripts include poems or songs about the Craft. Some of them are not very good ('Come all you Masons, hear what I do say ...' **D.c.37**; 'Masters kind, prove true in mind ...,' **D.h.24**; 'Master Hiram from near the sea ...' **D.sundry. 54**; 'To our Lodge we invite Lords, Gentlemen, and Knights ...,' **E.a.23**; 'Of all the world a part it is inferred ...,' **H.7**). One or two are quite amusing ('The Prophecy of Brother Roger Bacon,' **D.e.13**; 'A *caput mortuum* here you see ...,' **H.1**). One of my favourites is a bit of verse written soon after 1600, and copied at the beginning of three versions of the Old Charges (**D.c.3, 27, 37**). It is an anagram; that is, if you take the first letter of each line in order, they spell a word: MASONRIE.

> **M**uch might be said of the noble art,
> **A** craft that's worth esteeming in each part.
> **S**undry nations' nobles, and their kings also –
> **O**h, how they sought its worth to know!
> **N**imrod, and Solomon the wisest of all men,
> **R**eason saw to love this science then.
> **I**'ll say no more, lest by my shallow verses I,
> **E**ndeavouring to praise, should blemish Masonrie.

Appendix 1.

A Tentative Reconstruction of the 'Standard Original.' Version of the Old Charges in Modern Spelling

The Purpose of Reconstituting a Lost Text. More than three-quarters of the known copies of the 'Old Charges of Masons' are descended from a text that was written in the first half of the sixteenth century. This text, which is conventionally known as the 'Standard Original' Version, was an edited and revised form of an older version that was current among masons in the Middle Ages. The 'Standard Original' does not survive, but it may be reconstructed by working backwards from its many descendants. When once recovered the text will be of interest for at least two reasons. (1) It will be earlier than any of the copies derived from it.

(2) It will be free of the scribal errors and additions that have crept into the later copies.

The Method. One who claims to give you a lost text may seem at first glance to be either a magician or a charlatan. The first glance is deceptive. The text is reconstructed in accordance with the same scientific principles that are used to edit *any* work that survives in a number of manuscript copies. The technique is regularly followed in the constitution of texts of the Greek and Latin Classics. The initial stage of the project is to work out the affinities of the various copies. Then we can draw up a family tree, or '*stemma*.'

It appears that only two copies were made of the Standard Original Version. One was the ancestor of Families **D** and **G**; the other gave rise to Families **T**, **E**, and **F**. We can reconstruct these two texts and compare them. Where the readings coincide, they will generally give us the reading of the Standard Original. For example, at 4.1, the ancestors of Families **T**, **E**, and **D** all had 'These be the seven liberal sciences,' and this must be inherited from their parent. (Here the two younger families, **F** and **G**, both have, 'Note, I pray you, that these seven . . .,' and are not relevant for our purposes.)

Where the descendants disagree, sometimes we can compare them with an earlier progenitor, the Mediaeval Version, which may be reconstructed from the members of the Plot Family and the Cooke Manuscript. If this older text coincides with either of the later texts, we can be reasonably sure that the shared reading is what stood in the Standard Original. For example, in chapter 7.5, Nimrod instructed his Masons 'that they should serve their lord truly for their pay,' and then his reason is given. The ancestor of Families **D** and **G** says 'so that he [i.e., the lord] might have worship and all that belong to him.' The ancestor of Families **T**, **E**, and **F** had 'so that he [i.e., Nimrod] might have worship for sending them to him.' Evidently several words in the text had been obliterated; the scribe could read only 'so that he might have worship . . . ng to him,' and he had to fill in the gap on his own. But which is the earlier reading, 'belong' or 'sending'? The Plot Family (**C**) has 'So that I may have worship and thanks for sending you . . .,' and the Cooke Manuscript (**B.1**) has almost the same thing in lines 403–406. We conclude that **TEF** preserve the true reading.

Again, in 20.1, Families **D** and **G** read, 'These be the charges in general that belongeth to every true Mason to keep,' while Families **T** and **E** read, ' . . . that every Mason should hold.' (Family **F** omits this clause.) Family **C** has ' . . . that every Mason should hold,' and this must be the original reading.

In passages where the Mediaeval Text is utterly different from the Standard Original, then we are forced to choose one of the two later readings on grounds that may be more or less subjective. For example, in Chapter 1. God is invoked to 'govern us in our living' (**T**, **E**, **F** has adapted this to 'govern our lives'), or to 'govern us here in our living' (**D**, **G**). I have chosen the latter, because it makes a more pointed contrast between man's transitory sojourn on Earth and the everlasting bliss of the next world. Again, in 13.1, the builders who spread Masonry abroad are called 'glorious craftsmen' (**T**, **E**; 'and these craftsmen' in **F**), or 'curious

craftsmen' (**D**, **G**). I prefer the latter, because the epithet 'curious' (in the sense of careful) is more appropriate.

Very occasionally neither branch is correct, and we may have to resort to Conjectural Emendation. For example, in 16.3, Prince Edwin decrees that the book must be read when a new Mason is made. Families **D** and **G** continue, 'and for to give him his charge.' Family **T** has either 'and to give him his charge' or 'for to give him his charge.' Family **E** has 'and to give him his charge.' Family **F** has a paraphrase, 'that he might fully understand what articles, rules, and orders he was obliged to observe,' which is clearly not original. The original version was 'and so to give him his charge;' the 'so' (with a long s) was misread as 'fo,' and corrected to 'for,' and then some scribes, instead of writing both 'and' or 'for,' chose between them. Again, in 20.6 we are told that he that shall be made Mason should 'be able in all manner of degrees' (**D**, **G**), or 'be able over all sciences [or syers]' (**E**), or 'be a man [or anena] on [or within] all sides' (**C**; Families **T** and **F** omit the clause). The original text was 'be able on all sides.'

There is one place where the text is demonstrably wrong. In 5.13 one of the two antediluvian pillars of stone was made of *laterus*. This must have been a misreading for *lateres*, the Latin word for baked brick. But 'baked brick' makes no sense here; it is not a kind of stone, and it will not float. So I have retained the nonsense word *laterus*, to which the scribe evidently assigned some meaning of his own.

The text offered below is closer to the original, and more accurate, than any other that has hitherto been available; it will not be correct in every detail. Further study will inevitably offer refinements. (Similarly, whenever a new text of a Classical author is published, the editor invariably introduces a certain number of improvements.)

In Classical texts it is usual to provide an *apparatus criticus*, or list of significant variant readings, that will show the sources of the text adopted by the editor. To do so in the present instance would add considerably to the cost of production without appreciably increasing the joy of the readers for whom it is intended. So we have, with regret, omitted it. The editor seeks consolation in the words of one of his teachers:

> We should hope ... for a seemly elegance in our editions and resent it as an outrage if we open a copy ... only to find a horrible *apparatus criticus* lurking at the bottom of the page like some open sewer at the end of a gracious promenade. ... Let an editor make the best text he can, and then present [it] in tranquil stateliness ... Textual criticism exists in order to give us a text; when that has been made the bye-products should be destroyed or hidden (Gilbert Norwood, *Pindar* [Berkeley, 1945], 7).

The text given below has been arbitrarily divided into chapters and sections. The chapters are marked by brief titles and figures in the margin. The sections are distinguished by raised numerals in the body of the text. These indicators were not present in the original, but have been inserted to facilitate reference.

In a version which is reconstituted from many texts, any one of which may be idiosyncratic and inconsistent in its spelling and punctuation, there would clearly be little use in attempting to reproduce the exact form of the original. Accordingly we have, with few exceptions, followed modern spelling and punctuation.

The Stemma. Rather than attempting to show the relationship of all 113 texts – indeed, some details are not yet clear – we shall content ourselves with a *stemma* that shows how the different families are connected.

A Tentative Reconstruction of the 'Standard Original' Version of the Old Charges in Modern Spelling

[*Chapter One. Invocation*]
1   The might of the Father of Heaven, with the wisdom of the glorious Son, through the grace and goodness of the Holy Ghost, that be three persons in one Godhead, be with us at our beginning, and give us grace so to govern us here in our living that we may come to His Bliss that never shall have ending. Amen.

[Chapter Two. Purpose and Contents]
2   'Good Brethren and Fellows, our purpose is to tell you how and in what manner this worthy Craft of Masonry was begun, and afterwards how it was founded by worthy kings and princes, and many other worshipful men; [2]And also to them that be here we will declare the charge that belongeth to every true Mason to keep. [3]For in good faith, an ye take heed thereto, it is well worthy to be kept for a worthy craft and a curious science.

[Chapter Three. The Seven Liberal Sciences]
3   [1]For there be seven liberal sciences, of the which it is one of them, and the names of the seven sciences be these. [2]The first is Grammar, that teacheth a man to speak truly and to write truly. [3]The second is Rhetoric, that teacheth a man to speak fair and in subtle terms. [4]The third is Dialectic, that teacheth a man to discern or know truth from falsehood. [5]The fourth is Arithmetic, that teacheth a man to reckon and account all manner of numbers. [6]The fifth is Geometry, that teacheth a man mete and measure of the earth and all other things, of the which science is Masonry. [7]The sixth is Music, that teacheth a man the craft of song, and voice of tongue, organ, harp and trumpet. [8]The seventh is called Astronomy, that teacheth a man to know the course of the sun, moon and stars.

[Chapter Four. Geometry: The Fundamental Science]
4   [1]These be the seven liberal sciences, the which seven be all found by one science, that is to say, Geometry. [2]And thus may a man prove that all the sciences of the world be found by Geometry. [3]For it teacheth mete and measure, ponderation and weight, of all manner of things on earth. [4]And there is no man that worketh any craft, but he worketh by some mete or measure; nor no man that buyeth or selleth, but by measure or weight, and all this is Geometry. [5]And these merchants and craftsmen find all other of the seven sciences; and especially the ploughmen, and tillers of all manner of grain (both corn and seeds), vine-planters, and setters of other fruits. [6]For Grammar nor Rhetoric, nor Astronomy nor none of all the other sciences, can find a man measure or mete without Geometry. [7]Wherefore methinketh that science is most worthy that findeth all other.

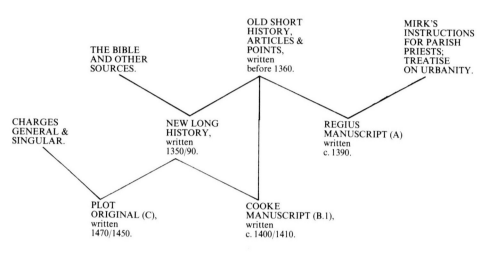

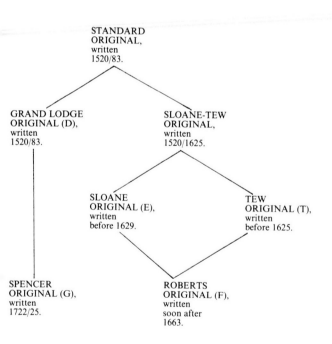

[Chapter Five. The Two Pillars]
5   ¹How this worthy science was first begun I shall you tell. ²Before Noe's Flood there was a man that was called Lamech, as it is written in the Bible, in the fourth chapter of Genesis. ³And this Lamech had two wives, the one hight Ada and the other Sella. ⁴By his first wife Ada he got two sons, the one hight Jabel and the other Jubal. ⁵And by the other wife Sella he got a son and a daughter. ⁶And these four children found the beginning of all the crafts in the world. ⁷And this eldest son Jabel found the craft of Geometry; and he departed flocks of sheep, and lands in the field, and first wrought a house of stone and tree, as it is noted in the chapter abovesaid. ⁸And his brother Jubal found the craft of Music, song of tongue, harp and organ. ⁹And the third brother Tubalcain found smith's craft, of gold, silver, copper, iron, and steel. ¹⁰And the sister found the craft of weaving. ¹¹And these children knew that God would take vengeance for sin, either by fire or water. ¹²Wherefore they wrote the sciences that they had found, in two pillars of stone, that they might be found after Noe's Flood. ¹³And the one stone was marble, that would not burn with fire; and the other stone was called *laterus*, that would not drown in water.

[Chapter Six. How the Pillars were found after the Flood]
6   ¹Our intent is to tell you truly how and in what manner these stones were found, that these sciences were written in. ²The great Hermarines, that was Chus's son, the which Chus was son unto Sem, that was Noe's son (the same Hermarines was afterward called Hermes, the father of wise men), he found one of the two pillars of stone, and found the sciences written therein, and taught them to other men.

[Chapter Seven. Nemrod]
7   ¹And at the making of the Tower of Babylon, there was Masonry first made much of. ²And the King of Babylon, that hight Nemrod, was a Mason himself and loved well the Craft, as is said with the Master of Stories. ³And when the city of Ninive and other cities of the East should be made, Nemrod, the King of Babylon, sent thither sixty Masons at the rogation of the King of Ninive his cousin. ⁴And when he sent them forth he gave them a charge on this manner: ⁵That they should be true each of them to other; and that they should love truly together; and that they should serve their lord truly for their pay, so that he might have worship for sending them to him. ⁶And other mo charges he gave them; and this was the first time that ever any Mason had any charge of his Craft.

[Chapter Eight. Euclid]
8   ¹Moreover, when Abraham and Sara his wife went into Egypt, and there he taught the seven sciences to the Egyptians; ²And he had a worthy scholar that hight Euclid, and he learned right well, and was master of all the seven sciences. ³And in his days it befell that the lords and estates of the realm had so many sons that they had gotten, some by their wives and some by other ladies of the realm, for that land is a hot land, and plenteous of generation, that they had no competent livelihood to find their children, wherefore they made much care. ⁴And when the

King of the land made a great council and a parliament, to wit how they might find their children, and they could find no good way. ⁵And then they did cry throughout the realm, if there were any man that could inform them, that he should come unto them, and he should be well rewarded for his travel, that he should hold himself well pleased.

[Chapter Nine. Euclid teaches Geometry in Egypt]
9   ¹After this cry was made, then came this worthy clerk Euclid, and said to the King and all his great Lords: ²'If ye will, take me your children to govern, and to teach them the seven sciences, wherewith they may live honestly as gentlemen should; ³Under condition that ye will grant me a commission, that I may have power to rule them as the science ought to be ruled.' ⁴Which the King and his council granted him anon, and sealed the commission. ⁵And then this worthy doctor took to him these lords' sons, and taught them the science of Geometry in practic, for to work in stones all manner of worthy works that belonged to building of temples and churches, castles, manors, towers, and all other manner of buildings.

[Chapter Ten. Euclid's Charge]
10   ¹And he gave them a charge on this manner. ²The first was that they should be true to the King and to the lord that they served. ³And that they should love well together, and be true each one to other. ⁴And that they should call each other his Fellow or else his Brother, and not servant nor his knave, nor none other foul name. ⁵And that they should truly deserve for their pay of the lord or Master that they serve. ⁶And that they should ordain the wisest of them to be Master of the Work, and neither for love nor great lineage nor riches nor favour, to set another that hath little cunning to be Master of the lord's Work, whereby the lord should be evil served and they ashamed. ⁷And also that they should call the governor of the work 'Master' in the time that they work with him. ⁸And other many mo charges that are too long to tell. ⁹And to all these charges he made them swear the great oath that men used at that time. And ordained for them reasonable pay that they might live honestly by. ¹⁰And also that they should come and assemble together every year once, how they might work best to serve their lord for his profit and their own worship. And to correct within themselves if they had trespassed. ¹¹And thus was the Craft grounded there. And that worthy clerk gave it the name of Geometry; and now it is called in this land Masonry.

[Chapter Eleven. David]
11   ¹Sithen long after, when the Children of Israel were come into the Land of Behest, that is now called amongst us the Country of Jerusalem, King David began the temple that is called *Templum Domini*, and is named with us the Temple of Jerusalem. ²And the same King David loved well Masons, and cherished them much, and gave them good pay. ³And he gave them the charges and manners as he had it out of Egypt, given by Euclid, and other charges mo that ye shall hear afterwards.

[Chapter Twelve. Saloman]

12   ¹And after the decease of King David, Salomon, that was son unto David, performed out the temple that his father had begun. ²And he sent after Masons of divers lands, and gathered them together, so that he had fourscore thousand workers of stone, and were all named Masons. ³And he had three thousand of them that were ordained to be Masters and Governors of his Work.

⁴And there was a King of another region that men called Hiram, and he loved well King Salomon, and gave him timber to his work. ⁵And he had a son that hight Aynon, and he was master of Geometry, ⁶And was chief Master of all his Masons, and master of all his graving and carving, and of all other manner of Masonry that belonged to the temple. ⁷And this witnesseth the Bible, *in Libro Regum tertio, caputulo quinto.* And this same Salomon confirmed both charges and manners that his father had given to Masons. ⁸And thus was that worthy Craft of Masonry confirmed in the country of Jerusalem and in many other kingdoms.

[Chapter Thirteen. Charles of France]

13   ¹Curious craftsmen walked about full wide into divers countries, some because of learning more craft, and some to teach their craft. ²And so it befell that there was a curious Mason that hight Naymus Grecus, that had been at the making of Salomon's temple. ³And he came into France, and there he taught the science of Masonry to men of France. ⁴And there was one of the royal line of France that hight Charles Martell. ⁵And he was a man that loved well such a craft, and drew to this Naymus Grecus abovesaid, and learned of him the Craft, and took upon him the charges and manners. ⁶And afterwards, by the grace of God, he was elect to be King of France. ⁷And when he was in his estate he took many Masons, and did help to make men Masons that were none, and set them on work, and gave them both charges and manners, and good pay, as he had learned of other Masons; ⁸and confirmed them a charter from year to year, to hold their assembly, and cherished them much. And thus came the Craft into France.

[Chapter Fourteen. Saint Alban]

14   ¹England in all this season stood void of any charge of Masonry, until the time of Saint Alban. ²And in his days, the King of England, that was a paynim, did wall the town about that is now called Saint Albans. ³And Saint Alban was a worthy knight, and was chief steward with the king, and had the governance of the realm, and also of the making of the town walls; ⁴And he loved well Masons and cherished them much. And he made their pay right good, standing as the realm did then; ⁵For he gave them two shillings sixpence a week, and threepence to their nuncheons. ⁶And before that time throughout all the land a Mason took but a penny a day and his meat, until Saint Alban amended it. ⁷And gave them a charter of the king and his council for to hold a general council, and gave it the name of assembly; ⁸And thereat he was himself; and helped to make Masons, and gave them charges, as you shall hear afterwards.

[Chapter Fifteen. Athelstan and Edwin]

15 ¹Right soon after the decease of Saint Alban there came great wars into England of divers nations, so that the good rule of Masonry was destroyed until the time of King Athelstan, that was a worthy King in England, and brought the land into good rest and peace, and builded many great works of abbeys and castles and divers other buildings. ²And he loved well Masons, and he had a son that hight Edwin, and he loved Masons much more than his father did. ³And he was a great practiser in Geometry, wherefore he drew him much to commune and talk with Masons, and to learn of them the Craft. ⁴And afterward, for love that he had to Masons and to the Craft, he was made a Mason. ⁵And he got of the King his father a charter and a commission, to hold every year once an assembly where they would within the realm, and to correct within themselves faults and trespasses that were done within the Craft. ⁶And he held himself an assembly at York; and there he made Masons, and gave them charges, and taught them the manners, and commanded that rule to be holden ever after, and gave them the charter and commission to keep, and made an ordinance that it should be renewed from King to King.

[Chapter Sixteen. The Assembly at York]

16 ¹And when this assembly was gathered together, he made a cry, that all old Masons and young that had any writing or understanding of the charges that were made before in this land or in any other, that they should shew them forth. ²And when it was proved, there were found some in French, some in Greek, some in English, and some in other languages, and the intent of them was found all one. ³And he made a book thereof, how the Craft was founded; and commanded that it should be read or told when any Mason should be made, and so to give him his charge. ⁴And from that day until this time Masonry hath been kept in that form, as well as men might govern it. ⁵And furthermore at divers assemblies have been put and ordained certain charges more by the best advice of Masters and Fellows.

[Chapter Seventeen. The Manner of Taking the Oath]

17 *Tunc unus ex senioribus teneat librum, ut ille vel illi ponant manus super librum, et tunc praecepta debent legi.*

[Chapter Eighteen. The Admonition before the Charge]

18 ¹Every man that is a Mason take right good heed to these charges, ²If that you find yourselves guilty in any of these, that you may amend you against God. ³And especially ye that are to be charged, take good heed that ye may keep these charges, ⁴For it is a great peril for a man to foreswear himself upon a Book.

[Chapter Nineteen. The Charges General]

19 ¹The first charge is that ye shall be true men to God and the Holy Church; and that ye use no error nor heresy, by your understanding or by discreet or wise men's teaching.

²And also that ye shall be true liege men to the King without treason or falsehood; and that ye know no treason or treachery, but that ye amend it if ye may, or else warn the King or his council thereof.

³And also ye shall be true each one to another; that is to say, to every Master and Fellow of the Craft of Masonry that be Masons allowed, ye shall do to them as ye would they should do to you.

'And also that every Mason keep true counsel of lodge and of chamber, and all other counsel that ought to be kept by the way of Masonry.

⁵And also that no Mason shall be a thief or thief's fere, as far forth as he may know.

⁶And also that ye shall be true to the lord and master that ye serve, and truly to see to his profit and advantage.

⁷And also you shall call Masons your Fellows or Brethren, and no other foul name; nor you shall not take your Fellow's wife in villainy, nor desire ungodly his daughter nor his servant.

⁸And also that ye pay truly for your meat and drink where you go to board.

⁹And also ye shall do no villainy in that house whereby the Craft may be slandered.

[Chapter Twenty. The Charges Singular]
20   ¹These be the charges in general that every Mason should hold, both Masters and Fellows. Rehearse I will now other charges singular for Masters and Fellows.

²First, that no Master shall take upon him no lord's work, nor no other man's work, but that he know himself able and cunning to perform the same, so that the Craft have no slander nor disworship, but that the lord may be well and truly served.

³And also that no Master take no work but that he take it reasonably, so that the lord may be well and truly served with his own good, and the Master to live honestly and pay his fellows truly their pay, as the manner of the Craft asketh.

'And also that no Master nor Fellow shall supplant other of their work; that is to say, if he have taken a work, or else stand Master of a lord's work, he shall not put him out, except he be unable of cunning to end the work.

⁵And also that no Master or Fellow take no apprentice to be allowed his apprentice, but for seven years; and that the apprentice be able of birth and limbs, as he ought to be.

'And also that no Master nor Fellow take no allowance to be made Mason, without the consent of his Fellows, at the least five or six; and that he that shall be made Mason be able on all sides, that is to say, that he be freeborn and of good kindred, and no bondman, and that he have his right limbs, as a man ought to have.

⁷And also that no Master nor Fellow take no lord's work to task that was wont to go to journey.

⁸And also that every Master shall give pay to his Fellow but as he may deserve, so that he be not deceived by false workmen.

⁹And also that no Fellow slander another behind his back, to make him lose his good name or his worldly goods.

¹⁰And also that no Fellow, within the lodge or without, misanswer another ungodly without reasonable cause.

¹¹Also that every Mason shall reverence his elder, and put him to worship.

[12]And also that no Mason shall play at hazard or at dice, nor no other unlawful games, whereby the Craft may be slandered.

[13]And also that no Mason shall be no ribald in lechery, to make the Craft to be slandered.

[14]And that no Fellow go into the town in the night time there as is a lodge of Fellows, without a Fellow with him, that may bear him witness that he was in honest places.

[15]And also that every Master and Fellow shall come to the assembly if it be within fifty miles about him, if he have any warning, to stand there at the reward of Masters and Fellows.

[16]And also that every Master and Fellow if they have trespassed shall stand at the reward of Masters and Fellows, to make them accord if they may; and if they may not accord them, to go to the common law.

[17]And also that no Master nor Fellow make no mould nor square nor rule to no layer.

[18]And also that no Master nor Fellow set no layer, within the lodge nor without, to hew mould stones with no mould of his own making.

[19]And also that every Mason shall receive and cherish strange Fellows when they come over the country, and set them to work, as the manner is; that is to say, if they have mould stones in place, he shall set him a fortnight at the least on work, and give him his pay; and if he have no stones for him, he shall refresh him with money to the next lodge.

[20]And also that every Mason shall truly serve the lord for his pay; and truly make an end of your work, be it task or journey, if you may have your pay according as you ought to have.

[Chapter Twenty-One. The Oath]
21   These charges that we have rehearsed, and all other that belong to Masonry, ye shall keep, so help you God and Halidom, and by this Book to your power. Amen.

APPENDIX 2
A LIST OF THE OLD CHARGES BY FAMILY AND BRANCH

The texts are listed below according to their conventional classification, which is in general terms correct. It has not been revised since 1947, when the Devonshire Branch (**D.e.**) was formed by the union of two closely related branches. Versions discovered since that date have been inserted in the same family or branch as their closest relatives. Still, it is clear that certain small adjustments will have to be made, particularly by dividing the Dowland and Dumfries branches (**D.b, D.h**), both of which as they are now constituted include widely divergent texts.

Dates are included for the sake of convenience. They are the conventional ones, except in a few instances in which fresh evidence has been uncovered. In those cases a correction has been entered without comment.

Poole's revision of *Gould's History of Freemasonry*, in volume 1 (London, 1951), on pages 48–76, provides brief descriptions of all the versions of the Old Charges

known up to that date, together with references to published facsimiles and transcriptions.

A.	REGIUS POEM.		c. 1390
B.	COOKE FAMILY.		
	B.1.	Cooke Ms	c. 1400–1410
	B.2.	Woodford MS	1728
	B.3.	Supreme Council MS	1728
C.	PLOT FAMILY.		
	C.1.	Plot Abstract	1686
	C.2.	Watson MS	1687
	C.3.	Crane MS No 2	c. 1780
	C.4.	Heade MS	1675
	C.5.	Poole Abstract	1665
	C.6.	Halliwell MS No 2	1840
T.	TEW FAMILY.		
	T.1.	Tew MS	1700/1750
	T.2.	Aitchison's Haven MS	1666
	T.3.	Buchanan MS	c. 1670
	T.4.	Beaumont MS	1690
	T.5.	Portland MS	1700/1750
	T.6.	Bolt-Coleraine MS	1728
	T.7.	Drinkwater MS No 1	c. 1710
	T.8.	Prichard Abstract	1730
	T.9.	Hadfeild MS	c. 1625
D.	GRAND LODGE FAMILY.		
	(a)	*Grand Lodge Branch.*	
	D.a.1.	Grand Lodge MS No 1	1583
	D.a.4.	Phillipps MS No 1	c. 1670/1690
	D.a.5.	Phillipps MS No 2	c. 1670/1690
	D.a.8.	Kilwinning MS	1675/1678
	D.a.29.	Cama MS	c. 1725
	D.a.39.	Bain MS	1670/1680
	D.a.43.	Dring-Gale MS	c. 1710
	D.a.47.	Talents MS	c. 1710
	(b)	*Dowland Branch.*	
	D.b.16.	Clerke MS	1686
	D.b.22.	Hughan MS	1700/1750
	D.b.30.	Papworth MS	1750/1800
	D.b.31.	Phillipps MS No 3	c. 1790
	D.b.32.	Haddon MS	1723

D.b.36.	Dowland Version	1815
D.b.40.	Langdale MS	c. 1650/1675
D.b.41.	Levander-York MS	c. 1740
D.b.50.	King George VI MS	1727
D.b.52.	Chadwicke MS	1600/1650
D.b.53.	Hathaway MS	1700/1750

(c) *York Branch.*

D.c.3.	York MS No 1	c. 1600
D.c.17.	York MS No 5	1650/1700
D.c.27.	York MS No 2	1704
D.c.37.	Newcastle College MS	1700/1750

(d) *Lansdowne Branch.*

D.d.2.	Lansdowne MS	c. 1600
D.d.15.	Antiquity MS	1686
D.d.33.	Probity MS	1700/1750
D.d.42.	Foxcroft MS	1699
D.d.48.	Fortitude MS	c. 1750

(e) *Devonshire Branch.*

D.e.13.	Stanley MS	1677
D.e.14.	Carson MS	1677
D.e.19.	Colne MS No 1	c. 1685
D.e.20.	Clapham MS	c. 1700
D.e.28.	Colne MS No 2	c. 1730
D.e.44.	Boyden MS	c. 1700
D.e.49.	Huddleston MS	1730
D.e.51.	Devonshire MS	c. 1640/1660

(g) *Harris Branch.*

D.g.25.	Dumfries MS No 3	1650/1700
D.g.26.	Harris MS No 1	1650/1700
D.g.34.	Harris MS No 2	1750/1800
D.g.45.	Heaton MS	1700/1750
D.g.46.	Brook-Hills MS	c. 1710
D.g.56.	Wakefield MS	c. 1710/1720

(h) *Dumfries Branch.*

D.h.18.	York MS No 6	1700/1760
D.h.21.	Dumfries MS No 1	1650/1700
D.h.24.	Dumfries MS No 2	1650/1700
D.h.55.	Lawson MS	c. 1689/1702

(i) *Stirling Branch.*

D.i.9.	Stirling MS	1650/1700
D.i.11.	Aberdeen MS	1670

(Sundry versions.)

D.sundry.6.	Wood MS	1610
D.sundry.12	Melrose MS No 2	1674
D.sundry.23	Dauntesey MS	c. 1690/1710
D.sundry.35	Melrose MS No 3	1762
D.sundry.54	Raymond MS	1705

E. SLOANE FAMILY.

(a) *Thorp Branch.*

E.a.10.	Alnwick MS	1701
E.a.16.	Thorp MS	1629
E.a.17.	Strachan MS	c. 1700
E.a.19.	Taylor MS	1650/1700
E.a.23.	Woodcock MS	1720/1740

(b) *Sloane Branch.*

E.b.1.	Sloane MS 3848	1646
E.b.2.	Sloane MS 3323	1659
E.b.3.	Harleian MS 2054	1650/1700
E.b.4.	Lechmere MS	1650/1700
E.b.14.	Tunnah MS	c. 1860
E.b.15.	Briscoe Pamphlet	1724
E.b.21.	Beswicke-Royds MS	1650/1700

(c) *Hope Branch.*

E.c.5.	Hope MS	1650/1700
E.c.8.	Wanstell MS	1693
E.c.9.	York MS No 4	1693
E.c.18.	Ramsey MS	1650/1700

(d) *Embleton Branch.*

E.d.7.	Embleton MS	c. 1680
E.d.12.	Crane MS No 1	1781
E.d.13.	Wren MS	1852
E.d.22.	Holywell MS	1749

(Sundry version.)

E.sundry.11.	Scarborough MS	c. 1700

F. ROBERTS FAMILY.

F.1.	Roberts Pamphlet	1722

F.2.	Grand Lodge MS No 2	c. 1650
F.3.	Harleian MS 1942	1650/1700
F.4.	Rawlinson MS	1700/1750
F.5.	Macnab MS	1722
F.6.	Drinkwater MS No 2	c. 1710

G. SPENCER FAMILY.

G.1.	Spencer MS	1726
G.2.	Jones MS	c. 1725
G.3.	Cole's Constitutions	1729
G.4.	Dodd Pamphlet	1739
G.5.	Songhurst MS	c. 1726
G.6.	Fisher MS	c. 1726

H. SUNDRY VERSIONS.

H.1.	Dumfries MS No 4	c. 1710
H.2.	Gateshead Orders	c. 1730
H.3.	Thistle MS	1756
H.4.	Langley Abstract	1738
H.5.	Krause Version	1810
H.6.	Hargrove Abstract	1818
H.7.	Carmick MS	1727
H.8.	Drake Fragment	1727

X. MISSING MSS.

X.1.	Melrose MS No 1
X.2.	Baker MS
X.3.	Morgan MS
X.4.	Dermott MS
X.5.	Wilson MS
X.6.	York MS No 3
X.7.	Masons' Company MS
X.10.	Newcastle Lodge MS
X.11.	Lamb Smith MS
X.12.	Anchor and Hope MS
X.13.	Folkes MS
X.15.	*London Chronicle* MS
X.16.	Stone MS
X.17.	Meehan MS

SELECTED REFERENCES

AQC is the abbreviation for *Ars Quatuor Coronatorum:* Transactions of Quatuor Coronati Lodge No 2076.

The literature on the Old Charges is immense, but see (other than the publications of individual texts) William James Hughan, *The Old Charges of British Freemasons* (London, 1872); Hughan, *The Old Charges of British Freemasons*, Second Edition (London, 1895; altogether different from the first edition); Wilhelm Begemann, 'An Attempt to Classify the "Old Charges" of the British Masons,' *AQC* 1 (1886–1888) 152–161; Begemann, *Vorgeschichte und Anfänge der Freimaurerei* in *England* 1 (Berlin 1909) 106–309; Herbert Poole, *The Old Charges* (London, 1924); H. Poole and F. R. Worts, *The 'Yorkshire' Old Charges of Masons* (York, 1935); Poole, 'The Descent of the Old Charges,' *Miscellanea Latomorum* 26.1 (July 1941) 1–6; 26.2 (September 1941) 17–22; 26.3 (October 1941) 33–41; Poole's revision of *Gould's History of Freemasonry* (London, 1951) 1.23–76; Douglas Knoop and G. P. Jones *A Handlist of Masonic Documents* (Manchester, 1942); W. McLeod, 'Saint Alban and Saint Amphibal in the Mediaeval Masonic Tradition: A Review Article,' *AQC* 89 (1976) 113–122; 'The Old Charges and the *Hathaway Manuscript:* An Exercise in Methodology,' *AQC 90 (1977) 177–193; 'The Old Charges,' Proceedings* of The Heritage Lodge No 730, Cambridge (Ontario), 1.2 (April 1978) 2–14; reprinted in *Transactions* of South Canterbury Lodge of Research No 436, 9.5 (June 1978) 3–7; 'Our Predecessors – Scottish Masons of about 1660,' *AQC* 92 (1979) 215–216; 'A Lost Manuscript Reconstructed: The Ancestor of One Branch of the Old Charges,' *AQC* 94 (1981) 15–42; 'Apleo and Voo,' *AQC* 94 (1981) 234–235; 'The Old Charges (with an Appendix reconstituting the "Devonshire Branch Hyparchetype"): The Anson Jones Lecture for 1983,' *Transactions*, Texas Lodge of Research, 18 (1982–1983) 104–132; 'The Old Charges (with an Appendix reconstituting the "Thorp Branch Hyparchetype"),' *Transactions*, Ancient Landmarks Lodge No 3579, Bloomington, Illinois, for 1983; 'Additions to the List of Old Charges,' *AQC* 96 (1983) 98–110; 'Batty Langley,' *The Philalethes* 38.2 (April 1985) 16–21; *The Old Gothic Constitutions* (Bloomington, Illinois; Publications of the Masonic Book Club, Volume Sixteen, 1985).

THE ROLE OF THE INNKEEPER IN MASONRY

THE PRESTONIAN LECTURE FOR 1987

CHRISTOPHER GOTCH

I have two confessions to make. First my title should have been, of course, From Labour to Refreshment. Secondly the etymology of my name is pertinent. A Gotch is a large beer jug specifically for use by bell ringers in olden times during an arduous programme of change-ringing. A few still exist. I am disappointed not to have one at my elbow.

Early speculative freemasonry, when lodges met twice monthly & refreshment was, so it seems, as important as labour, has always been a combination of good work & good fellowship & the feast, the festive board, the banquet or simple refreshment – call it what you please – is still a vital & convivial part of our proceedings. It has given rise to many varied customs peculiar to the Craft, customs often as esoteric as some forms of ritual.

Take, for example, this outsiders' account from a 1737 pamphlet:

> This ceremony (*that is Initiation*) being performed & explained, the recipiendary is called Brother after which they sit down &, with the Grand – Master's (*that is the Worshipful Master's*) leave drink the new Brother's health. Everybody has his bottle. When they have a mind to drink they say 'Give some powder' (that is fill the glass). The (Grand)Master says 'Lay your hands to your fire-locks'; they then drink the Brother's health & the glass is carried in three different motions to the mouth. Before they sit it down on the table they lay it to their left pap, then to the right & then forward, & in three other pauses they lay the glass perpendicular upon the table, clap their hands three times & cry three times VIVAT. If they perceive or suspect that some suspicious person has introduced himself amongst them, they declare it by saying 'It rains' which signifies that they must say nothing...'

THE TAVERN

Up to the mid seventeenth century the main building materials in England were stone or timber. In 1666 London, the largest city in England and built mainly of timber, was ravaged by the Great Fire, preceded a year earlier by the Great Plague. The latter decimated the number of native operative Masons; the former caused an influx of masons from the provinces and abroad to cope with the rebuilding under the aegis of the City Commissioners. This threw the long established territorial operative Masons' Lodges into disarray thus paving the way for non-operative members, the admittance of whom proved a shrewd move to boost the then parlous state of Lodge Benevolent Funds. Successful in the short term, this move spelt the demise of the operative Masons' Lodge. Before Grand Lodge was

founded in 1717, specifically to control speculative masonry in London, operative lodges were formed arbitrarily to serve purely local needs, where building work was in progress. On completion of the work, they were deserted by the itinerant operatives and only kept alive by the speculative brethren if so inclined or numerous enough.

The original lodge, or loge in mediaeval times, had been the site hut adjoining the works such as the castle, cathedral or church. Here the operatives quaffed porter, mead or ale; here boiled meat, fish or cheese, assuaged noonday hunger during the long hours of labour; here trade secrets were exchanged and apprentices quizzed on their proficiency in the art. It was here, too, that the mysteries and secrets of the master masons' skill were imparted by word of mouth with a guardian at the door to prevent all intruders or lesser skilled workmen from entry. The catechism was regular, ritualised, and intended to indoctrinate. Eventually, it proved more feasible to conduct such meetings in the nearby tavern. This move from site hut to tavern, and the introduction of non-operative brethren, gave the impetus to the philosophical movement of freemasonry then evolving. The innkeeper played an important role in this process.

Taverns were rarely large; hence their proliferation. At best they were clean and cosy, at worst squalid and uncomfortable; but all were venues for the exchange of gossip, scandal, confidences, contracts, money and even trysts for sex. Business folk, masons included, invariably spent as much time at the tavern as at their offices such was the hubbub and multitude there and more often than not, a handshake over a pot of porter clinched a business deal. The tavern kept open hours from morn to night. Depending upon the season, dinner – the main meal of the day – was partaken from late noon and consisted of a gargantuan repast by our standards. It was not until the early nineteenth century that dinner became an evening meal and then only amongst those of rank and relative fortune.

The main delights of masonic refreshment were pipe smoking – long clay pipes being supplied free by the landlord – and quaffing punch, from a large bowl common to all, or wine or port, with much song singing; all carried on during proceedings. As our brethren at that time tended to be extremely rumbustious, the gavel was in constant use to keep order. A chamber pot was kept handy in a sideboard to provide much relief with little privacy. Calling Off was then a necessity to differentiate labour from refreshment but rarely involved members leaving the Lodge room. Lodges were small because the tavern was small and the private room available for Lodge use equally small, probably not much more than 12 ft square.

Many other societies met, perforce, at taverns so the demand for private accommodation was acute. Such societies, often termed clubs, built their own premises in due course, and played the host to many a Lodge.

Some alleviation of this problem was provided by both inns and coffee houses which served much the same purpose as taverns but were patronised by a wealthier, higher strata of society. At first coffee houses were unlicensed but as the eighteenth century progressed they became more a restaurant, a club or an hotel catering to those with bibulous propensities.

HOGARTH

Hogarth, perhaps unwittingly, played a singular role in early speculative masonry. A member of several Lodges, he was Grand Steward in 1735, the year Grand Stewards' Lodge was founded, and had the gall to elope with the daughter of a Past Senior Grand Warden, Sir James Thornhill. Hogarth's engravings characterising, or satirising, masonry at that time are well known. Less familiar is the tale of his weekend jaunt with his brother-in-law, John Thornhill and three companions, all fellow masons, except perhaps one, down and around the Thames estuary in May 1732.

In the small hours of 27 May that year, having set out from a tavern in the Strand, they sought another at Billingsgate from which 'they hired a tilt-boat which brought them at dawn to Gravesend, after a rainy, windy, sleepless passage. The next four days were spent meandering by land and water around the mouth of the Medway and Isle of Sheppey before returning home. Ebenezer Forrest, a member of one of Hogarth's Lodges, composed a prose and verse version of the escapade. John Thornhill, who made a map, and William Tothall, a cloth merchant, definitely were fellow masons as was probably Samuel Scott, a 'prospect painter'.

At Rochester, after viewing the town, they repaired to The Crown Inn for dinner soon after noon. Forrest records the scene;

> With due attention then prepare
> Yourself to hear our bill of fare.
> For our first course a dish there was
> Of soles & flounders with crab-sauce,
> A stuff'd & roast calf's-heart beside,
> With purt'nance minc'd & liver fry'd;
> And for a second course, they put on
> Green pease & roasted leg of mutton,
> The cook was much commended for't;
> Fresh was the beer, & sound the port;
> So that NEM.CON. we all agree
> (whatever more we have to see)
> From table we'll not rise till three

On to Hoo went our merry band of Brothers to visit the churchyard where Hogarth disgraced himself when his guts began to grumble;

> Which he to ease, turn'd up his tail
> Over a monumental rail   etcetera

On reaching the church at Stoke, Forrest slyly inserts masonic references into his doggerel;

> But near a farm, or an elm tree,
> A long pole fix'd upright we see,
> And tow'rd the top of it was plac'd
> A weathercock, quite in high taste,
> Which all of us, ere we go further,
> Pronounce of the COMPOSITE ORDER.

First, on a board turned by the wind,
A painter had a cock designed,
A common weathercock was above it,
This turn'd too as the wind did move it;
Then on the spindle's point so small
A shuttlecock stuck o'ertopped them all.
THIS TRIPLE ALLIANCE GAVE OCCASION
TO MUCH IMPROVING SPECULATION

At the Nag's Head that evening;

Supper we get &, when that's o'er,
A tiff of punch drink at the door,

On the way home they sat up at Gravesend carousing late;

That wednesday morn we lay till eight,
Tobacco then, & wine provide,
Enough to serve us for this tide.
Get breakfast, & our reckoning pay
And next prepare for London, Hey;
So hiring to ourselves a wherry
We put off, all alive & merry

Such was a long weekend's outing for masons in 1732.

EARLY LODGE PROCEEDINGS

Early lodges were accorded numbers but no names and were referred to as the lodge meeting at The Devil's Tavern or The King's Arms, and so forth. Taverns provided, in addition to public space, upstairs accommodation for private meetings. This was limited for most taverns were no more than ordinary houses with a street frontage of about twenty feet and a depth much the same; such private rooms often formed part of the landlord's residential accommodation. This space limitation had a considerable bearing upon the development of the Lodge. As many as fifteen members could prove an embarrassment, seven, occasionally as few as five even, proved the rule rather than the exception. Such venues had considerable drawbacks and depended entirely upon the goodwill of the landlord.

Lodges were held usually between 6.00 and 10.30 pm Adjustments were made for the season and late arrivals to achieve a quorum. As Chapter meetings were often held later the same night, it was not unusual for the landlord to have to cope with our masonic forefathers from 5.00 pm until well after midnight. Once upstairs, someone had to act as doorkeeper. Originally he was not even a mason, but merely a waiter or potboy in the landlord's employ. One of his tasks, before the days of post, was to deliver notice of meetings by hand. In effect, this was the landlord's responsibility delegated to a minion. It was clearly impossible for the non-mason doorkeeper to be entrusted, as Tylers were to be later, with the delineation in sand, chalk, charcoal or clay on the floor of the meeting chamber, of the masonic symbols now represented by the tracing boards; so this task – an onerous one – was performed by a lodge member.

When assembled the brethren, properly dressed, sat down around a table on which were candelabra, and also three separate candles, placed in a triangle to light the proceedings, as well as the large bowl of punch for refreshment. Clay pipes were lit up and, as the evening progressed, snacks were demanded and delivered by the doorkeeper. On completion of any business, such as the making of a mason or the election of officers, toasts were proffered and drunk on the spot; songs, usually masonic, but occasionally bawdy, were sung. The newly initiated brother washed off the tracing board, contributions to the Lodge Benevolent Fund were made, the bill for the evening's refreshment settled with the landlord and gratuities made to the doorkeeper. Most of the brethren then went home. Should the weather be particularly inclement, the (Right) Worshipful Master sometimes postponed business and commanded the brethren to gather round the fire for comfort and discussion. The making of masons formed but a minor part of the proceedings; masonic catechisms, talks on architecture or science, Grand Lodge affairs, elections and fellowship being the prime consideration of masonic brethren at that time. The Master held sway and always wore his hat – the only member to do so; like the gavel, it invested him with power and authority.

Meetings were often arranged to coincide with periods of full moon to ensure light, and thus greater safety from footpads, on the journey home. Masonry was essentially a local affair; the landlord and his tavern equally so. Should either prove a disappointment, lodge membership dwindled. Fire, too, was a further hazard in this era of candlelight and many early Lodges lost minute books & furniture due to tavern conflagrations.

Candles were indeed a menace; as wicks flared incessantly so a deficient candle had immediately to be snuffed and the wick trimmed with a pair of scissors – that is until twisted wicks were invented. According to a contemporary freemason;

There could be no greater discovery made
Than candles to burn without snuffers aid.

THE MEETING PLACE

Freemasonry could not have survived, let alone thrive, had it not been for the tavern, the inn, the coffee house and later the club, the pub and the hotel. There is one omission, the common alehouse. This was a mere shop or front room of a lowly dwelling where equally lowly people drank to excess a contemptible liquid called ale. Made from 'Wicked Weeds', the growth of which in Kent was sanctioned by Henry VIII, ale gave rise to a contemporary doggerel;

'Hops, Reformation, Boys & Beer,
Came to England all in one year'.

The reference to boys is a paradox; even so, the alehouse was not a suitable place for masons to meet.

The word tavern comes from the Latin taberna – a hut: the same meaning as the word Lodge. Inn was an anglo-saxon word for a house of entertainment – not necessarily of ill-repute. By 1473 the Hostellers of London had adopted the name of Innkeepers and where chartered as a Livery Company in 1514.

In 1778 Thompson's, an Hotel in Exeter, claimed the first use of this term derived from hostel, and there the St. John the Baptist Lodge No. 39 met for several years. The Methuen Arms, Corsham, became a hotel around 1805 whereas The Acorn, Birmingham, changed to The Imperial Hotel as late as 1879. Earlier in 1617 the traveller, Fynes Moryson, claimed 'The World affords not such Innes as England hath', probably the result of the distinction, made a decade previously between alehouses and inns when the innkeeper was given both duties and privileges the mere alehouse-keeper did not possess. It was later said that; 'the English law regards the highest class of hotel as little more than an Inn and little less than a disorderly house'.

Inn signs, like current logos and Lodge emblems, provided instant recognition particularly for the illiterate of previous centuries. Earliest taverns displayed a bush, adapted from a bundle of leaves and boughs, the Roman sign for a taberna. Later signs echoed historical events, legends, heros, sports and occupations. Thus, The Lamb and Flag or Saracen's Head reflect the crusades, The Sun the badge of Richard the First, and The Three Compasses carpentry and so forth with, naturally, The Square and Compass for the Freemasons' Tavern. In those days, all visitors dined at a common table but in the eighteenth century each party had a private room, whilst only the poorest traveller ate in the kitchen – the dining room with separate tables was a mid-Victorian innovation. A feature of the eighteenth century town inns was the Assembly Room at piano nobile level designed for select social activities, hence its use by Masons as an obvious and respectable place to meet.

Innkeeping was an honourable calling. The host was expected to be 'a seemly man, bold of speech, wise, well taught and a merry man'. Often a member of the local council, sometimes Mayor or maybe Justice of the Peace, the innkeeper was a man of import in the community; not a fine gentleman, but a vital link between classes, familiar to each and known for courteous devotion to service. The exact role of inn and tavern was then clearcut and not allowed to overlap.

By Queen's Anne's reign at the start of the eighteenth century, just when English freemasonry was developing, nearly five hundred coffee houses existed, the majority in London. As alternatives to taverns they fast became centres of the bon ton. The earliest handbill advertising the delights of coffee proclaimed that it 'quickens the spirits, and makes the heart lightsome' and, as an added boon, cured sore eyes, dropsy, gout and scurvy being 'neither laxative nor restringent'.

The new coffee houses possessed better facilities than most taverns providing spacious rooms for private gatherings. Little wonder, therefore, that numerous Lodges and other groups moved to such premises especially as landlords made no charge for the use of rooms, relying on the profit made from food and drink and the distinction conferred upon the house by the presence of notable men. As a result the term 'club', in the modern sense, became common. 'We now' said John Aubrey, the noted seventeenth century antiquary, 'use the word clubbe for a sodality in a taverne', or as later in a coffee house.

A letter dated 9 October 1787 from one mason to another provides a consise picture of a coffee house in Bath at that time:

I am lodged very well & very quietly at the Coffee House I spoke of when you were here. A very good room & good bed. I board with the family the Mistress of which is well behaved & sensible – a coffee room to lounge in with all the London & country newspapers. The Lodgings are half a guinea a week – breakfast, dinner & supper; candles & small beer for one guinea more – so that there is nothing extra but wine, punch & tea in the afternoon! Our company at dinner are (sic) but 4 boarders, & our table is sufficiently, nay well supplied. We have a world of Irish here & Lord Yelverton at their head.

The coffee house was, therefore, not much different from the inn.

Around the period of the Union in 1813, Grand Lodge made a determined effort to rescue older outlying Lodges in London from meeting in squalid taverns in equally squalid areas. Certain Grand Officers joined these Lodges and effectively took control by packing the Lodge with joining members of, shall we say, a higher calibre who then voted to transfer to more respectable premises in the City and West End. In so doing, these lodges forewent mere refreshment during labour to become proper dining lodges. Fees increased accordingly with a consequent decrease of less affluent members. There were instances of Vintner, Victualler and Innkeeper masons aiding this form of rescue operation, not always from blameless motives.

With the advent of the railway early in the nineteenth century, many urban roadside inns lost their wayfarer trade. Those that survived were reduced to taverns or pubs catering only to the local community and, as such, continued to provide Lodge venues for the district. The railway spawned the Station and other hotels; they, too, served the same purpose.

In Victorian times the lowly alehouse, and its counterpart the gin shop, was supplanted by or transformed into the Pub with its rigid class divisions of bars, public, saloon and private. The alehouse was reconstituted as the public bar, roughly speaking, the tavern as the saloon, while the private bar, a new innovation, allowed the guilt-ridden to drink unseen and undisturbed by Rechabites. And who were the Rechabites? Those Biblical masterminds present, who immediately quote 2 *Kings*; ten; 15–31, may pass on this one.

Jehonadab, son of Rechab, exhibited much zeal in assisting Jehu to destroy Baal 'out of Israel'. He applied this fervour to promulgate regulations for his own tribe foreswearing a settled agricultural and vinicultural existence for a furtherance of nomadic life. In other words he banned alcohol and achieved notoriety as the first temperance fanatic!

The Victorian Pub, a complex affair, had apart from the main bars numerous other spaces such as the snug, news room, smoking room and tap room all carefully screened one from another. On the first floor, small or large rooms could be hired by local clubs, societies, and masonic groups. Indeed, this pattern continued, certainly outside the largest urban centres, until well after World War II.

A social survey 'The Pub & the People', published in 1943, yields an intriguing and somewhat sly passage:

Another sort of selective Pub group with rules of order, passwords & taboos, is the Dolly Club. The password is, so to speak, showing your dolly. Every member of the Dolly Club (which has no formal constitution) carries a small cheap doll. When one member meets

another both must produce their dollies – or pay a fine. Membership is purely masculine & it is a little strange, perhaps, to see a miner meeting a navvy in the street, each producing a dolly. There is a great deal in common between clubs of these types & the more organised semi-masonic gatherings that take place in reserved rooms & in secret in Pubs.

The Temperance Movement combined with Victorian middle class aversion to pubs did much to popularise the restaurant where meals with refreshment might be partaken in suitable social surroundings and, when required, in complete privacy, an aspect obviously essential to masonic Lodges.

THE MASONIC HALL

After its first Assembly and feast at the Goose & Gridiron the Grand Lodge of England, the premier Grand Lodge of the world, met in various inns, taverns and City Livery Company Halls over the next sixty years. The first real feast, or Grand Festival, was held at The Stationers' Hall in 1721, thereafter more often than not, at that of the Merchant Taylors. This was clearly inconvenient and as early as 1763 the proposal for a special hall for both functions was mooted. It took the Premier Grand Lodge eight years to plan, build and open, its first Masonic Hall in Great Queen Street fronted by a combined tavern and coffee house, called The Freemasons' Tavern. A further Hall, incorporating the site of the latter, superceeded the original in 1869 and in turn was replaced by the present building in 1933, with a restaurant, The Connaught Rooms, in place of the former tavern.

The opening of the first Freemason's Hall in 1776 created a precedent which Lodges, adherent to the Premier Grand Lodge, were not slow to follow throughout the country wherever several Lodges co-existed in cities and towns. Elsewhere, the tavern and inn still held sway with the respective landlord a key member of the Lodges concerned.

The Union of the two Grand Lodges in 1813 gave further impetus to the founding of Masonic Halls; Masonic Centres are a later innovation. The Masonic Hall was the first step to provide a suitable and permanent Temple where one or more Lodge could meet in total privacy, even if feasts still had to be held at a nearby hostelry. Now, most Lodges meet and dine at Masonic Halls or Centres and the caterer is the servant of the management.

The history of masonry, however, makes it clear that the innkeeper of any establishment where lodges met was a prominent factor in the future of those Lodges. Generally speaking, landlords proved less a liability than an asset, a fact not always evident from early Lodge minutes which usually refer only to recalcitrant innkeepers.

Perhaps the most damning stricture on record refers to Bro Goldsmith, landlord of the Coach & Horses Inn at Ipswich who, on being committed to Marshalsea Prison in 1821, begged assistance from the British Union Lodge No. 114 of which he was a member. The W/M wrote a withering reply. I quote:

> If Masonry has taught you that to assist our distressed Brethren is an essential duty, it ought also to instruct you that to render its charity efficiently it selects for its objects the Moral & Good, & that it rejects from a participation in its Benevolence the dissolute & the vicious.

FROM LABOUR TO REFRESHMENT

The premier Grand Lodge of England created a landmark with the building of the first Grand Temple, but recognised the importance of retaining Brother Luke Reilly's tavern and coffee house to provide the necessary refreshment. By this one act labour and refreshment were separated and it was but a short step to disallowing any form of refreshment and smoking in the Lodge itself. The division was complete. Refreshment was now the concomitant of Labour.

The dining Lodge weeded out a number of undesirable and less worthy brethren, particularly those who treated masonic meetings as an excuse for an unbridled binge. To the delights of feasting further unofficial ritual was added such as Victorian sentimental songs, extra toasts and speeches of a mutual self-congratulatory nature, and methods of fire peculiar to individual Lodges. Pity the poor landlord who, until the advent of the solid based 'firing glass', had perforce to clear up masses of broken glass.

I once assumed, naively, that those Lodges called Temperance – there are thirteen – had foresworn alcoholic refreshment. How wrong I was! The Temperance Movement began in 1831 reaching its apogee twenty or so years later. It need not detain us for it is a creed to which happily only a minority subscribe. I am assured, however, that at least one Lodge of this nature does exist with a festive board as parched of alcohol as a desert of water. I am equally assured – apocryphal no doubt – that, by the time dinner commences, the Brethren are curiously elated. Clearly temperance and fortitude go hand in hand.

A comic once summed up the Temperance movement succinctly. 'Imagine' he said 'Imagine waking up in the morning knowing that you had reached the HIGH of the day'. I sometimes ponder the exact meaning of Calling Off and On when the Worshipful Master asks the Junior Warden what time it is. It is all a matter of emphasis. 'HIGH Time, Worshipful Master' or 'PAST high time, Worshipful Master. It also adds pertinence to Brotherly Love, RELIEF and truth. So much for the Temperance Movement, with which the Masonic landlord obviously had no truck.

THE INNKEEPER AS A MASON

It could be said that just as Lodges needed inns so the innkeeper needed Lodges and thus became a Mason for purely commercial reasons. The Grand Lodge edict forbidding landlords to be members of any Lodge meeting at their taverns must give substance to the suspicion.

It was good business for a landlord to have one or more Lodges meeting at his house, but few other clients made such demands upon him. If not a Mason at first he soon became one as it was rare for a Lodge to meet at a tavern whose landlord was not a Brother. In so doing the Lodge naturally expected duties which could prove extremely onerous. Apart from delivering the summons, he had to store the Lodge furniture such as minute books, jewels, working tools, candelabra and, indeed, all the aprons. He not only held the latter but provided new ones too. From where he obtained them is uncertain but it is no coincidence that the now familiar firm, Toye, Kenning and Spencer, supplier of Masonic regalia, was

founded by Huguenots at about the same time that Dr Desaguliers, also a Huguenot, was Grand Master of the premier Grand Lodge.

The innkeeper was expected also to collect fees from Initiates and joining members as well as the fines imposed upon erring brethren for unpunctuality, intoxication or other misbehaviour, and defects of dress. He had to account for these and for all refreshment provided to the Lodge. In other words, he acted as Secretary, Treasurer, Tyler & Steward of the Lodge, until these offices were separately established. Barely surprising then that many an innkeeper not only fell short of these duties but decided the custom of the Lodge was not worth his while. The Mason landlord had to be dedicated in every sense of the word. Such dedication had to be equated with commercialism & that proved the rub.

Few innkeepers ever reached the chair until this office became a matter of proper election rather than the perquisite of influential members of the Lodge, but then he could hardly be expected to act as Master when already discharging the multifarious duties demanded of him. Instances of disgruntled landlords are not rare.

Take Bro Brusby of The Castle Inn at Highgate where a new Lodge had met for just two years. The final minutes, dated 7 April 1733, state:

> The Lodge being then acquainted by Bro Brusby that it did not suit his interest or convenience to accommodate the Lodge with the room they used to meet in of a Saturday; it was unanimously agreed to incorporate ourselves with the Right Worshipful the Lodge who (sic) meet at The Swan at Hampstead.

A member of this transitory Highgate Lodge was Thomas Crawford, host of The Bear & Harrow in Butchers' Row off the Strand. In 1730 he was a founder member of two new lodges that met at his own tavern. One, The University Lodge, the first ever to be named, was as short-lived as that at Highgate; the other, now St George's & Cornerstone No. 5, owes its survival almost entirely to Crawford who nursed it for several years until it thrived. Why did he not help The University Lodge? Because, it is claimed, the latter formed the nucleous of the Grand Stewards' Lodge, founded in 1735.

Thirty or so years later, No. 5, then Cornerstone Lodge No. 34, met at the Albermarle in Dover Street the host of which Thomas Eyre – not a Mason – recorded amounts charged for initiations, joining members, refreshment & cash in hand signed by him up to 11th October 1766, shortly after which he died. At the following meeting the cash received was acknowledged by his wife who, unable to sign her name, made her mark. This led to the appointment of a Lodge Treasurer and a move to a neighbouring tavern run by a Mason. A successful landlord, therefore, had a vested interest in being a Mason and it was to his advantage that Lodges should flourish.

OUTSIDE LONDON

Elsewhere in England the pattern was no different. The name of the inn or tavern where early Lodges first met was usually but not always adopted. Lodge No. 103 in Bristol, referred to in its warrant dated 1765 as meeting at 'a house on the Quay' called The Duke of Beaufort, adopted this name in 1771, the last year the then

Duke of Beaufort was Grand Master. In twenty years between 1781 and 1801 the Lodge moved six times, until in 1813 it found a permanent home at a Freemasons' Hall. Rutland Lodge No. 1179, likewise, was named after the Rutland Hotel in Ilkeston, Derbyshire, where it met for no less than a century; at first in a bedroom over the Billiard Room. In 1879 Bro Hall, the proprietor, built a special Lodge room which by 1951 had been leased to the area Masonic Association until the latter built its own Hall.

The story of the Lodge of Sincerity No. 1 of the Wigan Grand Lodge provides a rich source of information, more about refreshment than labour, I fear. But then it was indeed a law unto itself. I have no time to recount the details of this aberrant movement except to say it rejoined the United Grand Lodge in 1913 and is now numbered 3677. During its first 122 years of existence it met at nine inns, all but two of the innkeepers being Masons. In 1826 the bi-monthly meetings lasted an hour and a half, with a ratio of two to one for refreshment, and many a member expelled for being 'in a beastly state of intoxication'. One innkeeper 'was removed' as all the funds had been lent by him on promissory notes. Between calling Off and On members passed 'a most glorious space of time by singing & other amusements' and at the Feast of 1884, the Brethren were;

> entertained by a substantial Dinner of which every member was perfectly satisfied with the viands provided by the worthy Host Bro Richard Birchall.

It must not be assumed that landlords never became Masters of Lodges. Bro Willey, host of the Sir John Falstaff in Sheffield was, in 1806, Master of the Britannia Lodge No. 139 which had met there for six years. For reasons unstated but almost certainly due to the Grand Lodge edict against such an event, the Lodge then moved elsewhere. His successor as innkeeper in 1825 was made a Mason three years later whereupon the Lodge returned to his house, remaining there until he left the premises in 1832, when it transferred to a Masonic Hall.

And so westwards where, on 28 December 1732, a new Lodge No. 41 'met at Bro Robinson's The Bear in Bath; & Regularly formed themselves' but, suffering from the mid-eighteenth century apathy towards the Craft, it merged in 1785, at Thomas Dunckerley's suggestion, with No. 458 to become the Royal Cumberland yet retained the earlier number.

And who was Dunckerley? None other than a natural son – so it is said – of the Prince of Wales, afterwards George II. It has been claimed too that Dunckerley saved freemasonry from extinction in the latter half of the eighteenth century. But that again is another story.

Mention of Dunckerley brings me to the Lodge of Harmony No. 255 founded by him in 1785 and the last Lodge of which he was Master. The Lodge met at The Toy Inn, Hampton Court, the landlord of which was Bro William Smart who on 31 December 1816 was proposed;

> to be admitted a regular subscribing member in consequence of the new regulation not prohibiting him as Master of that House from that privilege.

Bro Smart had joined the Lodge originally in 1808, but four years later demanded more money to accommodate the Lodge. Negotiations became acrimonious, and

the Lodge, threatening to move elsewhere, expelled him from membership. Bro Smart apologised but, although re-admitted, never attended the Lodge again. When he sold his premises the Lodge was forced to find alternative accommodation and was thereby outsmarted!

It moved in 1819 to the nearby Red Lion run by Bro Lawrence then Senior Warden and several times secretary. There was an immediate squabble about 'the expense of building a closet for the Lodge'. An uneasy truce continued for several years until the Lodge finally decided in 1828 to quit the Red Lion, Hampton, for the Greyhound Inn, Richmond, the house of Bro Furze. Here it remained for over eighty years.

> In Bro Furze (I quote in 1885 history) the Lodge found a firm & staunch friend (who) contributed to the prosperity of the Lodge by the liberal & kindly manner in which he provided for the comforts of the Brethren.

Praise indeed! It can be no coincidence that within the space of 75 years The Lodge of Harmony No. 255 had, as members, four innkeepers & eight waiters. This particular innkeeper had proved his worth because to him harmony was the name of the game.

The minutes of many other Lodges reveal, similarly, the constant struggle to find satisfactory standards of accommodation and refreshment. But why, for instance, did the Liverpool Lodge of Harmony No. 220 make twenty moves in half a century whereas Ipswich British Union Lodge No. 114 had but eight in a whole century. This same Ipswich Lodge had no less than thirty innkeepers as members in its first century but none in the next. Brewers were a safer bet.

CONCLUSION

English speculative masonry at its inception, so it has been said, was little more than 'a tavern affair of tradesmen and artisans' and remained so until 1767 when Thomas Dunckerley and the Duke of Beaufort combined to inject a wider, and more noble purpose, to the Craft. The stigma of meeting in a mere tavern was slowly but surely removed as Lodges accepted separation of refreshment from labour. Consequently, Masonry burgeoned and with a mammoth nudge from the United Grand Lodge, dining Lodges became the rule rather than the exception by the early nineteenth century.

In one guise or another the innkeeper played a vital and often dramatic, role in this On the one hand he proved vulgarly commercial; on the other he contributed a service essential to the comfort, happiness and refreshment of the brethren without which masonry, as we know it, could not have flourished.

Let us salute him in the words of the traditional song which, for all we know, may well have been Masonic in origin:

Come landlord fill the flowing bowl
Until it doth run over.
For tonight we'll merry be,
Tomorrow we'll be sober.

His ghost is with us still, enthusiastically echoing the curious headings of a Liverpool Lodge menu;

'Tis ever common that men are merriest when away from home!

And perhaps more pertinently;

He who observes the Speaker more than the sound of words will seldom meet with disappointment!

So, Worshipful Master, the spectre of the innkeeper must fade away, and I with him, to the plaint of PAST HIGH TIME.

SOURCES

My sources are too numerous to list. Most of them derive from my own masonic library. It contains those standard publications which any mason interested in the history of the Craft might possess including a number of *A.Q.C.* and other transactions.

Information on inns, taverns and other meeting places has been garnered from more general sources. By far the largest source has been individual Lodge histories which I list under acknowledgements.